THE
AMERICAN
BLACK MALE

THE
AMERICAN
BLACK MALE

His Present Status and His Future

EDITED BY

Richard G. Majors
The Urban Institute, Washington, D.C.

Jacob U. Gordon
University of Kansas

Nelson–Hall Publishers / Chicago

This book is dedicated to the National Council of African American Men (NCAAM) in hope that it inspires the seeds of hope and prosperity for all Black males, both young and old.

Cover painting: *Four Dudes*, by Cynthia Scott

Library of Congress Cataloging-in-Publication Data

The American Black male : his present status and his future / edited
  by Richard G. Majors and Jacob U. Gordon.
     p.   cm.
  Includes bibliographical references and index.
  ISBN 0-8304-1236-0
  1. Afro-American men. I. Majors, Richard. II. Gordon, Jacob U.
E185.86.A42   1991
305.38′896073—dc20
                                          93-4948
                                            CIP

Manufactured in the United States of America

10 9 8 7 6 5 4 3

CONTENTS

ACKNOWLEDGMENTS

I am indebted to several people for their help, support, and advice. First of all, I would to thank one of my best friends and secretary, Sandy Parker; also, Viola Scott, Ronald E. Hall, Glen Martin, Greg Foster, Mario Anderson, Allan Curtis, Eugene Scott, Robert Hall, Roy Cochran, Josh Koenig, the Love Family, Klaus Witz, Robert Sprague, Tara Huebner, the late J. McVicker Hunt, Larry Halicek, and Stuart Jones; and finally, all the students in my Psychology of African-Americans (P337) classes at UWEC. I would also like to thank the following family members: my grandmothers, Lillian A. McGill and Viola Hughes; my grandfathers, Richard Majors and Charles Hughes; my mother, Fannie Sue Majors; my father, Richard Majors; my sisters, Lynn, Holly, Lisa Doi, Stacy, Tish, and brother, Chan. I would also like to thank my uncle, Charles Hughes, and aunts, Yvonne Hughes and Josephine Yeaton; and the following deceased relatives, little William, my uncles, Claude and Wally Reed and George; my aunts, Marie, Marizetta and Ruth, and my late step-mother, Daisy.

RICHARD G. MAJORS

The completion of this book has required collaborative effort on five levels: (1) my co-editor, Richard Majors, and I; (2) Nelson-Hall's staff; (3) the contributors to the volume; (4) my colleagues and students in my Civil Rights classes at the University of Kansas; and (5) my family. I am grateful to all of the people at each of these levels for their support, challenge, encouragement, and counsel. I am especially indebted to my wife, Thelma, my three sons, Jacob, Jr., Jason, and Jevon, and my daughter, Edythe, for their love and faith in me. Finally, I am indebted to my mother, Atiomatse, who died at age 106 in Nigeria before the publication of this book.

JACOB U. GORDON

INTRODUCTION:
The Purpose of the Book

by Richard Majors and Jacob U. Gordon

Historically, racism and discrimination have inflicted a variety of harsh injustices on African Americans in the United States, especially on males. Being male and Black has meant being psychologically castrated—rendered impotent in the economic, political and social arenas that whites have historically dominated.

This passage, which begins Richard Majors' and Janet Mancini Billson's book *Cool Pose: The Dilemmas of Black Manhood in America* (1992), is worth quoting here because it epitomizes the situation of urban Black men in today's America. They have poorer health, both physical and mental, than Black women or white men and women. They are more likely to be in trouble with the law, and they are more likely to die before their time, often by violence. Society, unfortunately, seems to recoil from rather than help them, with further devastating consequences.

Yet most Black men are good fathers, good husbands, and good citizens, in spite of the odds against them. The intent of this book is to educate society about issues that affect Black males, to help counter the predominantly negative stereotypes of Black men, to help build understanding of the normal and healthy personality of Black men, and to explore strategies that empower them.

The Facts

experience higher rates of a wide variety of health, labor market, and social problems (see Majors and Billson 1992; Mincy 1994; Hatter and Wright 1993, for discussion). Health problems include more heart disease, hypertension, cirrhosis of the liver, tuberculosis and other lung diseases, and diabetes (Heckler

1985). Labor market problems include unemployment, underemployment, poverty, education deficits, and illiteracy. Social problems include higher rates of drug and alcohol abuse, delinquency, crime, imprisonment, and unwed teenage parenthood (Cordes 1985; Gite 1985; Majors and Billson 1992). Black males also have the highest rates of homicide and the shortest overall life expectancy save one category of people—those 85 years or older (see Bulhan 1985; Cordes 1985; Gite 1985; and Heckler 1985). Finally, Black Americans, and especially Black males, are more likely to be mentally ill and to be hospitalized for psychiatric reasons. And they are prescribed more psychotropic drugs (Bulhan 1985).

The problems of young Black urban males are, indeed, severe. To use Ralph Ellison's famous adage, Black males have become "invisible" in this country. In *Young, Black and Male in America: An Endangered Species* (1988), Taylor Gibbs addresses the conditions that contribute to this invisibility: "[Black males] have been miseducated by the education system, mishandled by the criminal justice system, mislabeled by the mental health system, and mistreated by the social welfare system." This treatment and neglect has devastated Black males to the degree that they are socially and economically worse off now than in 1960 (Gibbs 1988). No wonder many Black males have become angry, frustrated, indifferent, and apathetic toward society and life in general. Unfortunately, these feelings often lead to self-destructive behavior, with its concomitants of violence, crime, and imprisonment. For example, Black males account for 6 percent of the U.S. population but they make up 46 percent of the nation's prisoners (see Mauer 1990; 1991; for discussion). For the first time in our history more Black males are in the American criminal justice system than in higher education (Mauer 1991). A recent report released by the Sentencing Project (Mauer 1991) compares the number of prison and jail inmates in the United States with those in other nations:

- The United States now has a higher recorded rate of incarceration than any other nation, surpassing both South Africa and the Soviet Union (before dissolution), the previous leaders.
- Black males in the United States are imprisoned at a rate four times that of Black males in South Africa: 3,109 per 100,000 compared to 729 per 100,000.
- The annual cost for the one million inmates of the U.S. penal system is $16 billion, and for the 450,000 Black male prisoners, almost $7 billion.

The Sentencing Project report recommends that Congress establish a national commission on crime to explore why American rates of incarceration are so high. Their recommendations to reduce the arrest and incarceration rates for Black males include:

- Analyzing racism in the criminal justice system.
- Redefining the "war on drugs" as a public health problem, not an issue of criminal justice.
- Repealing mandatory sentencing laws.

- Expanding the focus on alternatives to incarceration.
- Creating jobs.

Damaging Stereotypes

This social and economic devastation has only been made worse by negative portrayals in the media (Hall 1993). Black males have been characterized as punks, troublemakers, dope addicts, gang-bangers, lazy, and hostile. Black males have also been stereotyped in the media by the five D's: dumb, deprived, dangerous, deviant, and disturbed (Gibbs 1988).

Similar stereotypes have dominated the academic literature on Black males. Historically, the literature has focused on the lower-class Black male (rather than middle-class Black males), low self-esteem and negative self-identity of Black males, female-headed families, delinquency, and father absence. This marginalized view of Black males has been referred to as a deficit orientation (Gibbs 1988). Historically, this deficit orientation or model has portrayed Black males as predominantly useless, unfit, powerless, irresponsible husbands/fathers, and burdensome to their spouses and children. Such a model gives us little insight into the lives of most Black males, who are hard-working, sensitive, and responsible family members. We desperately need more balanced scholarly work if we are to understand Black males in their totality.

Needed Research

Major contributions toward understanding Black males have been made by Wilkinson and Taylor (1977), Gary (1984), Gibbs (1988), Lee (1992), Madhutbuti (1990), Mincy (1994), and Bowser (1991). However, a major purpose of this volume is to address important issues that have not been addressed or not addressed in depth. These include AIDS, gangs, African-American immersion schools, Afrocentrism, the use of coping mechanisms, black masculinity, anger and rage, and self-help strategies.

With regards to research on Black males, high on the priority list is the role of Black fathers/husbands in intact families. Robinson, Bailey, and Smith (1985); Cazenave (1984); Staples (1994); and Cheatham and Stewart (1990) have made invaluable contributions, but more studies are urgently needed. Research is also crucial that attempts to understand the lower-class urban Black husband/father in his role as provider, decision-maker, caretaker, protector, religious person, teacher, authority figure, companion, and productive American citizen. Finally, more research is needed in the areas of male-headed families, and nondeviant Black males.

This volume also focuses on the political climate, issues, movements, and events—particularly over the past five years—that have helped to shape stereotypes, prejudices, and attitudes toward Black males. Sociopolitical ideologies that have been critical in shaping opinions, attitudes, and social policy toward Black males today include:

- The proliferation of neoconservative policies (for example, an emphasis on punitive and treating-the-symptom kinds of crime policies: building more prisons, longer sentences, and an increased emphasis on capital punishment).
- Rise of neo-white supremacist hate groups.
- The more sophisticated and subtle, but equally deadly, forms of racism that flourish in the 1990s.

Another objective of this volume is to explore solutions that empower Black males. Solutions and recommendations include manhood training programs, Afrocentric philosophy, African-American immersion schools, and role modeling and mentoring programs that foster positive self-images and constructive life-styles.

Organization of the Material

Announcement of the multidisciplinary content and character of this book has attracted contributions from many scholars in diverse fields with a wide range of interests. Needless to say, this diversity has made our jobs more difficult in terms of selecting and organizing the material in a coherent and balanced fashion. After careful consideration of this task, we have divided the book into six parts: (1) Historical Perspective; (2) Present Status; (3) Search for Empowerment; (4) Psychosocial Development and Coping; (5) The Future; and (6) Conclusions and Recommendations.

Audience

We have designed this book to reach a wide audience: public policy specialists, social scientists, legislators, government officials, educators, health care workers, social welfare workers, clergy, civil rights leaders, youth workers, business executives, political and civic leaders, labor leaders, and criminal and juvenile justice officials. We hope the book will be useful also for undergraduate and graduate courses in Afro-American studies, ethnic studies, cross-cultural psychology, community psychology, urban and planning studies, social and public policy, health sciences, education, social welfare, criminal programs, and law.

A final and extremely important audience is the group of dedicated professionals in organizations that design and operate programs specifically for inner-city youths and their families. These include the National Council of African American Men's (NCAAM) First and Ten Program and Boys of Character Program, City, Inc., Side by Side Sabathan Community Center, Inner City Youth League, and the Omega Club, among others. Without their efforts, the prospects for Black males in America would be much more bleak.

PART 1

Historical Perspective

CHAPTER 1

Men's Studies, the Men's Movement, and the Study of Black Masculinities: Further Demystification of Masculinities in America

by Clyde W. Franklin II

Two important developments in the 1980s related to men's studies form the basis for the discussion in this essay. The first development took place throughout the 1980s, beginning with college-level textbooks in men's studies like Elizabeth Pleck and Joseph Pleck's *The American Man* (1980), James A. Doyle's *The Male Experience* (1983), and Clyde W. Franklin, II's *The Changing Definition of Masculinity* (1984). During this period, the field of men's studies was delineated and defined by several scholars (August 1982, Brod 1987, Davis 1985, Morgan 1981, Pleck 1981, Richards 1982, Spender 1981). Harry Brod, more than any other, gives the most concise and encompassing conceptualization of the fledgling academic discipline. He responds brilliantly to those who would offer the criticism that traditional societal patriarchy has resulted in academics historically being "male based" and "male oriented." Brod contends that traditional scholarship was only "seemingly about men" and excluded from consideration what is unique to men qua men (Brod 1987, 2). He goes on to state the following:

> The overgeneralization from male to generic human experience not only distorts our understanding of what, if anything, is truly generic to humanity but also precludes the study of masculinity as a specific male experience, rather than a universal paradigm for human experience.

Brod, in making the case for men's studies, succinctly defines men's studies as "the study of masculinities and male experiences as specific and varying social-historical-cultural formations."

Developments in Black Masculinities

The gradual recognition of Black masculinities in America was another emergent academic phenomenon related to men's studies in the 1980s. Over twenty years ago two noted Black psychologists, William H. Grier and Price M. Cobbs, published the compelling and polemical *Black Rage* (1968). Based on their professional work with Black men as well as examination of their own lives as Black men, Grier and Cobbs responded to the voices of many who were observing the growing unrest of Blacks in America. The authors countered that the revolt in the 1960s was against societal norms, laws, and customs proving to be deadly and humiliating for large numbers of Black people, especially Black men.

To be sure, developments in Black masculinities have a much longer and richer legacy than the past twenty or so years. Black masculinities in the United States began their development as "the boat" inched closer to Jamestown, Virginia, in 1619, with twenty male slaves chained below deck in wretchedly filthy conditions—the first of millions of Black Americans to follow. Uprooted from their country, their tribes, their families, these males and those who followed were taken to various Southern port cities, auctioned off like cattle, and enslaved for the duration of their lives. Kitano (1985) contends that living under the conditions of slavery has been the single most important experience for the Black person in the United States. Furthermore, Kitano states, slavery "has stamped both slave and slave owner with an indelible mark that has been difficult to erase even though the Emancipation Proclamation is well over one hundred years old . . ." (p. 106). Just as important for our purposes here is Kitano's contention that "the system that classifies people into human/subhuman, master/servant, adult/child, owner/owned, and the techniques for maintaining this disparity have survived in both overt and subtle forms" (p. 106).

On January 1, 1863, the signing of the Emancipation Proclamation formally ended slavery even though the Civil War continued to rage for a time after. Following the end of the war, a series of reconstruction acts, the Civil Rights Act of 1866, the Fourteenth Amendment (extending to Black Americans citizenship rights), and the Fifteenth Amendment (enfranchising Blacks) provided the opportunity for a *new* relationship between America and Black Americans. However, the relationship did not materialize due to American culture's violence toward Blacks, as well as racist customs and practices that all but recreated and reinstitutionalized slavery. In fact, by 1896 blatant segregation, discrimination, and violence toward Black people were commonplace enough to secure the *Plessy* v. *Ferguson* Supreme Court decision strengthening Southern segregation laws for "Jim Crow" adherents. "Separate but equal" became the law of the land.

Numerous accounts of Black life in America during and after Reconstruction prior to the twentieth century suggest that even after slavery was abolished, Black American masculinity had a tenuous or uncertain heritage at best. Still not understanding what was expected of them, Black males during this period were assigned an inferior nonmasculine status by law, by custom, and in some instances by violence.

For a variety of reasons, basic tenets of what would become known as "American masculinity" evolved beyond the grasp of Black men during this period. This is not difficult to understand because the model of masculinity in America had been constructed by the patriarchal slave-master system. Clearly, the denial of Black male leadership in America had been promoted, if not dictated, through various and sundry means. First, the *concubinage of Black women following the Civil War* undermined the Black male's efforts to become a "man." As long as the Black male was a slave, property, a thing, he had no claims to being a man. In freedom, however, he was suddenly a human . . . maybe, even a man? But . . . a man *provides* . . . as the *master did*, a man is *strong* . . . as the master was, a man protects . . . as the master did, . . . a man is . . . well . . . a man. He is not a Negro . . . he is a *man!* By this time the Black male is begrudgingly recognized as a Negro, but it *is* questionable whether he is recognized as a man. John O. Killens' novel, *And Then We Heard the Thunder,* has a passage that illuminates the point. Killen states, "The only thing they will not stand for is for a

Black man to be a man. And everything else is worthless if a man can't be a man."

The twentieth century ushered in an impetus for a new definition of Black masculinity. Such Black men as Langston Hughes, Marcus Garvey, W. E. B. Du Bois, George W. Carver, and Booker T. Washington became prominent figures during the first four decades of the century. Separately, and together, these men and others promoted Black self-sufficiency, Black self-determination, Black achievement, Black persistence, and essentially, the American definition of Black success.

The men mentioned above and many others of the period manifested hegemonic masculine traits despite America's reticence to extend to them the gender "man" or "masculine." In fact, many Black males continued to exhibit many of the traits that American society decreed American males needed to manifest in their social interactions. However, the majority were frustrated in their efforts to assume the American male role, which was reserved for white American males only during the beginnings of the twentieth century.

In 1964, sociologist Nathan Hare wrote of the "frustrated masculinity" that many "Negro" males experienced. He lamented the fact that Black males were denied access to the provider-protector role in Black families because of structural barriers that thwarted their full participation in American society. Hare, as we see, was concerned particularly about the structural barriers to Black males' occupational opportunities and participation.

When many Black males were blocked in their efforts to assume aspects of the male role, they constructed and developed alternative definitions of the male role—ones that could be fulfilled with minimum interference from societal blockage of goals. Since the provider-protector role could not be assumed, many Black males developed a nurturing role with wives and children similar to the role reserved for white females. Black males also developed an aspect of the altered male role white males only recently have begun to develop—intrasex intimacy. The primary reasons for this altered aspect of masculinity are explained in the following section.

The Emerging Men's Movement and Black Men

The modern-day men's movement in America grew out of the concerns of a small group of men regarding problems men experienced following the onset of the women's movement in the late 1960s and early 1970s. Increasingly, some men found it difficult to perform traditional male sex roles; as a result they experienced feelings of frustration, lowered self-worth, decreased self-esteem, and, in some instances, general feelings of confusion.

Coming out of widespread feelings of anomie among males at this time were attempts by some of them to examine critically the male sex role. As Henry Brod (1986) later would say, such early efforts were initial attempts to examine issues affecting "men as men"—a perspective never before used within or outside of academia. This point will be returned to later.

These disgruntled men began to question the traits, roles, and expectations society assigned them solely on the basis of their biological characteristics. Also unacceptable from their perspectives were societal expectations that men's emotions should be suppressed, their intellect superior to women's, their warmth and sensitivity unmanly, and their sexuality compulsively heterosexual.

The following statement, constructed by courageous men at the Berkeley Men's Center in Berkeley, California, during the late sixties and published in 1970, serves as a classical manifesto for both the fledgling men's movement today and the emerging academic discipline Men's Studies.

Berkeley Men's Center Manifesto

We, as men, want to take back our full humanity. We no longer want to strain and compete to live up to an impossible oppressive masculine image—strong, silent, cool, handsome, unemotional, successful, master of women, leader of men, wealthy, brilliant, athletic, and "heavy." We no longer want to feel the need to perform sexually, socially, or in any way to live up to an imposed male role, from a traditional American society or a "counterculture."

We want to love ourselves. We want to feel good about and experience our sensuality, emotions, intellect, and daily lives in an integrated way. We want to express our feelings completely and not bottle them up or repress them in order to be "controlled" or "respected." We want to enjoy masturbating without feeling guilty or that masturbation is a poor substitute for interpersonal sex. We want to make love with those who share our love, male or female, and feel it should not be a revolutionary demand to be either gay, heterosexual, or bisexual. We want to relate to our own personal changes, motivated not by a guilt reaction to women, but by our growth as men.

We want to relate to both women and men in more human ways—with warmth, sensitivity, emotion, and honesty. We want to share our feelings with one another to break down the walls and grow closer. We want to be equal with women and end destructive competitive relationships between men. We don't want to engage in ego battles with anyone.

We are oppressed by conditions which make us only half-human. This conditioning serves to create a mutual dependence of male (abstract, aggressive, strong, unemotional) and female (nurturing, passive, weak, emotional) roles. We are oppressed by this dependence on women for support, nurturing, love, and warm feelings. We want to love, nurture, and support ourselves and other men, as well as women. We want to affirm our strengths as men in areas such as childcare, cooking, sewing, and other "feminine" aspects of life.

We believe that this half-humanization will only change when our competitive, male-dominated, individualistic society becomes cooperative, based on sharing of resources and skills. We are oppressed by working in alienating jobs, as "breadwinners." We want to use our creative energy to serve our common needs and not to make profits for our employers.

We believe that Human Liberation does not stem from individual or social needs alone, but that these needs are part of the same process. We feel that liberation movements are equally important; there is no hierarchy of oppression. Every group must speak its own language, assume its own form, take its own action; and when each of these groups learns to express itself in harmony with the rest, this will create the basis for an all embracing social change.

As we put our ideas into practice, we will work to form a more concrete analysis of our oppression as men, and clarify what needs to be done in a socially and personally political way to free ourselves. We want men to share their lives and experiences with each other in order to understand who we are, how we got this way, and what we must do to be free.

From the first National Men and Masculinity Conference held in Knoxville, Tennessee, in the spring of 1975 to the 1992 Conference held in Chicago, Illinois, relatively small but growing numbers of men and a few women have convened annually.

The yearly meetings of this conference have spawned both activist and academic organizations and activities. For example, local and regional organizations closely and loosely affiliated with the national organizations have emerged; national campaigns (e.g., Central Ohio Men's Network, Brotherpeace, Church Ladies for Choice, and the like) are monthly and annual events; and local and national activities supporting an end to racism, sexism, and homophobia, all promoting social equality, are participated in regularly by men aligning themselves with what can be called loosely the Men's Movement.

Interestingly, while the above activities seldom are grouped under the umbrella of a "men's movement" and people always wonder what is being referred to when reference is made to a "men's movement," many activities of the past fifteen years do portend a Men's Movement, albeit a relatively small one. In fact, a continuum of men's organizations exists, ranging from those that are politically conservative to those that are politically liberal. Especially active has been the National Organization for Changing Men (NOCM), a liberal group of men who define themselves as supportive of such men's issues as improved fathering, antihomophobia, improved men's mental health, ending violence against women, and antisexism. The organization recently changed its name to the National Organization of Men against Sexism (NOMAS). Also active have been Men's Rights, Inc., and the National Congress for Men, two conservative groups also concerned with sexism and men's problems. Their concern, however, is with fostering the understanding that the provider-protector roles have dehumanized, damaged, and limited men, and, in essence, have had lethal effects on men. Such organizations have yet to find a comfortable alliance with NOCM, now known as NOMAS.

As NOMAS begins where NOCM left off, and as Men's Studies achieves legitimacy as an academic discipline in colleges and universities throughout the country, perhaps greater recognition of a men's movement in America will penetrate the lives of increasing numbers of women and men of various races, ethnicities, nationalities, and sexualities. Consider NOMAS's revised statement of principles:

NOMAS (formerly NOCM)
Revised Statement of Principles

The National Organization for Men Against Sexism is an activist organization of men and women supporting positive changes for men. NOMAS advocates a perspective that is pro-feminist, gay-affirmative, and committed to justice on a broad range of social issues including race, class, age, religion, and physical abilities. We affirm that working to make this nation's ideas of equality substantive is the finest expression of what it means to be men.

We believe that the new opportunities becoming available to women and men will be beneficial to both. Men can live as happier and more fulfilled human beings by challenging the old-fashioned rules of masculinity that embody the assumption of male superiority.

Traditional masculinity includes many positive characteristics in which we take pride and find strength, but it also contains qualities that have limited and harmed us. **We are deeply supportive of men who are struggling with the issues of traditional masculinity. As an organization for changing men, we care about men and are especially concerned with men's problems, as well as the difficult issues in most men's lives.**

As an organization for changing men, we strongly support the continuing struggle of women for full equality. We applaud and support the insights and positive social changes that feminism has stimulated for both women and men. We oppose such injustices to women as economic and legal discrimination, rape, domestic violence, sexual harassment, and many others. Women and men can and do work together as allies to change the injustices that have so often made them see one another as enemies.

One of the strongest and deepest anxieties of most American men is their fear of homosexuality. This homophobia contributes directly to the many injustices experienced by gay, lesbian, and bisexual persons, and is a debilitating restriction for heterosexual men. We call for an end to all forms of discrimination based on sexual-affectional orientation, and for the creation of a gay-affirmative society.

We also acknowledge that many people are oppressed today because of their race, class, age, religion, and physical condition. We believe that such injustices are vitally connected to sexism, with its fundamental premise of unequal distribution of power.

Our goal is to change not just ourselves and other men, but also the institutions that create inequality. We welcome any person who agrees in substance with these principles to membership in the National Organization of Men Against Sexism.

From its tenuous inception, the men's movement—or at least that branch of the men's movement emerging from the National Men and Masculinity Conferences—and local and regional organizations devoted to men's issues, have welcomed and sought Black men's participation. Over the years, however, few Black men have participated in local, regional, and national activities centered around changing the lives of men and promoting gender and sex equality. Certainly there are numerous reasons for the dearth of Black male participation in the emerging Men's Movement. Reasons range from Black men's lack of knowledge about the men's movement to their complete disinterest in such a movement.

Generally, rationales given by Black males for their nonparticipation in men's movement activities are embedded in several cognitive schemata characterizing Black men. Major features of the cognitive schemata are based on the following perceptions: (1) the men's movement is a white middle-class "luxury"; (2) men's movement issues are not relevant for Black men because Black men enjoy little power in the social structure; (3) dysfunctions associated with masculinity are not Black male problems because of societal barriers to Black males' "masculine" role assumptions; (4) the men's movement does not address issues of great importance to Black males; (5) the problems white males have are not recognized as important by Black males; (6) Black males have not held the oppressive power that white males have held; and (7) Black men's interests are better served if Black men devote their energies to fighting for racial equality.

Succinctly, Black men's lack of cultural, institutional, and interpersonal assimilation in America contributes to an overall feeling by many Black males that the men's movement has little or no relevance for the lives of Black men. This accounts, in part, for the scarcity of Black men in the men's movement. Whether Black men's perceptions are based on accurate or inaccurate cognitive schemata really is unimportant. The fact that the perception persists and results in minimal Black male participation in the men's movement is the issue here. Only if there can be some alteration in Black men's cognitive schemata related to the men's movement will increased Black male participation in men's movement activities occur.

Undoubtedly, it is a risky endeavor to convince Black men that there is merit in freeing themselves socially and politically, and that individualism, competition, aggression, and independence are traits to be exchanged for cooperation, the sharing of resources and skills, and nurturing. Black men have never enjoyed the privileges and prerogatives white men have enjoyed, and they have often been chided for not being competitive enough, for not being aggressive enough, for not being emotionally stoic enough. Surely, they will see this as an effort to once again *trick them*.

Certainly one can quarrel with the notion that Black men's masculinity bears some resemblance to white men's masculinity and so Black men, like white men, can benefit from a men's movement. However, a convincing case for similarity between the two can be made. Being mindful of the fact that similarity does not negate the existence of *critical differences between the two*, we will explore Black men's male sex rule prescriptions and proscriptions.

Political science professor William Strickland writes: "It's a rare day when there's good news about the lives of Black men. Countless articles tell us our fathers and husbands, our lovers and brothers are approaching extinction due to an unholy combination of social ills, political misdeeds, and social wrongs" (1989, 48). According to Strickland, the political misdeeds and racial wrongs are external factors affecting Black men's social ills. In other words, there are intrusions on Black men's lives in the United States that are absolutely unavoidable—ones that are based on one simple fact—the men are *Black* and therefore *unacceptable*. The intrusions that are unacceptable and thus define Black men in America are couched in the socialization process most Black men undergo. This is a process that is conflictual, contradictory, and often sends mixed messages to Black men. The result is devastating, as society is discovering.

The secret is out. What the Black community for years has known, been quiet about, dreaded and feared, finally has become public knowledge—thousands of young Black men are in trouble. In fact, based on numerous indicators of social mobility and social pathology, an entire generation of Black men may be in serious jeopardy. Jewelle Taylor Gibbs (1988, 258) reports that suicide rates among Black males aged fifteen to twenty-four have tripled since 1960. Gibbs also reports that the leading cause of death for Black males in this age group is homicide, with the estimate that a young Black male has a one in twenty-one lifetime chance of being murdered. Moreover, overwhelmingly, young Black males are murdered by young Black males. Gibbs and her colleagues also report disturbing and somewhat alarming statements related to Black male substance abuse, unemployment rates, and incarceration rates.

What is causing this most recent destruction of Black men in America? Less than twenty-five years ago African-American males, in a courageous, proud and militant movement, gained recognition as newly arrived "men" in America. They did so despite decades of societal resistance, often of a violent nature, to recognizing adult Black males as Black men. Still, the Black man presently being recognized by mainstream society is not the Black man who invented the cotton gin; he is not the Black man who pioneered the development of blood transfusions; he is not the Black man who performed miracles with the peanut; he is not the Black man who fought tirelessly for civil rights and women's rights in the 1800s; and, he is not the Black man who in the late 1960s led Black people on a journey to the "promised land."

Instead, the Black man recognized by mainstream society today is fearsome, threatening, unemployed, irresponsible, potentially dangerous, and generally socially pathological. Black men who *do not* share these characteristics are thought to be anomalies despite their increasing numbers. There are various types of Black masculinities in America. Some of these masculinities are compatible with American society, and some are not. Let us consider these masculinities and the factors producing them.

Black Masculinities in America:
Three Sources of Socialization

Many Black males in America experience what may be called a lethal socialization triangle. The triangle consists of: (1) a type of primary group socialization providing mixed messages regarding the meaning of Black masculinity; (2) a peer group socialization source that teaches innovative Black masculine traits; and (3) a mainstream societal socialization source that sends Black men mixed messages regarding competitiveness, aggressiveness, passivity, inferiority, and invisibility.

These three sources of Black male socialization, though complex, correspond with the realities of Black men's lives in America today. Black men's lives are complex because of oftentimes conflicting expectations held by people in the three worlds making up Black men's society. If, as G. H. Mead (1934) suggested, self reflects society, then Black men can be typed according to the extent that their socialization reflects predominantly the influence of one of three worlds: the Black male's primary group, the Black male's peer group, and the mainstream society. This point is discussed in greater detail in the next section. Below, the nature of Black men's socialization sources is explicated.

The Black Male's Primary Group

The typical Black male's primary group mirrors mainstream societal values and norms, but usually from a Black community perspective. Important to note is (1) the fact that the poverty rate of Blacks is three times that of whites; and (2) Blacks increasingly are becoming an underclass due to the effects of unemployment or employment in dead-end, low-wage jobs, and changes in governmental policy, especially during the 1980s, which curtailed governmental poverty programs while massively increasing military spending. Despite these factors, which imply that many Black males' primary group experiences are quite different from those of their white counterparts, some version of American values and beliefs is a part of Black male primary group socialization. The version of American values and beliefs imparting Black male socialization typically is tempered by the Black experience in this country. It is not necessary in this paper to discuss the nature of the Black experience in America historically. It is a documented fact that Blacks have a legacy of slavery, segregation, lynchings, de facto segregation, blocked opportunities, and in contemporary times, an emerging trend threatening to start the cycle all over again. Black males becoming men in America typically experience a primary group socialization influence which teaches them such beliefs and values as freedom, democracy, individualism, equality of opportunity, competitiveness, the work ethic, practicality, humanitarianism, and the like. These are ideal values and beliefs shared by the majority of Americans and are felt to be core aspects of American culture (Williams 1970; Kluegal and Smith 1986). Of importance here is the fact that these core values and beliefs are "ideal" rather than "real." The values and beliefs may not be practical in the real world, though they may be accepted in principle. Primary group caretakers in charge of Black males' socialization generally alter their instructions to Black males. The alteration accounts for "real" practices of American values and beliefs in American society that Black males may be experiencing at a given time and ones that will be experienced in the future.

The Black Male Peer Group

The Black male peer group may be especially influential in Black men's lives during early adulthood. The influence is significant because Black men, during this stage, are highly vulnerable to directives from others. Levinson et al. (1978) have defined the age period from seventeen to twenty-four as the Early Adult Transition period. This period, which may be earlier for many Black males, links adolescence and early adulthood. These Black males are exploring, modifying the self, and attempting to create a life in the adult world. For the Black male experiencing much conflict in attempts to separate from this primary group, the Black male peer group often serves as an anchor. He often finds refuge with those who are undergoing the same conflicts, apprehensions, pleasures, and preparation for adulthood. By this time, too, many teachings of the primary group have been severely tested by the Black male's own experience as well as the experiences of his peers.

Fortunately or unfortunately, the peer group slowly becomes more and more a significant self-validating agency supplanting, for a time, the primary group's importance to the Black male. Certainly, it is not unusual for the Black male peer group to become the young Black male's most significant other nurturing his masculine identity. In fact, this significant other, a kind of "social world," is reflected in the young Black male's self—consistent with G. H. Mead's idea that self reflects society.

Mainstream Society and Black Males

Mainstream society completes the triangle, and for many Black males, this point of the triangle is the most lethal. When it is linked with the other two points (the Black male primary group and the Black male peer group), and the socialization process is the result of interaction between the three points, many Black males are devastated, as I discuss later.

It is not an overstatement to say that perhaps the most reviled, mistreated, misunderstood, and neglected human being ever to live in America is the Black male. Mainstream society, in teaching young Black males, fails them miserably because it wants nothing to do with them. Because of this, most Black males' societal conditioning consists solely of proscriptive teaching (what Black males are not supposed to do), with little emphasis on prescriptive teachings. Perhaps the emphasis on proscriptive teaching is to be expected, since most of this socialization occurs within such restrictive institutions (as juvenile detention centers, prisons, and halfway houses) or via vicarious, subtle, exclusionary practices (most Black males are subjected to this kind of mainstream societal socialization). Moreover, the reluctance to teach Black males directly what they *should do* as men in society may be due to a reluctance to accept Black males as men on a level with other recognized men in American society. This would mean full recognition of the various masculinities of Black men and some alterations in hegemonic definitions of masculinity. American society may not be prepared to do this at the present time.

The Nature of the Lethal Socialization Triangle: Production of Types of Black Masculinities

The triangle Black males experience produces types of selves that make Black males enigmas in American society, not only because of the complexity of Black men's selves but also because of the complexity of their interactions. In fact, the complexity of interactions derive from the complexity of selves. Of great importance for this analysis is sociologist Sheldon Stryker's assumption that "self is cause rather than consequence of behavior" (1980). This assumption is consistent with the idea that Black male behavior is a function of Black male social construction, which is related to Black male socialization. The sources of Black male socialization are conflicting expectations held by people in three related, though distinct, social worlds comprising Black males' society: (1) the Black males' peer group; (2) the Black males' primary group; and (3) "mainstream society." For a variety of reasons, the influences on Black males of any one of the above socialization sources will be variable. Black males entering the first phase of the adult life cycle are especially susceptible to peer group influences, as noted earlier. Structure of family of origin (presence or absence of father, older male siblings, and older male relatives) also may affect the extent to which the male peer group influences the Black male. Number and type of responsibilities assumed by males during the entering adulthood phase also impact variables with respect to Black male socialization. Black males can be typed according to the predominant influence of any one of these worlds at a given time in life. Peer group controlled Black males generally are involved in a number of social relationships dependent on their commitment to the peer group. Moreover, the relationships entered into usually are quite deep and far-reaching. Perhaps, as Sheldon Stryker (1980) implies, Black males become committed to Black male peer groups because numerous relationships between themselves and significant others are related directly to their membership in Black male peer groups. In addition, such relationships are quite likely to be perceived as in-depth ones by these Black males, further increasing commitment to the peer group. For example, today many Black males are poised to enter adulthood with limited education, no developed skills outside of mainstream society, and with little or no support from societal structures (e.g., the economic institutions, the political institutions, the educational institutions). Many of these men suffer truncated relationships with their primary groups and look to their peer group for the basis of their male identity. William Strickland contends that for males in mainstream society, the primary basis of identity is work (1989, 52, 110). Black males, like much of the Black community, realize that persistent discrimination, the decline of smokestack industries, the suburbanization of jobs, and generally stagnating urban economics all have led to decreasing employment and chronic unemployment for large numbers of Black males during the 1990s (Larson 1988, 109–10). As a result, Black males along with much of the Black community have constructed alternative general definitions of masculinities for Black males.

Black Male Peer Group–Controlled Masculinity

One such definition may be termed "Black male peer group–controlled masculinity." The peer group not only constructs this type of masculinity but enforces adherence to its prescriptions and proscriptions. In terms of Robert Merton's classification of modes of individual adaptation in society, the tendency for Black men to turn to the Black male peer group for their masculine identity is both innovative and resourceful. Many do not participate in societal institutions for reasons of exclusion or voluntary nonparticipation (William Harris contends that many Black men choose not to attend church because they find it hypocritical and untenable [Harris 1990, 22]). Thus, construction of Black masculinities may bear little resemblance to mainstream masculinity or at the very least, drastically alter forms of mainstream masculinity. Still, the versions of masculinity constructed and adopted by many Black males must be considered viable alternatives in a society such as ours. Strickland contends that "as we enter the last decade of the twentieth century, we face a danger more covert, more insidious, more threatening and potentially more final than these: the apparently sly conspiracy to do away with Black men as a troublesome presence in America" (Strickland 1989, 48).

When Black males are peer group controlled, the types of masculinities evolving generally are based on the key traits of aggressiveness, violence, competitiveness, heterosexuality, cool poses, dominance, sexism, and passivity/indifference in mainstream society. While some may feel that these traits are dysfunctional in today's society, for many Black males, internalizing and displaying such traits are logical strategies to follow in a society that produces, at best, men who must develop multiple personalities in order to function reasonably well in their day-to-day activities.

Black Male Primary Group Controlled Masculinity

As noted earlier, the Black male's primary group is a second side of the lethal triangle socializing American Black males. These groups are as diverse as the Black male population, and numerous varieties of the Black male's primary group exist. The groups vary in makeup, function, and emotional climate. The Black male's primary group may consist of two parents and siblings, a single parent and siblings, or an extended family with several generations living together. The socioeconomic status of the Black male's primary group also may range from upper class to lower class; and the emotional climate of the group can be a source of unparalleled value for the Black male or one of little significance. Needless to say, economic factors often intervene to affect the extent to which the Black male's primary group influences the Black male.

Poverty is a major problem for the Black males' primary group in the United States. Because of the high incidence of households in which single females are responsible for rearing Black males, and the fact that three-quarters of such families are below the poverty level, their socializing influence on many Black males may be minimal. Gibbs (1988) feels that "Black youth are the ultimate victim of a legacy of nearly 250 years of slavery, 100 years of legally enforced segregation, and decades of racial discrimination and prejudice in every facet of American life." She goes on to reiterate numerous authors' views that "the brutality of slavery, the cruelty of segregation, and the injustice of discrimination" all have resulted in Blacks enduring inferior schools, substandard housing, menial jobs, and other indignities of poverty. Still, many Black parents, from generation to generation, held on to the idea, through all of these travails, "that their children would eventually merge into the mainstream of American society."

The fact that Black parents traditionally have held on tenaciously to the idea that their children would become a part of the mainstream did not eradicate barriers in the social structure that deny Black males full societal participation. It is because such obstacles to Black male upward mobility have persisted through the generations that presently a crisis exists in the Black community. Certainly there has been a modicum of progress for Black males since the late 1960s, but there also have been only disappointing increases in the status of Black males since the early 1980s. Susan Tiff, writing for *Time* magazine (1990, 83) reports that "the signs of crisis are everywhere, with nearly one in four Black men ages 20 to 24 in jail, on probation, or on parole." She goes on to report that Black males are less likely to attend college than Black females or white females or white males. Tiff notes that homicide is the leading cause of death for Black males ages fifteen through thirty-four; and she quotes Secretary of Health and Human Services Louis Sullivan: "When you look at a long list of social pathologies, you find Black men Number 1" (1990, 83). Through all of these difficulties, however, many Black males experience a type of socialization that is fundamentally primary group controlled with modifications that are consistent with American societal values. This type of socialization experience, where the primary group predominates, produces Black male behavior that is more likely to be conforming to mainstream society's norms and values. It also produces a fairly great number of Black men who bear the brunt of a racist and violent society. Usually it is due to their primary group influences, which teach them the necessary survival skills, that these Black men remain socially functional males in American society with a minimum of social pathologies.

Mainstream Society Controlled Black Men

Mainstream society forms the third point of the lethal socialization triangle for Black males and the third controller of Black males. Understanding this point of the triangle is relatively easy. Informed socializing agents such as television, radio, newspapers, and movies portray Black males in ways quite contradictory to the messages given them by their Black peer groups and the Black community. The mainstream media seem to portray young Black males as "roving, irresponsible predators." Ishmael Reed contends that President Bush's "Willie Horton ad campaign in 1988 was successful because it was created after a decade of Black male bashing by the mass media" (1992, 40).

For Black males, the result of mainstream society's socialization into manhood is to inform these men that they are outside of mainstream society. Black men are invisible in American society, the media contend. Certainly there are some Black men with influence, such as Louis Sullivan, Secretary of the United States Department of Health and Human Services; Virginia Governor Douglas Wilder; Gen. Colin Powell; and New York City Mayor David Dinkins. However, these men are seen as exceptions to the rule. By and large, mainstream society and Black males themselves overwhelmingly receive images of Black males that link them with highly publicized statistics of social pathologies. Reed (1992) asks the question, "Why are Black faces and bodies used to illustrate most social pathologies—illegitimacy, crime, illiteracy, alcoholism, drug addiction, spousal abuse, prostitution, AIDS, family abandonment, and abuse of the elderly—when there are millions more whites involved in those activities than Blacks?"

That Black males particularly are vulnerable to a kind of mainstream society socialization inimical to their well being is not a new phenomenon. Black males receive the same kind of generic socialization messages as White males. While there has been some alteration in traditional masculinities during the last two decades, much of the alteration has been less real than imagined or hoped for. Males in America still are expected to assume aggressive, competitive, dominant, and powerful roles in society. This is true despite the fact that lip service is paid to the notion that males today can be sensitive and nurturing in their relationships with others, including other males. Yet, the everyday activities of men remain constrained by rather rigid definitions of appropriate or acceptable masculinities.

The definitions of masculinities deemed acceptable have the following broad themes: dominance, competitiveness, violence, homophobia, sexism, and misogyny. Mainstream society subtly and not so subtly teaches Black males that it is manly to hold dominant roles in society's basic institutions (e.g., the family, the economy, politics, religion, and education). Those men who hold such positions are rewarded with status, prestige, esteem, and even more, legitimate power.

In the case of Black men, however, the necessity to prepare for occupancy of such roles often is learned. However, all too often Black men also learn that numerous impediments lie in their paths to occupancy of prestigous and powerful positions. Sociologist William J. Wilson (1987, 56) contends that "the exodus of middle- and working-class families from many ghetto neighborhoods removes an important 'social buffer' that could deflect the full import of the effects of prolonged periods of joblessness in Black inner-city neighborhoods." Wilson reasons that basic institutions (church, schools, stores, recreational facilities, etc.) remain viable if much of the base of their support comes from economically stable and secure Black families. He goes on to state that the very presence of such families means that children may observe increasing joblessness and idleness, but they also see people regularly going to work; they may see many children dropping out of school, but they also learn a connection between education and meaningful employment; they may recognize an increase in crime, but they also learn that many residents in the neighborhood are not involved with crime. Wilson concludes that it is not so much discrimination in current mainstream society that spells doom for many Black families and, by inference, Black males. Rather, Wilson feels that social isolation is the culprit. Social isolation, according to Wilson, results in exclusion from the job network, lack of interaction on a sustained basis with people who are employed and steady breadwinners, and underdevelopment of cognitive, linguistic, and other educational and job-related skills necessary for the field of work, among other debilitating consequences for Blacks in the ghetto.

While Wilson's analysis is penetrating, it does not pay sufficient attention to deliberate attempts to keep the Black male in place. The fact that Black males face numerous obstructions in their efforts to assume visible masculine roles in American society is an issue that must be addressed if we are to understand the Black males' plight in America. How Black males construct their various masculinities in the face of such obstructions must be subjected to analysis in any viable study of Black masculinities in America. It is quite possible that when Black males are mainstream society–controlled they are in the greatest danger. Mainstream society–controlled Black masculinity is the type of masculinity that is most contradictory and conflictual and the least supported for Black males. When mainstream society socialization predominates, the Black male's masculine identity is tied to contradictory and conflictual bases. Thus, the behavior that is likely to be produced can be expected to be contradictory and conflictual. This likelihood will become more apparent as the influence of mainstream society increases.

Sex Role Strain and Black Masculinities

Joseph Pleck first introduced the sex role strain model as an analytical tool that can be used to explain the male sex role. This analytical model, following Pleck's lead, suggests usage of the lethal sociological triangle model to understand the impact of socialization experiences on the Black male. In addition, it also proposes a link between the socialization experiences and Black male behavior, suggesting that such behavior will be most intimately linked to the socialization point to which a particular Black male is most committed. Different identities are likely to be invoked in various situations.

To trace consequences of the lethal socialization triangle involves empirical study—questions Black male studies should explore. For example, it is possible that the identity salience and commitment variables related to the Black male peer group become increasingly interwoven and influential as social class and social status decrease. In other words, the higher the socioeconomic status, the less the influence of the Black male peer group, and, conversely, the lower the socioeconomic status, the greater the influence of the Black male peer group. Needless to say, this influence is not always positive. Since mainstream society stresses male power and success while simultaneously blocking Black male opportunities, when primary group influences are weak or nonexistent and when the Black male peer group tends toward an exaggeration of those negative aspects of traditional masculinity, we get a case like 2 Live Crew's "As Nasty as They Wanna Be" 10 million seller. What is striking about the recording is not so much the sexually explicit language as it is the virulent and pervasive debasing of women. It is a perfect example of what the lethal socialization triangle has done to some Black males in America. These Black men hate their parents, their women, their religion, their "bitches," and finally, themselves, while all the time remaining enslaved to their white masters. The triangle strangles these Black males. I contend this is a consequence that occurs when mainstream society stresses male success, dominance, aggressiveness, misogyny, and *keeping Black males in oppressive conditions.* Only when Black masculinities become integral aspects of the men's movement and the academic men's studies area will the Black man in America become less of an enigma.

CHAPTER 2

Klansmen, Nazis, and Skinheads: Vigilante Repression

by Ken Lawrence

In its routine functioning, white supremacy denies people of color a fair share of society's resources and power through its economic, political, legal, and cultural structures—which together are often called institutional racism. By definition, institutional racism operates automatically; that is, specific and deliberate acts of discrimination are not required to achieve a white-supremacist result. Often all that is necessary is to preserve previously existing economic, political, and social differentials.

In the United States, the principal victims of institutional racism, and white supremacy generally, are African-Americans, both because they are the largest group oppressed racially and because they have been kept in an oppressed condition longer than any other people with the exception of Native Americans. (The oppression of Native Americans is institutionalized, but not in the sense meant here, and the specific mechanisms are beyond the scope of this chapter.)

Institutional racism can only persist to the extent that its routine functioning is not effectively challenged, but oppressed people are rarely docile for long. Insurgency, whatever its character—legal or illegal, violent or nonviolent—is a political act, and the response designed to preserve the white-supremacist system is political repression. Often the situation appears otherwise, because ruling classes typically attempt to criminalize acts of insurgency.

Three basic forms of political repression exist together in our society. The most precise of these, the activities of the secret police, tend to be most effective when their political targets can be defined as specific individuals or organizations (Lawrence 1985). The most amorphous and diffuse, police brutality, is the typical method of stifling insurgency in oppressed communities, nations, and classes. The third variety, which is our subject here, falls somewhere in between but intersects both of the others: *vigilante violence*—right-wing terrorism committed by ostensibly private (nongovernmental) individuals and organizations.

Violent repression is almost always gender specific, directed by and against males, although there are exceptions. One example is the well-known beating of civil-rights leader Fannie Lou Hamer in the Grenada, Mississippi, jail on June 9, 1963 (Zinn 1965). The reason that incident caused a public outcry and revulsion, even in the white community, was that such violence committed against a woman was socially taboo, even among militant racists. But during 1963 and 1964, Hamer's organization, the Student Nonviolent Coordinating Committee, documented hundreds of cases of racist violence and terror directed against Black men, including instances of murder, that did not evoke comparable public concern and condemnation.

The other taboo was killing whites who participated in the freedom movement. A number of Black men were murdered by racists in Mississippi in the summer of 1964, but only one, James Chaney, is widely remembered, because he was killed in the company of two white colleagues, Michael Schwerner and Andrew Goodman (Huie 1968). As long as Black men were the sole victims, little media attention was directed at the problem, and few perpetrators were brought to justice.

From the viewpoint of the white ruling class, the existence of right-wing terrorists is quite literally a necessary evil (except for its members who embrace them with enthusiasm). The stench of Nazism continually wafting from that fringe is an embarrassment to a class whose self-justifying mythology is based on its hegemony over an open and (within limits) pluralistic society. But when the need arises to employ violence and terror, liberal welfare workers can't be sent to do the job.

For their part, the fascists are not content to be mere hirelings, goon squads serving at the pleasure of plutocrats. Their aim is revolutionary, to seize power and remake the country according to their own vision, purging society of the people they regard as parasites and racial inferiors. For that reason there is always a risk when the rulers choose the vigilante method of repression. When all else is equal, the police and military, loyal to and commanded by official authority, are the preferred instruments.

The fact that the ruling class has a recurring need for Ku Klux Klan and neo-Nazi ruffians to carry out its dirty work when its preferred repressing authorities are not up to the task means that from time to time it is also necessary to repress those fascists too, lest they develop sufficient political following and momentum to take power in their own name.

Some Ku Klux Klan History

Ever since the end of the Civil War, vigilante terrorism has typically been white supremacist and conspiratorial, epitomized by the Ku Klux Klan, but it has not always been fascist. The KKK was born in 1866. Fascism was not born until the ruins of World War I darkened Europe. The Klan was around for half a century before fascism existed in the world and actually taught the fascists a great deal in their early years.

In the 1860s the Klan, led by the notorious Nathan Bedford Forrest, represented the guerrilla continuation of the war he had fought as a Confederate general. In essence Forrest, who had been a Memphis slave trader before the war, and the worst war criminal of the Confederacy, exchanged his grey uniform for a white sheet. The earliest Klan, then, was a restorationist movement of the Confederacy.

The Invisible Empire was something quite different when it arose in the 1920s. It was essentially a bourgeois nativist movement and was not primarily based in the South. The KKK had the potential to go further than it actually did because in many places a person had to be a Klansman, or at least have the active endorsement of the Klan, to be elected to public office. The Klan came very close to capturing control of the national Democratic and Republican parties. It was a right-wing, white-supremacist, xenophobic, but essentially mainstream bourgeois movement, which intended to control the politics of the United States government and as many state and local governments as possible, through the traditional legal political apparatus (Chalmers 1981).

Revived in the 1960s, the KKK was essentially a backward-looking movement attempting to preserve what was most reactionary and most peculiar of the institutions of the segregated white South. It was under that banner, represented everywhere by the battle flag of the Confederacy, that it went out and committed beatings, bombings, lynchings, mutilations, and castrations.

It is something quite different today.

Now it is as likely to fight under the banner of the crooked cross, the Nazi swastika, as under the banner of the Confederacy. In fact, it is the genius of the Klan leaders of today that they have managed to merge these two movements into a single whole and to create a coherent ideology out of those two divergent strains (Lawrence 1982).

The Background of U.S. Fascism

The fascist movement got its real insurgent birth in the United States from Henry Ford through his newspaper, *The Dearborn Independent*. Today the neo-Nazis and the Klan consider his book *The International Jew* (1920) to be one of their bibles. Ford modeled his automobile empire as much as he could on the New Order fascist dictatorship to which he aspired for society as a whole. He even established an entirely segregated two-city system for his workers. Dearborn, home of what was then the largest factory in the world, the Ford River Rouge plant, was for whites; Inkster was its Black suburb. That little fascist ministate was not broken until the United Auto Workers CIO organized it in the 1940s, the last of the automobile trusts to be unionized.

Building on the movement that Henry Ford had founded, the fascists, but not the Ku Klux Klan, flourished in the 1930s. One of the largest mass movements in the United States, and one of the few outside the mainstream political parties that was capable of packing Madison Square Garden in those years, was Father Charles Coughlin's Christian Front. Huey Long built a similar movement in the state of Louisiana, called Share the Wealth, which was organized by the notorious anti-Semite Gerald L. K. Smith. (Smith later became one of the most important figures in the reconstitution of the fascist movement in the 1950s, bringing it into a working coalition with the Klan over a period of time.) Aviation pioneer Charles A. Lindbergh was their man on a white horse, while William Dudley Pelley and Gerald Winrod headed up the storm troopers (Carlson 1943, 1946; Seldes 1943).

Today's merged fascist movement has an ideology quite different from that of Nathan Bedford Forrest's Confederacy, or the nativism of David C. Stephenson, the main figure of the KKK's 1920 rebirth, or of 1960s Klan leaders Sam Bowers and Robert Shelton. On the other hand, many of the leading

Klansmen of the sixties have accommodated themselves quite well to the new line, which they had shunned as un-American twenty-five years ago. The new line was exemplified by the United Racist Front in North Carolina, responsible for the 1979 Greensboro massacre when five members of the Communist Workers party were murdered (Lawrence 1981).

How the Ku Klux Klan Became Fascist

The Ku Klux Klan did not become fascist overnight. But racists, even when divided by important points of doctrine, have considerable areas of political agreement, so it is no accident that one of the leading fascists of the thirties, Gerald L. K. Smith, was also close kin to the Klans of the fifties and sixties, and that most of the Klans borrowed heavily from his journal *The Cross and the Flag.*

The earliest attempt at merging the two movements was in 1940 at Camp Nordland, New Jersey, when the German-American Bund and the Ku Klux Klan met, 3,500 strong, on a Bund platform beneath a fiery cross. Anti-Semite Edward James Smythe presided, having spent three years working to consummate such a coming together. Arthur H. Bell, the KKK's Grand Giant, shook hands with August Klapprott, the Bund's vice-president, and Klapprott declared, "The principles of the Bund and the Klan are the same."

But that merger was not to be. A storm of unfavorable publicity forced the Klan's Imperial Wizard, James Colescott, who had originally authorized participation in the meeting, to recant and to repudiate the Nazis. Eventually Colescott's literature listed fascism among the foreign "isms" the Klan officially opposed, and Smythe's dream was stillborn (Carlson 1943).

But from that time on, some of the most committed Nazis viewed the KKK as their most likely road to power. Among these was J. B. Stoner, who was a Klan Kleagle (organizer) in Tennessee during World War II but was also organizing a "national anti-Jewish political party" and distributing the favorite tract of the Jew-haters, *The Protocols of the Learned Elders of Zion,* a document forged by the secret police in czarist Russia to justify anti-Jewish pogroms. In 1958 the National States Rights Party (NSRP) was founded by Edward Fields, who had worked with Stoner in the forties, and Matthias Koehl. Koehl later succeeded George Lincoln Rockwell as head of the American Nazi party.

Stoner's Nazi sympathies were never veiled. He told the *Atlanta Constitution* in 1946 that Hitler had been too moderate and that his party wanted "to make being a Jew a crime, punishable by death." But he also practiced law jointly with KKK leader James Venable of Atlanta (Carlson 1946). During the early years of the NSRP, Stoner's role was low profile (the 1958 Birmingham church bombing for which he served a prison term was committed during this period), but he eventually emerged as its national chairman and main spokesman.

After the United Racist Front, a Klan/Nazi umbrella organization formed in September 1979 in North Carolina, carried out the Greensboro massacre in November of that year, NSRP leaders Stoner and Fields saw the opportunity to hasten the fascist development of the whole movement. Fields organized the New Order Knights of the Ku Klux Klan, combining the two movements in the name. The New Order Klan simultaneously projected its politics (by organizing a union, then calling a strike to protest the hiring of Mexican workers at the Zartic Frozen Foods plant in Cedartown, Georgia) and promoted "Klan unity" (by inviting leaders of the various competing Klan factions to a meeting to "honor" two of the Greensboro killers). One Klan leader after another aligned himself with Fields, and the Nazification of the Ku Klux Klans was achieved (Lawrence 1981).

The Government Role

During the 1960s, civil rights workers in the South frequently reported that the Federal Bureau of Investigation was on the side of the Ku Klux Klan and Citizens Council white supremacists who were waging a war of terror and intimidation against them. Often when racists administered public beatings to freedom riders and voter registration workers, FBI agents would observe and take notes. They would never intervene to protect the victims, let alone arrest the perpetrators of violence.

In November 1962, Dr. Martin Luther King, Jr., publicly complained about the attitude of FBI agents in the South. "To maintain their status, they have to be friendly with the local police and people who are promoting segregation," he said. FBI director J. Edgar Hoover, whose grudge against King predated that statement, and who worked secretly to undermine, smear, and discredit King as a popular leader from then until the civil-rights leader was assassinated in 1968, publicly blasted back in 1964, branding King "the most notorious liar" in the United States.

Justice Department documents made public many years later confirmed what civil-rights activists had said all along. John Doar, an attorney in the Justice Department's Civil Rights Division during the 1960s, wrote, "During 1961 to 1963 the Bureau investigated many intimidation cases. The fact that it had conducted an investigation did some good but it made few, if any, cases and its performance—for the Bureau—was far from adequate. This was due, in part, to the limited size and scale of the Bureau's operation in Mississippi, part due to the attitude of some Mississippi agents, and part was certainly due to the fact that the Bureau's civil rights section at the seat of government did not understand the problem of intimidation in Mississippi, nor the inefficiency and corrosion of some—but not all—of the Mississippi resident agents."

Doar gave a specific example of the latter problem. In the summer of 1964, Attorney General Robert Kennedy sent a team of Justice Department lawyers to Mississippi, headed by Walter Sheridan, to investigate the escalating campaign of violence in the southwestern part of the state. "About the middle of

June, two lawyers from Sheridan's unit contacted Clarence Prospere, the resident agent in Natchez. They reported that Prospere was very uncooperative. He stated that in many matters the FBI considered the Justice Department attorneys 'outsiders.' He advised that no report would be sent unless he was specifically instructed to do so from the New Orleans field office. He would not agree to telephone if violence broke out, unless, again, he was specifically instructed to from New Orleans. He would give no background information on the area and on the identity of known extremists" (Senate Select Committee 1976b).

In the summer of 1964, members of the White Knights of the Ku Klux Klan of Mississippi murdered three civil-rights workers—James Chaney, Michael Schwerner, and Andrew Goodman—in Neshoba County. Under pressure from the public outcry that followed, the FBI set up a field office in Mississippi and solved the case. Director Hoover also ordered that "White Hate Groups" be a new subject for "counterintelligence" (Hoover's euphemism for covert action) under the now infamous COINTELPRO operation. Previous targets had been communists and other leftists, Black activists, and Puerto Rican nationalists.

But the anti-Klan COINTELPRO was quite different from the others. Whereas the order targeting "Black Nationalist–Hate Groups" instructed FBI field offices "to expose, disrupt, misdirect, discredit, or otherwise neutralize the activities of black nationalist, hate-type organizations and groupings, their leadership, spokesmen, membership, and supporters," the "white hate" COINTELPRO aimed at "the relatively few individuals in each organization who use strong arm tactics and violent actions to achieve their ends." The COINTELPROs directed against the Communist party, the Socialist Workers party, and the New Left went well beyond their memberships; the anti-Klan COINTELPRO did not (Senate Select Committee 1976a).

To establish this new COINTELPRO, the FBI actually created a statewide Ku Klux Klan organization from scratch (the state has never been disclosed), and recruited two hundred members to it. The Senate Select Committee on Intelligence (1976a) concluded that this tactic "risked increasing violence and racial tension." At a speech to one Klan rally, the FBI's undercover man told his KKK followers, "We are going to have peace and order in America if we have to kill every Negro."

Gary Thomas Rowe, an FBI informant in the Alabama-based United Klans of America, was one of the most vicious when it came to terrorizing civil-rights activists. He surfaced in March 1965 as an eyewitness to the murder of Viola Liuzzo, a participant in the Selma-to-Montgomery voting rights march. Many people believe the testimony of Rowe's fellow Klansmen, who swear that Rowe himself was the killer.

In some cases in the 1960s and 1970s, the United States government sponsored fascist terrorist organizations without even the pretense of being opposed to violence. It actually financed them, armed them, and directed their activities.

The United States Army's 113th Military Intelligence Group based in Evanston, Illinois, and the Chicago Police Department's Red Squad jointly operated a fascist organization called the Legion of Justice from 1969 to 1972. Legionnaires clubbed and maced members of socialist and antiwar organizations, broke into their headquarters and stole their files, and planted bugging devices; vandalized a progressive bookstore; stole films from Newsreel, a left-wing film making and distributing collective; and teargassed performances by a Soviet dance company and a Chinese acrobatic troupe with grenades supplied by a police Intelligence Division officer. In one case a legion member attended an antiwar rally, burned the rally organizer's hand with a cigarette, and then made his escape with police help.

The legion's founder, S. Thomas Sutton, had participated in Nazi and Ku Klux Klan mob violence against demonstrations for open housing and school desegregation in the 1960s. He ran as an independent segregationist candidate for governor of Illinois in 1968. On university campuses he agitated for the formation of a "right-wing terrorist underground." The post office box address Sutton used for the Legion of Justice in Elgin, Illinois, was also used by Robert B. DePugh's Minutemen, a supersecret right-wing guerrilla organization that had waged vigilante violence against the left until DePugh was captured and sent to prison on kidnapping, blackmail, and illegal weapons charges.

The legion had overlapping memberships with other fascist organizations, including the American Nazi Party, the National Socialist White People's Party, and the National States Rights Party. Besides the Legion of Justice, Sutton founded and led a racist organization called Operation Crescent from 1966 until his death in 1974. A Cook County, Illinois, grand jury report (1975) condemned the police and the army for operating the Legion of Justice (Stern 1976).

In the summer of 1971 the Secret Army Organization was founded by former members of the Minutemen on the West Coast. The main SAO target was Peter Bohmer, an antiwar activist in San Diego, California. On one occasion, two SAO members drove past Bohmer's home, firing shots into the house and wounding a woman inside. Other Secret Army vigilante acts against the peace movement included slashing tires, telephone death threats, destroying property, arson, and firebombing, but the police never managed to catch the perpetrators.

After the SAO bombed a theater in 1972, the San Diego police could no longer look the other way. They knew the FBI had an undercover informer inside the SAO, and they demanded to know his identity. The FBI supplied his name: Howard Berry Godfrey, a former Minuteman and the commander of the SAO's terror squad. In the arrests that followed, police confiscated quantities of explosives and munitions that had been acquired from Camp Pendleton, with the tacit approval of the police and the FBI as it turned out. Even with the Secret Army Organization fully exposed, the FBI remained loyal to Godfrey, obstructing the investigation and concealing the evidence (Committee for Action/Research 1973).

In 1973 Lyndon LaRouche's National Caucus of Labor Committees (NCLC), which had started out five years earlier as a bizarre left-wing cult, suddenly emerged as a vigilante organization. LaRouche ordered his storm troopers to launch violent attacks on communists, socialists, labor, and welfare rights activists in a terror campaign he called Operation Mop-Up. The violence continued over the next three years as Operations Counterpunch and Amsterdam, broadened to add Maoist organizations as targets. In 1975, former members reported that LaRouche was sharing intelligence reports about the left with the U.S. military. By 1977, NCLC members were serving as auxiliary spies and provocateurs for the FBI and the New Hampshire police. During the Reagan years, NCLC intelligence agents enjoyed direct access to officials at the Central Intelligence Agency and the Defense Intelligence Agency (King 1989; Liberation News Service 1973; Terrorism Information Project 1976a, 1976b; Kahn et al. 1977).

The Klansmen and Nazis who murdered five members of the Communist Workers party in Greensboro had been infiltrated by two provocateurs, Bernard Butkovich of the U.S. Treasury Department's Bureau of Alcohol, Tobacco, and Firearms, and Edward W. Dawson, an informant for the Greensboro Police Department and the FBI, who urged the fascists to make an armed attack on the CWP's "Death to the Klan" demonstration, and who led them to it while other Greensboro police looked on but made no move to prevent violence (Lawrence 1981; Bermanzohn and Bermanzohn 1980).

The Role of the Military-Industrial Complex

The August 7, 1967, *Los Angeles Times* carried a front-page photo showing a big, burly white man viciously beating two peace marchers on Wilshire Boulevard. Reports at the time noted that antiwar demonstrators in Los Angeles and San Francisco had been attacked by members of a motorcycle gang, some said by Hell's Angels. These assaults, and similar ones in other places, were generally assumed to be unorganized, spontaneous outbursts of patriotic passion.

Actually, the man in the *Los Angeles Times* photo was Michael Halsey Brown, even then a veteran Nazi, founder and leader of the Iron Cross Motorcycle Club and the Oakland Suicide Squad. In the 1950s he had been a member of George Lincoln Rockwell's American Nazi Party and headed Rockwell's U.S. Nazi Motorcycle Corps. Many years later, Brown told how key backing for his terrorist activities had been provided by retired Lt. Gen. Pedro A. del Valle (James 1983).

Del Valle's admiration for fascism may have begun when he was the official U.S. military observer posted with the Italian forces in Eritrea in 1935. During World War II he commanded the First Marine Division during the battle of

Okinawa. After the surrender of Japan, he retired from the Marine Corps (*New York Times* 1935, 1945).

Del Valle became a vice-president of International Telephone and Telegraph Corporation and later president of ITT of South America (*The Reaper* 1984). He was in the news during the fifties as a spokesman for ultraconservative causes: publicly defending Sen. Joseph McCarthy against censure by the U.S. Senate and urging U.S. military backing for attacks on China by Chiang Kai-shek's nationalists and on North Korea by Syngman Rhee's forces in the South (*New York Times* 1954, 1955). He was prominent in anti-Semitic organizations, including Merwin K. Hart's National Economic Council and his own Defenders of the American Constitution (Forster and Epstein 1964; Janson and Eismann 1963).

Despite his emergence on the fringe regarded as too extreme even by the John Birch Society, del Valle remained well connected. As commander at the United States Central Naval Academy at Annapolis, he invited a prominent Italian fascist to conduct a three-day seminar for Pentagon and CIA representatives on "The Techniques and Prospects of a Coup d'Etat in Europe" (Christie 1984).

During the Vietnam War, del Valle served as a go-between linking the U.S. commander in chief of the Pacific fleet with mercenaries who mounted operations against targets off limits to the military, which the Navy could not officially condone (*The Reaper* 1984). While he was orchestrating some of the dirtiest actons against North Vietnam, he sat on the advisory board of the National Youth Alliance, a neo-Nazi organization that had emerged out of the Youth for Wallace movement after George Wallace's 1968 presidential campaign (Lipset and Raab 1970). NYA became the National Alliance; its commander was and still is William Pierce, author of *The Turner Diaries* (Macdonald 1978). And, as mentioned above, del Valle was providing powerful backing for the biker-stormtroopers hired to break up antiwar demonstrations in California, led by Mike Brown.

Later, in 1974, when "Pete" (del Valle's code name to his Nazi contacts) "wanted to flex a little muscle," he turned to Mike Brown, who "wanted very much to be that muscle," to bomb the United Nations building in New York. The bomb didn't go off, Brown was captured, and he served a term in federal prison.

Even after del Valle died in 1978, nobody suspected that he had been the link connecting the mighty U.S. military machine in Asia, the mercenary efforts that exceeded the few constraints imposed on the military there, and the vigilante terrorists back home battling in the streets against the antiwar movement. This true Daddy Warbucks story remained secret until Mike Brown reminisced to *The Spotlight*, the weekly tabloid published by Willis Carto's anti-Semitic and racist Liberty Lobby, in 1983 (James 1983).

But once Brown had told all, it made sense. Without that kind of support and direction, his neo-Nazi bikers really could not have sustained much of a threat. Just a year later, in the fall of 1984, a Nazi publication announced that Mike Brown was coming out of retirement. *National Socialist Vanguard Report* wrote, "He asks that former members of the Oakland Suicide Squad, the Iron Cross Motorcycle Club and other fighters who are interested in 'hitting the bricks' with him again to contact him" (1984, 8).

To date, no specific person or connection has been publicly identified as providing the military-industrial backing for the new wave of Klan-Nazi terrorism in the United States; but many 1980s activities of the sort backed by Pedro del Valle internationally in the 1960s have been the handiwork of Major General John Singlaub, former commander of U.S. troops in South Korea, and chairman of the World Anti-Communist League, an organization that has worldwide connections with right-wing governments and death squads and with neo-Nazi movements. Singlaub was one of the principal recruiters of private financial backing for the Nicaraguan contras from wealthy industrialists during the years of Ronald Reagan's presidency (Anderson and Anderson 1986).

Although links connecting the corporate elite and the current generation of vigilante terrorists have not been proven, it would be folly to assume they don't exist.

United States Fascism in the 1980s and 1990s

The difference between the new face of the Ku Klux Klan and its earlier expressions is that the role of racism and anti-Semitism and scapegoating in general is quite different ideologically for a fascist movement from that of a right-wing conservative movement or a traditional Klan-type movement. It is not to put people in their place; it is not to make a subclass out of them and to exploit, or superexploit, their labor. It is *genocidal*. It is *exterminationist* (Lawrence 1982).

The manual of the current Klan/Nazi strategy is a 1978 and 1980 novel, *The Turner Diaries*, written by William Pierce, fuehrer of a Nazi group called the National Alliance, under the pseudonym Andrew Macdonald (Gearino 1980, Macdonald 1978, 1980). It is a stirring call to arms. To cast it in literary terms, it turns *The Iron Heel* upside down. Where Jack London projected a look back at the future revolution to see its horrors, William Pierce employs the same literary strategy to extol the revolution that creates the New Order and to show how he wants it to take place.

The fictional strategy for the Nazi seizure of power presented in *The Turner Diaries* is very similar to the actual strategy of the neo-Nazis in Europe. The French fascist who devised the strategy, Michel Faci, who uses the nom de guerre LeLoup, calls it the *strategy of tension*. He recommends resorting to bombings and other terrorist atrocities as attempts at social destabilization. The time for them is ripe, he says, because the fascist movement has reached its peak "respectable" legal strength. Now it is time to polarize society and build on the fears, the tensions, and the disarray that can be created by disrupting the fabric of politics as usual, and at the same time highlight the relative weakness of official authority (Edgar 1982; Lawrence 1982).

The Turner Diaries begins, after a period of difficulty and repression of the right, with the bombing of the FBI building in Washington. It goes from there, with ever-escalating violence, to its climax, a nuclear war launched by the fascists after they have captured a portion of the U.S. nuclear arsenal. Along the way, Pierce includes a lot of dialogue designed to differentiate the politics of his movement from conservatism:

> [The conservative] didn't understand that one of the major purposes of political terror, always and everywhere, is to force the authorities to take reprisals and to become more repressive, thus alienating a portion of the population and generating sympathy for the terrorists. And the other purpose is to create unrest by destroying the population's sense of security and their belief in the invincibility of the government.

Other passages indicate a similar desire to destabilize society. The culmination of this he describes as follows:

> *August 1, 1993.* Today has been the Day of the Rope—a grim and bloody day, but an unavoidable one. Tonight, for the first time in weeks, it is quiet and totally peaceful throughout all of southern California. But the night is filled with silent horrors; from tens of thousands of lampposts, power poles, and trees throughout this vast metropolitan area the grisly forms hang.
>
> In the lighted areas one sees them everywhere. Even the street signs at intersections have been pressed into service, and at practically every street corner I passed this evening on my way to HQ there was a dangling corpse, four at every intersection. Hanging from a single overpass only about a mile from here is a group of about 30, each with an identical placard around its neck bearing the printed legend, "I betrayed my race." Two or three of that group had been decked out in academic robes before they were strung up, and the whole batch are apparently faculty members from the nearby UCLA campus.

He describes how they did this:

> Squads of our troops with synchronized watches suddenly appeared in a thousand blocks at once, in fifty different residential neighborhoods, and every squad leader had a long list of names and addresses. The blaring music suddenly stopped and was replaced by the sound of thousands of doors splintering, as booted feet kicked them open. . . .
>
> One of two things happened to those the troops dragged out onto the streets. If they were non-Whites—and that included all the Jews and everyone who even looked like he had a bit of non-White ancestry—they were shoved into hastily formed columns and started on their no-return march to the canyon in the foot-

hills north of the city. The slightest resistance, any attempt at back talk, or any lagging brought a swift bullet.

The Whites, on the other hand, were, in nearly all cases, hanged on the spot. One of the two types of preprinted placards ["I defiled my race" or "I betrayed my race"] was hung on the victim's chest, his hands were quickly taped behind his back, a rope was thrown over a convenient limb or signpost with the other end knotted around his neck, and he was then hauled clear of the ground with no further ado and left dancing on air while the soldiers went to the next name on their list.

The hangings and the formation of the death columns went on for about 10 hours without interruption. When the troops finished their grim work early this afternoon and began returning to their barracks, the Los Angeles area was utterly and completely pacified. The residents of neighborhoods in which we could venture safely only in a tank yesterday were trembling behind closed doors today, afraid even to be seen peering through the crack in drawn drapes. Throughout the morning there was no organized or large scale opposition to our troops, and by this afternoon even the desire for opposition had evaporated.

That spells out the aim and the strategy of today's neo-Nazis and Klansmen. It's very different from bombing a church here, lynching a civil-rights worker there, in order to keep people in their place. It is actually a vision of seizing control of the entire society, exterminating minorities, Jews, and white "race traitors," and creating something quite different. When the fascists' apocalypse comes, there will be no grace given to women and children, obviously, but until that day arrives, they will probably continue to focus on males of the inferior races and treasonous classes.

A white-supremacist group called Aryan Nations center in Hayden Lake, Idaho, spawned a gang called the Order, modeled after the fictional organization of that name in *The Turner Diaries*, which sought to implement the novel's vision literally, in real life. Financing themselves with the proceeds from activities such as counterfeiting, holding up banks, and robbing armored trucks, members of the Order carried out dramatic acts of exemplary violence, including the 1983 machine gun murder of Alan Berg, a Jewish radio personality in Denver (Singular 1989).

Tolerating, even creating, fascist organizations to terrorize the left and insurgent minority protestors is one thing; permitting a fascist group to embark on a path aimed at the overthrow of the government is quite another. Even a Washington administration insensitive to the meaning of Bitburg wasn't about to permit that kind of activity to grow unchecked. Over the past few years, the government has vigorously pursued the Order, killing its founder, Robert Mathews, "turning" or otherwise corrupting some of its members, and jailing others. But a trial of fourteen top white supremacists in Fort Smith, Arkansas, ended in acquittals, enhancing the prestige of the main three: Louis Beam, believed to be the underground movement's top commander, former head of the most violent Klan faction in Texas, best known for its attacks on Vietnamese fishermen in Galveston Bay; Richard Butler, founder of the Aryan Nations; and Robert Miles, head of the racist Christian Identity Church, who served six years in prison for bombing school buses in Pontiac, Michigan, in 1971. The Fort Smith acquittals were celebrated by 250 white supremacists who gathered at Hayden Lake for the Aryan Nations World Congress in July of 1988.

Despite that setback, the government isn't likely to let up on its attempts to suppress these forces in the Nazi movement, and its concern is understandable. Robert Miles once regaled his KKK followers, "When a Klansmen finds he has cancer, or is ill or something and doesn't have long to live, he should cash in his insurance, send his family away, and buy himself a rifle. He can then go hunting for big game—judges, politicians, and government guys." But this Medusa monster won't die. As the government packed the surviving members of the order off to prison in 1985, its successor, the Order II, was formed, emerging in 1986 to carry on the Nazi revolution. It soon launched another wave of robberies, bombings, and murder, but its members, too, were captured, and in 1988 four Order II terrorists pleaded guilty to charges of racketeering, counterfeiting, and firearms violations (Lawrence 1989).

While federal, state, and local authorities have kept the heat on the sectors of the terrorist right that include the government itself among their principal targets, other overlapping branches of the Klan/Nazi movement have been relatively unscathed by prosecutions. These include the most menacing of the vigilante street fighters, who aim their violence at protest movements among oppressed people, peace activists, progressives, and leftists.

Today's storm troopers are being organized by different factions of the neo-Nazi right. David Duke is a former Ku Klux Klan leader and head of the National Association for the Advancement of White People. He was an elected member of the Louisiana legislature, but after he lost a hotly contested race for governor in 1991, his popularity waned both in his home state and nationally. In 1988 he was the presidential candidate of the Populist party, whose principal vehicle is the tabloid newspaper of Willis Carto's Liberty Lobby, *The Spotlight*, the most widely circulated anti-Semitic weekly in the United States. *Spotlight* circulation has dropped below 100,000, down from its peak of 340,000 in the early 1980s, but Liberty Lobby reaches untold thousands more through its weekly satellite radio broadcast, "Radio Free America." This is also the faction that sponsors the Institute for Historical Review, a pseudo-scholarly center in California that specializes in adducing evidence that the Nazi Holocaust never happened, that it's simply an invention by Jews to secure permanent special status for the state of Israel. The mass constituencies pursued by this wing of the fascists include family farmers driven to desperation by the agricultural crisis. Allied with them are other groups, such as former members of the militant Posse Comitatus (now defunct), followers of the martyred "tax protester" Gordon Kahl, and blue-collar workers who feel their jobs are threatened by minorities, immigrant workers, and foreign imports.

More violent and dangerous at present are the so-called Third Position fascists who oppose both the "communist East" and the "capitalist West," mirroring the line that has a broad following among Nazis in Europe. The tendency is called "Strasserite," after the brothers Gregor and Otto Strasser, who represented the most radical anticapitalist wing of German National Socialism until Adolf Hitler brought them to heel. The main U.S. advocates of the Third Position are Gary Gallo, leader of the National Democratic Front, and Tom Metzger, head of the insurgent White Aryan Resistance (WAR). As a vigilante leader, Metzger, a former California Ku Klux Klan leader, is probably the most dangerous right now. An excerpt from his speech to the 1987 Aryan Nations World Congress sums up his political line:

> WAR is dedicated to the white working people, the farmers, the white poor. . . .
> This is a working class movement. . . . The conservative movement in this country is dead. The right wing is dead. The Marxist left never was alive, so don't worry about that. This is the white wing. . . . Our problem is with monopoly capitalism. The Jews first went with capitalism and then created their Marxist game. You go for the throat of the capitalist. You must go for the throat of the corporates. You take the game away from the left. It's our game! We're not going to fight your whore wars no more! We've got one war, that is right here, the same war the SA fought in Germany, right here, in the streets of America.

Metzger's WAR promotes racial solidarity of white people in the United States and Russia, opposes U.S. intervention in Central America, supports the environmental "green" movement, and backs militant strikes by mainly white workers, such as the 1988 P-9 strike against Hormel in Austin, Minnesota. But the main recruits for battle are alienated street youth, neo-Nazi "skinheads," organized by Metzger's son John and trained in hand-to-hand combat and knife fighting by John Metzger's White Student Union/Aryan Youth Movement (Anti-Defamation League 1987). Tom Metzger's call-in taped Aryan Alert spells out the vigilante aim when he gives the addresses of various minority, left, and progressive organizations and says to his followers, "Why don't you pay them a visit?" He got even more specific about members of the John Brown Anti-Klan Committee (which has fought Metzger every step of the way), calling upon his members to find out "where they eat, where they meet, and where they sleep." Metzger specifically builds on the militancy of other sectors of the fascist movement. He led a demonstration in support of the Fort Smith defendants, for example, and despite serious disagreements, he endorsed David Duke's gubernatorial campaign. Yet Metzger is not harassed or stopped, even in ways the government could carry out routinely. His weekly television show, "Race and

Reason" (named after Carlton Putnam's 1961 segregationist bible which holds a special place in the racist pantheon), airs in more than forty cities with nary a raised eyebrow from the Federal Communications Commission.

The Metzgers and their neo-Nazi skinheads have taken every advantage of public exposure. Even a face-to-face confrontation with antiracists on the Oprah Winfrey show helped them more than it hurt, and skinhead violence is now the main form of vigilante terror in the United States. Nurtured by racist rock music, Nazi youths have perpetrated such atrocities as nailing a man to an eight-foot plank after he defected from their ranks; hurling a teenaged boy through a plate glass window after he tried to prevent them from putting up an anti-Semitic poster; and kidnapping and torturing a prostitute. They threatened to lynch a Black woman (Lawrence 1989).

On November 13, 1988, three Portland, Oregon, skinheads beat to death Mulageta Seraw, an Ethiopian man, with a baseball bat. The three have since pled guilty and are serving long prison terms. In one of the very few published case studies of Nazi skinhead activities, Elinor Langer (1990) has shown the Metzgers' importance in organizing the skinheads in Portland.

Skinhead violence has spread to every part of the United States, erupting in California, Florida, Illinois, Massachusetts, Michigan, Nevada, Ohio, Oklahoma, Oregon, and Texas. During the first six months of 1988, the Klanwatch project of the Southern Poverty Law Center documented twenty assaults, four arsons, three murders, thirty incidents of vandalism, and twelve cross burnings, all committed out of extreme racial or religious bias. "Half of the assaults and two of the murders were officially attributed to neo-Nazi skinheads," says the Klanwatch report, and to those should be added the explicitly political acts of violence against antiracist organizers. As Langer (1990, 85) notes, more recent estimates are unavailable: "Everyone agrees [the number of incidents of hate-motivated violence] are dramatically increasing, but there are no reliable figures."

Even the numbers of adherents to the various Klan and Nazi organizations cannot be estimated with precision, she writes. "Estimates made by [the Klanwatch Project of the Southern Poverty Law Center, the Center for Democratic Renewal, and the Anti-Defamation League of B'nai B'rith] range from about 10,000 to about 20,000 members of these groups nationally, with the organizations agreeing on a rule of thumb of about ten passive supporters for every hard-core member—and thus a possible total of up to 200,000—and agreeing as well that the numbers are conservative" (Langer 1990, 85).

Conclusion

Because white-supremacist vigilante repression has become Nazified, it is politically more complicated than in the past incarnations of both the Ku Klux Klans and the Nazi/facists. Langer commented on the significance of this development:

Although one group may start with the Jews and end with the blacks and another may start with the blacks and end with the Jews, they are linked by the newer idea that blacks are the latest woe that the Jews are heaping on the world. These are not the only convictions held in common, of course. Hostility to homosexuals and aliens, to name only the two other groups, is also universal, though reflected less in the current ideological libraries than in the streets. But it is above all else the centrality of the Jew, even in the wake of the Holocaust, that makes me believe that "neo-Nazi" is the proper label for the movement in question. The quality of its hate and the direction of its intentions go beyond what we have seen in America before. As anomalous as it seems in a country in which blacks are not only the primary historical but also the primary daily victims of racism of every description, the Jew is, increasingly, the ultimate target; and lest the logic elude you, it is that, out of fear of being recognized as a race themselves, the Jews have conceived and implemented a variety of political strategies, of which integration is only the most offensive, designed to minimize racial differences in general. The significance of the historic shift on the far right from the dominance of the Klan to the dominance of the Nazi-influenced skinheads and others is in fact precisely the linkage of blacks and Jews in an explicitly genocidal context. . . . However much some Jews, and some blacks, may now wish to part company, from the neo-Nazi viewpoint they are part of the same problem, as are gays and every other minority as well. (Langer 1990, 84–85)

These are the politics that drive today's vigilante terrorists, who make up one leg of the triangle of political repression. Ironically, their most fertile recruiting ground is among alienated white youths who just a few years ago seemed more attracted to the left's vision of peace, equality, and social justice, but today have turned away from those ideals in favor of the white-supremacist new order. Vigilante repression, like government repression, is now a permanent feature of the U.S. political landscape. Black freedom organizations, liberals, and leftists have developed fairly sophisticated organizing networks and political/legal strategies to combat state repression, both that of the secret police directed against specific targets and the more diffuse and generalized repression of entire communities by random police violence. Far less attention and resources have been devoted to this other aspect of political repression. If that doesn't change fairly soon, the situation will get a lot worse.

It can happen here.

CHAPTER 3

Neoconservative Attacks on Black Families and the Black Male: An Analysis and Critique

by James B. Stewart

This chapter examines aspects of the treatment of race and culture in the analyses and public policy prescriptions of neoconservatives. Particular emphasis is placed on how the circumstances facing African-American males are conceptualized. In traditional conservative thought, males have precedent over females, and a special importance is attached to the family as a primary social unit. Males are treated as the principal mediators between the family and external institutions, particularly political-economic structures. As a consequence, neoconservative portrayals of Black males decry the perceived retrogression from this traditional role. Caricatures that project images of disproportionate involvement in criminal activity by Black males and welfare dependency of Black women have been used to promote the broader neoconservative agenda. The most familiar example of such image creation is the Willie Horton ad used by the Republicans during the 1988 presidential campaign.

First, this chapter explores the intellectual foundations of neoconservative theories of gender roles, families, and society. Aspects of traditional conservative thought relevant for understanding the specific character of neoconservative attacks on Black males and Black families are presented in the second section. The foundations of contemporary neoconservative analyses in the work of E. Franklin Frazier are then explored in the third section. That section includes a critique of Frazier's model based on an alternative perspective advanced by W.E.B. Du Bois. Neoconservative analyses of Black family life and Black males are presented and critiqued in the fourth section. Many of Frazier's formulations are shown to be similar to those of contemporary neoconservatives. These views are then counterposed to an alternative perspective on the historical and contemporary realities of African American life in America that is informed by the work of Du Bois. In the alternative framework, metaphors such as "endangered species" and "institutional decimation" are used to describe the linkage of African American males to the larger society. The essence of this perspective, in the words of Barbara Solomon (1988, 304), is that public policy is the source of "difficulties for black males in social functioning generated by circular and dysfunctional transactions vis-à-vis family, school, and work."

The analysis is concluded with a summary of the state of intellectual discourse about Black males, the Black family, and the significance of race and culture in American society.

Foundations of Conservative Thought

The image of the Black male as predator is used by neoconservatives to illustrate what they interpret as the result of a social experiment gone awry. Black males are portrayed as the equivalent of Frankenstein's monsters created by permissive social policies. These social policies have allegedly produced a rejection of fundamental values and beliefs required for acceptance as functioning members of society. This "deficit" model focuses on the failure to conform to "mainstream" behavioral expectations. "Dysfunctional" behavioral patterns supposedly result from weak intermediary social institutions, for example, family and church, that are the major vehicles through which inculcation of core values occurs. Governmental intrusion is opposed by neoconservatives because it presumably reinforces unproductive behaviors.

One of the distinguishing characteristics of traditional conservatism is its emphasis on the rights of church, social class, family, and property. These rights are asserted as primary relative to the authority of the state and to the forces fostering both individualism and nationalism (Nisbet 1986, 22).

Conservative thought embodies a profound emphasis on historical continuity in human relations. Nisbet attributes to Burke the suggestion that: "People will not look forward to posterity who never look backward to their ancestors" (1986, 24). History is treated not as a linear process but rather in the context of "the persistence of structures, communities, habits and prejudices generation after generation" (1986, 24).

Democracy was treated with suspicion by traditional conservatives: "One of the great dangers of democracy was its creation of the mass . . . through emphasis upon the majority and through egalitarian values which tended to level populations" (Nisbet 1986, 46). Liberty and equality are viewed as incompatible because while "the abiding purpose of liberty is its protection of individual and family property . . . the inherent objective of equality . . . is that of some kind of redistribution or leveling of the unequally shared material and immaterial values of a community" (Nisbet 1986, 47). From this perspective efforts through law and government to counteract differences in outcomes resulting from variation in innate talents and abilities cripple the liberties of all, "especially the liberties of the strongest and the most brilliant" (Nisbet 1986, 47).

Conservatives emphasize the importance of intermediate associations in democracies because "they offset, by their very existence and the loyalties they win from their members, the ever-mesmerizing power of the social democratic state and its creed of equality" (Nisbet 1986, 37). Given the family's stature as the foundation of society, "the authority—and thereby the freedom or autonomy of the family—is sacrosanct; neither the state nor the church may rightfully transgress upon the prerogatives belonging to kinship" (Nisbett 1986, 38). Nisbet (1986, 52) argues that "much of the conservative veneration for the family lies in the historic affinity between family and property." The role of custom and law is to protect the family character of property, as seen in definitions of the role of women in ways that gave primacy to family inheritance of property.

In conservative thought it is intermediate groups that have a responsibility to provide direct aid to those in need rather than government. The rationale is that these groups are closer to the individual. By extension, the primary purpose of government is seen as nurturing the strength of intermediate groups. To bypass these groups through welfare aid provided directly to classes of individuals is argued to be both an invitation to discrimination and inefficiency and a source of group erosion (Nisbet 1986, 62).

As a transition to the examination of the treatment of the lives of people of African descent in neoconservative thought, it is critical to keep in mind that many of the initiatives undertaken during the "Reagan Revolution" were not consistent with traditional conservative ideology as summarized above. To illustrate, Nisbet argues that "tireless crusades to ban abortion categorically, to bring the Department of Justice in on every Baby Doe, to mandate by Constitution the imposition of 'voluntary' prayers in the public schools, and so on" are inconsistent with the views of conservatives that "the surest way of weakening the family . . . is for the government to assume, and then monopolize, the family's historic functions" (1986, 104).

This disjunction would be understood as reflecting the linkage between a body of thinking and particular sociopolitical developments. Traditional conservatism had its roots in the reaction to the French Revolution, while, as Nisbet (1986, 99) notes, neoconservatism is a product of the 1960s.

The image of Black males that is found in contemporary neoconservative thought also has historical roots. Its historical political roots lie in the ideology of racial oppression that has undergirded race relations in this country. Its historical intellectual roots have been a mirror image of that ideology. The propagation of that image in intellectual circles was accomplished most effectively by the Black sociologist, E. Franklin Frazier. Although Frazier could hardly be described as a conservative, he laid the groundwork for the contemporary harnessing of quasi-conservative ideology and a distorted image of Black males through his decidedly negative portrayal of Black family life and Black males.

Pouring Old Wine into New Bottles

Frazier's (1926) discussion of Black families could easily have been incorporated into a contemporary neoconservative tract. Black families, in his view, suffer from a "lack of traditions, knowledge, and ideals which all people acquire by living in the social and physical environment to which they have become adopted" (210). However, Frazier's methodology was much more coherent than that of contemporary neoconservatives. Frazier (1927, 165–66) maintains that investigations of African-American families must both take an historical approach and apply the method of cultural analysis, which was designed to take "into account all the factors, psychological, social, and economic, which determine the character of any group. . . ."

Assessing how this methodology would relate to the study of Black families, Frazier (1927, 166) claims that the Black family "would not present the unique characteristics which a family group like the Chinese, where the family is based upon blood, land, law, and religion, and is the 'practical unit of social control in the village,' would present if placed in the American social environment."

This indicates that Frazier, like traditional conservatives, insists that the examination of contemporary issues be undertaken within the context of an understanding of the evolution of societal institutions. Following his line of reasoning there is no need for a separate analysis of African-American culture, because European-American culture is the only appropriate frame of reference. "Generally," he suggests, "when two different cultures come into contact, each modifies the other. But in the case of the Negro in America it meant the total destruction of the African social heritage" (Frazier 1927, 166). Frazier argues that African Americans had failed not only to introduce innovative familial adaptations, but also to conform to European-American norms. For Frazier, then, pathology was endemic in African-American families rather than an institutionalized feature of the social structures that constrained the opportunities of Blacks.

Frazier (1966, 367) went so far as to suggest that it is only within the context of the American milieu that Black life has meaning: "When one views in retrospect the waste of human life, the immorality, delinquency, desertions, and broken homes which have been involved in the development of Negro family life in the United States . . . the Negro has found within the patterns of the white man's culture a purpose in life and a significance for his strivings which have involved sacrifices for his children, and the curbing of individual desires and impulses indicates he has become assimilated to a new mode of life."

For Frazier, the institution of slavery was the source of the deculturation of African Americans. As a consequence, it is no surprise that when Frazier looked for positive examples of family life during the era of enslavement he could locate them only among free Blacks. He insisted that it was within this group "that family traditions became firmly established before the Civil War" (Frazier 1966, 362).

This desirable pattern of family development was contrasted to a matriarchal pattern that Frazier saw as the norm. He argues that "only the bond between the mother and her child continually resisted the disruptive effect of economic interests that were often inimical to family life among slaves. Consequently, under all conditions of slavery, the Negro mother remained the most dependable and important figure in the family" (Frazier 1966, 32).

The modal pattern of development described by Frazier was clearly inconsistent with the ideal of family centrality and stability projected through traditional conservative thought. Only the experiences of the free Black family remotely resembled conservatives' image of the family.

Frazier (1966) maintains that the two distinct lines of family development continued to diverge after the Civil War. One line of development extended the tradition of free Blacks such that "the authority of the father was firmly established, and the woman in the role of mother and wife fitted into the pattern of the patriarchial household . . . [and] the father became the chief, if not the sole breadwinner" (88). The second pattern of family development entailed women becoming "responsible for the maintenance of the family group . . . [after severance of] the loose ties that had held men and women together in a nominal marriage relation during slavery" (p. 88).

Frazier (1966) applauds the urbanization of Blacks in the early twentieth century, although he recognizes the potential for the exacerbation of problems of family organization and functioning. His positive assessment stems from his belief that urbanization combined with a transformation of the linkage of Black males to the new economic order would strengthen partriarchal family structures. Thus, he argues that "the most significant element in the new social structure of Negro life is the Black industrial proletariat. As the Negro has become an industrial worker and received adequate compensation, the father has become the chief breadwinner and assumed a responsible place in his family" (1966, 366). Unfortunately, the industrial sector did not generate the magnitude of employment opportunities for Black males envisioned by Frazier, and a new chapter in the continuing history of economic subordination was written.

This model of underdeveloped patriarchal family life among African Americans was adopted by Moynihan (1967) to describe subsequent developments. Neoconservatives have resurrected Moynihan but have been less forthcoming about the legacy of Frazier. In fact, as will be presented in the succeeding discussion, the only deviations from Frazier's paradigm that can be found in neoconservative writings about Black families and Black males have been retrogressive and have involved a weakening of the explanatory framework by (a) transforming a dynamic historical model into a static ahistorical framework and (b) substituting governmental programs for the institution of slavery as the vehicle for "underdevelopment" of the Black family.

Given the significance of Frazier's work as a foundation for neoconservative projections of Black families and Black males, it is important to understand the limitations of Frazier's analysis. These can be identified by contrasting Frazier's analytical framework with that of a contemporary, W.E.B. Du Bois.

Du Bois, like Frazier, understood that Black family life had undergone extraordinary stress in the American environs. Du Bois (1908, 31) acknowledges that "we have striking evidence of the needs of the Negro American home. The broken families indicated by the abnormal number of widowed and separated, and the late age of marriage, show sexual irregularity and economic pressure." However, Du Bois (1908, 31) argued that "these things all go to prove not the disintegration of Negro family life but the distance which integration has gone and has yet to go."

While Du Bois was very much an integrationist and shared many of Frazier's views about the "civilizing" effect of slavery, he did not advocate total assimilation of values and behaviors. As an example, in discussing sex mores he argued that "the Negro attitude in these matters is in many respects healthier and more reasonable. Their sexual passions are strong and frank, but they are, despite example and temptation, only to a limited degree perverted or merely commercial. The Negro mother-love and family instinct is strong, and it regards the family as a means, not an end, and although the end in the present Negro mind is usually personal happiness rather than social order, yet even here radical reformers of divorce courts have something to learn" (1908, 42).

The major difference between the views of Du Bois and Frazier is associated with the assessment of the implications of integration of Blacks into the industrial order. Du Bois (1908, 36) warns that "low wages and a rising economic standard is postponing marriage to an age dangerously late for a folk in the Negro's present moral development" [and that] "present economic demand draws the [N]egro women to the city and keeps the men in the country, causing a dangerous disproportion of the sexes." Thus, even in the early period of industrialization, in some cities males had less access to employment opportunities created by industrialization and urbanization than Black women had.

Unlike conservatives and neoconservatives, Du Bois (1924, 142) saw the movement of Black women into the labor market as a harbinger of future developments rather than as an indicator of incomplete assimilation of the norms of white family life: "The Negro woman more than the women of any other group in America is the protagonist in the fight for an economically independent womanhood in modern countries. Her fight has not been willing or for the most part conscious but it has, nevertheless, been curiously effective in its influence on the working world."

Du Bois thus offers a direct challenge to the model of family organization advocated by the Frazier/Moynihan/conservative/neoconservative school of thought. Du Bois' model, which rejects traditional patriarchal organization, serves as the basis for the contemporary critique of neoconservative analyses of African-American families and African-American males. In addition, as will be noted below, neoconservative commentators have weakened their own case by failing to draw on the work of Frazier.

Neoconservativism, Black Families, and Black Males

Denial of Persisting Structural Barriers

The foundation of neoconservative examinations of Black life and culture is the frontal assault on the public policies associated with the Great Society and the War on Poverty programs initiated during the 1960s. Governmental programs originating during this era are now under attack on charges that they exacerbate rather than ameliorate contemporary social problems. The overt discriminatory behavior and social disadvantages that previously existed have presumably been eradicated by Civil Rights laws. Neoconservatives selectively emphasize carefully chosen social indicators of "progress" in reducing inequalities to make their case. This type of rationale is exemplified by Gilder's (1981) discussion of labor market trends. Gilder argues that during the last twenty-five years, since the massive dismantling of legal barriers, African Americans have outperformed other Americans as measured by various indices. While Gilder acknowledges that discrimination persists in some pockets of the labor market, he argues that "it has only a small impact on the relative incomes of Blacks and whites" (1981, 132–33). The extension of Gilder's argument is that such progress is threatened by the perpetuation of policies developed in the 1960s, because they engender dysfunctional behavior and handicap the potential for further improvement through deregulation of market mechanisms.

Gilder's analysis is consistent with that of Williams (1982, 2), who challenges the general intellectual thrust that "there are collective forces that seek to deny Blacks socioeconomic opportunity which must be offset by some other force in order to give Blacks equal changes." He observes that "when choices are made in the market arena, people, including poor people, have a higher probability of getting *some* of what they want, even if they are a minority. When choices are made through the political arena, they very well may get *none* of what they want" (1982, 142).

The analyses of Gilder, Williams, and others are used to project images of rife sexual and familial irresponsibility permeating predominantly Black communities. Consider, for example, a description used by Gilder of "hundreds of thousands who are not necessarily fathers of the particular children they happen to be living among . . . who live for a while with a welfare mother before moving on to another one [and] are not forced to marry or remain married or learn the disciplines of upward mobility" (Gilder 1981, 116). Gilder's imagery is remarkably similar to that used by Frazier (1966). All that has been done is to update the linguistic referents from the post–Civil war era to the post–civil rights era.

Ahistoricism in the Examination of Contemporary Patterns

Although the principal points of attack of neoconservatives are the social programs developed during the 1960s, in some cases there is also reinterpretation of events and processes at work during earlier periods. Such reinterpretations are always limited to the post–Civil War period, however. Thus, Black conservative Orlando Patterson (1972) has argued for Blacks to move "toward a future that has no past." This perspective is also implicit in the title of the journal published by Black conservatives, *The Lincoln Review*, which invokes the spirit of the republicanism of Abraham Lincoln to provide a guiding vision.

The importance of the foregoing discussion is that although traditional conservatives emphasize the preservation of tradition and the critical role of history in providing guidance for the present, neoconservatives are curiously unwilling to engage in serious assessment of the relevance of the era of chattel slavery for contemporary American culture. Instead, they declare, without serious intellectual discourse, that all historically conditioned barriers have been overcome. This line of argumentation is wholly inconsistent with traditional conservative thought and has the effect of reducing lived history to irrelevancy. In addition, it is totally opposed to the methodology advocated by Frazier (1927). Thus, although Frazier and the neoconservatives wind up in the same camp, he reaches his destination through systematic application of an analytical framework while their journey is a meandering quasi-intellectual safari.

The grounds for the curious aversion to history exhibited in neoconservative analyses are largely political. The goal is to avoid the issue of whether compensation is due for past wrongs. Neoconservatives reject such compensation on the grounds that to do so would violate the liberties of the contemporary "innocent" generation. These intellectual gymnastics fuel the general denial that there are still structural barriers associated with earlier periods that adversely impact the contemporary life chances of African Americans.

The Role of Theories of Sex Roles and Beliefs in Black Genetic Inferiority

The themes identified above are virtually invariant across authors regardless of race/ethnicity and include, in addition to Gilder (1981) and Williams (1982), other white neoconservatives such as Murray (1984) and Black neoconservatives like Sowell (1975). Most neoconservative writers, with the exception of Gilder (1981), fail to ground their analyses directly in traditional conservative philosophy and, instead, frame their arguments using questionable analogies and cursory intergroup comparison.

Gilder's work is of particular interest because he reverts to the traditional conservative model of sex roles to describe the plight of Black males. Gilder (1981, 114) criticizes the expansion of public assistance on the grounds that "the benefit levels destroy the father's key role and authority." These circumstances described by Gilder are portrayed as violating basic societal organizational norms in which the male is the provider, "the definitive male activity from the primal days of the hunt through the industrial revolution and on into modern life" (1981, 115). He argues that "unlike the mother's role, which is largely shaped by biology, the father's breadwinner duties must be defined and affirmed by the culture" (1981, 115).

The male's response to the weakening of his role is described as a "combination of resignation and rage, escapism and violence, short horizons and promiscuous sexuality" (Gilder 1981, 115). But in this instance, Gilder argues, "the pattern is often not so much a necessary reflection of economic conditions as an arbitrary imposition of policy—a policy that by depriving poor families of strong fathers both dooms them to poverty and damages the economic prospects of the children" (1981, 115).

In the end, however, Gilder's principal concern is not with the micro-level behaviors, per se; rather, he bemoans the fact that "welfare, by far the largest economic influence in the ghetto, exerts a constant, seductive, erosive pressure on the marriages and work habits of the poor, and over the years, in poor communities, it fosters a durable 'welfare culture' . . . [that] continuously mutes and misrepresents the necessities of life that prompted previous generations of poor people to escape poverty through the invariable routes of work, family, and faith" (1981, 122). The question, however, is that if the primal urges and sex roles dictates that Gilder ascribed to African Americans are so ingrained in the long history of humankind, how can twenty-five years of public policy so easily distort and misdirect them?

The failure to address this issue is highly problematic, because Gilder relies heavily on argumentation that relies on changes in sex roles to explain trends in earnings and labor force participation. But his argumentation references only contemporary phenomena and abstracts from what is supposed to be primal conditioning. He maintains, for example, that there is no way to reconcile the interests of Black men with the cause of feminism and insists that "the main impact of feminism is to take jobs and promotions away from . . . men and give them to educated women" (1981, 137).

Gilder proposes increased aggressiveness of African-American males as a solution: "In their present pass, black men need a dimunition of the emphasis on credentials and qualifications in the American economy and an increased stress on aggressiveness, competitiveness, and the drive to get ahead. . . . It is the greater aggressiveness of men, biologically determined but statistically incalculable, that accounts for much of their earnings superiority" (1981, 137).

Gilder's resort to biological determinism is problematic for several reasons. First, historically such arguments have been associated with claims about the genetic inferiority of Blacks. Second, to suggest that Black males should diminish efforts to obtain higher levels of schooling in an era during which the Black male presence in higher education is declining borders on the ludicrous for two reasons: (1) with respect to contemporary labor market outcomes, acquisition of higher order credentials constitute a necessary strategic competitive strategy; and (2) as it relates to marital patterns, the consensus of scholars who examine patterns of marriage formation is that comparability in educational attainment and social status increases marriage probabilities (see Macpherson and Stewart, 1991, for a discussion of this research). Third, a declining emphasis on academic achievement serves simply to reinforce the arguments of proponents of the genetic intellectual inferiority of Black who use differences in educational achievement to buttress their position.

The extent of Gilder's subscription to a biological model of Black inferiority cannot be overemphasized. He observes, for example, that "the biological factor is particularly important in giving black men their small edge over black women. Unlike the larger advantage of white men over white women, the black male superiority, according to statistical analysis, is almost entirely attributable to sexism. Because of the difficulty female-headed families face in disciplining boys, black women are several times more likely to have high IQs than black men and are substantially superior in academic performance. On credentials alone, black men would not be able to complete with either black or white women in employment or to function as preferable providers" (1981, 136).

Thus, in Gilder's view, Black males are inferior intellectually to all other racial/gender cohorts and must compensate by increased aggressiveness if the traditional male role is to be re-established. For Gilder the critical question is why "the black males' edge over their women . . . is so inadequate to sustain the male role as provider and the father's place in the home" (1981, 137). The policy implications of his views follow directly: "Even if disguised by regular litigation in favor of black men, the antidiscrimination drive can only reap a harvest of demoralization, work-force withdrawal, and family breakdown, and a decay in the spirit of work, family, and faith on which enduring upward mobility depends. The crucial goal of an antipoverty policy must be to lift the incomes of males providing for families and to release the current poor from the honeyed snares of government jobs and subsidies" (1981, 152).

Segregation and Labor Market Behavior

Other neoconservative commentators, especially Black neoconservatives, shy away from such overtly biological models that gaily pronounce the inferiority of Blacks. However, their implicit subscription to associated premises is evident through their aggressive defense of segregation as a desirable residential pattern and in their treatment of criminal activity. Most Black neoconservatives argue that racial segregation is not a critical source of persisting inequality. Public policy initiatives to reduce segregation are seen as violating the rights of individuals to associate voluntarily. As an illustration, Williams (1982, 10) argues that "it is efficient for people with similar tastes and the means to pay for public goods to reside together. If communities exhibit a high degree of homogeneity, it is less likely that local budget and expenditure decisions will be highly offensive to any one individual's set of tastes." But Williams ignores the extent to which limited choices of Blacks produce involuntary location relative to access to public goods.

The issue of segregation and its impacts is closely linked to the question of the labor market behavior of Black males and the general economic condition of peoples of African descent. As noted by Boston (1988), "To conservatives numerous factors explain this [disadvantagement] better than racial discrimination. These include ethnic differences in age, education, geographical location, job experience, occupational distribution, family size, and culture." Boston (1988) has presented a detailed critique of the specific interpretations offered by Thomas Sowell. He suggests that the explanations offered by the neoconservatives do not stand up under careful scrutiny. Boston argues that "not only are qualified blacks relegated disproportionately to lower status jobs, but their concentration in such positions is reinforced by occupational mobility barriers" (1988, 159). More generally, a variety of studies have convincingly documented the continuing barriers to employment that Black males experience as a result of their disproportionate numbers in central city areas (see Cain and Finnie 1990; Farley 1987; Hughes and Madden 1991; Ihlanfeldt and Sjoquist 1989; and Leonard 1987).

Darity and Myers (1986, 173) have mounted an equally forceful challenge to the work of Murray (1984). They suggest that Murray's account of an apparent power shift in the 1960s associated with the transformation of poverty policy is "embarrassingly oversimplified" and that "understanding growth of welfare in the 1970s requires a history that begins at least in the 1930s, when the competition between the business and managerial elites originated" (1986, 173). While acknowledging the accuracy of Murray's description of the weakening labor market attachment of Black teenage males and increased involvement in illicit activities, they criticize the lack of an explanatory paradigm to account for these patterns. In particular, they argue that no prescription is offered regarding "where all the jobs would come from to employ these young black males, or how marriages will suddenly materialize out of a new 'responsibility' urgently pressed upon youths who are now in prison, or about to be imprisoned." Darity and Myers (1986, 176) suggest that "what is clear is that this pool of marginalized black males poses so serious a puzzle for Murray that, in his few encounters with them in the course of the discussion of black poverty, he must acknowledge his utter ignorance.

Illicit Economic Activity (Crime)

Conservatives and neoconservatives treat the high level of criminal activity in predominantly Black communities as an indicator of the breakdown of traditional civic values. However, this view is at odds with that which has emerged from the analysis of criminal activity by economists. As noted by Vicusi (1986, 301), "The economic analysis of criminal behavior has focused on the economic incentives to engage in illegal actions. . . . According to this model if the expected rewards from criminal behavior exceed the net benefits of alternative pursuits, the individual will choose to engage in crime. Crime is not fundamentally different from legitimate occupational pursuits." Vicusi concludes that "although minor changes in the economic environment may not dramatically alter the overall youth crime problem, the criminality among those who are not in school or employed is very sensitive to economic incentives. Since members of this group are responsible for most of the youth crime, they comprise a major, economically responsive component of the criminal population (1986, 344). The problem, as noted by Thompson and Cataldo (1986) is that the expected earnings from illicit activity are extraordinarily high. In Vicusi's (1986) study average earnings are $22,495 on an annualized basis. As observed by Thompson and Cataldo (1986, 348), "Such levels are hardly comparable to either expected legal earnings ($3,800 for the crime-committing subgroup), nor are they at all comparable to actual crime income ($1,570)." Thompson and Cataldo conclude that "expectations of illegal income opportunities are overly influenced by a few relatively good opportunities close at hand and by the fact that the youths do not adequately discount their longer-term crime prospects once these short-term options are used up" (1986, 348).

The larger issue at stake is the model of criminality that underlies both conservative and economic theories. Georges-Abeyie (1978, 37) claims that "the current array of popular criminological and criminal justice theories fail, for the most part, to offer insight into the dynamic of Black criminality, and criminal justice processing." Georges-Abeyie (1981, 99) advocates a social-ecological model that attributes above-average rates of Black criminality in large part to "the fact that blacks reside in 'natural areas' of crime. According to Georges-Abeyie, Blacks disproportionately reside in an ecological complex with characteristics that engender high rates of criminality. The characteristics of this socio-geographical space that condition high levels of criminality are identified as (1) deteriorated or deteriorating housing, (2) limited or nonexistent legitimate employment and recreational opportunities, (3) amonic behavior patterns, (4) a local criminal tradition (which started prior to the duration of the current Black ethnic group in residence), (5) abnormally high incidence of transient or psychopathological individuals, (6) a disproportionate number of opportunities (due to mixed land use) to engage in criminal deviance or to develop subcultures that are extra-legal (criminal or quasi criminal), (7) an area where poverty and limited wealth is the norm rather than the exception."

It is interesting to note that the model proposed by Georges-Abeyie for the study of behavioral patterns is similar to that championed by Frazier. As noted in Stewart (1990), Frazier adapted the human ecology model developed by the Chicago Sociological School. The model requires the segmentation of a geographical space into zones with differing physical characteristics so that the processes of urban expansion and change can be measured along the main thoroughfares radiating from the center of the city. The metrics employed in this approach include rates of poverty and home ownership.

Neoconservatives tend not to engage in detailed systematic investigations required by the method of social ecology or by other accepted traditions of empirical investigation. The closest example is Wilson's (1987) analysis of the so-called permanent Black underclass. As a member of the Chicago school, Wilson has been careful to ground his analyses within the social-ecological tradition.

Neoconservative Policy Recommendations

In general, the critiques that have been integrated into the presentation of neoconservative analyses of Black families and Black males demonstrate a failure of this school of thought to generate conclusions that are supported by available data. This derives from the propagandist as opposed to scientific thrust of their analyses. This thrust carries over to the sphere of policy recommendations.

As noted previously, in traditional conservative thought there are two related desirable policy thrusts: (a) the reduction of intrusion by government into private affairs, and (b) the empowerment of intermediate institutions as the cement of healthy societies. Neoconservatives have transformed proposition (a) into blind advocacy of the market mechanism as an alternative to government intervention. They have failed, however, to examine the extent to which expansion of the scope of market-conditioned activity weakens the specific intermediate institutions that are central to the traditional conservative model of viable societies. Neoconservative attacks on public policy directions originating in the 1960s fail to take into account the extent to which these policy directions in fact represent a negotiated arrangement between government and intermediate institutions that undergird the viability of African-American life and culture.

Black neoconservatives in particular rail against the traditional leadership of Black intermediate institutions and argue vociferously for de-emphasis of political activity as a vehicle for addressing inequality. Thus, they would have one type of intermediate institution relegated to an invisible background role despite the acknowledged importance of intermediate institutions as a check against governmental hegemony. Intermediate institutions that operate specifically in the political arena are probably the best equipped to challenge governmental excess.

Sowell's (1975, 147–48) commentary is illustrative of Black neoconservatives' assessments of Black leadership: "Leadership patterns among minorities tend to fit the rest of their social patterns. Groups given to excitement, violence, and emotionalism in general tend to produce flamboyant leaders, great orators, and individuals with personal charisma. Both the Irish and the American Negroes have produced numerous men of this sort, over the years. . . . The charismatic leadership tends heavily toward politics and other grand designs as means of advancing the race."

Sowell's analysis attempts to dissociate leadership from the organizations with which they are associated. This constitutes simply another example of the selective and biased interpretations that are characteristic of the neoconservative view of Black life and culture. Leadership that is chosen by a constituency and advances the agenda of that constituency is operating in a manner consistent with the expectations of traditional conservatives. As long as the interests of the constituents are being served by their leaders, traditional conservative thought would suggest that little attention should be focused on the criticisms advanced by neoconservatives.

Summary

In concluding this discussion and critique of neoconservative thought it is useful to summarize several of the principal charges levied against the neoconservatives. First, the accuracy of their characterizations of the contemporary status of

Blacks and behaviors in Black communities are highly suspect and are refuted by sophisticated empirical analyses. Second, the assignment of responsibility for producing current patterns of family organization and individual behavior to government policies of the 1960s is theoretically and empirically untenable even within the traditions of conservative scholarship. Third, the neoconservative analyses embody models of biological determinism to prescribe outmoded sex roles and posit the genetic inferiority of Blacks. Fourth, the policy recommendations offered by neoconservatives are advanced on the basis of dubious empirical support that are inconsistent with the tenets of conservative thought.

The preceding critique provides a foundation for presentation of an alternative "model" of the dynamics of the linkage of Black males and Black families to the dominant social order that is informed by the line of thinking introduced by W.E.B. Du Bois that was discussed previously.

Black Males, Black Families, and the Social Order: An Alternative Framework of Analysis

A large body of literature is available to provide the broad outlines of a functional model of how peoples of African descent have been and are linked to the social order and the specific effects of that linkage on Black males. The major requirements of such a model is to avoid the ahistorical character of the neoconservative speculations and to use the historical evidence to generate an assessment of the underlying objectives of public policy. The model must also critically examine the assumptions regarding sex roles that are embedded in traditional thought, utilizing the available knowledge about Black male-female relationships and sex roles in Black families.

Neoconservatives uncritically assume that the direction of public policy is to reduce inequalities between Blacks and whites. This conclusion derives from (a) a truncated historical analysis that gives inappropriate weighting to the post–1960 period and (b) the use of selected inaccurate measures of the linkage of African Americans to the social order.

Although neoconservatives are silent on the issue of slavery, modern perspectives on the institution have generated insights that undermine their interpretations of later developments. The modern perspective goes beyond even Du Bois, because he, like Frazier, accepted the now outmoded view that slavery destroyed African traditions among the enslaved, leaving in the wake an uncivilized mass. To illustrate, Du Bois was ambivalent on the question of the importance of African origins for contemporary culture patterns, noting that the attempt to relate contemporary conditions to an African past was "not because Negro-Americans are Africans, or can trace an unbroken social history from Africa, but because there is a distinct nexus between Africa and America which, though broken and perverted, is nevertheless not to be neglected by the careful student" (1908, 9).

A variety of research has discredited the traditional view and has documented the continuing importance of African survivals as part of the cultural repertoire of African Americans (see Blassingame (1972), Genovese (1974), Gutman (1976), Herskovits (1958), and Sudarkasa (1981)). This body of literature soundly refutes the simplistic view adopted by Frazier, Moynihan, and neoconservatives that African Americans constitute simply an incompletely assimilated subgroup of "Americans." Rather, the implications of the new scholarship are, first, that African Americans are bi-cultural and, second, that interventions designed to enhance their lived experiences must taken into account this enlarged and complex cultural repertoire.

This perspective is of critical importance not only in examining the dynamics of family functioning and sex roles but also in the context of transactions with other institutions in the society. Both Du Bois and Frazier analyzed the family as an institution that interacts with other institutions as part of a closely interconnected network. Unlike neoconservatives, they recognized that the market constitutes simply one of the many institutional structures within society. Neoconservatives portray the market as an apolitical, color blind, detached vehicle to which anyone can connect at will to achieve economic success.

Neoconservatives also attempt to depict government as detached from other institutions and to portray its functioning as being at odds with the well-being of society. But government is also part of the complex of institutions that constitute the social organism. It is charged, in part, with the maintenance of social order and the promotion of well-being for its principal constituents. African Americans have never been designated as a constituency whose interests are paramount. Rather, public policy has always operated to promote the well-being of other groups at the expense of Blacks.

Mechanisms to accomplish this subordination have included vehicles to (a) restrict the political and social status of African Americans and avoid revolts, (b) use Black labor as a stopgap to cover shortages of more desired labor sources, and (c) structure economic flows to prevent accumulation of sufficient economic resources by African Americans to challenge (a) and (b). Regulation of access to markets and public goods has been a key strategy in achieving these objectives. Economic flows are managed in part by the segmented character of labor markets that facilitates disproportionate over-representation of Blacks in low-wage jobs. Access to relatively high-paying jobs has been greatest in times when labor shortages existed, for example, during major wars. After both the first and second world wars, many of the employment gains were reversed. In periods during which employment opportunities have expanded, as well as during those in which job prospects have worsened, the diversion of income flows to external agents has been facilitated by the absence of a strong indigenous business sector. The absence of a strong network of Black businesses has necessitated the purchase of goods and services from outside suppliers. Demand for products and services external to Black communities has been artificially strengthened by advertising that reinforces dysfunctional consumption patterns, for example, luxury automobiles, cigarettes, and alcohol.

This historical and contemporary pattern has spurred the development of new models to characterize the relationship of African Americans in general, and Black males in particular, to the larger social order. Precedents for such re-examinations include Willhelm (1970) and Yette (1971). More recently, Stewart and Scott (1978) used the construct of "institutional decimation" to characterize the processes that reduced the sex ratio among Blacks by about 10 percent between 1920 and 1970. Stewart and Scott maintain that institutional decimation "leads to the temporary and permanent removal of Black males from the civilian population through the operation of labor market mechanisms, the educational system, the health care delivery system, the public assistance complex, the subliminal institutions of crime and vice, the penal correction system, and the military" (1978, 90). These authors suggest that the process operates organically rather than as a result of some complex conspiracy. Even in the absence of a formal means of co-ordinating the mechanisms of exploitation, however, Stewart and Scott contend that the interests of the dominant group are clearly served in part by "contain[ing] pressures in Black communities in which the potential for violent uprising exists [and] maintain[ing] a balance between the number of Black and white males" (1978, 83).

Using the "endangered species" metaphor, Solomon (1988, 304) indicts public policy as the source of "difficulties for black males in social functioning generated by circular and dysfunctional transactions" vis-à-vis family, school, and work." In a complemetary manner Gibbs (1988, 1–2) argues that Black males have been "miseducated by the educational system, mishandled by the criminal justice system, mislabeled by the mental health system, and mistreated by the social welfare system."

The plight of Black males has worsened over the last two decades as the pace of technological change has accelerated. Increasing rates of technological change and economic transformation beginning in the 1950s set in motion a set of forces that particularly disadvantage Black males. As an example, Cogan (1982) argues that the mechanical cotton picker destroyed Black males' southern employment opportunities. This job loss induced migration to northern urban areas where job opportunities were insufficient to absorb the influx. The result has been a monotonic increase in Black male unemployment since the 1950s. In commenting on the economic prospects for Blacks twenty years after the publication of Gunnar Myrdal's classic study, *An American Dilemma*, Arnold Rose, one of Myrdal's collaborators observes: "The Negro is frequently the most rapidly displaced worker when changing technology requires an upgrading of skills. . . . Hence, Negroes are the hardest hit by technological unemployment, and technological change and low seniority have for all practical purposes replaced discrimination as the main forces in excluding Negroes from factory jobs in the North and West. Negroes thus again constitute a disproportionately

large number of the 'permanently unemployed,' and the rate of becoming unemployed was about double that of white workers during the several recessions
that have occurred since 1955" (1962, xxx).

The importance of structural constraints in limiting employment options
for Blacks was summarized succinctly by Charles Killingsworth (1967, 71–72):
"Certain broad implications for policy are rather obvious from the conclusion of
this analysis. The first is that some of the remedies most often prescribed for Negro unemployment are to yield disappointingly small results. Anti-discrimination
laws, higher rates of attendance at today's schools, faster economic growth, the
normal push-pull forces in the labor market . . . none of these seem to hold the
promise of substantial impact on the basic source of Negro disadvantage. A second implication is that the mere passage of time without the application of powerful remedial measures will probably increase Negro disadvantage."

Regulation of the Black male population since the mid-1970s has taken on
a new character. Changes in the structure of the economy have reduced the demand for traditional blue-collar jobs. The growing service sector has produced
jobs requiring skills disproportionately not possessed by Black males. As a consequence, increasing numbers of immigrants and increased labor force participation of white women, especially married women, are now preferred suppliers
of labor. The all-volunteer military is providing a release valve in the form of
"employment" opportunities not available in the civilian sector. However, this
option is being increasingly foreclosed by expected cuts in the defense budget
and the end of the Cold War. Consistent with the view of Georges-Abeyie discussed previously, for some Black males increased involvement in the "underground economy," or what may be characterized as the "exonomy," has been
the principal response to worsening labor market opportunities.

In general, as noted by Stewart (1984), "the overall impact of economic
policy on the black experience has been, and continues to be, the exploitation of
black labor coupled with parallel exploitation of black consumer purchasing
power. The aggregate policy thrust can be seen by examining policies affecting
the structure and functioning of labor markets, policies shaping the configura-
tion of the economy and the location of economic activity, and policies affecting
the acquisition of skills and general training" (p. 142).

One of the issues raised by neoconservatives that does require attention is
the extent to which greater socio-economic class differentiation among Blacks is
producing greater divergence of social goals. The modern Civil Rights movement eliminated the possibility of maintaining the old caste system that had reduced the impact of class differences among African Americans in fostering political disunity. Despite the efforts of neoconservatives to lump the War on
Poverty and Affirmative Action as one generic public policy thrust, these two
initiatives were actually targeted at different socio-economic classes. The
former, as the name implies, addressed the lower class, while, in contrast, Affirmative Action programs were targeted at the creation of a new Black middle

class. Public policies attacking residential segregation were designed to selectively facilitate the migration of the middle class from the central cities, thereby isolating the lower class.

The encouragement of a class-based residential location schism effect is evident in the limited extent to which public housing has been introduced into suburban areas. The suburbanization of the Black middle class increased the diversion of income flows to the larger economy as the Black middle class took on the consumption patterns of the white middle class.

Elements of the preceding discussion are amplified by the comments of Darity and Myers (1986); "We agree with Piven and Cloward that the changing demographics of the poverty population had an important influence on the *politics* of poverty policy. Thus, the coincidental rise in single-parent families with the expansion of welfare was really the reflection of policy responding to demographics rather than demographics instantaneously responding to policy" (pp. 173–74). These demographic changes have facilitated a new control strategy focused on the cooptation of new Black middle class. Black neoconservatives are simply one manifestation of this strategy. The strategy also involves accentuation of conflicts between Black males and females (see Scott and Stewart, 1979).

Afrocentric analyses of the relationship of Black males to American society seek to examine the linkages among policy areas and the most critical vehicles for affecting change. In some cases Afrocentric and neoconservative analyses agree on the importance of an approach but base the conclusion on very different frameworks of reference. As an example, the two perspectives agree to some extent that self-help is required to address persisting inequities. For the neoconservatives, however, self-help is a *substitute* for government initiatives, and government is not seen as being allied with the private sector in exploiting Blacks. In the Afrocentric framework self-help is a complement to government action if and when government is committed to reducing inequities. At other times self-help must be directed toward empowerment to counter government and private sector initiated oppression. It is critical that self-help efforts be designed in ways that utilize the specific strengths of African-American culture and be implemented as part of a comprehensive strategy. As Stewart (1984, 154) notes, "Coordination is required if efforts including boycotts and negotiated settlements . . . [and collective] accumulation strategies . . . are to coalesce into a momentum that will alter the pattern of historical continuity. . . ."

Toward a Future Informed by the Past

Neoconservatives argue that current social policies are misguided as efforts to improve the lives of African Americans. This is hardly a new or insightful observation. Public policies targeted at African Americans during periods in which fears of revolt were minimal have never been directed toward reducing inequality. Destabilization of Black families and control of Black males has always been in the interests of the dominant group. Use of a group of intellectuals to further those interests is also not new.

The 1980s was a decade during which the threat of internal revolt was minimal and substantial retrenchment in social welfare expenditures occurred. Rising levels of racial tension and racially motivated violence is likely to induce increases of such expenditures during the 1990s. Advocates of a humanistic world order seek to establish a regime that genuinely seeks universal empowerment. The outlines of a public policy agenda to accomplish this would certainly bear no resemblance to that advocated by neoconservatives. Rather, as Harrison (1977, 262–63) notes, there is a need "for a change in emphasis away from concentration on the alleged defects of the ghetto poor themselves toward the investigation of defects in the market system which constrain the poor from realizing their potential." Movements toward such an approach are likely to be incremental, but short-term changes should be "consistent with the long-range vision of more radical reform involving guaranteed employment, . . . vocational training, . . . and family allowances" (p. 314).

The system of public assistance requires reform not only to reduce work disincentives, as advocated by neoconservatives, but more importantly to eliminate the use of such assistance as a vehicle of social control for managing the aggregate levels of dissatisfaction experienced by the disadvantaged. Balkin (1989) provides examples of pilot programs that enable women on welfare to engage in self-employment activities in conjunction with modification of rules governing benefit reductions. In many cases these enterprises lead to employment of others, potentially adolescent sons or unemployed males. This constitutes a domestic variant of the tradition of market women in West Africa and the historical role of free women of color as entrepreneurs in the North during the slavery era described by Curry (1981).

Afrocentric perspectives are also useful in developing strategies to respond to the proliferation of youth crime and alienation from local community institutions. Adaptation of the tradition of socializing cohorts of males in African societies through structured rites of passage is now being explored in many communities.

Ultimately, all peoples within the orbit of the American economy have a stake in the empowerment and elevation of African-American males. Collectively, perhaps people of conscicence can help to realize the vision offered by Gibbs (1988, 360): "[If] black youth are given real opportunities for education, if they are provided with meaningful jobs, if they have adequate income to care for their families, if they have hope for future mobility, then they will act responsibly and will contribute their fair share to the larger community."

Whether the policy mix proposed by Gibbs is sufficient to achieve the desired results is, of course, an open question. The option of maintaining current directions, however, can only have the effect of adding momentum to the current downward spiral, which, if unchecked, will eventually produce a national and global disaster of unprecedented proportions.

CHAPTER 4

The Black Male in American Literature

by William L. Andrews

Like "jes grew," the Black cultural phenomenon whose history is chronicled in Ishmael Reed's novel *Mumbo Jumbo* (1972), the topic of this chapter is "an influence seeking its text." The following brief remarks cannot be the text that my topic, the Black male in American literature, has been seeking. Obviously a big and multifaceted book—more likely a series of such books—will be necessary to do justice to the topic of this essay. That no one has attempted to write a book on the Black male in American literature is eloquent testimony to criticism's inability still to find a way to confront, let alone comprehend, this topic. Failing to come to grips with this question, however, leaves us literary critics and scholars open to the charge that because of our benign neglect the general reading public may assume that like Topsy the Black male in American literature "jes grew" without recognizable origins or intelligible purposes. Although this essay can be termed little more than notes toward a study of the Black male in American literature, it is offered as a preliminary effort to historicize the question at issue here.

Instead of trying to classify various images or stereotypes of the Black male in American literature, the aim of this paper is to focus on a few nodal points in the literary history of the United States *and* in the history of the Black male's depiction in that literary history. The two genres of American literature in which the Black male has figured most importantly are the novel and autobiography. White Americans have met more Black men in novels or through their own self-portraits in autobiographies than through personal acquaintance. Because these two narrative forms, more than poetry or drama, have so extensively and profoundly affected America's notion of Black people (female as well as male), this essay will concentrate on the status of the Black male in American narrative literature. Since it is impossible to comment on more than a handful of key texts, I would like to account for my choice of texts by noting just two principles of selection at work here. The texts discussed in this essay all share this in common: (1) they are best-selling books that have been read and continue to be read by a sizable American audience; and (2) they have been accorded serious attention by reviewers, critics, and literary and cultural historians. In short, the texts to be discussed have been taken seriously by both the popular and the scholarly audience, which is a good indication that these texts have exerted a considerable influence on the mind of the United States, broadly conceived.

This essay examines a handful of widely influential texts from the nineteenth and the twentieth centuries in order to make at least some tentative comments on how the image and status of the Black male has been developing since American literature first began to take account of this figure. The discussion incorporates writing on the Black male by both white and Black authors of the United States in equal proportion. In pairing Frederick Douglass and Harriet Beecher Stowe, Ralph Ellison and William Styron, my intention is not to suggest that one writer necessarily influenced another, but rather to show how

Black and white writers have addressed similar social and cultural issues bearing on the status and fate of the Black American male.

In the opening paragraph of Ralph Ellison's *Invisible Man* (1952), the Black male narrator says that he is invisible "simply because people refuse to see me." "When they approach me they see only my surroundings, themselves, or figments of their imagination—indeed, everything and anything except me." This peculiar brand of invisibility informs the portrayal of Black males in both of the white-authored texts to be discussed in this essay. These texts—Harriet Beecher Stowe's *Uncle Tom's Cabin* ([1852] 1965) and William Styron's *The Confessions of Nat Turner* ([1967] 1968)—constitute the most widely read and most critically controversial narratives of Black male experience in both nineteenth- and twentieth-century American literature. The differences between these novels—technically, thematically, and ideologically—are of course pronounced. Yet both texts share at least one thing in common: the Black man at the center of each of these novels is hardly visible at all, in Ellison's sense of the term, because the Black man's individual humanity has been for the most part veiled by an abstracted identity projected onto him by the white author's notions of what a Black man represents, or ought to represent.

In suggesting that the authors of each of these crucial American novels project an abstract identity onto their Black male characters, I do not wish to imply that this process of abstracting is limited solely to Black male characters in American literature. A great many critics have argued that one of the more familiar qualities of the American novel is its abstractedness, its tendency to turn characters—regardless of color or sex—into symbols whose interaction seems to point beyond the world of human experience toward larger philosophical, religious, or ethical issues of central concern to the author (Chase 1957). Thus in arguing that the Black male is abstracted in the novels of Stowe and Styron I am not suggesting that the process of abstracting is itself peculiar to the treatment of the Black male in American literature. Nor would I say that the process of abstracting is in and of itself inherently detrimental to the representation of the Black male in literature. Endowing a character's identity with a certain abstract quality, thus making him or her representative of something greater than himself or herself, is one of the oldest and most familiar means by which characters from Achilles to Kafka's Joseph K have been given a lasting significance.

The question, therefore, is not whether writers ought to abstract the Black male character in fiction. The questions are: First, in the key texts under examination in this essay, is the Black male an abstract, a *representative*, of something indigenous to *his* culture—or does he represent something in the author's psyche or in the author's culture? Second, does the abstractness, the representativeness, of the Black male character overshadow and subtly deny his individuality—or is there a creative tension between what he represents as a cultural and social figure and what he seems to be as an individual person?

The first major portrait of a Black male in American narrative literature appeared in the *Narrative of the Life of Frederick Douglass, An American Slave, Written by Himself* ([1845] 1982). Selling more than thirty thousand copies in the first five years of its existence, Douglass's *Narrative* was an international best-seller in its own time, its contemporary readership far outstripping that of Thoreau's *Walden*, for instance, or Melville's *Moby-Dick*. Today the *Narrative* is probably the only work by a Black writer that is universally granted a place in the American literature canon by critics and literary historians. Like all the antebellum slave narratives, Douglass's autobiography was written to combat white Northern ignorance about slavery as an institution and the slaves as human beings. Douglass's mentor, the abolitionist William Lloyd Garrison, introduced the *Narrative* by stressing how representative Douglass's experience of slavery had been (Douglass [1845] 1982). But even as he sought to argue the typicalness of Douglass's slave experience, Garrison also could not help but note the extraordinary individuality of the Black author's manner of rendering that experience. For most students of the *Narrative* today, it is the style of self-presentation, the manner in which Douglass recreates the slave as an evolving self bound for mental as well as physical freedom, that makes his autobiography so memorable. Douglass fully understood how important it was for his autobiography to be, as its subtitle proclaims, "written by himself." For in writing his own story, rather than dictating it to a ghostwriter (as many slave narrators did), Douglass made sure that his representativeness as a slave would be counterbalanced by his individuality as a writer. No matter how his white readers might attempt to sum him up as a symbol, they could not do so without coming to terms with the words he himself had chosen to reveal himself as an individual.

In the last thirty years, as critics have given Douglass's *Narrative* increasing attention, there has been much debate over which models Douglass himself may have used to help him create the image of himself that he wanted to impress on his readers. Doubtless Douglass was influenced by models of selfhood implicit in a variety of American literary traditions, from the Protestant spiritual autobiography to the romantic individualism of Emerson. In the climax to the *Narrative*, Douglass states that his forcible resistance to Covey the slave breaker "rekindled the few expiring embers of freedom, and revived within me a sense of my own manhood" (Douglass [1845] 1982). What Douglass meant by the term *manhood* in this context—his human dignity, his self-determination, his male pride?—is by no means a settled matter among literary scholars of the *Narrative*. What is clear, however, is that Douglass did not have to wait until he escaped slavery to discover an ideal of manhood that inspired him to seize his own liberty. He points out that he won several fellow slaves over to his plan for escape by reminding them "of our want of manhood, if we submitted to our enslavement without at least one noble effort to be free." Thus the idea of Black manhood in Douglass's *Narrative* is traced back to its origins in the slave community. Whatever literary traditions from the majority culture Douglass the writer enlisted to enhance the resonance and significance of this ideal of Black manhood for his white readers, the *Narrative* shows that the ideal at its basis was a Black cultural construct. By plainly identifying this source of his ideal of manhood, Douglass's *Narrative* refuses its white reader the luxury of seeing Douglass as simply an abstracted blackfaced version of white cultural ideals. In other words, the richness and complexity of that which Douglass does represent as both an individual man and a symbol of the slave community depend ultimately on the tension between his African-American cultural roots and his Western cultural acquisitions.

Comparing Douglass's self-portrait with Harriet Beecher Stowe's image of Uncle Tom helps us see the problem with the latter character as representative either of Black culture or an individual Black male. In response to charges that the world of *Uncle Tom's Cabin* was mainly the product of her overheated abolitionist imagination, Stowe claimed that many of the incidents and most of the characters, particularly the prominent Black male characters, of *Uncle Tom's Cabin* were drawn from life and had their analogues in slave narratives that she had read. That Stowe drew on a variety of slave narratives for the materials of her novel is unquestionable. But it is one thing to import Black images and slave experiences into a work of fiction and quite another to situate those images and experiences in a context that allows them to speak fully to and for their cultural origins.

When Stowe read *The Life of Josiah Henson* (Henson 1849), the slave narrative that she claims most influenced her idea of Uncle Tom, what struck her the most was not the way in which Henson managed to spirit himself and his entire family to freedom but rather an episode of "self-renunciation" in which Henson described how he once resisted the temptation to undertake an escape from slavery by murdering his young master (Stowe 1853). Thus, in *The Key to Uncle Tom's Cabin* (1853), Stowe presented Henson, the man whose "Christian principle was invulnerable," as the key to Uncle Tom, the Christian hero of her novel. Like many romantic racists in the white antislavery community, Stowe was convinced that "the negro race is confessedly more simple, docile, childlike, and affectionate, than other races; and hence the divine graces of love and faith, when in-breathed by the Holy spirit, find in their natural temperament a more congenial atmosphere." Stowe may have sincerely believed that Henson's act of "self-renunciation" legitimized her portrayal of Uncle Tom as the self-sacrificial lamb, the archetypal Black suffering servant. But the greater likelihood is that Uncle Tom's saintly character stems primarily from Stowe's own cultural prejudices and sociopolitical agenda.

The antithesis of Uncle Tom among the Black characters of Stowe's novel is a mulatto firebrand named George Harris, whom his creator claimed to have modeled at least in part on Frederick Douglass. The fact that Stowe's novel divides its attention between the "truly African" Uncle Tom and the very light-complexioned George Harris compels us to recognize the division between spiritual and political heroism that underlies *Uncle Tom's Cabin* (1965). This division between Stowe's two African-American heroes is also basic to an understanding of the bifurcated image of the Black male that *Uncle Tom's Cabin* impressed on the consciousness of nineteenth-century America. Uncle Tom's spiritual heroism is expressed ultimately in his resistance to slavery's demand for the subservience of his soul to the satanic Simon Legree. George Harris's political heroism is epitomized in his resistance to slavery's demand for the service of his body (and that of his wife and child) to the chattel principle. Why should Harris be the active, even the aggressive, resistor to injustice, while Uncle Tom maintains a passive resistance to evil? The answer lies in Stowe's conviction that Harris's so-called Anglo-Saxon blood would never tolerate the ill-treatment that Tom's African nature can patiently bear. In other words, neither individual choice nor cultural training have much to do with the type of hero that George Harris or Uncle Tom turns out to be. Their behavior can be explained simply by their racial heritage, in accordance with the notions of race that Stowe had imbibed from her own cultural tradition.

These racial assumptions are also probably behind the striking similarity of fate shared by both Uncle Tom and George Harris. In the end of the novel both men are removed from the American scene—Tom to heaven as a result of his self-sacrificial death, Harris to Africa via voluntary exile. Stowe tries to justify this outcome by suggesting that both men have earned the right to be free from the trials and temptations of their caste condition in America. But it is obvious, nevertheless, that disposing of Tom and Harris in this way allows Stowe to avoid coming to grips with the profoundest question raised by her novel: What is the future of the free Black male in the United States?

This question would become one of the most hotly debated in all of American narrative literature after the Civil War. In *Huckleberry Finn* ([1884] 1977) Samuel Clemens (Mark Twain) tried to soothe nervous whites by suggesting that the Black man's desire for freedom was no more threatening—and no more serious—than the desire of any white boy for a loosening of the bonds of maternal control. But many white novelists of the late nineteenth and early twentieth centuries took a grimmer view of the arrival of the Black man on the threshold of civil rights. The fear of miscegenation as a direct outgrowth of equal rights for blacks made the mulatto a figure of morbid fascination in many popular American novels (Kinney 1985). Disturbingly sexual, aggressive, and psychologically conflicted mulattoes, descendants of George Harris by virtue of their mixed blood and their inability to find a place for themselves in the social order, haunt the imagination of the immensely influential novelist William Faulkner, for instance. In both *Light in August* ([1932] 1972) and *Absalom, Absalom* ([1936] 1972), Faulkner retools mulatto stereotypes from the nineteenth century to portray the Black man as inevitably doomed, a scapegoat who must suffer for the sins of white Southern fathers. Joe Christmas, the protagonist of *Light in August*, inevitably invites comparisons to Jesus Christ, yet even as Christmas's white lover articulates her sense of the pathos of "the black shadow in the shape of a cross" looming over humanity, she also acknowledges a sense of unbearable oppression under that shadow, as though she and all whites "were nailed to that cross." No wonder this woman's surname is Burden—she represents for Faulkner white America's outraged acknowledgment and resentment of the moral onus it must bear for the tragedy of race in the twentieth-century United States.

In "Everybody's Protest Novel" ([1949] 1968), James Baldwin states that *Uncle Tom's Cabin* "is activated by what might be called a theological terror, the terror of damnation" in its author and like-minded whites who fear the evil of Blackness and yet feel obliged to purify that evil not only for the salvation of the lost Negro but also for the redemption of unregenerate white America. Similar contradictory motives compel Faulkner to sacrifice Joe Christmas in *Light in August* and to bring about the apocalyptic conclusion of *Absalom, Absalom*. In the midst of multiple social revolutions during the 1960s, another visitation of "the terror of damnation" came to white America in the form of the Black man as avenging angel, epitomized in the hero of Styron's *The Confessions of Nat Turner*. In Nat Turner, whose 1831 insurrection in Southampton, Virginia, forced America to confront the possibility of a bloody racial Armageddon over slavery, Styron's imagination conjured up yet another version of the Christ-haunted Black male, an amalgam of suffering servant and executioner, at war with himself and all the white race.

As is the case among a number of the more prominent Black males created by white fiction writers, Styron's Nat, like Mark Twain's Jim ([1884] 1977), Stephan Crane's Henry Johnson ([1899] 1960), Sinclair Lewis's Kingsblood Royal (1947), and Faulkner's Joe Christmas ([1932] 1972), is a singular man in several respects, particularly as a result of his isolation not only from the adult white community, but from sustaining contact with African Americans as well. Styron's Nat has but two confidants—the God of the Old Testament and the (evidently white) reader of his new testament. Rarely does Turner share with Black people his innermost anxieties or his highest aspirations, for according to his estimate, "like animals they relinquished the past with as much dumb composure as they accepted the present, and were unaware of any future at all." Like Prometheus, Prophet Nat tries to be a kind of revolutionary Black man-maker, yet when the time for bloody action comes, he finds he lacks the stomach to lead his troops in their ruthless mission.

To prove himself equal to and worthy of the violent ideal he espouses, Turner kills an adolescent white girl whose innocence, kindliness toward Blacks, and almost flirtatious attraction to him have throughout the novel tempted him to indulgence in a most profoundly felt mix of lust and rage. The slaying of Margaret Whitehead would seem to signify a final resolution of Turner's long-standing pity for and yet hatred of whites who cannot be judged complicitous in the outrage of slavery, a resolution necessary to his eventual triumph as a messianic purveyor of Jehovah's justice on the good and evil alike. But in the final scene of *The Confessions,* in an agony of separation from his God and beset by anxiety about whether he can or will be redeemed, Turner imagines himself reclaimed by Margaret Whitehead, whose profession of love for him enables him to discover a new gospel—"We'll love one another"—of biracial salvation through Christ.

Calling in his last moments on the Lord Jesus, a name Turner acknowledges having almost forgotten until the spirit of Margaret Whitehead reinvokes it, illustrates a climactic turning of Styron's hero away from a peculiarly African-American religious vision centered on God the deliverer of Black people and toward a twentieth-century liberal's notion of Christianity founded in Jesus' boundless mercy for all (Harding 1968). This was no doubt a comforting conclusion for a novelist who wanted to suggest a way out of the cycle of racial fear, hatred, and retribution that seemed to enclose American society in the 1960s. But more than one critic has objected to the price Nat Turner has to pay for his salvation—and that of white America—in Styron's novel. While any novelist has the right to revamp a historically mythic figure to make him speak to a contemporary reader, the process by which Styron sought to individualize Turner necessarily diminished him. It becomes clear that only by losing hope in his people and by doubting his faith in the God whose vengeance he sought can Styron's Turner find ultimate balm in the bosom of a latter-day sexualized version of Stowe's evangelical Eva and in an integrationist's ideal of Christ. Thus the confessions of Nat Turner dematerialize finally into his creator's book of (self-serving) revelations.

The Confessions of Nat Turner was the last white-authored novel of Black experience to seize the attention and engage the conscience of the United States. Having made such a crucial issue of the terms by which Black manhood should be defined in contemporary fiction, Styron's novel was succeeded by a number of African-American texts that implicitly, if not explicitly, offer alternatives to what most Black writers now consider Styron's negative object lesson in Black male portraiture. While some may regret the refusal of white novelists in the last two decades to attempt a Black male as a protagonist, one should note several particularly important narratives of recent vintage, such as Alex Haley's *Roots* ([1976] 1977), Toni Morrison's *Song of Solomon* (1977), and David Bradley's *The Chaneysville Incident* ([1981] 1982), that record heroic Black men's quests to discover their genealogy, their cultural heritage, and by implication key aspects of their own identity. Even the much-celebrated renaissance of Black American women's writing that has taken place in the 1980s may be read as testimony to a continuing and vital discourse about the meaning of gender and the nature of male as well as female roles in African-American culture and society.

It would be short-sighted, however, to suggest that the impetus behind contemporary African-American fiction's concern with the origins and significance of Black male identity stems from *The Confessions of Nat Turner.* If one were to recognize a single text as having enabled and set the tone for the post–World War II debate on the Black man in America, one would have to point to Ellison's *Invisible Man*. Like Frederick Douglass, Ellison's protagonist understands that freedom and fulfillment for a Black man in America depend on the recovery of his cultural antecedents and the assertion of his individual identity against those forces that would deny him either one. But Douglass's struggle was waged primarily against those who tried simply to deny him knowledge of his past and the right to an identity of his free choosing. Ellison's unnamed protagonist, on the other hand, is faced with a more complex problem of deciding which aspects of his culture, whose traditions he has partially accepted, rejected, repressed, and misperceived, he wants to identify with. Repeatedly, false and manipulative mentors offer Ellison's protagonist a variety of names and personae—from "the next Booker T. Washington" to Reverend B. P. Rinehart—that promise to simplify his quest for his own invisible selfhood. The Invisible Man's story shows how he tries on one after another of these personae in an attempt to please others or to aggrandize the man he thinks he is or can be, only to discover time and time again the ruinous cost of his many charades. In the end, the Invisible Man discovers that "all my life I had been looking for something, and everywhere I turned someone tried to tell me what it was. I accepted their answers too, though they were often in contradiction and even self-contradictory. I was naive. I was looking for myself and asking everyone except myself questions which I, and only I, could answer." Ultimately, the Invisible Man realizes that he is just that, invisible, possessed of an identity waiting to be socially delineated. His great discovery is that he holds the responsibility for either creating himself into what his own imagination tells him he is capable of becoming, or allowing others to impose their own semblance of selfhood on his character.

Through the Invisible Man's realization of the potential within himself, Ellison affirms the Black man's future in modern America, allying his quest for freedom and fulfillment with both sides of his African and American heritage. Contemplating the unscrupulous Rinehart, an urban hustler who plays virtually every role available to a Black man in the ghetto, the Invisible Man is struck by the fact that, regardless of this man's antisocial character, his life has a profound lesson for men like the Invisible Man: "His world was possibility and he knew it. He was years ahead of me and I was a fool. I must have been crazy and blind. The world in which we lived was without boundaries. A vast seething, hot world of fluidity, and Rine the rascal was at home."

The question is, can a socially responsible Black man turn this "hot world of fluidity" to a positive purpose, not only for himself but also for his people and American society at large? *Invisible Man* ends with the narrator's affirming of just this conviction, though he does not specify the kind of socially responsible action he intends to pursue. All he is sure of is that his grandfather, spokesman for the perplexing and contradictory wisdom of the Southern Black folk culture, was right when he advised his offspring on his deathbed to "overcome 'em [the whites] with yeses, agree 'em to death and destruction." Through most of his life the Invisible Man thought (quite erroneously) that by agreeing with powerful white men he would somehow still be able to overcome them or the racial barriers that stood between himself and the success he craved. What he finally understands, however, is that he must "affirm the principle on which the country was built and not the men, or at least not the men who did the violence." This principle—that all men are created equal? that liberty is every person's inalienable right? the Invisible Man never says—is part of this Black man's birthright as an American, but he does not come to understand its peculiar application to him *as* a Black man, until he comes to terms with his cultural heritage, as old as his long-deceased grandfather and as young as Rinehart his contemporary. From the dialectic of his dual African-American heritage, the Invisible Man at the end of his story comes into sharper focus as an individual, as well as a Black American man, than at any previous juncture in the novel. As a result, he achieves his ultimate fulfillment, his greatest completeness as a self, in his teasing request of Blacks and whites, male and female, to consider whether "who knows but that, on the lower frequencies, I speak for you?" In this suggestion that Americans may finally learn to read who they are in and through a Black man rather than merely projecting what they fear or fantasize onto his person, Ellison brings the Black man in the literature of the United States to his apotheosis as potentially representative of America's dream, not just its nightmare. It remains to the readers as well as the writers of American literature to recognize that potential and in so doing help to realize that dream.

CHAPTER 5

The Black Male: Searching beyond Stereotypes

by Manning Marable

What is a Black man? Husband and father. Son and brother. Lover and boyfriend. Uncle and grandfather. Construction worker and sharecropper. Minister and ghetto hustler. Doctor and mineworker. Auto mechanic and presidential candidate.

What is a Black man in an institutionally racist society, in the social system of modern capitalist America? The essential tragedy of being Black and male is our inability, as men and as people of African descent, to define ourselves without the stereotypes the larger society imposes upon us, and through various institutional means perpetuates and permeates within our entire culture. Our relations with our sisters, our parents and children, and indeed across the entire spectrum of human relations are imprisoned by images of the past, false distortions that seldom if ever capture the essence of our being. We cannot come to terms with Black women until we understand the half-hidden stereotypes that have crippled our development and social consciousness. We cannot challenge racial and sexual inequality, both within the Black community and across the larger American society, unless we comprehend the critical difference between the myths about ourselves and the harsh reality of being Black men.

Confrontation with White History

The conflicts between Black and white men in contemporary American culture can be traced directly through history to the earliest days of chattel slavery. White males entering the New World were ill adapted to make the difficult transition from Europe to the American frontier. As recent historical research indicates, the development of what was to become the United States was accomplished largely, if not primarily, by African slaves, men and women alike. Africans were the first to cultivate wheat on the continent; they showed their illiterate masters how to grow indigo, rice, and cotton; their extensive knowledge of herbs and roots provided colonists with medicines and preservatives for food supplies. It was the Black man, wielding his sturdy axe, who cut down most of the virgin forest across the southern colonies. And in times of war, the white man reluctantly looked to his Black slave to protect him and his property. As early as 1715, during the Yemassee Indian war, Black troops led British regulars in a campaign to exterminate Indian tribes. After another such campaign in 1747, the all-white South Carolina legislature issued a public vote of gratitude to Black men, who "in times of war, behaved themselves with great faithfulness and courage, in repelling the attacks of his Majesty's enemies." During the American Revolution, over two thousand Black men volunteered to join the beleaguered Continental Army of George Washington, a slaveholder. A generation later, two thousand Blacks from New York joined the state militia's segregated units during the War of 1812, and Blacks fought bravely under Andrew Jackson at the Battle of New Orleans. From Crispus Attucks to the 180,000 Blacks who fought in the Union Army during the Civil War, Black men gave their lives to preserve the liberties of their white male masters.

The response of white men to the many sacrifices of their sable counterparts was, in a word, contemptuous. Their point of view of Black males was conditioned by three basic beliefs. Black men were only a step above the animals—possessing awesome physical power but lacking in intellectual ability. As such, their proper role in white society was as laborers, not as the managers of labor. Second, the Black male represented a potential political threat to the entire system of slavery. And third, but by no means last, the Black male symbolized a lusty sexual potency that threatened white women. This uneven mixture of political fears and sexual anxieties was reinforced by the white males' crimes committed against Black women, the routine rape and sexual abuse that all slave societies permit between the oppressed and the oppressor. Another dilemma, seldom discussed publicly, was the historical fact that some white women of all social classes were not reluctant to request the sexual favors of their male slaves. These inherent tensions produced a racial model of conduct and social control that survived the colonial period and continued into the twentieth century. The white male–dominated system dictated that the only acceptable social behavior of any Black male was that of subservience—the loyal slave, the proverbial Uncle Tom, the ever-cheerful and infantile Sambo. It was not enough that Black men must cringe before their white masters; they must express open devotion to the system of slavery itself. Politically, the Black male was unfit to play even a minor role in the development of democracy. Supreme Court Chief Justice Roger B. Tawney spoke for his entire class in 1857: "Negroes [are] beings of an inferior order, and altogether unfit to associate with the white race, either in social or political relations; and so far inferior that they have no rights which the white man was bound to respect." Finally, black males disciplined for various crimes against white supremacy—such as escaping from the plantation, or murdering their masters—were often punished in a sexual manner. On this point, the historical record is clear. In the colonial era, castration of Black males was required by the legislatures of North and South Carolina, Virginia, Pennsylvania, and New Jersey. Black men were castrated simply for striking a white man or for attempting to learn to read and write. In the late nineteenth century, hundreds of Black male victims of lynching were first sexually mutilated before being executed. The impulse to castrate Black males was popularized in white literature and folklore, and even today, instances of such crimes are not entirely unknown in the rural South.

The relations between Black males and white women were infinitely more complex. Generally, the vast majority of white females viewed Black men through the eyes of their fathers and husbands. The Black man was simply a beast of burden, a worker who gave his life to create a more comfortable environment for her and her children. And yet, in truth, he was still a man. Instances of interracial marriage were few, and were prohibited by law even as late as the 1960s. But the fear of sexual union did not prohibit many white females, particularly indentured servants and working-class women from soliciting favors from

Black men. In the 1840s, however, a small group of white middle-class women became actively involved in the campaign to abolish slavery. The founders of modern American feminism—Susan B. Anthony, Elizabeth Cady Stanton, and Lucretia Mott—championed the cause of emancipation and defended Blacks' civil rights. In gratitude for their devotion to Black freedom, the leading Black abolitionist of the period, Frederick Douglass, actively promoted the rights of white women against the white male power structure. In 1848, at the Seneca Falls, New York, women's rights convention, Douglass was the only man, Black or white, to support the extension of voting rights to all women. White women looked to Douglass for leadership in the battle against sexual and racial discrimination. Yet curiously, they were frequently hostile to the continued contributions of Black women to the cause of freedom. When the brilliant orator Sojourner Truth, second only to Douglass as a leading figure in the abolitionist movement, rose to lecture before an 1851 women's convention in Akron, Ohio, white women cried out, "Don't let her speak!" For these white liberals, the destruction of slavery was simply a means to expand democratic rights to white women: the goal was defined in racist terms. Black men like Douglass were useful allies only so far as they promoted white middle-class women's political interests.

The moment of truth came immediately following the Civil War, when Congress passed the Fifteenth Amendment, which gave Black males the right to vote. For Douglass and most Black leaders, both men and women, suffrage was absolutely essential to preserve their new freedoms. While the Fifteenth Amendment excluded females from the electoral franchise, it nevertheless represented a great democratic victory for all oppressed groups.

For most white suffragists, however, it symbolized the political advancement of the Black male over white middle-class women. Quickly their liberal rhetoric gave way to racist diatribes. "So long as the Negro was lowest in the scale of being, we were willing to press his claims," wrote Elizabeth Cady Stanton in 1865. "But now, as the celestial gate to civil rights is slowly moving on its hinges, it becomes a serious question whether we had better stand aside and see 'Sambo' walk into the kingdom first." Most white women reformists concluded that "it is better to be the slave of an educated white man than of a degraded, ignorant black one." They warned whites that giving the vote to the Black male would lead to widespread rape and sexual assaults against white women of the upper classes. Susan B. Anthony vowed, "I will cut off this right arm of mine before I will ever work for or demand the ballot for the Negro and not the [white] woman." In contrast, Black women leaders like Sojourner Truth and Frances E. Watkins Harper understood that the enfranchisement of Black men was an essential step for the democratic rights of all people.

The division between white middle-class feminists and the civil rights movement of Blacks, beginning over a century ago, has continued today in debates over affirmative action and job quotas. White liberal feminists frequently use the rhetoric of racial equality but often find it difficult to support public policies that will advance Black males over their own social group. Even in the 1970s, such liberal women writers as Susan Brownmiller continued to resurrect the myth of the "Black male-as-rapist" and sought to define white women in crudely racist terms. The weight of white history, from white women and men alike, has been an endless series of stereotypes used to frustrate the Black man's images of himself and to blunt his constant quest for freedom.

Confronting the Black Woman

Images of our suffering—as slaves, sharecroppers, industrial workers, and standing in unemployment lines—have been intermingled in our relationship with the Black woman. We have seen her straining under the hot southern sun, chopping cotton row upon row and nursing our children on the side. We have witnessed her come home, tired and weary after working as a nurse, cook, or maid in white men's houses. We have seen her love of her children, her commitment to the church, her beauty and dignity in the face of political and economic exploitation. And yet, so much is left unsaid. All too often the Black male, in his own silent suffering, fails to communicate his love and deep respect for the mother, sister, grandmother, and wife who gave him the courage and commitment to strive for freedom. The veils of oppression, and the illusions of racial stereotypes, limit our ability to speak the inner truths about ourselves and our relationships to Black women.

The Black man's image of the past is, in most respects, a distortion of social reality. All of us can feel the anguish of our great-grandfathers as they witnessed their wives and daughters being raped by their white masters, or as they wept when their families were sold apart. But do we feel the double bondage of the Black woman, trying desperately to keep her family together and yet at times distrusted by her own Black man? Less than a generation ago, most Black male social scientists argued that the Black family was effectively destroyed by slavery; that the Black man was much less than a husband or father; and that the result was a "Black matriarchy" that crippled the economic, social, and political development of the Black community. Back in 1965, Black scholar C. Eric Lincoln declared that the slavery experience had "stripped the Negro male of his masculinity" and "condemned him to a eunuch-like existence in a culture that venerates masculine primacy." The rigid rules of Jim Crow applied more to Black men than to their women, according to Lincoln: "Because she was frequently the white man's mistress, the Negro woman occasionally flaunted the rules of segregation, . . . The Negro [male] did not earn rewards for being manly, courageous, or assertive, but for being accommodating—for fulfilling the stereotype of what he has been forced to be." The social by-product of Black demasculinization, concluded Lincoln, was the rise of Black matriarchs, who psychologically castrated their husbands and sons. "The Negro female has had the responsibility of the Negro family for so many generations that she accepts it, or assumes it, as second nature. Many older women have forgotten why the responsibility developed upon the Negro woman in the first place, or why it later became institutionalized," Lincoln argues. "And young Negro women do not think it absurd to reduce the relationship to a matter of money, since many of them probably grew up in families where the only income was earned by the mothers: the fathers may not have been in evidence at all." Other Black sociologists perpetuated these stereotypes, which only served to turn Black women and men against each other instead of focusing their energies and talents in the struggle for freedom.

Today's social science research on Black female-male relations tells us what our common sense should have indicated long ago—that the essence of Black family and community life has been a positive, constructive, and even heroic experience. Andrew Billingsley's *Black Families in White America* illustrates that the Black "extended family" is part of our African heritage that was never eradicated by slavery or segregation. The Black tradition of racial cooperation, the collectivist rather than individualistic ethos, is an outgrowth of the unique African heritage that we still maintain. It is clear that the Black woman was the primary transmitter and repositor of the cultural heritage of our people and played a central role in the socialization and guidance of Black male and female children. But this fact does not by any way justify the myth of a "Black matriarchy." Black women suffered from the economic exploitation and racism Black males experienced—but they also were trapped by institutional sexism and all of the various means of violence that have been used to oppress all women, such as rape, "wife beating," and sterilization. The majority of the Black poor throughout history have been overwhelmingly female; the lowest paid major group within the labor force in America is black women, not men.

In politics, the sense of the Black man's relations with Black women are again distorted by stereotypes. Most of us can cite the achievement of the great Black men who contributed to the freedom of our people: Frederick Douglass, W. E. B. DuBois, Marcus Garvey, Martin Luther King, Jr., Malcolm X, Paul Robeson, Medgar Evers, A. Philip Randolph. Why then are we often forgetful of Harriet Tubman, the fearless conductor on the Underground Railroad, who spirited over 350 slaves into the North? What of Ida B. Wells, newspaper editor and antilynching activist; Mary Church Terrell, educator, member of the Washington, D.C., Board of Education from 1895 to 1906, and civil rights leader; Mary McLeod Bethune, college president and director of the Division of Negro Affairs for the National Youth Administration; and Fannie Lou Hamer, courageous desegregation leader in the South during the 1960s? In simple truth, the cause of Black freedom has been pursued by Black women and men equally. In Black literature, the eloquent appeals to racial equality penned by Richard Wright, James Baldwin, and Du Bois are paralleled in the works of Zora

Neale Hurston, Alice Walker, and Toni Morrison. Martin Luther King, Jr., may have expressed for all of us our collective vision of equality in his "I Have a Dream" speech at the 1963 March on Washington—but it was the solitary act of defiance by the Black woman, Rosa Parks, that initiated the great Montgomery bus boycott in 1955 and gave birth to the modern civil rights movement. The struggle of our foremothers and forefathers transcends the barrier of gender, as Black women have tried to tell their men for generations. Beyond the stereotypes, we find a common heritage of suffering, and a common will to be free.

The Black Man Confronts Himself

The search for reality begins and ends with an assessment of the actual socioeconomic condition of Black males within the general context of the larger society. Beginning in the economic sphere, one finds that the illusion of Black male achievement in the marketplace is undermined by statistical evidence. Of the thousands of small businesses initiated by Black entrepreneurs each year, over 90 percent go bankrupt within thirty-six months. The Black businessman suffers from redlining policies of banks, which keep capital outside his hands. Only one out of two hundred Black businessmen have more than twenty paid employees, and over 80 percent of all Black men who start their own firms must hold a second job, working sixteen hours and more each day to provide greater opportunities for their families and communities. In terms of actual income, the gap between the Black man and the white man has increased in the past decade. According to the Bureau of Labor Statistics, in 1979 only forty-six thousand Black men earned salaries between $35,000 and $50,000 annually. Fourteen thousand Black men (and only two thousand Black women) earned $50,000 to $75,000 that year. And in the highest income level, $75,000 and above, there were four thousand Black males compared to five hundred and forty-eight thousand white males. This racial stratification is even sharper at the lower end of the income scale. Using 1978 poverty statistics, only 11.3 percent of all white males under fourteen years old live in poverty, while the figure for young Black males is 42 percent. Between the ages of fourteen and seventeen, 9.6 percent of white males and 38.6 percent of Black males are poor. In the age group eighteen to twenty-one years, 7.5 percent of white males and 26.1 percent of all Black males are poor. In virtually every occupational category, Black men with identical or superior qualifications earn less than their white male counterparts. Black male furniture workers, for example, earn only 69 percent of white males' average wages; in printing and publishing, 68 percent; in all nonunion jobs, 62 percent.

Advances in high technology leave Black males particularly vulnerable to even higher unemployment rates over the next decades. Millions of Black men are located either in the "old line" industries such as steel, automobiles, rubber, and textiles, or in the public sector—both of which have experienced severe job contractions. In agriculture, to cite one typical instance, the disappearance of Black male workers is striking. As late as forty years ago, two out of every five Black men were either farmers or farm workers. In 1960, roughly 5 percent of all Black men were still employed in agriculture, and another 3 percent owned their own farms. By 1983, however, less than 130,000 Black men worked in agriculture. From 1959 to 1974, the number of Black-operated cotton farms in the South dropped from 87,074 to 1,569. Black tobacco farmers declined in number from 40,670 to barely 7,000 during the same period. About three out of four black men involved in farming today are not self-employed.

From both rural and urban environments, the numbers of jobless Black adult males have soared since the late 1960s. In 1969, for example, only 2.5 percent of all Black married males with families were unemployed. This percentage increased to about 10 percent in the mid-1970s, and with the recession of 1982–1984 exceeded 15 percent. The total percentage of all Black families without a single income earner jumped from 10 percent in 1968 to 18.5 percent in 1977—and continued to climb into the 1990s.

These statistics fail to convey the human dimensions of the economic chaos of Black male joblessness. Thousands of jobless men are driven into petty crime annually, just to feed their families; others find temporary solace in drugs or alcohol. The collapse of thousands of black households and the steady proliferation of female-headed, single-parent households is a social consequence of the systematic economic injustice inflicted upon Black males.

Racism also underscores the plight of Black males within the criminal justice system. Every year in this country there are over 2 million arrests of Black males. About three hundred thousand Black men are currently incarcerated in federal and state prisons or other penal institutions. At least half of the Black prisoners are less than thirty years of age, and over one thousand are not even old enough to vote. Most Black male prisoners were unemployed at the time of their arrests; the others averaged less than $8,000 annual incomes during the year before they were jailed. And about 45 percent of the thirteen hundred men currently awaiting capital punishment on death row are Afro-Americans. As Lennox S. Hinds, former National Director of the National Conference of Black Lawyers has stated, "Someone black and poor tried for stealing a few hundred dollars has a 90 percent likelihood of being convicted of robbery with a sentence averaging between 94 to 138 months. A white business executive who embezzled hundreds of thousands of dollars has only a 20 percent likelihood of conviction with a sentence averaging about 20 to 48 months." Justice is not "color blind" when Black males are the accused.

What does the economic and social destruction of Black males mean for the Black community as a whole? Dr. Robert Staples, associate professor of sociology at the University of California–San Francisco, cites some devastating statistics of the current plight of younger Black males:

Less than twenty percent of all black college graduates in the early 1980s are males. The vast majority of young black men who enter college drop out within two years.

At least one-fourth of all black male teenagers never complete high school.

Since 1960, black males between the ages of 15 to 20 have committed suicide at rates higher than that of the general white population. Suicide is currently the third leading cause of death, after homicides, and accidents, for black males aged 15 to 24.

About half of all black men over age 18 have never been married [or are] separated, divorced or widowed.

Despite the fact that several million black male youths identify a career in professional athletics as a desirable career, the statistical probability of any black man making it to the pros exceeds 20,000 to one.

One half of all homicides in America today are committed by black men— whose victims are other black men.

The typical black adult male dies almost three years before he can even begin to collect Social Security.

Fred Clark, a staff psychologist for the California Youth Authority, states that the social devastation of an entire generation of Black males has made it extremely difficult for eligible Black women to locate partners. "In Washington, D.C., it is estimated that there is a one to twelve ratio of black [single] males to eligible females," Clark observes. "Some research indicates that the female is better suited for surviving alone than the male. There are more widowed and single black females than males. Males die earlier and more quickly than females when single. Single black welfare mothers seem to live longer than single unemployed black males."

Every socioeconomic and political indicator illustrates that the Black male in America is facing an unprecedented crisis. Despite singular examples of successful males in electoral politics, business, labor unions, and the professions, the overwhelming majority of Black men find it difficult to acquire self-confidence and self-esteem within the chaos of modern economic and social life. The stereotypes imposed by white history and by the lack of knowledge of our own past often convince many younger Black males that their struggle is too overwhelming. Black women have a responsibility to comprehend the forces that destroy the lives of thousands of their brothers, sons, and husbands. But Black men must understand that they, too, must overcome their own inherent and deeply ingrained sexism, recognizing that Black women must be equal partners in the battle to uproot injustice at every level of the society. The strongest ally Black men have in their battle to achieve Black freedom is the Black woman. Together, without illusions and false accusations, without racist and sexist stereotypes, they can achieve far more than they can ever accomplish alone.

PART 2

Present Status

CHAPTER 6

A Generation behind Bars: Black Males and the Criminal Justice System

by Marc Mauer

Discussion regarding the crisis of the African-American male has continued for a number of years now. Whether or not the African-American male is an "endangered species," it is clear that the dimensions of this crisis are broad. Perhaps nowhere are they so startling as within the criminal justice system. Consider a few statistics:

- As of 1989, almost one in four (23 percent) Black males between the ages of twenty and twenty-nine was under the control of the criminal justice system—in prison, in jail, on probation, or on parole. This compared with one in sixteen white males and one in ten Hispanic males (Mauer 1990).
- The number of African-American males in prison and jail—499,000— exceeds the number of African-American males enrolled in higher education (Mauer 1992).
- Forty-four percent of all prisoners in the United States are Black; Black males make up 40 percent of the condemned on death row.
- Black males in the United States are incarcerated at a rate almost five times that of Black males in South Africa (Mauer 1992).

These statistics only begin to describe the complexity of the criminal justice crisis, a crisis defined by the pervasiveness of the criminal justice system in the lives of Black men and its devastating consequences for the health and survival of the Black community.

The problems that Black males face in the criminal justice system are not new, of course. Lynchings as one form of "justice" defined a significant period in our history. And the fact that 90 percent of the 455 men executed for the crime of rape were Black tells us much about the system's contributions to the perpetuation of racism.

Certainly, in recent years, some of the most egregious problems within the justice system have been challenged. Police brutality—the beatings in the back room of the police station, harassment on the street corner—now occurs with less frequency in some jurisdictions, due to greater scrutiny of the Black community and the courts. Blacks and other minorities are also now much more prominent in a variety of criminal justice leadership positions—as police chiefs, judges, and wardens. But as the Rodney King experience shows us, long-established patterns of abuse still exist.

Despite these changes, the most dramatic and ominous trend within the justice system is its vast expansion, dating back almost two decades. Since 1973, we have witnessed an unprecedented growth in the system. Even though the justice system has long been a major feature of the life cycle for many Black men, never before have we had a period in which such a substantial portion of the community has come under the control of the system. In this sense, we can only surmise what the consequences of this situation will be for current and future generations.

For the young Afro-American men caught up in the system, it is clear that their prospects for engaging in a productive career and family life will be severely postponed and diminished by their involvement in the system. Employers, educational institutions, and potential marriage partners display little enthusiasm for the young man who has little work history or potential earnings, and whose long-term stability in the community is uncertain.

There are those who would say that, unfortunate as this situation may be for the Black community, these are Black "criminals," after all, who are being placed under criminal justice supervision. Had they not chosen a life of crime, they would not be suffering the ill effects of the justice system. Furthermore, the Black community is being afforded protection from those who rape, rob, and assault its citizens with such frequency.

At a time when the Black community is suffering from high rates of crime, this argument is persuasive for many. Further, if it could be demonstrated that the high incarceration rate of Black men were having a sustained impact on crime, some would argue that this would justify the financial and human cost of such policies.

What we see instead is a twenty-year progression of criminal justice policies which have had little impact on crime and have taken a great toll in human lives. Consider the past decade, for example, a time when the nation's prison and jail populations have doubled. If one assumes that a high level of incarceration has a significant impact on crime, then we should have seen dramatic effects during this period. Yet, overall, there was little change in the crime rate. Even more disturbing to the "law and order" perspective is that trends in crime rates were not at all consistent during the eighties. During the period 1980–84, crime fell steadily, by a total of 15 percent. Then, from 1984 to 1989, crime rates steadily increased, by a total of 14 percent. Thus, over the course of a decade, first prison populations increased and crime went down, then prison populations continued to increase and crime went up. Any cause-and-effect relationship is far from clear.

Advocates of a continued "get tough" approach to crime control are faced with the challenge of defining an optimal level of control, a point at which such a policy will have a demonstrable impact. If putting one out of four young Black men under the control of the system is not sufficient to substantially cut crime, does the level of control need to be increased to two out of four, or three out of four? Would we tolerate such levels if young white men were thus involved in the system?

Aside from the human costs for the Black community, the overall financial costs to the nation are substantial and increasingly problematic for the health of our communities. A conservative estimate of the cost of incarceration for the 499,000 African-American males in prison is $8.9 billion a year (Mauer 1992, 3). Overall corrections costs in 1990 were $20 billion nationally, representing the fastest growing expenditure in state budgets. Rising criminal justice costs are now resulting in painful choices for state and local officials faced with cutbacks in education, transportation, and other services.

Why Do African-American Men Have Such Disproportionate Rates of Involvement in the Criminal Justice System?

If we are to begin to develop strategies by which to reduce the disproportionate impact of the criminal justice system on Black men, we need to understand the complex set of factors that have created this situation. These factors include both criminal justice policies and socioeconomic issues affecting the Black community.

Crime Rates

A starting point for an analysis is to look at why so many Black men enter the justice system in the first place. Except for the relative handful who have been unjustly convicted, clearly all the Black men in the system have committed a crime (or have been charged with a crime, as is the case for pretrial detainees in jail). Do Black men commit more crimes than other groups, or are their high numbers in the justice system a result of a discriminatory system?

Later, we shall look at some of the factors relating to differential criminal justice processing, but for now, we can see that Black males do have higher offense levels for a range of crimes. Homicide rates are perhaps the best indicator of this, since virtually all homicides are reported to the police, and the rates of arrest, prosecution, and conviction are also high. Overall, Blacks make up 48 percent of all arrests for murder, clearly very disproportionate to their representation in the total population (*Report to the Nation* 1988). While arrest data may reflect some racial bias in police priorities, it is unlikely that the overall arrest rates for homicides are dramatically different than actual offense rates.

Victimization studies conducted by the Justice Department confirm the higher Black male rate of offending for a number of crimes. The victimization studies, in contrast to FBI crime reports which only account for crimes reported to the police, survey households to determine levels of victimization regardless of whether crimes are reported to the police. Thus, the victimization studies yield a higher, but presumably more accurate, rate of actual crime. For crimes of violence, Blacks are the perceived perpetrators for 27.1 percent of all single-offender crimes, about twice their proportion of the total population (*Criminal Victimization* 1992, 60). (Although these figures are for all Blacks, and not just males, the vast majority of crimes among Blacks and whites alike are committed by males.) Other studies show that for crimes against persons—rape, robbery, assault, and larceny from the person—Black males ages eighteen to twenty commit these crimes at a rate five times that of white males in this age group (Currie 1985, 154).

It would be surprising indeed if Black male rates of offense for certain crimes were not higher than for white males. For, if we believe that there is even some causal relationship between social and economic conditions and rates of crime, then certainly the Black community, with its disproportionate levels of poverty and other social ills, should exhibit higher rates of crime as well.

If we accept the fact that Black males commit serious crimes at higher rates than white males (and both groups at much higher rates than for women of any race), then we need to explain why this is so. The historical legacy of racism is certainly a key part of the analysis. But the dramatic increases in criminal justice populations over the past twenty years suggest other factors as well.

Structural Changes in the U.S. Economy

Not all poor people commit crimes, nor do all wealthy people refrain from committing crimes. We need only look at the large numbers of law-abiding poor people or the Wall Street insider traders to see this. Yet, it is also true that the stresses, strains, and lack of income associated with poverty create needs and temptations that lead a portion of poor people to engage in criminal activities.

While we have always had poverty, and the Black community has suffered from this in great numbers, the economic changes the United States has undergone in the past twenty years have had a profound impact on the life prospects of the Black community. The declining position of the United States in the world economy, the loss of cheap energy sources, and outmoded production techniques all have combined to yield a period of social and economic uncertainty. As the manufacturing economy has been replaced in large part by a service economy, our urban areas have experienced severe dislocations, leaving them with fewer jobs, an eroding tax base, and financially strapped families. Relatively high-wage manufacturing has been replaced by lower-wage service work. An auto worker in Detroit with a high school education who could support a family on a single income now may have a son selling computer software at half the salary of his father. These structural changes have created the framework for a political climate featuring social divisions, racism, and a less charitable view of one's neighbors and community.

The Criminal Justice Response

The beginnings of the "get tough" movement can be traced to the late 1960s, but the framework for its success is clearly ingrained within the priorities of the criminal justice system. Living in a time of high crime rates and daily crises in the criminal justice system, we tend to forget that the system is one in which new policies for crime control are being chosen every day, both consciously and unconsciously.

In the most basic way, our history of criminal justice control is one of controlling the crimes of the poor. One need only visit almost any prison in the country to note the vast inmate population of low-income and primarily non-white prisoners. Nowhere in the Constitution is it written that theft of an auto shall be taken more seriously than insider trading, yet in practice, that has been an unwritten assumption of our system.

Some would argue that while it is unfortunate to focus on crimes of the poor, their "street crimes" are more violent than those crimes of the wealthy, and so close attention to them is warranted. Looking at street crimes, or the FBI Index crime rate, though, we find that only about 13 percent are violent (Federal Bureau of Investigation 1991). Further, we need to question what constitutes a "violent" offense. Many offenses of environmental pollution or workplace safety are much more violent in their long-term consequences than individual street crimes. Do we pay more attention to street crimes because they are immediate and direct, or because they are more likely than white-collar crimes to involve nonwhite offenders?

How do these priorities manifest themselves in daily routines of law enforcement? Many are built into the discretionary nature of the system, starting with the cop on the beat, and working through the prosecutor, judge, and parole board. If the local police officer sees two drunk men staggering down the street—one a white man in a three-piece suit and the other a disheveled looking Black man—which one is likely to be arrested and which one likely to get a call home for a ride?

Resource allocation within the criminal justice system also tells us much about the priorities placed on various types of crime. It is estimated that the total national loss for all street crimes is $11 billion a year, compared to $175 billion to $231 billion a year for white-collar crime (Austin and Irwin 1987). Until relatively recently, little attention was paid to white-collar offenses. Although this has changed somewhat with higher rates of apprehension and conviction in the 1980s, the system remains overwhelmingly focused on crimes of the poor.

The Rise of the "Get Tough" Movement

The "formal" inauguration of the "get tough on crime" movement can in many ways be seen in the 1968 presidential campaign. Prior to that, criminal justice reform, while perhaps not in vogue, was considered a worthy topic of discussion. Public support for the death penalty was at an all-time low, only a handful of executions took place during the 1960s, and incarceration rates had been declining for almost a decade.

But underlying this seemingly liberal public atmosphere were the growing seeds of a more repressive social climate. Crime rates, particularly in urban areas, increased markedly in the 1960s, leading to the "white flight" and heightened security measures that now are commonplace. The impact of the civil rights movement, the urban rebellions of 1967, and the social divisions caused by the Vietnam War all served to polarize American society, often along racial lines. In a world seemingly changing by the day, those who could not or would not understand the changes sought a return to "normalcy," or as described by Richard Nixon, "law and order."

Nixon's successful campaign captured these themes well for his targeted audience. Upon taking office, he moved to implement quickly "tough" crime-control policies. Under the guise of criminal code reform, the Nixon Administration took a draft bill prepared under the Johnson Administration and developed the notorious S.1, a compilation of some of the most repressive legislation in the areas of civil rights and civil liberties seen in many years.

Since that time, the "get tough" movement has taken hold. No longer merely the brainchild of a Republican administration, it now represents a political statement and set of policies that have worked equally well for both Democrats and Republicans. Liberal governors in New York and conservative governors in Texas alike boast of their achievements in building prisons and incarcerating ever greater numbers of offenders. Politicians attempt to outdo each other on their support for the death penalty and more repressive crime-control measures.

The movement reached its zenith, in terms of public attention, in the 1988 presidential campaign, as George Bush's media advisors succeeded in making Willie Horton into a household name. Little attention was paid to the overwhelming success rates of most prison furlough programs, or even to Governor Dukakis's boasting of his own prison-construction accomplishments in Massachusetts.

Unfortunately, the "get tough" movement has meant more than just empty campaign slogans. Once elected, legislators have often pursued repressive criminal justice policies with a vengeance. They have taken the form of mandatory minimum sentences, habitual offender laws, cutbacks in parole and "good time," and other policies that cumulatively have served to swell institutional populations. The overall dimensions of this buildup are staggering. Since 1973, the prison population has quadrupled, rising from 204,211 sentenced felons in 1973 to 823,414 in 1989 (Fundis et al. 1990; Morton and Snell 1992). Overall, the prison and jail population doubled during the 1980s, with more than 1.2 million Americans now behind bars. Probation and parole populations have experienced similar increases, rising 34 percent and 77 percent respectively between 1985 and 1990. Since the 1976 Supreme Court ruling reinstating the death penalty, the death rows of the nation have filled quickly, with well over two thousand inmates now awaiting execution.

For African-American males, already involved in the criminal justice system in substantial numbers, these developments have led to the current crisis. Even more distressing, Black and Hispanic rates of criminal justice control are increasing at an even greater rate than that of whites. As we shall see, much of this increasing disparity is a result of the renewed "war on drugs."

An irony of the "get tough" movement is that after twenty years of implementing "tough" policies, there still exists an image of the criminal justice system as being "soft on crime"—"revolving door justice" in which "soft" judges "coddle" prisoners. Seemingly there is an insatiable public appetite for "tough" rhetoric on crime. This craving, though, may have been misrepresented in the media and by pollsters. A distinction needs to be made between getting tough and controlling crime. If we can control crime in a cost efficient manner through *less* repressive policies, we should expect that public support will be forthcoming.

The "War on Drugs"—A War on the Poor?

Overall crime rates did not change substantially during the 1980s and cannot explain the rise in prison populations. In fact, the renewed war on drugs has fueled much of the dramatic increase:

- Adult arrests for sale or manufacture of drugs increased by 293 percent between 1980 and 1989, from 102,714 to 404,275. Arrests for drug possession rose by 128 percent during this period, from 368,451 to 843,488 (*Drugs and Crime Facts* 1991, 8).
- Drug offenders make up an increasing share of the prison population. In the federal system, the proportion of drug offenders rose from 25 percent of all prisoners in 1981 to 53 percent in 1991 (Isikoff 1991). In state prisons, offenders accounted for 6 percent of all prisoners in 1979 and 22 percent of inmates in 1991 (Greenfeld 1992).

Although drug use cuts across class and racial lines, drug law enforcement has been disproportionately directed toward inner city, and thereby Black and Hispanic, drug use. The National Institute of Drug Abuse has reported that Blacks make up 12 percent of people who use drugs regularly and 16 percent of regular cocaine users. Yet, more than 48 percent of those arrested for heroin or cocaine drug charges in 1988 were Black (Meddis 1989). As Delaware prosecutor Charles Butler recently observed, "Sure, it's true we prosecute a high percentage of minorities for drugs. The simple fact is, if you have a population—minority or not—that is conducting most of their illegal business on the street, those cases are easy pickings for the police" (Bearak 1990).

Thus, although drug prosecutions and convictions are up nationally, Blacks are making up an increasing percentage of these figures. From 1984 to 1989, the Black share of drug arrests nationally rose from 30 percent to 41 percent (Meddis and Suides 1990). In Michigan, drug arrests overall have doubled since 1985, while Black drug arrests have tripled (Mitchell 1990). Unless there is a dramatic change in direction in the war on drugs—currently 70 percent of federal funding is devoted to law enforcement—we can expect ever greater numbers of Black males to swell our prisons over the coming decade.

Racism and the Criminal Justice System

The evidence upon which to determine whether the criminal justice system has a racist impact is not as clear as one might expect. On the one hand, as we have seen, Black males do commit serious offenses at greater rates than do white males. In this regard, if the criminal justice system responds to those offenses equally, then the determination of racial bias would have to be sought in social and economic conditions preceding the criminal justice system.

In the most extreme case—capital punishment—the evidence is quite strong for a racially determined outcome. Several authoritative studies in recent years have concluded that the race of both offender and victim in a potentially capital case plays a strong role in determining in which cases a prosecutor will seek the death penalty and whether it will be imposed by a judge or jury (Amnesty International 1987). The studies find that the Black offender/white victim combination is far more likely to result in a death sentence than any other pairing. (When presented with this evidence, the Supreme Court majority responded by saying that an overall pattern of racism was not sufficient to overturn death statutes, and that death row inmates would need to prove specific racial bias in their own cases.)

For other offenses, though, the research literature is more mixed. Blumstein, for example, found that 80 percent of disparity in sentencing could be explained by factors not related to race, primarily seriousness of offense and prior criminal history. The remaining 20 percent, he concluded, might be explained by race or by other factors (Blumstein 1982). A recent RAND study of sentencing in California determined that race was not a factor in sentencing when other variables were controlled for (Klein et al. 1990).

How does this evidence fit with the experience of Black defendants, prisoners, and their attorneys who report on racially determined criminal justice outcomes every day? The seeming contradiction may depend on which part of the system is being examined. As described previously, much of the disparity in the justice system may lie in the early stages, at the level of arrest and prosecution. Thus, a Black drug offender and a white drug offender may be treated equally at sentencing, but the Black drug offender may be more likely to be arrested and prosecuted in the first place. Thus, we cannot conclude that the system is fair just because sentencing outcomes appear to be. One new study, for example, examined the impact of federal mandatory sentencing statutes and found that prosecutors used their discretion to plea bargain below the mandatory minimum sentence in a manner that "appears to be related to the race of the defendant" (*Mandatory Minimum Penalties* 1991, ii).

Life Prospects for Black Males

Perhaps the most troubling explanation for the high rate of criminal justice control for African-American men relates to their real and perceived lack of opportunity and their hopelessness about the future. Young Black men growing up today have a radically different perception of the criminal justice system than young white men do. When one in four young Black men come under the control of the system, Black men find it hard not to view that system as an almost inevitable part of one's life cycle. This is not to say that it is a "rite of passage" but that it is a part of growing up, taken for granted almost as many young whites assume they will go to college.

The sense of limited opportunity, of course, is not just an assumption but a perception based on disturbing reality. As the National Center for Children in Poverty of Columbia University has documented, one of every two Black children under the age of six is now living in poverty (as are 40 percent of Hispanic children) (Rich 1990). Unless current policies are altered seriously, this group represents the next generation of "prison bound" offenders.

How Can We Respond to the High Criminal Justice Control Rate?

Much of the solution to the high rate of Black male involvement in the criminal justice system lies, of course, in addressing racism and social and economic inequities, and in strengthening community support for young people. In the course of developing these broad strategies, though, we should not neglect reforms within the criminal justice system that can contribute to a lessening of the system's negative impact on Black males. Following is an outline of policy reforms that could begin to address the problem.

Increase Diversion from the Criminal Justice System

Many young and first-time offenders are only stigmatized by their contact with the criminal justice system, without necessarily receiving either appropriate supervision or support. Opportunities exist to divert many of these offenders to organizations and individuals who can better focus on the problems of Black, Hispanic, and poor youth. Organizations such as 100 Black Men exist in many communities. The courts can use them as resources to divert defendants and to develop preventive measures for work with "at risk" youth before they become enmeshed in the justice system.

Focus the "War on Drugs" on Prevention and Treatment Rather Than Law Enforcement

The law enforcement approach to drug abuse is hardly a new strategy. It has been tried for decades with little impact. The consequences of current and proposed policies of large-scale arrests of casual users as well as dealers threatens to overload completely the judicial and corrections systems, while avoiding discussion of more profound underlying issues.

A comprehensive study by the Special Committee on Criminal Justice in a Free Society of the American Bar Association's Criminal Justice Section illustrates the problem well. The committee reported that, of approximately 34 million serious crimes committed against persons or property in 1986, 31 million never resulted in arrest, and only several hundred thousand resulted in felony convictions and imprisonment. Even if we assume that a good number of those offenders had committed multiple crimes that were not detected, we are still left with a situation in which a small portion of criminals are prosecuted. Clearly, continued excessive reliance on the criminal justice system can have only a limited impact on drug crimes, and at great cost.

In some jurisdictions, criminal justice officials have come to recognize and respond to the limitations of incarceration. Pretrial diversion programs in several jurisdictions now screen drug defendants and refer some to treatment programs in lieu of prosecution. A new police chief in New Haven, Connecticut, has adopted a policy of discontinuing mass drug arrests; officers now go door-to-door in certain communities encouraging residents to make use of city-sponsored treatment programs.

The larger policy question, of course, concerns the funding priorities for treatment and law enforcement. Current federal policy, as articulated by the Office of National Drug Control Policy (the "drug czar") and funded by Congress, has directed 70 percent of anti-drug funding toward law enforcement and only 30 percent toward treatment and prevention. With waiting lists to enter drug treatment of six months or more in many communities, can we really say that the criminal justice system is our only alternative, and that nothing else has worked?

Reduce Lengthy and Inefficient Prison Terms

Mandatory sentencing laws and lengthier prison terms have resulted in high costs with only relatively modest gains in crime control. Prisoners cannot commit crimes in the community while they are locked up, but such measures prevent only a small fraction of all crimes. A 1978 report by the National Academy of Sciences concluded that to achieve a 10 percent reduction in crime, New York would have had to increase its prison population by 263 percent and Massachusetts by 310 percent (*Overcrowded Time* 1982, 15–16).

The massive increase in incarceration and lengthening of prison terms provides almost no long-term benefits in reduction of recidivism. The most recent Justice Department study of this issue shows that recidivism rates, while very high, are virtually identical for prisoners who serve anywhere from one to five years. Therefore, "getting tough" results in high corrections costs but leaves us with offenders who are no less likely to commit future crimes.

Reduction of lengthy prison terms by itself is not the answer to crime. What it would accomplish, though, is to relieve the burden on an overcrowded system, reduce the impact of the system on minorities, and free up tax dollars to be used for more preventive measures.

Sentence to Ameliorate Racial Disparities

Judges, prosecutors, defense attorneys, and probation officers together have an important opportunity to lessen the drastic impact of the justice system on Black males. That opportunity comes at the time of sentencing. The courtroom sentencing process should include a full examination of the circumstances of both victim and offender and an analysis of community support and supervision mechanisms that may represent appropriate sentencing options. The goals of this process should be several: to assess public safety concerns; to restore victims to the extent possible; to order appropriate and constructive sanctions in the community; and to reduce the chances that offenders will return to the system.

Increase the Use of Alternatives to Incarceration

For far too long, we have equated punishment with prison. Aside from the fact that incarceration is by far the most costly component of the criminal justice system, it has also not proved to be very productive as a means of reducing crime. If we want our justice system to punish, treat, or supervise offenders, we may turn to a variety of community-based sanctions that can accomplish these ends in some cases without resorting to imprisonment. These programs are varied but include restitution to victims, community service work, intensive probation supervision, and provisions for treatment programs, education, and employment. Programs that provide alternative sentencing options for judges have been established throughout the country and have demonstrated that they are more appropriate than incarceration in many cases. Far too often, though, they are underfunded or fail to have clear goals established for diverting offenders from a prison system. In some jurisdictions, too, white offenders are more likely to receive the benefits of alternative sentencing, while Blacks continue to receive prison terms in large numbers. Programs providing alternatives to incarceration need to be monitored to ensure that minority offenders are appropriately represented in these sanctions.

Conclusion

The criminal justice system is not the primary cause of the distressing plight of African-American males, nor is it unique in its operations regarding racial disparities. Its impact on Black males and the Black community, though, is potentially devastating for the life prospects of both current and future generations. Of particular significance is the fact that long-established trends in the criminal justice system have worsened considerably over the past two decades, with little relief in sight.

The potential for political and community change does exist, even if reform forces appear to be weak at times. Two factors appear to be critical in developing broad public support for change. First is the ever escalating cost of building and operating prisons. The public and policymakers appear increasingly conscious of limited resources and the competition for tax dollars; they may well be receptive to arguments pointing to the fiscal crisis that a growing corrections bureaucracy will create.

Tied in with this is the limited effectiveness of the justice system in controlling crime. Even though they pay the enormous costs of courts and prisons, most Americans still do not feel safe in their homes and communities. A strategy designed to link these issues together, along with alternative crime-control proposals, has the potential of building a broad coalition to support more effective, and less destructive, policies. The life prospects, not only of African-American males, but of our whole society depend on these policies.

CHAPTER 7

The Case Against NCAA Proposition 48

by Gary A. Sailes

Sidney Prince, a Black all-star high school football player, lay on his bed at 12:08 A.M. unable to sleep. His mind was filled with thoughts about the English exam he had the next day. A smile appeared on his face as the confidence he felt came to the surface; he was prepared to "ace" an exam in a subject he enjoyed very much. One of the brightest students in his senior class, he was totally unaware that he would graduate number two in his class in the spring. He was also unaware that he would be labeled "not good enough" by a system he was about to enter, the college sports system.

Sidney Prince was one of the most sought-after high school football players in Oklahoma in 1986. He was recruited by and signed a letter of intent to play football at the University of Oklahoma. The high school scouting reports listed him as an honor student, a top football prospect, a bona fide "Blue Chipper"—a college coach's dream. But Sidney Prince did not play football in his first year of college. He failed to meet the minimum academic standards set by the NCAA that year for incoming freshman student athletes. His score on the math portion of the SAT exam was too low. Sidney Prince was a sacrificial lamb in a college sports system much bigger than his school, his teachers, his family, and himself. He was a Proposition 48 casualty, another statistic in a seemingly cold and insensitive institution whose harsh rules and hypocritical ethical code altered his life. He was victimized before he ever had a chance to play the big game, and his dream had to be postponed for at least a year.

Background Information

In January 1983, at its annual meeting, the National Collegiate Athletic Association (NCAA) enacted Rule 5-1-(j), better known as Proposition 48. In an attempt to tighten admissions standards for incoming freshmen student athletes, the rule stipulated that, to participate in varsity competition at an NCAA-affiliated college or university, new recruits must graduate from high school with a minimum grade point average of 2.0 on a core curriculum of eleven courses, including three years of English, two years of social science, two years of mathematics, and two years of a natural or physical science. In addition, they had to score at least 700 points out of a possible 1600 on the Scholastic Aptitude Test or a minimum of 15 points out of a possible 36 on the American College Test.

A supplemental proposition, Rule 49-b, stated that Proposition 48 would go into effect at the beginning of the 1986–87 school year and would only affect the 277 institutions competing at the Division I level. Students who did not qualify could be admitted and attend class but could not participate in either varsity practices or competition. Nonqualifiers could compete as sophomores after demonstrating satisfactory academic progress, and they would receive four years of varsity eligibility if they continued to maintain satisfactory academic progress. Partial qualifiers (those who met one but not both of the requirements) could receive an athletic scholarship, but they would thereby forfeit one year of varsity eligibility.

Public Reaction

Proposition 48 initiated an outcry from Black university presidents, educators, and coaches and from the civil rights establishment. They claimed the rule was biased against Blacks, that standardized tests like the ACT and SAT favored whites and would adversely effect the eligibility of Black freshmen student athletes and the recruitment efforts of athletic coaches at historically Black colleges and universities.

A *USA Today* report ("Fewer Athletes" 1987) revealed that Black student athletes and Black colleges and universities in the United States had, in fact, been most adversely affected by NCAA Proposition 48. The American Institutes for Research (1988) reported that in its first year, 65 percent of all Proposition 48 casualties were Black. Moreover they reported, Blacks accounted for an alarming 91 percent of the Proposition 48 casualties among recruits for Division I basketball. The so-called emotional response from the African-American establishment served as an early warning to the NCAA. As predicted, Black athletes were more adversely affected by the new rule than were white athletes.

As mentioned earlier, partial qualifiers could receive an athletic scholarship but were not allowed to compete in their freshman year and would lose one year of varsity eligibility. That door was slammed shut in January, 1989. At its annual conference, the NCAA passed another rule called Proposition 42. This new rule denied first-year eligibility, an athletic scholarship, and school financial aid of any kind to entering college freshmen student athletes not showing both the minimum grade point average and the minimum SAT/ACT score upon graduation from high school.

The implementation of Proposition 42 outraged the Black establishment. Georgetown University basketball coach John Thompson and Temple University basketball coach John Chaney, outspoken critics of Proposition 48, publicly protested its enactment. The NAACP and the National Urban League publicly took a hard stand against Proposition 42, arguing the new rule could keep many Black athletes from attending college. Joseph Johnson, president of Grambling State University and chairman of the National Association for Equal Opportunity in Higher Education, strongly opposed Proposition 42, arguing it was discriminatory against Blacks and economically disadvantaged Americans in particular. He maintained most Black athletes would not be able to attend college without an athletic scholarship. In support of his contentions, the American Council on Education (1989) has reported that approximately 87 percent of African-Americans attending college require financial aid. These findings support the assertion that Proposition 42 was blatantly discriminatory and partially blocked Black high school students' access to higher education.

The academic establishment also supported Black college presidents, educators, and coaches, asserting that the NCAA had stepped out of bounds with rules regulating who could and could not receive financial assistance at their respective institutions. The academics were incensed by the NCAA's seemingly outrageous arrogance and ill-founded claim of authority. Intense pressure from the public and academic arenas influenced the NCAA to amend Proposition 42; now partial qualifiers could receive school financial aid but not athletic scholarships. However, partial qualifiers lost one year of eligibility, having to sit out both practice and competition during their first year.

Implications of Proposition 48

The discussion surrounding Proposition 48 seemed extremely one-sided. The arguments against the rule are far more extensive and consequential than those arguments for it. At the time of the rule's inception, approximately 43.5 percent of all senior student athletes participating in football and basketball at Division I institutions were graduating, but only 38 percent of Black athletes were graduating. The NCAA felt that if tighter academic requirements were implemented, more disciplined and capable student athletes would enter college as freshmen, and so national graduation rates would increase. Such an improvement would help to decrease public criticism, diminish congressional scrutiny, and perhaps ameliorate the tarnished image of the NCAA. At best, this notion was ill-founded and embarrassingly naive.

Establishing academic eligibility requirements for incoming freshmen student athletes would never resolve the serious problem of low graduation rates among college athletes. The variables affecting the academic performance of the student athlete are diverse and complex, and they require considerably more than a quick fix. The academic and athletic demands on the typical student athlete at a Division I school are immense, requiring more than sixty-five hours per week of the athlete's time. The rule served as nothing more than a pathetic attempt on the part of the NCAA to restore some degree of academic integrity to college athletics, to eliminate media pressure, and to influence public opinion about the internal operations and state of affairs of college athletics in the United States.

Most of the freshmen student athletes who failed to meet Proposition 48 eligibility requirements were blocked by low standardized test scores. Yet, the admissions network at American colleges and universities believes standardized tests have cultural biases that favor middle- and upper-income whites. Thus, the SAT and ACT are unfair to minorities and the economically disadvantaged. Appropriately, admissions offices do not base their entire decisions on standardized test scores; they also look at high school grade point averages, letters of recommendation, class rank, national origin, gender, race, declared major, and other factors. The experts in college admissions do not feel that high school grades and standardized test scores alone adequately determine the typical high school student's capability to successfully manage college academics.

The NCAA stands alone basing academic eligibility requirements solely on grade point average and SAT/ACT scores. After reviewing the literature, I can only conclude that the NCAA's hard stand is unjustified and unethical. For example, a 1987 University of Michigan (Walter, et al. 1987) study of more than seven hundred football players between 1974 and 1983 found no relationship between GPA in high school or the first year of college and SAT scores. Further, only high school GPA served as an accurate predictor for GPA during the first year of college. Furthermore, 86 percent of players who would have been ruled out by Proposition 48 because of low test scores actually graduated from college. In support of the Michigan study, (Walter et al. 1987) the American Institutes for Research (1989c) reported that 79 percent of all 1986 and 1987 Proposition 48 casualties playing Division I basketball and football were still in college making normal progress towards a degree. Over 60 percent of those student athletes did not meet Proposition 48 eligibility requirements because of deficient standardized test scores.

Further evidence against employing standardized test scores as valid admissions criteria is provided by Crouse and Trusheim (1988), authors of *The Case against the SAT*. They not only found that SAT scores do not correlate well with college grades, but they also uncovered an economic bias in the SAT: for every $18,000 increase in family income, SAT scores increased by an average of 200 points. This is particularly significant in view of the fact that African-Americans at the time of the study earned half the income ($18,000) of white Americans; 33 percent of Black Americans lived in poverty, and 16 percent in extreme poverty. Moreover, the American Institutes for Research (1989B) reported that approximately 50 percent of the Black student athletes who play Division I football and basketball emanate from impoverished backgrounds, compared with 13 percent for whites. It seems clear that Black high school student athletes are more adversely effected by Proposition 48 than are their white counterparts.

An examination of recent national test score norms from the Educational Testing Service appear to support the assertion that African Americans were targeted by the NCAA's new rule. Black high school students had average scores of 712 and 13.0 on the SAT and ACT respectively in 1987. Their average ACT score was two points below the minimum requirements established by the NCAA, and their average SAT score barely met the minimum. In 1990, the NCAA raised the ACT requirement to 18, making it even more difficult for African Americans to comply with the rule. The 1987 averages for white high school students on the SAT and ACT were 890 and 19.7 respectively, well above the minimum requirements established by the NCAA.

While the desire of the NCAA to eventually graduate more student athletes is noble, its current method of pursuing this goal is not only discriminatory, but victimizes Black and economically disadvantaged student athletes. For that reason alone, the rule should be amended or abandoned altogether.

The element most universally damaging to the scholarship and gradua- tion rates of student athletes is the business mentality of the college sports sys- tem. College sports in fact constitute a thriving business generating hundreds of millions of dollars in income every year. College sports observe all the unwritten rules of corporate businesses: they perpetuate the philosophy of capitalism and profit; establish marketing and promotion strategies based on product demands and consumption; sabotage, control, and/or eliminate competitors; bend or cir- cumvent the rules of fair trade to gain a market edge; strive to win at all costs; and acknowledge expendable commodities (coaches and student athletes) in the name of profit.

However, only about 13 percent of NCAA Division I schools project a profit on their own. Coming to the rescue, the NCAA offers huge sums (over $2 million to the basketball national champion and a $16 million split at the Rose Bowl) to winning schools and/or conferences at national championships. CBS's recent agreement to pay the NCAA $100 billion over seven years to broadcast the National Basketball Championship will only magnify the problems perme- ating college athletics. The drive for the great financial rewards made available by the NCAA and its sponsors creates more competition between athletic pro- grams and places more pressure on coaches to win, encouraging cheating in the system. This system also increases the time-consuming demands and pressures on student athletes, encouraging them to believe that athletics are more impor- tant than academics.

The research supports this contention. The Women's Sports Foundation (1989) released a study entitled *Minorities in Sports*. It was reported that student athletes had higher GPAs coming out of high school than they earned in college. Also, the American Institutes for Research, (1989a) reported student athletes cited lack of time to pursue their academic studies as the chief problem facing them during their college experience. Division I student athletes also reported that approximately two-thirds to three-quarters of their time was monopolized by athletics, leaving them little time to attend class or to manage their studies.

Discussion

Most Black college presidents and educators and the civil rights establishment feel Proposition 48 is not a fair rule. Many arguments have surfaced regarding the rule's ethical and philosophical implications. Some argue that the eligibility standards established by Proposition 48 are so minimal that anyone not able to meet them does not belong in college. That assumption is elitist and demon- strates a lack of awareness of and sensitivity to the mission of historically Black colleges and universities. The literature has demonstrated on numerous occa- sions that standardized test scores do not accurately predict an individual's ability to manage college course work. Yet, it is the standardized test scores that are preventing over 66 percent of Proposition 48 casualties from obtaining freshman eligibility and athletic scholarships to attend college. Moreover, the literature has also shown that over 80 percent of Proposition 48 casualties probably will graduate from college. Further, among historically Black colleges and universities there is the conviction that all persons have the right to pursue an education, and no one who chooses to attend one of these schools shall be discriminated against. Denying anyone access to higher education because of elitist philosophies based on the results of culturally biased standardized tests violates the principles of freedom that are the foundation of this country's Constitution, which guarantees the rights of its citizens.

Still, some argue that "anyone against Proposition 48 is against academic excellence!" That assumption is terribly naive. In fact, Proposition 48 bars student athletes from demonstrating their capacity for academic excellence. Not all students who earn low scores on standardized tests are poor or marginal students. It is well known to educators that the quality of instruction in American inner-city public high schools is not consistent with the instruction taking place in financially better off private, rural, or suburban schools. Quality of high school instruction has an impact on how well the student scores on standardized tests. The ACT and SAT standardized tests reveal more about the disparities in the American educational process than about the capability of students to handle college course work.

The following question was raised: "Were the architects of Proposition 48 motivated by prejudice or bigotry?" It is apparent that the rule was not clearly thought out, its consequences were not thoroughly investigated, and its implementation demonstrated a lack of racial and cultural awareness and sensitivity. The NCAA's biggest mistake was to exclude officials representing historically Black colleges and universities from the committee that conceptualized Proposition 48. Had such officials been included, the NCAA could have avoided controversy and bad press.

Proposition 48 should be abandoned primarily because it serves no viable purpose and survives only on principle. Proposition 48 demonstrates a power play on the part of the NCAA and has created distance between the NCAA and academia, Black educators, and the civil rights establishments. The NCAA has overextended its authority by implementing a rule that undermines and attempts to regulate the admissions and financial aid policies of American colleges and universities. It simply does not have that right nor is it qualified to do so. Proposition 48 prevents deserving and capable young student athletes from receiving their only possible means of financial aid to attend college. From an educational standpoint, that is totally unacceptable.

Common knowledge dictates that the problem with college sports isn't the type of student athlete who is being recruited; the problem is the system within which the athlete must compete. Student athletes are not given adequate time to pursue their college studies leading to the degree. The business mentality of athletic programs is in direct conflict with the philosophy of amateurism and scholarship the NCAA is so nobly trying to reestablish in college sports. That the two ideologies are not compatible is especially clear in view of the current state of affairs in college sports. Unless the NCAA exercises more control over its governing institutions, it will continue to experience its current problems, drawing unwanted negative media exposure and pressure from the general public.

Recommendations

The NCAA will probably never control the business side of college sports. It can, however, recapture part of their integrity and reestablish scholarship among student athletes by implementing and enforcing sweeping reforms to protect the rights of student athletes. Many reforms have been proposed by the NCAA University Presidents Committee and by a Congressional committee called the Knight Commission (1991). Many of the proposed reforms have met extreme resistance and criticism from the body of Division I athletic directors and coaches. They maintain that the proposed reforms would diminish their capacity to generate revenues which would in turn reduce the competitiveness of their athletic programs, most notably in football and basketball, the two major revenue-producing sports at most schools.

The primary focus of the two reform committees was to protect the rights of student athletes to pursue an education and to graduate with their classmates. To accomplish this, they concluded, the pressures associated with intercollegiate competition would have to be reduced, freeing more time for student athletes to pursue their academic studies. The proposal generating the most criticism from coaches was to reduce weekly practices to twenty hours per week. Currently, most Division I football and basketball teams practices between thirty and forty hours per week (Knight Commission 1991). Other reforms included eliminating spring football practice, reducing the number of contests played in a given season, and having later starting dates for intercollegiate seasons. On the average, Division I basketball teams play thirty contests per year, more if they make it to the NCAA tournament. Intercollegiate baseball teams play an average of sixty contests per year. On average, Division I basketball and football players miss approximately six classes per semester. In many cases, professors are either required or encouraged to make bothersome arrangements to allow student athletes to take make-up examinations. Implementing restrictions on the number of allowable contact hours in athletics for student athletes would greatly reduce the pressures and demands they experience and allow them more opportunity to pursue academic work leading to a degree.

Another proposal submitted by the NCAA Presidents Committee was to eliminate athletic dormitories (Knight Commission 1991). This recommendation would have two major benefits. First, it would eliminate the athletic department's expense of maintaining housing for student athletes, turning over this responsibility to the campus housing office. Second, "mainstreaming" student athletes would help to dispel the traditional jock mentality, increase the student athlete's competitiveness in the classroom, and expose athletes to a more balanced social experience. In fact, studies have demonstrated that students who involve themselves in the social environment of college and university campuses do better academically and have a greater chance of graduating. Living in a restricted environment centered around athletics diminishes that possibility.

The Knight Commission (1991) proposed that academic safety nets be developed and maintained for student athletes. Tutoring, counseling, and academic monitoring programs would help to ensure the academic success of student athletes. Studies have demonstrated that many student athletes require some type of counseling or tutorial assistance to balance the demands of being both a student and an athlete.

It was recommended that individual schools as well as the NCAA establish scholarship funds to pay the educational expenses of student athletes who exhaust their eligibility before graduating (Knight Commission 1991). Currently, only 43.5 percent of student athletes actually complete their major course requirements to earn their bachelors degree in four years. For all students, studies have demonstrated, an average of five years is required to obtain a bachelor's degree; however, most athletic scholarships are awarded for only four years. Since the majority of Black athletes come from families who are unable to pay their college expenses, establishing and maintaining posteligibility or five-year athletic scholarships become very important issues.

Athletes should receive a monetary stipend in addition to their athletic scholarships. Currently, the NCAA does not allow student athletes to hold jobs or to receive funds in addition to their athletic scholarships (Knight Commission 1991). Generally, it has been reported, athletic scholarships do not cover normal expenses. The monetary restrictions imposed by the NCAA limit the activity and sociability of student athletes to an extent that can adversely affect their adjustment to the college environment. Studies have shown that becoming involved in normal social activities on the college campus contributes to the student's identification with the school and to academic achievement leading to graduation (Fleming 1988).

First-year student athletes should not be allowed to compete in varsity athletics. The NCAA enforced this rule until the late 1970s. Eliminating the first year of eligibility would give the student athlete the opportunity to mature, to become socially and educationally adjusted to the university, to focus on and become serious about their studies. These developments would increase their chances of earning a degree. To maintain four years of eligibility, they would need five-year scholarships. Granting them would demonstrate the institution's and the NCAA's commitment to the educational attainment of the athletes.

The NCAA should make coaches more accountable for graduating their athletes and placing them in degree-granting curriculums. For failing to graduate their student athletes, coaches should be penalized (fewer scholarships, no postseason play, fewer recruitment visitations). The NCAA should also encourage college and university presidents and chancellors to exercise more control over their athletic programs, including those academic programs that service student athletes. If academically marginal student athletes are recruited, remedial programs, such as the one at the University of Georgia, should be established to provide such student athletes with the opportunity to develop those skills and to become competent and competitive in the classroom.

There should be widespread support for current legislation, recommended by the Knight Commission, requiring colleges and universities to publicize the graduate rates of their student athletes. Prospective student athletes can then make informed decisions about the schools they will attend and avoid programs that are not graduating their athletes.

Summary

Proposition 48 discriminates against Blacks, and the research confirms that it does. An overwhelming majority of Proposition 48 casualties are African American. If parity existed in the educational system and if Proposition 48 were a fair rule, only 12 percent of the casualties would be Black, since African Americans represent 12 percent of the American population. However, cultural and socioeconomic biases are built into the rule; they emanate from the biases built into the SAT and ACT tests. As long as standardized test scores are utilized to establish eligibility requirements for college athletic participation, discrimination will continue.

The implementation of Propositions 48 demonstrated a lack of foresight and poor judgment on the part of the NCAA. Student athletes are not the problem in college sports; given the chance, they could succeed in the classroom. Integrity can be restored to intercollegiate athletics by implementing policies that protect the rights of the student athlete to receive a college athletic scholarship and a college education. The number of athletes who exploit the college system so as to enter professional sports is minimal. Implementing a rule that attempts to exempt them from the college sports system at the expense of denying access to deserving student athletes is unfair and unethical. The implementation of sweeping reforms in the college sports system, and not a quick fix, is the only logical alternative for the NCAA. Only then will the Sidney Princes in our high schools get the opportunities they deserve.

CHAPTER 8

African-American Males and Homelessness

by Billy E. Jones and Vincent P. Christmas

One of the most critical issues facing this nation and its government today is the ever-increasing problem of the homeless. The phenomenon is present in the industrial Northeast and the rural South, the Pacific Northwest, the Sun Belt, and the Midwest as well. In 1984, estimates on the numbers of homeless persons in the United States ranged from a low figure of 250,000 to a high of 3 million (U.S. Department of Housing and Urban Development 1984). However, no responsible advocate, politician, or researcher can, with any degree of accuracy, claim to know the extent of this population. Although estimates can be developed based on average shelter census figures and contacts made by street outreach programs, soup kitchens, and hospital case records, the nature of this diverse and constantly growing population precludes accurate figures. Unfortunately, debates about those numbers continue to inhibit decision and policy-makers from examining the causes of as well as the solutions to this problem.

Similarly, there are no reliable data on the numbers of African Americans who are homeless or particularly of African-American men who are homeless. More can be learned about this population by examining such subgroups as those with hospital admissions, either medical or psychiatric, and those with histories of drug or alcohol abuse. Within a particular service system, information can be gathered. Clearly, homeless persons are not part of any service system as a whole; they fall into categories as conditions warrant.

At a time when poverty and economic inequities take their toll on all Americans, it is certain that for the almost 9 million African Americans who live below the arbitrary and imaginary line of poverty, survival is a real and present issue (Jaynes and Williams 1989, 279). Per capita earnings for African-American individuals, before taxes, have remained at about 57 percent of the per capita income for their white counterparts since the mid-eighties (Jaynes and Williams 1989, 279). Further differences between African Americans and whites are evident when one looks at median family income and at single heads of households. In the African-American community those families headed by women earn 59 percent of white womens' earnings in similar living situations. (Jaynes and Williams 1989, 281).

For both families and individuals, poverty not only exacerbates deleterious living conditions, sometimes leading to homelessness, but may also make it difficult to escape the conditions that have plagued this nation's poor.

How then does a society or government address the needs of the nation's homeless? How can concerned advocates and social service personnel provide the care and compassion required to assist the homeless? It is fairly certain that a place of residence for those without one will make the task of attending to other related needs more successful. When one has a home, issues of health, mental health, alcohol, and other substance abuse can be more effectively addressed. What does this mean for the millions of homeless persons in America and for the thousands who annually join their ranks? Since the beginning of the Reagan legacy in 1980, there has been a loss of 2.7 million low-income housing units nationwide. At the same time the level of federal support for low/moderate income housing has been reduced by 60 percent. In addition, an average of 500,000 units are lost annually due to demolition, fire, abandonment, or conversion (Institute of Medicine 1988, 4).

There are a myriad of conditions that severely restrict the ability of homeless people to utilize available, yet limited, resources to their advantage. Many of these conditions are social and medical in nature. For homeless people who are also suffering from mental illness, alcohol and substance abuse, AIDS, or other physical ailments, the battle against these conditions becomes even more critical. This chapter examines the problems facing the estimated 40,000–60,000 homeless single adults in New York City, with particular attention paid to the African-American homeless males in the city. Subgroups of this population will be discussed as well—i.e., those who are suffering from mental illness, alcoholism, and other substance abuse. Objectives of various service systems will also be examined, such as model programs and innovative initiatives that have been successful in addressing the needs of this heterogeneous population.

It is difficult to address the issue of homelessness, particularly homelessness among African-American men, without dealing with other societal factors that may contribute to or relate to the causes and conditions of homelessness. Politicians, policymakers, and advocates cannot eliminate the condition of homelessness unless concomitant progress is made in other areas of society such as health care, employment and educational opportunities, housing, and the judicial system.

It is easy to understand why the numbers of this nation's homeless so drastically increased during the decade of the eighties. When national economic trends fall, the poor are the first and hardest hit. In 1982, almost 12 million people were unemployed. This was the first time the national unemployment rate exceeded 10 percent since the Great Depression of the 1930s. Although by 1984 that figure had dropped to about 8.5 million jobless and by 1988 to below 6 million, the devastation of this prolonged period of high unemployment will effect this nation's economy well into the 1990s (Joint Economic Committee 1988, iv). An unprecedented rate of inflation, home and farm foreclosures, and the reduced buying power of the dollar also significantly affected how goods and services were delivered and which sections of society received them.

For African Americans with low and moderate incomes and for those who are homeless and may also suffer from disabilities, the past decade has been a particularly devastating period. The limited resources earmarked for the needy became even more scarce, while at the same time the individualism touted by Ronald Reagan became a license for some to turn their backs on African Americans and the poor. Many Americans felt that whatever African Americans required politically and socially had been achieved in the 1960s; now they should receive no special treatment or priority. In fact, many gains made in the federal courts during the 1960s continue to be reversed in this climate of empty morality, individualism, and blind militarism as this quote from Bruce Wright's book, *Black Robes, White Justice,* explains: "A wave of right-wing sentiment has descended on America. One of its by-products is the feeling that blacks have too much; that they are the beneficiaries of preferences to the detriment of whites; that black quotas mean that whites will be discharged so blacks can take their places" (Wright 1987, 6). Consequently, underserved communities continue to be underserved, and the needs of the African-American community continue unmet. But as professionals, families, and African-American elected officials struggle to survive and understand this era, so do the homeless and those who live on the verge of homelessness. However, for this group the consequences of the struggle can be fatal.

The neighborhoods of New York City where many African Americans reside are plagued by readily available drugs and alcohol as well as high crime and unemployment. The underserved community has become another defacto arm of the institution of a racially divisive America. Many other African Americans reside in correctional institutions, and still others on the streets, in public places, and in shelters. Homelessness among African-American men is but one inevitable result of the forces of this nation's ubiquitous institutionalized racism. This racial discrimination is deeply rooted in American society, and its effects are felt in numerous areas. It inevitably imposes greater handicaps on the 13,000–20,000 homeless mentally ill individuals estimated to live in New York City (New York City Human Resources Administration 1990, 1).

For African-American men, homelessness may result from institutionalized forces that significantly and negatively affect their coping ability. Homelessness can therefore be viewed as an inevitable consequence of practices that prevent African Americans from reaping the benefits of the society. Fighting these oppressive forces may be all-consuming, yet it enables individuals and families to mold their own destinies to some degree. Unfortunately, there are African Americans who cannot break down the oppressive walls of racism.

Many young African-American men are unable to overcome the barriers created by poor educational and employment opportunities and what mainstream society defines as poor job skills. Their problems are magnified by a distrust of those few government programs that serve the specific needs of African Americans. As a result, many young men become adept at manipulating the system; others simply dispense with it altogether, a decision that often leads to illegal activities. Some end up living on the streets, in transportation centers, or in other public places, and there are those who adapt to life in large city shelters. All of these persons utilize survival techniques learned and mastered in the streets. Unfortunately, the homeless mentally ill are not so adept because of their impaired functional ability, and so it is more difficult for them to manage.

Although much research has been devoted to the causes of homelessness among the mentally ill, much less has been done regarding the social, political, and health factors that cause homelessness among mentally ill African-

American men. And it is impossible to accurately determine the numbers of African-American men living on the streets. A correlation between the proportion of African-American men in New York City, based on the current census figures, and total numbers of homeless persons cannot easily be made, as African-American men are clearly overrepresented among the homeless in the city in comparison to their numbers in the general population.

There are three generally accepted explanations for the phenomenon of homelessness among the mentally ill. The first is that mental illness decreases the ability of people to avoid homelessness. The loss of job and home, for the mentally ill person living alone with few or no social supports, can be devastating. It is a prime contributor to homelessness, which in many instances could have been avoided if the individual had the ability to utilize available resources. Of course, the mental health delivery system may also be culpable by providing neither adequate outreach initiatives nor culturally relevant programming.

A second school of thought contends that when states introduced deinstitutionalized mental health, they provided few community-based resources, hardly any outreach programs, and inadequate residential facilities. Also absent were sufficient psychiatric in-patient beds and hospitals willing to accept homeless people and the poor. In fact, beginning in 1955 and continuing for the next two decades, there was a 70 percent decline nationally in the numbers of patients in state psychiatric centers. In 1955 there were 559,000 persons on inpatient psychiatric wards, but by 1980 there were approximately 150,000 (Steering Committee on the Chronically Mentally Ill 1980), and in New York state the in-patient census was 93,000 in 1955 and about 20,000 by 1987 (Caton 1990, 79).

Finally, there are those who believe that the tragedy of homelessness among the mentally ill population resulted because they were deinstitutionalized into an environment lacking affordable housing and community based supportive residences. The debate about the causes of homelessness among the mentally ill continues, but one thing is certain: an individual's mental health significantly deteriorates when he or she is living on the streets (Lamb and Lamb 1988, 301–5). Only by addressing all the factors that give rise to homelessness can we end the condition.

Life on the streets means living with a constant sense of fear and uncertainty, and one must adapt by using a range of survival techniques. The most basic and primary techniques aim toward obtaining shelter. For the purpose of this discussion, obtaining shelter means finding a public place to live that an individual can call his or her own. It can be in a park or on a subway station bench, a doorway, a heating vent, an alcove or "well-hidden sites known only to their users" (Baxter and Hopper 1981, 7).

It is also necessary to understand the skills needed to live on the street, how time living in public places is spent, and how African-American men in particular adapt to this unnatural life-style. Many homeless African-American men are able to reach into their vast reservoir of internal resources to survive in a society where the doors of opportunity have been closed to them. For the man who is homeless, these skills become paramount. In addition to the homeless who are visible to the passerby in lower Manhattan and the busy sections of the other boroughs, there are large numbers of persons living in subways, in Grand Central Station, Penn Station, the Staten Island Ferry terminals, and in parks, abandoned buildings, and vacant lots. For the most part, these homeless persons are African American and Hispanic American. Many have developed support groups and share space as well as daily tasks. Estimates on the numbers of persons residing in these areas are based on contacts made by various city-funded outreach programs. Specifically, the New York City Department of Mental Health, Mental Retardation, and Alcoholism Services funds five outreach programs serving the homeless mentally ill; the New York City Human Resources Administration staffs its own outreach services. In addition, the New York State Department of Substance Abuse Services operates outreach programs serving homeless substance abusers. For example, the outreach programs in contract with the Department of Mental Health, Mental Retardation and Alcoholism Services, made contact with a combined total of over 3,000 different individuals during 1990 (New York City Department of Mental Health, Mental Retardation, and Alcoholism Services 1990a; 1990b). Individuals frequent the terminals, transportation depots, and public parks and plazas. Still, many do not reside in easily accessible places, and they are hard to find and to count. What is known is that large groups live in the subway system, in the tunnels beneath Grand Central Station, and in Riverside Park, where they occupy the abandoned railroad tunnels.

The homeless mentally ill person living on the street is generally not part of such a group but tends to be more isolated and alone. Yet, like other homeless people, the homeless mentally ill require the basic necessities: food and a safe place to sleep. These requirements dictate where people reside and congregate. In midtown and downtown Manhattan, round-the-clock activity and a visible police presence offer some sense of security to those who sleep outside. Busy public places also offer greater opportunities for financial gain, whether by collecting cans for redemption or panhandling. In less active parts of the city, there is less apparent protection; persons residing there must provide for their own security and so fewer homeless people choose to reside there.

Mobile outreach program staff visiting the homeless find it increasingly difficult to determine whether a homeless person is mentally ill, a substance abuser, dually diagnosed, simply poor and hungry, or on the street to prey on the frail and unsuspecting. The conditions that gave rise to homelessness have also created an understandably desperate and sometimes violent cohort of street-smart individuals who live on the street yet sometimes use shelters. This group is comprised primarily of African American and Hispanic American young men, who strike fear into the hearts of many and are often equated with common criminals. Initiatives or plans to "sweep" or "clean up" areas frequented by the homeless usually mean that government wants to take action against this "dangerous" segment of the homeless population. For this reason, it is sometimes difficult to whom the outreach initiatives seek to serve or why they are undertaken. It is clear that certain myths and perceptions about race and sex cloud the judgment of many well-meaning bureaucrats.

Shelter life, specifically life in large municipal shelters, is difficult and dangerous, and living in one requires mastering certain techniques of survival. All the ills that plague society exist in concentrated form in New York City shelters. As in other institutions established as a means of control, the New York City shelters house an overrepresentation of African-American men in proportion to the general population.

In 1979, as a result of the Callahan v. Cary decision, New York City and the State of New York were compelled to provide shelter to all in need. Municipal facilities, originally intended to be emergency shelters, gradually became places where homeless persons languished for years. At this writing, the single adult population housed in large municipal shelters averages just under nine thousand during the cold months. About 85 percent are African-American and Hispanic-American. Another seven or eight hundred homeless persons utilize smaller facilities in churches and synagogues operated by the Partnership for the Homeless (New York City Human Resources Administration 1990, 8, 9). According to data compiled by Elmer Struening of the New York State Psychiatric Institute, approximately 25 to 30 percent of the New York City shelter population have experienced some form of mental illness (Struening 1986, v). Additionally, 30 percent of the general homeless population have reported a history of alcohol abuse, and this figure increases to 40 percent when other drugs are taken into account (Wright et al. 1987, 22–27). Approximately 15 percent of the homeless with alcohol and drug problems are also suffering from mental illness (Fischer 1990, p. 4). These are conservative estimates. The issues encountered by those who serve the homeless become even more problematic when one considers that alcohol and drug use not only compromise service and treatment plans but may lead to criminal activity as well. In a recent Johns Hopkins University study, 50 to 75 percent of the homeless with alcohol and drug histories had been arrested at least once within the prior six months and had at least one incarceration (Fischer 1990, 17). Most of the arrests were for assaults and disorderly conduct.

Shelter life for the mentally ill resident is characterized by an on-going struggle to protect one's life and property and by a series of interactions with shelter residents and staff. For many mentally ill shelter residents, isolation is a constant companion. Participation in a group situation is rare unless it is part of an organized shelter activity. For this reason, the New York City Department of Mental Health, Mental Retardation and Alcoholism Services has funded rehabilitation programs in nine of the twenty-four New York City municipal shelters serving single adults as well as four specialized units called Transitional Living

Communities. These programs provide six months of intensive preparation for independent living. These programs serve an average of 4,500 persons annually (New York City Department of Mental Health, Mental Retardation, and Alcoholism Services 1990c, 2).

However, mentally ill and frail elderly shelter residents often fall victims to theft and physical abuse in the shelter. For this reason some homeless mentally ill persons do not utilize the shelter system. They opt to live in smaller private shelters, public places, streets, or with family and friends for occasional stays whenever possible.

The experiences of service providers and the research on the homeless mentally ill offer valuable information on what services must be provided to homeless mentally ill African-American men (although more research must be compiled specifically on African Americans in general). Unfortunately, real solutions are often ignored, partly because they require a level of services that exceeds the budget available for programs to this population. Even programs that have proven successful and cost effective are not given priority unless they are politically advantageous.

However, when experience and research are allowed to dictate policy, they can produce satisfactory results. A case in point is the recent collaboration between the city and state on housing, providing for the development of 5,225 beds for the homeless mentally ill at a total cost of over $14 million. This initiative, the New York/New York Agreement to House Homeless Mentally Ill Individuals (1990) was signed by Gov. Mario M. Cuomo and Mayor David N. Dinkins on August 22, 1990.

Much of the research on the homeless and homeless mentally ill has taught policymakers that the supportive single-room residence is the home of choice for the majority of persons in shelters. According to residential placement statistics compiled by the Residential Development Unit of the New York City Department of Mental Health, Mental Retardation, and Alcoholism Services, persons who are placed in single-room supportive residences remain there the longest and with the most successful results (Christmas and Douglas 1989). This is precisely the type of residence that the New York/New York Agreement will provide.

The health and social status of a group is, as a rule, determined by that group's economic status. This is certainly true for the millions of Americans who live in poverty without health insurance or other benefits. These people seldom seek professional intervention until physical and emotional problems become quite severe. The poor are also more susceptible to the vagaries of economics and unemployment and thus must stretch what few resources they have, such as food stamps and other public aid.

For many African-Americans, poverty is compounded by a history of racial discrimination which perpetuates and intensifies the cycle of poverty, disease, and despair. As Jaynes and Williams note in *A Common Destiny*,

> Who will live and who will die and how much handicap and disability will burden
> their lives depend in large part on conditions of education, environment and em-
> ployment as well as on access to adequate medical services. Health is not only an
> important "good" in itself, it is also a determinant of life options during the entire
> life span. Health status is, therefore, an important indicator of a group's social
> position as well as its present and future well-being. Although multiple factors
> contribute to the persistent health disadvantages of Blacks, poverty may be the
> most profound and pervasive determinant. (Jaynes and Williams 1989, 393)

> Poverty, crime, drug abuse and the judicial and prison systems are inter-
> twined to such a degree that a young Black man growing up in such an environ-
> ment may view these factors as being beyond his control and therefore exhibits
> behavioral patterns [that] are often detrimental to self-improvement. (Jaynes and
> Williams 1989, 21).

This may, in part, be a reaction to the perception that to survive in a society
offering nothing, an individual must choose behaviors that are controllable. Examples include drug sales or use, burglary, robbery and influence over others,
particularly young women.

> Significant improvement in the health status of Blacks will depend on reducing
> health-damaging personal behaviors such as substance abuse, injuries, homicide
> and sexual activities that can cause ill-timed pregnancy or risk infection with sex-
> ually transmitted diseases. (Jaynes and Williams 1989, 22)

This sense of powerlessness in young men also causes many to feel that
little can be gained from academic advancement. In fact, most young African-
American men who have been educated in "poorly-staffed, dilapidated schools
populated with underachieving students can easily fall into the trap of perceiv-
ing the pursuit of academic excellence as a poor investment" (Jaynes and Williams 1989, 10). Differences in the quality of early educational experiences in
predominantly Black and white schools directly affect an individual's level of
achievement. This problem is graphically demonstrated by New York City's
high school dropout rate, which in mid-1990 was twice as high for African
Americans as for whites (p. 23).

Homeless children are also hard hit by missed educational opportunities.
The New York advocacy group Advocates for Children reported that in the
spring of 1990 the average daily attendance rate for homeless students was 51
percent compared to a citywide rate of 84 percent. A Board of Education report
of 1990 indicates that 55 percent of homeless high school students were absent
at least four days per week. This does not augur well for the future growth and
development of this segment of this nation's youth.

Crime and its potential punishments are also factors that significantly affect the lives of young men. African-American males are arrested, convicted,

and incarcerated at a rate much higher than any other group in the country. At present, African Americans account for almost half the entire prison population (Jaynes and Williams 1989, 259–60). They are also "disproportionately victims of crime: they are twice as likely to be the victims of robbery, vehicle theft and aggravated assault and 6 to 7 times as likely to be victims of homicide, the leading cause of death among young Black males" between the ages of fifteen and twenty-four (Quaison-Sackey 1986, 3–4). Although the African-American community accounts for 13 percent of the general population, African Americans comprise 40 percent of all murder victims (Centers for Disease Control 1990, 870). The escalating street battles for a piece of the drug profits and the preference for the use of powerful automatic weapons have no doubt been responsible for these staggering estimates. In fact, between 1978 and 1988, 78 percent of all homicides among African-American males were committed with guns by other young African-American males; the majority of victims were fifteen to nineteen years old (Centers for Disease Control 1990, 870).

The institutionalized impediments that all African Americans must overcome are great. Obviously, for an African-American homeless mentally ill man who must cope with such impediments and with the failures and flaws of the mental health and health care delivery systems, life can be devastating and often fatal.

Government services must evolve to meet the changing needs of people, and society must ensure that people are able to survive. New York's mental hygiene system and the experiences of its service providers and policymakers over the past three decades offer a key to understanding what needs to be done for the mentally ill homeless in the future. New policies and programs must be based upon experiences in order to address the real problems facing this nation.

The mental hygiene system of the nineties needs to be concerned about more than the delivery of good quality mental health services. It must ensure the delivery of services to various populations, with the coordination and cooperation of other service systems. Fully integrating health, mental health, substance abuse, and residential services for homeless African-American men is a fundamental ingredient in responding to the needs of this population. Problems affecting families and children, such as inadequate education and employment opportunities, health and medical care, and housing must also be addressed. Until government, communities, professionals and advocates respond to all the needs of the African-American community, the problems of this segment of the society will continue.

The resources are there as well as the knowledge and experience to contend with these issues. The task requires the reprioritization of funding and commitments coupled with the willingness to provide new initiatives in a culturally relevant manner. Until one examines the needs of this community in toto and evaluates the critical requirements of that community, the plight of the homeless will continue to confront this nation for the rest of this decade and into the next century.

CHAPTER 9

Black Men and AIDS: Prevention and Black Sexuality

by Benjamin P. Bowser

Acquired Immunodeficiency Syndrome (AIDS) epidemic is poised to strike the Black community severely. In order to prevent this from happening, Black men will have to make more radical changes in their sexual attitudes and behaviors than any other group of Americans. It is not an exaggeration to say that the physical survival of Black Americans as a community into the next century is immediately dependent upon Black men changing their sexual attitudes and behaviors. Of all the things that all Black Americans can do to improve their health and reduce the risk of disease (stop smoking, eat low-fat foods, get regular checkups), changing sexual behavior and attitudes will be the most difficult. The nature of the AIDS epidemic is the reason for this urgency, and each year the evidence becomes more compelling.

The vast majority of sexually active Black men and women are now aware that the virus that leads to AIDS can be spread through unprotected sexual contact without a condom (Dawson and Hardy 1989). However, compared to whites, young Black men and women are less likely to use condoms and, when they do, they use them inconsistently (Morrison 1985). In recent years, Black women have shown an increasing inclination to use condoms (Tanfer and Horn 1985). The group that is most resistant to taking precautions comprises young Black men (Rivara et al. 1985). Yet the survival of Black Americans in the long run against the AIDS epidemic will require practicing sexual abstinence, single partner fidelity, or uncompromising condom usage. Clearly, there is a conflict between current sexual behaviors and what needs to be done to prevent AIDS. The conflict between practicing unprotected sex with multiple partners and doing what is necessary for survival, centered around Black males, is now one of the main challenges of AIDS prevention among Black Americans (Bouknight and Bouknight 1988).

What is so difficult to appreciate about AIDS is that its deadly consequences are separated by years from the event and behaviors that cause the infection. There are no immediate signs or warnings of infection. Furthermore, for the general public the epidemic does not seem immediately important if they know few people who have been diagnosed with AIDS and died from it. What eludes public attention is that diagnosed AIDS cases represent only a small proportion of all infected persons (Redfield and Burke 1988). Those who have been diagnosed with AIDS represent only those in the final stage of the Human Immunodeficiency Virus (HIV) infection, and only a small proportion of all infected persons. The vast majority of HIV-infected persons show no symptoms while they are infected with an irreversible, incurable, and communicable disease. Ultimately, the probability of illness and death, as much as ten or more years after infection, is almost 100 percent (Institute of Medicine 1988).

The virus now spreads through two routes. The first is through sexual contact. During the time that a person is infected and asymptomatic, he or she can infect sexual partners, and those partners can in turn infect others. The second route of infection is by using contaminated hypodermic needles. Individuals who use contaminated needles expose themselves to a second and even more efficient route of HIV infection.

Clearly, AIDS is not simply another venereal disease. The prominence of Black men among known AIDS cases suggests the extent to which Black male sexual behaviors and needle use are on a collision course with AIDS and that HIV infections are spreading quietly and without signs among Black Americans. Table 9.1 illustrates how the AIDS epidemic, as reflected in diagnosed AIDS cases, has progressed overall and for Black men (CDC 1989, 1990).

The first line of table 9.1 in each transmission category looks at Black men as percents of the cumulative numbers of all AIDS cases reported since the beginning of the epidemic, as of May 1989 and April 1990. The second line in each category gives two pieces of information. First, there are the percents of all Black male AIDS cases by transmission category for each year. Second, there are the percents of all AIDS cases by transmission category for each year. Each measure gives important comparative information about the role of Black men in the epidemic. Black men make up approximately 6 percent of the U.S. population. Yet, when we look at the third row of statistics, in every transmission category Black men represent from three to six times their proportion of the U.S. population. The one exception is receipt through blood transfusion (hemophilia). Following is a discussion of Black men in each transmission category.

Table 9.1 Black Men as Percents of All AIDS Cases. May 1989–April 1990, and Means of Transmission for Black Men and All AIDS Cases

| Means of Transmission | May 1989 | | | April 1990 | | | Percentage Inc.1989–90 |
	Black Men/Total (%)	Total (%)	=%	Black Men/Total (%)	Total (%)	=%	Black Men/Total
Homosexual and bisexual sex	9367 (45)	58389 (61)	(16.0)	12927 (44)	78212 (60)	(16.5)	+38.0 +33.9
Intravenous drug users	7189 (34)	19497 (20)	(36.9)	10242 (35)	27842 (21)	(36.8)	+42.5 +42.8
Homosexual sex/ intravenous drug use	1743 (8)	6824 (7)	(25.5)	2349 (8)	8948 (7)	(26.2)	+34.8 +31.1
Homophilia	54 (0)	912 (1)	(05.9)	74 (0)	1171 (1)	(06.3)	+37.0 +28.4
Heterosexual sex	1429 (7)	4305 (5)	(33.2)	2030 (7)	6532 (5)	(31.1)	+42.1 +51.7
Transfusions	182 (1)	2361 (2)	(07.7)	273 (1)	3119 (2)	(08.8)	+50.0 +32.1
Undetermined	929 (4)	3273 (3)	(28.4)	1262 (4)	4428 (3)	(28.5)	+35.8 +35.3
Totals	20893 (100)	95561 (100)	(21.9)	29157 (100)	130252 (100)	(22.4)	+39.6 +36.3

Gay and Bisexual Men

The AIDS epidemic began spreading through the social networks of gay and bisexual men before it hit other groups of Americans. Because of this early start and direct experience with the epidemic, gay and bisexual men are the most conscious of the disease and the most diligent in practicing safe sex—using condoms. The continued high rate of AIDS cases among gay and bisexual men reflects those who were infected before the dramatic change in gay and bisexual men's behaviors toward safe sex. But note that, between the two trend years, Black gay and bisexual men increased as a proportion of all gay and bisexual AIDS cases and that the rate of increase was one-half percent higher than for all diagnosed AIDS cases among gay and bisexual men (first row and last two columns of table 9.1).

There are several related explanations for the overrepresentation of Black men among gay and bisexual AIDS cases. Black men are a hidden population within the gay world (Icard 1986; Dalton 1989). They have to be hidden because of the Black community's intense homophobia and because of racial discrimination among white gay men. As a consequence, in comparison to white gay men, Black gays had sexual networks that were more anonymous and less organized. Contact with sexual partners was more likely to be concentrated in public places and less likely to be characterized by steady partnerships. All of these factors increased the probability of being infected with the AIDS virus within the gay world.

The rates of infection among gay and bisexual men is approximately five years ahead of that in other high-risk groups. There are also three times as many total AIDS cases among gay and bisexual men as there are in the next-largest group, intravenous drug users. But if we look at the distribution of AIDS cases among Black men (the second row of each transmission category), we find a different view. By May 1989, Black gay and bisexual men made up 45.0 percent of all AIDS cases among Black men, and Black intravenous drug users (IVDUs) accounted for 34.0 percent of all cases among Black men. The difference is only 11 percent, and the difference was 1 percent less by the following year. This means that the distribution of AIDS cases in the general population and then among Black men is not the same. The AIDS epidemic among Black male IVDUs is far more advanced, when compared to the epidemic in the general population, in its comparability with Black gay and bisexual men. This difference between all AIDS cases and those cases among Black men has important implications for the AIDS epidemic among Black Americans.

Intravenous Drug Users

While there is little evidence at this point, Black male IVDUs AIDS cases may very well equal if not surpass AIDS cases among Black gay and bisexual men in coming years. The reason for this possibility is that Black gay and bisexual men are reducing their long-term infection rates by being diligent with safe sex practices. Black male IVDUs have yet to exercise the same caution. If the AIDS virus continues to move through the intravenous-drug-using population, the potential grows each year for bringing the AIDS epidemic into the heterosexual Black community. This point can be illustrated.

It was estimated in 1987 that there were from 147,000 to 244,500 Black IVDUs who were HIV infected, asymptomatic and mostly male (Centers for Disease Control 1987). After three additional years, a conservative estimate of the upper range of Black male, HIV infected IVDUs increased to approximately 350,000. This number reaches the lower estimate of the number of HIV-infected Black gay and bisexual men (Centers for Disease Control 1987). What is significant about AIDS among Black intravenous drug users is that they are the first group of Black heterosexuals to be infected. This means that heterosexual, HIV-infected IVDUs are sexually active in the non-IVDU heterosexual population and therefore can transmit the AIDs epidemic into the Black community at large. In contrast, Black gay and bisexual men have relatively self-contained sexual and social networks.

It is not true that all heroin addicts are down and out street corner men who have little or no contact with the public. Most are in the general population and are unrecognizable. It is also not true that heroin addicts are sexually passive. In San Francisco, the City Public Health Department and the Bayview Hunter's Point Foundation conducted a National AIDS Demonstration Research Project.* The team interviewed 376 out-of-treatment male IVDUs recruited from the streets. Twenty-five percent had jobs; 63.7 percent were at least high school graduates; 42.3 percent lived with a spouse or sex partner, and 92.8 percent had had two or more female sex partners in the six months prior to their interview. Virtually all the men interviewed were sexually active, and 14.7 percent were HIV positive.

Street outreach workers report that IVDUs are becoming increasingly aware that AIDS is spread through contaminated needles and, as a result, are taking precautions. This is especially true for IVDUs who now know others who have died from AIDS. In our survey of out-of-treatment IVDUs, 67 percent report that they cleaned their needles at least half the time with bleach in order to prevent HIV infections. But they still continue to have high rates of unprotected sexual contact—only 14.4 percent used condoms at least half the time.

There is a final point that makes the world of Black male, heterosexual IVDUs so central to the AIDS epidemic among Blacks. It involves two groups of Black women. The first group comprises Black female IVDUs. Most of these women were introduced to injection drug use by IVDU men with whom they were emotionally and sexually involved. So, HIV infections among Black female

*This research was conducted as part of the National AIDS Demonstration Research Project, grant R18DA04899, funded by the National Institute on Drug Abuse with Dr. Patricia Evans as Principal Investigator.

IVDUs are secondary infections from Black male IVDUs. The consequence of this pattern of drug use leads to high rates of HIV infection among Black female IVDUs (Centers for Disease Control 1990). While Black women comprise 6 percent of the U.S. population, through April of 1990, they accounted for 57.7 percent of all female IVDUs diagnosed with AIDS. These women make up 48.8 percent of all Black women diagnosed with AIDS. The second group of Black women consists of those who do not use intravenous drugs but who are sexually involved with male IVDUs. This second group of Black women accounts for 48.9 percent of all female heterosexuals who contracted AIDS from sex with male IVDUs and 14.2 percent of all Black women with AIDS.

Heterosexual Contact

It is assumed that men diagnosed with AIDS who are not intravenous drug users and who are not gay and bisexual contracted their HIV infection through vaginal sex. Table 1 shows that there were 2,030 Black heterosexual men diagnosed with AIDS through April 1990—a 42 percent increase over the previous eleven months; these men account for 7.0 percent of all Black men with AIDS. This rate of increase is actually lower than the 51.7 percent increase for all heterosexuals with AIDS. In comparison to gay and bisexual men and IVDUs, the number of Black male heterosexuals with AIDS is still relatively low, but the rate of increase is high.

Of these Black heterosexual men diagnosed with AIDS, 1,318 (64.9 percent) were born in Pattern II countries such as Haiti, and are presumed to have contracted HIV through sexual contact before coming to the United States. Five hundred and forty-five (26.8 percent) were infected by sexual contact with female IVDUs. These relatively low numbers and the foreign origin of most cases do not suggest that there is an epidemic among Black non–IVDU male heterosexuals in the United States. In table 1, the proportion of Black males who contracted AIDS from heterosexual contact actually declined between 1989 and 1990 by 2.1 percent. But this is not a reason to be relieved or complacent.

It is quite possible that the current AIDS incidence rate among Black male and female heterosexuals can increase sharply if the AIDS epidemic moves into crack cocaine–using social networks. Currently, Black men and women addicted to crack cocaine have one of the highest rates of sexually transmitted diseases as well as high levels of HIV risk behaviors (R. Fullilove et al. 1990). Their risk derives from compulsive sex-for-drugs practices. The HIV risk among crack addicts is considerable, not simply because they engage in frequent and unprotected sex, but also because their social networks overlap sexually with IVDUs who are already HIV infected. In addition, crack users are starting to inject heroin to reduce the "crash" of coming down from the crack cocaine's high. Similarly, IVDUs are starting to use crack along with heroin because it produces a better high than heroin.

If nothing is done, we can anticipate that HIV-infected crack addicts will accelerate HIV infections and, eventually, the number of AIDS cases among Black heterosexuals. Again, at the center of this potential to increase HIV infections are Black men who comprise the majority of crack addicts and who see no need to practice safe sex. Clearly, the problem that needs to be addressed is not simply informational. It is a problem of overall sexual attitudes and beliefs.

AIDS Prevention versus Black Sexuality

The behaviors necessary to prevent AIDS are in direct opposition to current Black attitudes toward sexuality. These attitudes will have to be changed with effective educational programs. But in order to do this, accurate and current information on Black sexuality is required, especially information on the behaviors and attitudes of Black men. One would presume that such information already exists. But a systematic and thorough review of the literature on Black sexuality turned up a big surprise—there is relatively little direct information on Black male sexuality.

Of approximately three hundred articles addressing some aspect of race and sex published between 1964 and 1989, only 191 address directly some aspect of Black sexuality—sexual practices, sexual orientation, fertility trends, attitudes and knowledge about sex (Weinstein et al. 1990). The largest category of these articles deals with adolescent women and teenage childbearing. Of those studies that focus on Black men and women, 83 percent are concerned with women. These studies rarely get beyond description, and they rarely attempt to systematically develop explanations. What are virtually nonexistent are direct studies of the sexual attitudes of a full range of Black men. We know almost nothing about Black men who are not patients being treated for sexually transmitted diseases, who are not teen fathers or male teens from troubled economically disadvantaged households (Robinson et al. 1985).

A series of generalizations about Black men is repeated in the research. These points were recently reviewed by Mindy Fullilove and associates (1990a). They are (1) that Black teen males consistently report earlier first sexual intercourse than any other race/gender group; (2) that Black teen males are less likely to use contraception than their white peers; (3) that Blacks overall and men in particular tend to endorse premarital relations; (4) that Blacks are more likely to have intercourse than whites and Black males are twice as likely as Black females; and (5) that Black men tend to maintain a sexual double standard.

The explanations for the extremes in Black male sexuality vary. A sample would include that Black males are more apt to view sex as physical pleasure, while women view sex as an occasion for intimacy (M. Fullilove et al. 1990). Black males internalize the masculine roles of dominance and aggressiveness, yet they have few legitimate outlets in society to be dominant or aggressive (Franklin 1984). The capitalist nature of American society has reduced Black male and female relations into commodities where men and women then treat themselves as sexual objects (Karenga 1982).

Social Class in Black Sexuality

One of the most enduring sociological findings is that marriages tend to be more stable among well-educated, well-paid white-collar workers than among poorly educated, poorly paid blue-collar workers (Aborampah 1989). Does this explanation explain the higher levels of sexual activity among Blacks in general and Black men in particular? In a study of the 1976 and 1981 National Survey of Children, Furstenberg (1987) found that, when mother's education or family income were controlled, racial differences in sexual activity were only partly accounted for. Social class made some differences. Middle-class Blacks were less promiscuous than lower-class Blacks, but they were still more sexually active than middle-class whites. In a second study by Weinberg and Williams (1988), racial differences in sexual promiscuity were not found to be explainable by social class. The conclusion drawn by these and other investigators is that the uniformly higher levels of sexual activity among Blacks, when compared to whites, were due to "cultural" differences.

An optimist would say that there is some progress in having exaggerated Black sexuality explained through culture rather than through biology as it was in the prior century (Harris 1968). But to use only a cultural explanation leads back over old ground into what is now the classical and continuing bias in research on Black Americans—to blame the victim (Valentine 1968; Ryan 1976). To view Black sexuality as cultural behaviors coming solely from Black people requires the following assumptions: (1) that the larger society and culture have no ongoing influence on Black life and culture; (2) that Black Americans are culturally and socially autonomous; (3) that the history of discrimination and poverty has had either little or no impact on Black sexuality; (4) that the increasingly marginal position of Black men in the economy does not impact their sexuality; (5) that there is one uniform Black culture; and (6) that there is in fact little diversity among Blacks, especially Black men, with regard to sexuality.

Furthermore, the apparent inability of social class to explain exaggerated Black sexuality in comparison to whites is based on an erroneous understanding of social class. Black and white social classes are not directly comparable. Students of race and social class have pointed out since the 1940s that objective measures of social class do not adequately account for the variability among Blacks in attitudes, beliefs, and values (Drake and Cayton 1944; Drake 1989). This means that even when Blacks and whites have the same educational level, the same income, and the same occupation, they are not necessarily in the same social class. They might not even be in the same economic class.

Among Black Americans, individuals who would be in the working class if they were white can identify with and be a part of the Black middle class. In the same way, an individual who might appear to be in the middle class if white can identify with and be a part of the Black working class. In each case, the basis of social class affiliation is group acceptance and identification with appropriate class-related attitudes, beliefs, and values. Social class among White Americans is much less conditional and more clearly bound. In contrast, because of the very narrow range in which Black social classes are bound, objective measures of their social class do not necessarily correspond to subjective social class.

The research strategy of measuring Black and white social classes by matching income, education, and occupation ignores major sources of intergenerational and intragenerational class differences—inherited wealth, savings, owning stocks and bonds, equity in property, the ability of relatives to give "gifts," access to financial information, number of generations in the middle class, percentage of one's extended family in the middle class, family as a mobility network, access to business, access to union crafts and professions based on family and ethnic membership, traditions of business ownership, and access to overseas investment. If just some of these factors were taken into account, we might very well find that the Black middle class is actually more comparable to the white working class. In that case, "exaggerated" Black sexuality might be social-class related after all, and the cultural explanation would be unwarranted.

An Alternative View of Black Sexuality

In order to understand the dimensions of attitude and behavior changes necessary to prevent the spread of AIDS, we have to fully appreciate sexuality's social context. Sexuality is an intrinsic part of a people's social experience. It is not isolated from their general experience or from the quality of their participation in the larger society. If Black sexuality is in some way different than it is for whites, then there must be something different about the respective social conditions of each group. This point can be extended to the apparent exaggerated sexuality of Black men. Are there some particular conditions common to Black men that might affect their sexual attitudes and behaviors?

A contextual and conditional explanation might begin by looking at the extent to which Black men are able and allowed to fully play out the male normative social and economic roles. I would propose that men in all social classes who experience frustrated instrumental and expressive roles place more emphasis on their sexuality. The degree of their frustration over time directly impacts the extent to which sexuality becomes emphasized. In addition to whether men are able to play normative roles, there is the concern of whether some traditional male roles can still be considered male roles. The broadening of the roles women can now play in the economy and in the community has reduced the roles that are clearly ascribed to men. Table 9.2 outlines the roles that men have traditionally played.

Table 9.2   Traditional Male Roles

Economic Male Role	Husband/ Manfriend Role	Father/ Male Role	Community Male Role
Primary income	Companionship	Protection	Leadership
Economic security	Protection	Emotional support	Protection of quality of life
Financial decisions	Emotional support	Guidance	*Physical upkeep
	Acceptance	Discipline	*Mutual support
	Social status		

The traditional male economic and community roles are now partly shared by women in the general population. In most white American house-holds the woman brings home a secondary income necessary to maintaining the quality of life and, optimally, shares in financial decision making. The man is still central to fulfilling the family's economic role. In households where the tra-ditional male economic role is shared, the role has become transitional.

The sharing is of a very different nature among economically disadvan-taged and middle-class Blacks. Increasingly, Black men in the working and lower classes are either underemployed or unemployed (Bluestone and Harri-son 1982). They are far more economically marginalized than Black women and have no social welfare safety net (Center for the Study of Social Policy 1986). Black men in professional and skilled jobs may not be economically marginal, but they are more likely than Black women to be socially marginal on the job and to be viewed as a threat by white men. Black men do not live or work in social contexts where they may play out male roles as fully as do white men in comparable circumstances. Among economically disadvantaged Blacks, increasingly, Black women are having to take on the full economic role—primary income and decision making. They are having to take on these responsibilities, not in order to maintain a high quality of life, but because they have to in order to survive due to the economic marginalization of Black working-class and lower-class men.

For Black men of all social classes who can no longer play the traditional male social and economic roles, tasks ordinarily assigned to men are not in tran-sition. These roles have been reassigned either permanently or temporarily to Black women. Social and economic role attrition for men sets into motion the attrition of other male roles as well. Many of these Black men become less able to serve as husbands (manfriends), fathers, and community leaders.

Male role attrition has negative social-psychological consequences. The fewer the traditional male roles these Black men are able to play, the less of "a man" they are perceived to be and the more they must struggle to see them-selves as men. This is why it is now not unusual to hear Black men and women refer in conversation to a man who is disappointing, a failure and unable to

Figure 9.1   Components and Process Leading to Exaggerated Male Sexuality

Economic and social marginality	→	Frustrated role fulfillment	→	Marginality as husband/father/manfriend	→	Compensation in sexuality in male relations

be a man, as a "bitch"—a term traditionally used to refer to degradingly to a woman.

One way for men to compensate for this clearly unacceptable social identity as a failure and a "bitch" is to exaggerate all that is left. And that is sex. In sex a man has not been replaced, and he cannot be simply left out. He has to be included, and what is left of his manhood demands that he control this last frontier. The result is exaggerated sexuality; high energy and high emotional investment in competition with other Black men; Black-on-Black violence; and, for some, chemical dependence as a way to escape the perception of threat to their self-identity as men. Figure 9.1 illustrates the components and process that result in exaggerated Black male sexuality.

One of the outcomes of economic marginality in the labor force and social marginality in larger society is the diminished opportunity to fulfill traditional and transitional male roles as man-friend, husband, father, and protector of the community. One way to compensate is to transfer frustrated motivation to competition with other Black males and to exaggerated sexuality. A parallel and reinforcing process is the understandable unwillingness of Black women, who have to assume the traditional male roles, to financially or emotionally support marginalized men or to defer to their diminished social manhood.

Effective AIDS Prevention

Given the social and economic context of Black male sexuality, it is going to require a lot more than information dissemination in order to get Black men to practice AIDS-preventive behaviors. Since there is no way to immediately solve the problem of Black male economic and social marginality, the prospects for changing Black male sexual behaviors appear to be quite dim. But there are reasons for optimism.

There have been successes in the AIDS-prevention effort that can serve as models for how Black males might be convinced to change their behaviors. Gay and bisexual men dramatically reduced their HIV-high-risk behaviors by first conducting AIDS education campaigns from within their communities (Coates 1990). This got the message out to everyone in their community. Then, through their own grass-roots discussions and persuasion, gay men developed a safe-sex social norm. HIV high-risk behaviors are now viewed as dangerous and as a reason for being cut off from the group. The most effective AIDS-prevention strategy has turned out to be for a group at high risk for AIDS to change its social norms. We have also had success in persuading intravenous drug users to bleach their needles to prevent HIV infections (Biernacki 1986). An important key to this success was to enlist as community educators ex-addicts who know the IVDU community and culture. They influenced IVDUs to change their norms in order to get wide-scale group compliance.

There is a need for the same grass-roots AIDS education among Black men, so that they will change their sense of what constitutes normative sexual behavior. The most effective way to develop such a new sexual norm would be to eliminate the motivation for exaggerated sexuality. To do so would require major structural changes in the position of Black men in American society and in the way that they are perceived. Such a social transformation would also solve virtually all of the other major crises and problems facing Black Americans. But short of a social transformation, Black male sexual norms can still be altered in favor of AIDS prevention.

Social norms of exaggerated sexuality can be changed by redirecting the underlying motivation for this overcompensating behavior toward, not away from, safe-sex norms. AIDS prevention efforts need to be directed at helping Black men (and women) to develop a new norm of what constitutes a Black man. There are a number of proposed components to this redefinition (Aborampah 1989). Part of this new definition should include nonexploitative sexuality and safe-sex practices. This is not impossible: there are Black men in the middle, working, and lower class who are already successfully practicing such behaviors, against current norms and perceptions. Change the sexual norms in favor of AIDS prevention, and these successful men will become the rule rather than the exception. But clearly, behavior and norm change has to come from within the world of Black men and women who support new Black sexuality and social norms.

CHAPTER 10

Anger in Young Black Males: Victims or Victimizers?

by Jewelle Taylor Gibbs

Young Black males in America have been described as angry, alienated, aggressive and antisocial (Gibbs 1988; Glasgow 1981).They are often portrayed in the mass media as hostile, sullen, brutal, and violent. The twin themes of Black male sexuality and aggression are inextricably linked in memorable images of Mister in Alice Walker's novel *The Color Purple*, of Shaft and Superfly in the Black exploitation movies of the 1970s, and of the infamous Willie Horton whose television commercial may have elected a president in 1988. The persistence of these images in American social, cultural, and political discourse raises the issue of their validity as an accurate portrayal of Black males in contemporary American society, as well as the issue of how these images are interpreted and manipulated by various interest groups.

Only a cynical ideologue would deny that young Black males are disproportionately involved in a range of self-destructive and socially nonproductive activities which frequently bring them into contact with the police. In fact, a recent study reported that nearly one out of four Black males, ages twenty to twenty-nine, are involved in the criminal justice system in prison, on parole, or on probation (Mauer 1990). Data from the Department of Justice further confirms this grim fact, showing that black juveniles who represent only 15 percent of all youth account for one-third of the juvenile arrests for major felony offenses in America (Federal Bureau of Investigation 1986).

In 1990 there were more young Black males in prison and in jail than enrolled in all the colleges and universities in America (Mauer 1991). The United States spent over $16 billion per year in 1988 to imprison 3,109 of every 100,000 black males, the highest rate of imprisonment of any country in the world. Yet 80 percent of these inmates were incarcerated for minor felony offenses such as parole violations and property, drug, and public disorder crimes (Wicker 1991).

Homicide rates provide another indicator of the explosive rage in Black males, who have a one in twenty-one chance of being murdered before the age of twenty-one (U.S. Department of Health and Human Services 1986). Homicide is the leading cause of death for Black males age fifteen to twenty-four, who are six times more likely to be murdered than their white male peers. The overall homicide rate for Black males age fifteen to twenty-four increased from 46.4 per 100,000 in 1960 to 101.1 per 100,000 in 1988. However, just in the five-year period from 1984 to 1988, the rate increased 67 percent. Guns accounted for more than 95 percent of the increase in homicide in this age group. Over 51 percent of the deaths occurred in six urban areas of California, Florida, Michigan, Missouri, New York, and Washington, D.C. (National Center for Health Statistics 1990). Cities characterized by large Black ghettos, high poverty rates, high unemployment, and high crime rates are those with the highest homicide rates; they include Washington, New York, Chicago, Detroit, Philadelphia, Houston, and Los Angeles. Contrary to popular mythology, most Black males are not killed by police or white vigilantes, but by other Black males using handguns (Hawkins 1986).

The recent dramatic increase in Black male homicide rates is associated with the growing drug and criminal activity in inner city Black communities, where illicit commerce in drugs and stolen goods has become a major source of income for Black males who have dropped out or been locked out of legitimate employment (Gary 1980; Gibbs 1988b). Unfortunately, these illegitimate activities foster gang rivalry, turf battles, and random violence directed against innocent bystanders in the streets. Fueled by their frustrations and poisoned by their own paranoia, these drug lords, street hustlers, and pimps discharge their anger and hostility, not only on their competitors and challengers, but also on those who simply get in the line of fire (Shapiro, McCall and Hull 1987).

Suicide rates for young Black males have tripled in the past three decades (U.S. Bureau of the Census 1990). While these rates are still lower than white male suicide rates, their increase mirrors the trend in homicide rates and suggests that there is a relationship. Suicide is conceptualized psychodynamically as a response to anger turned against the self, and so the increase in this ultimate act of self-destructiveness indicates a growing inability of Black males to cope constructively with their overwhelming feelings of anger and rage (Gibbs 1988a; Hendin 1969). Moreover, this trend also suggests that the social and cultural mechanisms in the Black community that previously protected Black males against suicidal behavior have been weakened or destroyed in the past three decades (Gibbs and Hines 1989). Many young Black males have come to view themselves as victims, triply disadvantaged by race, poverty, and social isolation, nonachievers in the schools, nonproducers in the labor market, and nonparticipants in the society. Thus, perceived as nonentities in every major social institution, too many Black males have decided to drop out permanently by literally destroying themselves as they can see no way out of their unendurable situations.

These self-destructive behaviors, troublesome as they may be, can be more easily comprehended, not simply as deviant activities of antisocial minority males, but more complexly as symptomatic indicators of the historically devalued status of Blacks in American society, the poverty of the Black family, the social and cultural isolation of the Black community, and the political and economic powerlessness of the Black male in a white male–dominated country. Since nearly one-third of Black families in America live below the poverty line, and nearly half of all Black youth are poor, many Black males begin life in severely disadvantaged situations where it is difficult, if not impossible, for them to envision a viable future for themselves as productive, well-functioning adults (Edelman 1987; Wilson 1987).

Factors Contributing to Anger in Black Males

Black males have been the principal victims of the legacy of racial discrimination and prejudice in American society. The historical record informs us that they were brutalized as slaves for nearly 250 years, during which they were not only treated as chattel property but also denied basic human rights to control their labor, to establish their households, and to protect their families. As Toni Morrison (1987) graphically describes in her prize-winning novel *Beloved*, Black males suffered psychological emasculation by helplessly standing by while white males raped their wives, sisters, and daughters. They also endured physical and sexual abuse, deprivation, and humiliation at the hands of white slave owners and their overseers. Unable to retaliate without fear of death or disfigurement, Black slaves were forced to suppress their anger and to develop coping strategies that would ensure their survival. In situations when the brutality became intolerable, their anger sometimes erupted into individual acts of defiance or collective acts of rebellion (Frazier 1967; Stampp 1956). Nonetheless, the price of rebellion was so high in repressive and cruel retaliatory measures that these rebellious acts were the exception rather than the rule. Black males learned very early on that the protests of the minority were no match for the power of the majority. They had to develop alternate ways of dealing with their anger over their inhumane and unjust treatment, such as passive resistance, childlike ignorance, self-denigrating humor, and sullen withdrawal (Grier and Cobbs 1968).

During the century between the end of the Civil War and the passage of the major civil rights bills in 1964 and 1965, Black males continued to be victimized by Jim Crow laws, which effectively segregated them in schools, housing, jobs, health care, public accommodations, and political participation in the South and many other areas of the nation. Lynchings and chain gangs replaced beatings and slave labor in the Old Confederacy, and Blacks were rendered powerless by their economic dependence and their political disenfranchisement. Again and again, Blacks learned the bitter lesson that angry confrontations or even peaceful protest would be met with Klan-like violence or massive armed resistance.

With the advent of a more liberal Democratic administration in the early 1960s, Blacks became more optimistic about their opportunities for economic mobility, equal justice, and political power. In spite of the New Frontier, the War on Poverty, and the historic civil rights legislation, the modest economic and political gains of blacks in the 1960s were short-lived and soon reversed by the late 1970s, as the country witnessed a conservative backlash to affirmative action programs, school busing, and social welfare programs. The group that suffered the greatest setbacks as a result of this backlash comprised Black males, whose problems during this period can be demonstrated in their declining employment rates, declining college enrollment rates, increased homicide and suicide rates, increased delinquency rates, and increased involvement in serious drug and crime activities (Gibbs 1988b; Wilson 1987). A case can be argued that these behaviors all reflect different ways in which Black youth gave vent to their anger, disappointment, and alienation over their dashed hopes and failed aspirations.

In the past two decades, the social and economic situation for the average Black family has worsened, and the gap has increased between the middle- and upper-income families and the lower-income and welfare-dependent families in the Black community (U.S. Bureau of the Census 1990). Since nearly one-half of all Black children grow up in poverty, many young Black males have never experienced the conditions that most white children take for granted, i.e., adequate nutrition, decent housing, access to health care, good schools, and safe neighborhoods. Since nearly half of Black children under eighteen are reared in female-headed families, many males have never known a strong male parent figure who can model appropriate masculine behaviors and provide positive models of identification (Wilson and Neckerman, 1984). By the time these Black males reach adolescence, they have often learned by experience that the world is a hostile, unwelcoming, and dangerous place; that they are viewed negatively by teachers, employers, and police; that their skin color is more important than their competence; and that society would rather incarcerate them than educate them.

As this generation of young Black males has witnessed a full-scale retreat from affirmative action, a dramatic resurgence in overt racism on college campuses as well as in suburban communities, an increasing conservatism in the Supreme Court's civil rights decisions, and a shrinking job market, they have become increasingly angry and agitated about their unequal access to the symbols of the American dream. Their grandfathers fought in World War II; their fathers fought in the Vietnam War, and they have been sent to defend democracy in Grenada, Panama, and even Saudi Arabia (where over one-third of the armed forces were black), but they are still not truly free and not really first-class citizens.

In just the last ten years these young Black males have seen differential standards of justice applied to middle-class stockbrokers and bankers whose financial crimes threatened the banking and securities systems of the entire nation. They have seen widespread misconduct by police and prosecutors who systematically harass, humiliate, and brutalize them in flagrant violation of their constitutional rights. They have seen the exploitation of talented Black athletes who are treated like pieces of property until their eligibility expires, usually without a diploma or any employable skills. They have seen differential treatment of middle-class white drug offenders and "date rapists," who are less likely to be arrested, tried and convicted than Blacks who commit the same offenses. They have seen judges mete out harsh sentences to young Black males found guilty of raping a young white stockbroker in New York, while giving lenient sentences to young white males involved in the gang murder of a poor Black teenager in Bensonhurst. To add insult to injury, at the end of the decade they have seen President Bush veto a major civil rights bill to increase their job opportunities, then only a few months later urge them to defend democracy in the Persian Gulf as American military personnel.

The anger of these young Black males is palpable; they are no longer willing to repress it, to sublimate it, or to deny it. Their rage erupts in muggings in the subway, robberies in the inner cities, gang shootings in the housing projects, racial fights in the schools, and protests on college campuses. Their anger is sometimes planned, sometimes random, but always destructive in its intent or its outcome. Their rage exploded in Los Angeles in the spring of 1992, after four white policemen were exonerated in the brutal beating of Rodney King, whose ordeal was captured on videotape for all the world to see. Nurtured in the crucible of the ghetto, labeled as antisocial misfits, treated as social pariahs, these youth will continue to act out their anger and frustrations in a vicious cycle of hostility, aggression, and violence. Understanding the historical roots and the current social context of this anger is merely the first step in analyzing its symptoms and its consequences for Black males, their families, their communities, and the broader society.

Perspectives on Anger

Anger has been defined as "a revengeful passion or emotion directed against one who inflicts a real or supposed wrong" (*American College Dictionary* 1969). As Tarvis (1989) points out, anger has been a perennial favorite topic of philosophers, psychologists, politicians, and pundits. So many theories have been advanced to explain anger as an emotional state that they could not be adequately summarized in this chapter. However, it is useful to describe three of these theories briefly, since they may shed some understanding on the psychological mechanisms that operate in the development and expression of anger in Black males, particularly in the relationship between anger and aggression.

In the late nineteenth century, Freud (1961) proposed that aggression was one of the basic human instincts, part of the unconscious psychic structure. Expression of this aggression induced anxiety because it was socially disruptive; so children had to learn how to control their aggressive feelings through repression, suppression, sublimation, or a number of other defense mechanisms. Anger was experienced as a conscious emotion and related to losses, failures, and disappointments in a person's life; extreme anger over the loss of a loved one created anxiety and was turned against the self, causing depression. This conceptualization of the relationship between anger and depression continues to influence the majority of mental health practitioners. It also helps to explain the angry responses of inner-city Black males who are so frequently confronted with failures and losses, yet do not feel social constraints against directing their anger toward external targets.

Anger is viewed by interpersonal psychologists as a reaction to early separation from a nurturing parent (Sullivan 1953). As the child matures, angry feelings will be evoked in situations where his or her emotional security is threatened. This concept of anger provides an explanation for the high rates of interpersonal violence in the Black community, where over half of the homicides of Black youth are committed by family members and acquaintances (Rose 1986).

The relationship between frustration and anger was investigated by a team of Yale psychologists over fifty years ago (Dollard et al. 1939). They proposed that frustration inevitably leads to feelings of aggression, which are then transformed into various behaviors, depending on the situation. Aggression may take the form of angry verbal or physical assaults, as in the case of Black males who experience high levels of frustration in their daily lives.

Finally, the social learning theorists have demonstrated the importance of modeling and reinforcement in the learning and maintenance of aggression (Bandura 1978). A child who is continually exposed to aggressive adult models will learn that aggression is an acceptable way to deal with angry feelings. Further, a child who is reinforced for aggressive acts even sporadically will incorporate them as a part of his or her behavioral repertoire. Clearly, many young Black males have ample opportunities to witness aggressive adults and to experience violence in their environments. They may be personally reinforced or obtain vicarious reinforcement for expressing direct anger or engaging in aggressive behavior when they see the material success and relative status of ghetto gang leaders, drug lords, and pimps.

These perspectives on anger and aggression are particularly relevant to the phenomenon of anger expression in Black males, as will become increasingly clear in the remainder of the chapter.

Ethnographic Studies

From Liebow's (1967) study of urban lower-class Black males in *Talley's Corner* to Glasgow's (1981) study of unemployed Black teenagers in *The Black Underclass*, Black males of all ages have expressed their frustration and anger, their rage and despair, their hurt and hostility at their poverty and lack of economic opportunities, at discrimination and social isolation, and at the daily indignities and humiliations they suffer in their interactions with whites.

"Talkin' and testifyin' " in their own words, as Smitherman (1977) describes the colorful idioms of Black dialect, these men have shared their experiences and voiced their resentments to Black and white scholars in a number of urban and rural communities over the past fifty years (Clark 1965; Drake and Cayton 1946; Monroe and Goldman 1988; Rainwater 1970; Schulz 1969). They have talked about the separate and unequal schools; the menial and low-wage jobs; the substandard housing; the inability to protect their wives, sisters, and daughters from sexual exploitation; the lack of medical care; the "last-hired, first-fired" employment practices; the political harassment; the brutality; and—especially for Southern Black males—the ultimate fear of lynching.

With resignation bordering on fatalism, these informants have exposed the world of "petty apartheid" incidents that most Blacks have endured daily in this country. These incidents range from lack of recognition or subtle forms of avoidance (e.g., white acquaintances who do not speak in public, whites who will not get into an elevator or sit down on a bus next to a Black male), to more overt forms of prejudice (e.g., refusing to admit a Black male into a store in certain neighborhoods, excluding Blacks from office social activities), to more extreme forms of discrimination (e.g., denying a home mortgage to a qualified applicant, refusing to hire or promote a qualified job applicant). As these incidents are reported, several themes emerge in these studies. First, the persistence of these practices over a long period of time and throughout all areas of the country is documented, and so Black males have been denied equal treatment in the North and South, in urban and rural areas, whether married or single, employed or unemployed, illiterate or college educated. Second, high socioeconomic status has never inoculated Black males against all forms of discrimination and prejudice. In some ways, middle-class Black males may be more vulnerable to the psychological stress resulting from such experiences, as will be discussed later. Third, Black males have recognized the powerful impact of their perceived sexuality and aggression on white males, who have always been alternately fascinated and repulsed by this myth. Their need to pacify white male anxieties about this potential threat has caused Black males to create a number of behavioral responses that simultaneously reduce their threat and reinforce other negative stereotypes of the passive, subservient, and asexual Uncle Tom (Grier and Cobbs 1968).

The high cost of this behavioral repertoire, which may be adaptive in some circumstances but very maladaptive in others, can be inferred from the physical and psychological symptoms found in Black males, who have high rates of hypertension, heart disease, stroke, premature mortality, and many somatic and psychiatric disorders associated with repressed rage, unsublimated anger, and high levels of anxiety (U.S. Department of Health and Human Services 1985). Findings about these relationships from empirical and clinical studies of Black males will be discussed in the following sections.

Empirical Studies

Evidence from a variety of sources sheds additional light on the relationship between anger and physical and psychological disorders in Black males. These sources include epidemiological data, community health surveys, and experimental studies of specific physical symptoms. While findings from these data do not always demonstrate a direct relationship between anger and health problems, there is widespread agreement that many illnesses are caused by or exacerbated by high levels of chronic anger, hostility, and anxiety that are suppressed and denied emotional expression (Tarvis 1989; Williams et al. 1985).

Epidemiological data indicate that Black males have higher rates than white males of hypertension (Myers 1990). The five leading causes of death for Black males age fifteen to twenty-four are homicide, accidents, suicide, cancer, and heart disease (U.S. Department of Health and Human Services 1985).

Community health studies also confirm the federal data that hypertension, cardiovascular diseases, and cirrhosis of the liver are major health problems for Black males (Myers 1990). As the Department of Health and Human Services report on black and minority health (1985) noted, many of these premature deaths are due to high-risk health behaviors including alcohol and drug use, smoking, and reckless driving. Williams and his colleagues (1985) summarize studies that suggest that smoking and substance use may be a means for Black men to alleviate tensions and to withdraw briefly from the stressful reality of their daily lives.

Experimental studies of hypertension have demonstrated a relationship between suppressed anger and hypertensive symptoms in Black males (Harburg et al. 1973; Myers 1990). These studies suggest that Black males are particularly at risk for hypertension in situations where they experience high environmental stress and/or are unable to fulfill their vocational aspirations due to external constraints.

Clinical Studies

Clinicians who have treated Black males in private or public psychiatric facilities have written extensively about anger as a major symptom in Black males (Gibbs 1988a; Grier and Cobbs 1968; Jenkins 1982; Pierce 1970; Poussaint 1983; Staples 1982). Although they may seek or be referred for treatment for a variety of psychological problems, anger is a common symptom that is never far from the surface and often the underlying cause of their emotional distress. It is also a tragic fact that many of these patients have erected elaborate defense mechanisms and developed dysfunctional behaviors in order to prevent their rage from overwhelming them or causing them constant distress.

Chester Pierce (1970) has coined the graphic term "micro-aggression" to describe the constant assaults on the self-esteem of Blacks in America. He notes that these negative interactions are particularly damaging to the sense of competence, efficacy, and dignity of Black males, who are more likely than Black females to face the brunt of these assaults. From a very early age, Black boys daily receive subtle and overt messages that they are expected to be unsocialized, unmotivated, and undisciplined. Teachers give more positive reinforcement to Black females (Reed 1988). Parents give more emotional support to Black females (Peters 1981). By the time Black males enter adolescence, many have unwittingly introjected negative views of themselves as "dumb, deviant, disturbed, disadvantaged and dysfunctional," the five d's that society has attributed to them and to their families (Gibbs 1988b; Gibbs and Hines 1989).

As Black males move into young adulthood, these negative attributions are consistently reinforced by potential employers, salesclerks, restaurant and hotel staff members, taxi drivers, and police. Their feelings of anger are fueled regularly by employers who refuse to hire them ("no Black males need apply"), by salesclerks who refuse to serve them ("Black males might rob you"), by restaurant hostesses who seat them near the kitchen ("Black males project the wrong image"), taxi drivers who refuse to pick them up ("Blacks live in dangerous neighborhoods"), and police who stop to question them ("Black males always look suspicious"). Obviously, there is no rational response to these stereotypes, nor can the Black male ever predict when and where he will be treated as an "invisible man," as an object of curiosity, as a symbol of aggression, as a token of affirmative action, or simply as a human being.

The uncertainty of his expected role in a given situation, that is, what others have projected upon him to fulfill their own neurotic needs, and the constant fear of overstepping the invisible caste barriers in this society create a free-floating anxiety in many Black males (Grier and Cobbs, 1968). I would argue that this anxiety, coupled with their chronic anger, is now the core of much of the psychological and social maladaptation of many young Black males in America.

Clinicians report that the anger in Black males may be suppressed or repressed, but it manifests itself in a wide variety of symptoms, attitudes, and behaviors (Grier and Cobbs 1968; Poussaint 1983). Symptoms include chronic fatigue, depression, anxiety, psychosomatic complaints (headaches, stomachaches, back pain, etc.), irritability, hostility, obsessive thoughts, and paranoid ideations. Attitudes that reflect pervasive anger include feelings of alienation, apathy, bitterness, hatred of specific individuals and groups, lack of motivation, suspiciousness, cynicism, and low self-esteem.

Anger is channeled into many self-destructive and socially maladaptive behaviors of young Black males, including delinquency, drug and alcohol use, extortion, gang activity, fighting, school failure, sexual promiscuity, and poor job performance. When anger turns into uncontrollable rage, Black males vent their aggression with weapons, committing family violence, assaults, and murders against each other and in the Black community (Dennis 1980; Gibbs 1988a; Hampton 1986; Poussaint 1983). Although sexual assaults are commonly associated with Black males, they actually commit fewer than 5 percent of the reported rapes in America. Yet Black males have high arrest rates for spouse abuse and family violence, suggesting that the primary victims of Black male anger are their wives, lovers, and children (Hampton 1986).

The past decade has witnessed an increase in gang activity among Black males in inner-city areas, particularly in urban areas such as Detroit, Washington, D.C., and Los Angeles. These gangs have flourished as the crack-cocaine trade has grown, but they have also become progressively more violent in their competition to control the distribution of drugs. Although there have been few actual studies of these gangs, reports in the mass media have created the impression that gangs fulfill several functions for their members, including mutual protection, social and recreational activities, and access to sources of money and power in their communities. I would propose that gangs also fulfill another important function for many of their members, that is, a social structure that permits, reinforces, and legitimizes the channeling of their anger and hostility at the dominant society. Thus, gangs provide a vehicle for group anger focused on illegitimate activities, thus symbolizing rejection and defiance of mainstream society.

Consequences of Anger

Anger is a powerful emotion and can have deleterious consequences, particularly when it is caused by situations that are chronic and that individuals perceive as beyond their power to change (Tarvis 1989). However, anger can also have positive outcomes in certain contexts. These consequences occur at four levels: the individual, the family, the community, and the broader society.

As noted earlier, anger at the individual level can affect the functioning of the Black male in numerous undesirable ways, including debilitating physical and psychological symptoms, negative and self-defeating attitudes, poor job performance, maladaptive and self-destructive behaviors, and loss of hope or limited aspirations for the future. Thus, anger exacts a high psychic toll on many young Black males who then become involved in a cycle of frustration, failure, and dysfunctional behaviors. Recent examples that have been widely publicized are the alleged gang rape of a young white stockbroker by a group of Black and Hispanic teenagers; the unintentional killing of several children in New York City by young Black males involved in drug turf battles or broken love affairs, and the college student riots at Virginia Beach, Virginia, in the summer of 1989.

If anger is acknowledged and channeled constructively, it can also be a powerful force for creativity, social change, unusual professional achievement, athletic excellence, or political leadership. Interviews with and autobiographical accounts of Blacks such as baseball pioneer Jackie Robinson, civil rights leader Martin Luther King, Jr., entertainer Sammy Davis, Jr., and champion boxer Muhammed Ali have all described the strategies these achievers used to transform anger over humiliating racial incidents into personal and professional triumph. The movies of Spike Lee, the lyrics of the rap groups, the poetry of Amiri Baraka, the choreography of Arthur Mitchell, the novels of James Baldwin—all are impressive examples of the use of anger as a creative force to address issues of race in American society.

In the family sphere, the Black male's anger makes it difficult for him to be a supportive spouse and a loving parent, so he becomes involved in antagonistic and competitive relationships. He may feel easily threatened by a more successful spouse who does not always sympathize with his need for recognition and respect. As the constant target of humiliation and harassment, the Black male often displaces his frustrations and vents his anger on the people who are most accessible and most vulnerable—his own family.

Anger of Black males in the family can quickly erupt into family violence with a potential for escalation into spouse abuse or child abuse. Since research has established a link between unemployment and family violence, Black males (whose unemployment rates are over twice as high as those of white males) are especially vulnerable to the frustration and anger of economic insecurity and forced idleness. Their families are thus at greater risk as targets of their anger; so it is not surprising that there are high rates of reported family violence among low-income Blacks (Hampton 1986). However, it is also important to bear in mind that dysfunctional Black families are more likely to be exposed to intervention by police and social welfare agencies; thus, arrest rates do not provide a valid picture for comparison of Black and white patterns of family violence. In fact, most researchers in this field, in their analysis of data from cross-sectional national surveys, have concluded that there are no significant differences in racial rates of family violence (Gelles 1979; Hampton 1986). Economic status rather than race appears to be a more significant factor in family violence, yet there is still some question concerning the relative insulation of middle- and upper-income families from police investigation and prosecution.

If the anger of Black males as heads of families could be channeled into concerns over creating more cohesive family units and more competent children, it could be a very constructive force for strengthening the functioning of the Black family. For example, husbands could play a more supportive role in encouraging their wives' careers, fathers could spend more time as mentors and advocates for their children, adult males could take more responsibility for their own economic self-sufficiency and could be more proactive in improving their housing and obtaining adequate health care for their families. Instead of allowing their anger to destroy their families, Black males must learn how to mobilize their anger to strengthen the defenses of their families against the constant pressures of the outside world (Madhubuti 1990).

Anger of Black males at the community level can be very destructive, or it can provide the impetus for community empowerment. Since the community organization movements of the 1960s, indigenous leaders and groups have emerged in many Black communities, ranging from the militant Black Panthers to the separatist Black Muslims. Some leaders of these groups have had criminal records and marginal educational qualifications, yet they have channeled their anger and hostility into efforts to improve their local communities and to energize social and political change in the inner cities.

These groups have established breakfast programs in the schools, after-school tutoring programs, health clinics, voter education workshops, youth recreation programs, and small businesses. Anger at the establishment has been a useful tool to harness the energies and aspirations of a segment of the Black community who often view themselves as passive victims rather than active initiators.

In the community sphere, the Black male's anger can easily spill over into relationships with neighbors, shopkeepers, professionals, and police, so that his hostile interactions may provoke counteraggressive responses and escalate into violent confrontations.

Moreover, the collective anger of Black males can transform a community from a ghetto into a battleground, as in the urban riots of 1965 in Watts, the riots following the assassination of Martin Luther King, Jr., in 1968, the demonstrations following the murder of Yusef Hawkins in Bensonhurst, Long Island, in 1989, and the most recent riot in Los Angeles following the Rodney King verdict. Although some Black women have been involved in all of these confrontations over racism or police brutality, Black males have been in the vanguard of the activities, venting their rage in vandalism, vulgarity, and violence directed against selective targets. These riots and demonstrations cannot always be predicted, but hindsight provides valuable insight into the conditions that foster these confrontations. In all of these situations, one incident of police brutality or racial injustice usually ignites the underlying frustrations and tensions of Blacks who feel shut out of the economic system, shut up in the political system, and shut into the ghetto (Report of the National Advisory Commission on Civil Disorders 1968).

On the broader societal level, the consequences of anger in Black males are multiple, both direct and indirect, in the areas of the mass media, social institutions, politics, and public policy. The barrage of violent images of Black males portrayed in the print and electronic media, such as the Republican party's infamous 1988 presidential campaign commercial about convicted murderer-rapist Willie Horton, certainly contributes to the fear and prejudice of whites and other minority groups toward all Blacks. These attitudes are channeled by the gatekeepers into the schools, the workplace, the financial institutions, the criminal justice system, the health care system, the social welfare system, the entertainment industry, the cultural institutions, etc. As a result, Black males are treated as pariahs, as predators, as provocative outsiders, as potential troublemakers. In turn, these attitudes are assimilated into the rhetoric of politicians and policymakers who use the spectre of Black violence as a convenient lightning rod to deflect the public from the real issues of poverty, racism, corruption, and bureaucratic mismanagement. With the support of both political parties, public policy is informed (or misinformed) by stereotypes and rhetoric rather than scholarly debate and logic, thus resulting in policies that further reduce the self-sufficiency of Black males, restrict their mobility, and reinforce their sense of frustration, alienation, and despair.

Implications for Prevention and Treatment

The anger in Black males will not simply be diffused, dissipated, or disappear over time. On the contrary, this anger will grow and fester as social conditions for Blacks in our inner cities continue to deteriorate. As their anger increases, so too will their alienation, their sense of exclusion, and their feelings of despair. This combination is a formula for violence, an invitation to destruction, and a program for social chaos.

Twenty-five years after the Watts riots, that fifty-square-mile area of south-central Los Angeles still festers with the wounds of poverty, unemployment, crime, drugs, and urban blight. The symptoms of anger are highly visible and ominous—increases in gang activity, drug dealing, high school dropout rates, and homicides, which occur at the rate of one every four days (*Santa Cruz Sentinel* 1990).

The conditions in Watts and Detroit are replicated on the south side of Chicago, in Harlem, in some sections of Washington, D. C., Boston, and other cities across the land. After thirty years of the War on Poverty, affirmative action programs, and civil rights demonstrations, the socioeconomic status and the social environment for the majority of Blacks is worse than it was in 1960. Young Black males have every right to be angry as the economic progress for the rest of the nation has largely passed them by, and as they have experienced the military sacrifices of the Vietnam War, the political rhetoric of affirmative action and "reverse racism," the economic exploitation of competition with immigrants, and the social isolation of disintegrating inner-city ghettos. Even college-educated Black males have had their professional ambitions blocked by the "glass ceiling" and seen their Black female peers move up the executive ladders more quickly and more successfully to reach near parity in income with professional white women (*Ebony Magazine* 1990).

How can this anger be diffused before it reaches explosive levels and literally destroys a generation of young Black males? This widespread anger cannot be treated merely as a symptom of *individual* psychological distress, but it must be approached as symptomatic of an underlying *social* disease. The disease analogy allows us to analyze the fundamental social factors that contribute to the anger in Black males, i.e., poverty, discrimination, social isolation, and political powerlessness. In order to address these factors, it is obvious that the *primary prevention* strategy must focus on the reduction and eventual elimination of poverty, racial discrimination, and their associated conditions, that is, slum housing, inadequate health care, poor schools, unemployment, crime, drugs, teenage pregnancy, and other social pathologies. Federal, state, and local government policies to accomplish these goals have been strongly proposed and carefully delineated in a number of recent policy-oriented books, a set of comprehensive recommendations too lengthy to repeat here (Edelman 1987; Gibbs 1988b; Schorr 1986; Wilson 1987). These policies would ultimately benefit future generations of Black youth, as legislative and judicial changes are slow to be achieved and even slower to be implemented. Thus, these are long-range goals that will require concerted effort by a coalition of civil rights, human rights, and other liberal advocacy groups.

Early intervention programs must also be established in order to identify those Black youth at high risk for school failure and ultimate social dependency. These programs should be designed to address the current generation of young parents, educators, health professionals, juvenile justice officials, and social welfare workers. Effective programs include such activities as parent-education training, Head Start, school-based health clinics, drug education, delinquency prevention, school dropout prevention, and community alternatives for first offenders (Committee for Economic Development 1987; Children's Defense Fund 1986; Edelman 1987; Gibbs 1988b). In addition, schools and community health centers need to develop programs of violence reduction, AIDS education, sex education, and reduction of other high-risk health behaviors which contribute to disproportionately high rates of morbidity and mortality in Black males (Brunswick 1988; Gibbs 1988b; U.S. Department of Health and Human Services 1985). Programs of health promotion are just as important for Black youth as programs of illness prevention in order to promote positive health behaviors.

Finally, mental health facilities must be expanded to meet the demand for the increasing number of Black males who need psychiatric treatment for psychological disorders, substance abuse, family problems, and job-related stress. These facilities have been woefully inadequate since the Reagan Administration dismantled so many of the community health centers and other community programs established during the 1960s (Edelman 1987; Schorr 1986). To be effective, mental health facilities should be available in the Black community, easily accessible by public transportation, and affordable for low-income clients (Children's Defense Fund 1986). Further, more funds should be allocated for the recruitment and training of minority mental health professionals who will commit themselves to serve the Black community and do not have negative attitudes or expectations about delivering services to Black male clients. Moreover, producing clones of the current mental health professionals is not the ideal solution because they have not been particularly empathic or effective in working with Black clients. It is essential for professional training programs to reform their curricula and internship opportunities to produce culturally competent mental health practitioners who will be knowledgeable about ethnic, social, and cultural differences; sensitive to variations in communication patterns and family structure; and tolerant of alternative norms, values, and behaviors as criteria for healthy psychosocial adjustment (Gibbs and Huang 1989; Jones and Korchin 1982; Sue and Moore 1984).

Summary and Conclusions

As the final decade of the twentieth century commences, young Black males in America find themselves in an increasingly marginalized position, the unwitting heirs to over 370 years of slavery, segregation, and discrimination; the helpless victims of persistent poverty, social injustice, and economic inequality; and the convenient targets of political demagogues who use them as scapegoats for the social and economic problems of the larger society. The cumulative impact of these forces has resulted in a hostile and unpredictable environment for young Black males in every major institution of this society—the educational system, the social welfare system, the health-care system, the criminal justice system, and the economic system. They have systematically been denied equal opportunity as well as equality of treatment in the schools, the social service agencies, the hospitals and the mental health clinics, the courts, and the labor force.

In response to this discrimination and exclusion from the mainstream society's channels for achievement, personal development, and social mobility, young Black males have found themselves increasingly socially isolated in inner-city ghetto neighborhoods, confined to low-skilled, dead-end jobs, subject to constant harassment by police and prosecutors, and manipulated by the mass media and unprincipled politicians to exploit the deeply entrenched cultural paranoia over the myth of their sexuality and aggression. With so many powerful barriers to prevent their assimilation and to limit their options for mobility in this society, young Black males have been forced into the defensive position of unwilling victims, caught between a rock and a hard place. They have responded to this victimization quite predictably, with feelings of rage and anger, fueled by even greater frustrations as they have seen the preferential treatment accorded to more recent immigrant groups who have been welcomed and encouraged to realize the American dream.

Only by understanding the depth of these frustrations and the intensity of this anger can one begin to comprehend the escalating violence and self-destructive behavior of these young Black males. The real tragedy is that many of these young men no longer see themselves as part of the larger society and do not subscribe to the mainstream values, the behavioral norms, and the goals of the society, which has failed them in nearly every respect. Thus, they have developed an alternative set of values that proclaim that life is to be lived in the fast lane, but its worth is cheap. Their norms are not based on the Ten Commandments, but on the skills necessary to survive life in the ghetto. Their goals are based on status and material success, but the means of attaining these goals are often illegitimate. They protect their turn and enhance their status by violent means, if necessary, always understanding how fragile and futile their lives really are. Thus, these victims of poverty and discrimination are gradually transformed into the victimizers of the vulnerable and disadvantaged, the mirror images of their own despair and alienation.

This society has chosen to address the symptoms and signs of Black male anger rather than attack the underlying causes and conditions that have created and fueled this anger. The government has chosen to build prisons rather than low-income housing; the educators have chosen to place Black males in "special classes" rather than to develop culturally appropriate approaches to educate them; the social welfare system has reinforced intergenerational dependency rather than provide education and training to encourage autonomy; and society has allowed the criminal justice system to warehouse young Black males into jails and prisons rather than provide them with employment opportunities and incentives to higher education, thus completing the vicious cycle.

If this country does not adopt effective prevention strategies to rescue young Black males from this escalating cycle of self-destruction and violence, it will lose another generation of Black youth. Can we afford to lose nearly 20 percent of the nation's work force as we enter the twenty-first century? Are we willing to discard millions of young Black men who have the potential to contribute to the economic, social, and cultural development of this nation? The answers to these questions will largely shape the future well-being of the Black community in America, the revitalization of the nation's cities, the economic productivity of the labor force, and the very stability of this emerging multicultural society.

PART 3

Search for Empowerment

CHAPTER 11

Black Males and Social Policy: Breaking the Cycle of Disadvantage

by Ronald L. Taylor

Federal social policy, whether in the area of employment, welfare, education, social insurance, poverty, or criminal justice, has often had a disproportionate impact on the lives of Black Americans. Their historically disadvantaged position in American society has magnified the impact of federal programs, whether their effect was to provide opportunities or to create obstacles to the achievement of racial equality. For example, the civil-rights legislation of the 1960s inspired an array of federally sponsored programs that contributed to significant improvements in the socioeconomic status and general well-being of Black Americans. In contrast, federal retreat from such programs and policies in the 1970s contributed to a deepening of Black social problems in the 1980s, especially in employment, education, health, and family stability.

Such reversals in federal initiatives have had a particularly adverse effect on the quality of life among young Black men, as evidenced by a number of social indicators. The status and well-being of young Black males in American society has always been problematic, and their condition had become the focus of concern and major government action in the 1960s (Moynihan 1965; Solomon 1988). For example, federal programs designed for disadvantaged youths and the poor, which enrolled some of the highest proportions of Black males (e.g., public service employment, and employment and training programs) were the targets for elimination or the severest cuts in federal funding during the 1980s (Center on Budget and Policy Priorities 1984).

Here we will examine how the shift in emphasis of federal policy during the past two decades—from a focus on the structural sources of Black inequality and social problems to one emphasizing the behavioral and value deficiencies of the Black "underclass"—contributed to the current crisis among young Black males in the inner cities and elsewhere in the country. The developments can best be understood by reviewing the historical context within which they were initiated.

From Blaming the System to Blaming the Victims

Federal initiatives designed to combat such national social problems as poverty, unemployment, ill health, and the shortcomings of the educational system are relatively recent developments in the United States. While the 1930s saw the beginnings of programmatic structures and social policy innovations designed to ameliorate the economic conditions of some segments of the population (e.g., public assistance for the needy over sixty-five, the blind, and dependent children under the Social Security Act of 1935), it was not until the 1960s that a more comprehensive system of income supports and other social provisions was established (Weir et al. 1988). One of the central objectives of federal programs and policies inaugurated during this period was the reduction of poverty and the myriad of social problems associated with it, especially among Blacks and other minority populations. Under the banner of the Great Society, the Johnson Administration declared a War on Poverty that included an expansion of existing entitlement programs and the establishment of such new programs as food stamps, Medicare, subsidized housing, and job training to enable the poor to break the cycle of poverty and become productive members of society.

Much of the impetus for increased federal activism in eradicating poverty in the early 1960s derived from the demands of the civil-rights movement, which aroused and focused public concern on the wide differences in the economic conditions of Blacks and whites, and from the emerging consensus among scholars and policymakers that poverty was a structural phenomenon embedded within the nature of the American system rather than a consequence of indolence or vice (Patterson 1981; Murray 1984). To deal with such a phenomenon, income supports or public assistance programs were not enough. What the poor needed to overcome the structural obstacles to stable employment and income was "a hand, not a handout." If poor youths and chronically unemployed adults were given the training and skills they needed to find employment, they would be well on their way to permanent self-sufficiency and productive lives. This premise, derived from the theory of human capital investment, and articulated in the 1964 *Economic Report of the President* (U.S. Council of Economic Advisors 1964) inspired a variety of federal initiatives targeted on the poor. Since it was assumed that the cycle of poverty could be broken most effectively among the young, many federal programs established during this period had a decided bias toward teenagers and young adults (Brown and Erie 1981).

Federal spending on human capital programs (i.e., education, training, and employment) rose sharply during the 1960s, from just under $1 billion in 1964 to $10 billion in 1968 (Burtless 1986). Expenditures for manpower training and work experience to bridge the gap in work skills between the poor and nonpoor included funding for the creation of such programs as the Job Corps, Neighborhood Youth Corps, and various other programs established under the Manpower Development and Training Act (MDTA). To address the educational needs of the poor, Head Start, Upward Bound, Teacher Corps, and Title I of the Elementary and Secondary Education Act were launched. The health and dietary needs of the poor were addressed through such programs as Medicaid, food stamps, neighborhood health centers, and school lunch programs. Through the community action and legal services programs, the poor acquired the political and legal means they needed for better access to jobs, goods, and services (Danziger, Haveman and Plotnick 1986).

Although nearly two-thirds of the poor population in the early 1960s was white, Black Americans had a higher incidence of poverty, and many of the most debilitating aspects of poverty were concentrated in the inner cities. Thus, the inner city became, as Sundquist (1968) noted, the crucial testing ground of President Johnson's conception of his Great Society: "There [the inner city] all of the programs devised by the activists to cope with unemployment, with poverty, with delinquency, with the shortcomings of educational systems, would undergo their trial by ordeal and succeed or finally fail" (p. 286). What effects did the broad range of government programs and policies have on the socioeconomic position and quality of life of Black Americans in general and Black males in particular? Early assessments of various antipoverty programs concluded that they had contributed to significant reductions in poverty among all segments of the poverty population (Plotnick and Skidmore 1975). For example, poverty fell from 18 percent to 13 percent for the population as a whole during the five years from 1964 to 1968. Among Blacks, reductions in poverty were even more dramatic. In 1959, 58 percent of working-aged Blacks (i.e., persons under sixty-five) were below the poverty line; by 1969 the percentage had dropped to 30 percent, a decline of 28 percentage points in ten years (Murray 1984).

Declines in Black poverty were accompanied by gains in education, facilitated in part through federal expenditures on education programs for disadvantaged students in nursery, elementary, and secondary schools and colleges. Although education was improving for all Blacks prior to federal initiatives in this area during the 1960s, progress toward closing the educational gap between Blacks and whites was accelerated by such programs (Murray 1984). By 1970, 54 percent of young Black men age twenty-five to twenty-nine, and 58 percent of young Black women had completed high school, as against 36 percent and 41 percent respectively who had done so in 1960. The 1960s also saw impressive and unprecedented increases in college attendance by Black students. From 1964 to 1970, total Black college enrollment increased by 101 percent (from 234,000 to 470,000). For young Blacks aged eighteen to twenty-four, the percent enrolled in college increased from 10 percent in 1965 to 18 percent in 1971.

The impact of federal programs on Black employment during the 1960s was more complex, since Black progress in education, evident prior to the initiation of such programs, would have been expected to have had a positive effect on Black employment, especially at the higher occupational levels (Taylor 1977). But as Brown and Erie (1981) have shown, "massive federal funding of State and local social welfare programs had substantial economic (and employment) effects on the Black community as a whole" (p. 306). They contend that social welfare policy of the 1960s generated a significant increase in the Black middle class largely as service providers for low-income service recipients. During the period from 1960 to 1976, more than half (55 percent) of the increase in Black professional, managerial, and technical employment occurred in the public sector (i.e., in local, state, and federal employment), compared with 34 percent for whites. Moreover, "social welfare programs accounted for nearly one-half of the Black middle-class increase, compared with one-quarter for whites" (p. 309). In short, expanding public social welfare employment during the 1960s and early 1970s served as a major port of entry for the emerging Black middle-class, which nearly tripled in size during this period (Brown and Erie 1981).

On the other hand, employment and training programs launched during this period and designed to enhance the job skills and employment prospects and earnings of more disadvantaged groups (e.g., low-income youth, welfare recipients, and the chronically unemployed) produced mixed results. The Job Corps, created under the Economic Opportunity Act of 1964, focused on the more severely disadvantaged youth between the ages of sixteen and twenty-one and provided a comprehensive program of services, including individual and group counseling, health care, occupational skills training, remedial and basic education, and job placement. It was developed as a residential program to remove youth from disruptive environments. Various assessments of this program found it to be very effective in producing employment, earnings, and educational gains by participants up to four years after completion (Mallar et al. 1980; Taylor 1990). Moreover, early results from an evaluation of the Manpower Development and Training Act (MDTA), passed in 1962, and initially designed to provide vocational and on-the-job training to male heads of households but later concentrated on meeting the needs of disadvantaged individuals with hard-core unemployment problems, revealed that the training participants received in this program had a positive and statistically significant effect on their earnings, from $200 annually for white males to more than $500 for Black females (Ashenfelter 1978).

However, later evaluations of the array of employment and training programs concluded that, with the exception of the Job Corps, few had much impact on the earning capacity or long-term employability problems of the Black poor, especially Black males (Levin 1977; Mallar et al. 1980) But as Levitan and Wurzburg (1979) point out, most of the early federal initiatives in this area were "implemented in an environment charged with emotional and political disagreement and subjected to a number of uncontrollable variables" (p. 9), which defied careful and systematic evaluation. As a result, many programs that were otherwise successful were branded failures on the basis of limited evidence and highly imprecise measures of evaluation (Bassi and Ashenfelter 1986).

Yet others contend that such programs were never designed to address the more serious structural problems the Black poor encountered in gaining access to long-term employment; rather, they were attempts to ease the deprivation among the poor and prevent the possibility of mass insurgency (Piven and Cloward 1971). Indeed, as Brown and Erie (1981, 315) contend:

> Almost from the beginning, the Neighborhood Youth Corps was less a training program than a means to put money in the pockets of inner-city youth. This became the pattern for many of the manpower and training programs of the Great Society. They were in a sense de facto income maintenance programs. Given the inability of the black poor to earn a living wage in the secondary labor market, due in part to the racial discrimination they still faced, they oscillated between working in the private sector, going on welfare, entering a training program, and engaging in illicit activities. Far from acquiring the ability to compete in the primary labor market, the black poor came to depend more and more on transfer payments and in-kind services.

Even if employment and training programs had been more successful in improving the job skills and earning capacity of their participants in the short term, it is doubtful whether the long-term employment prospects of poor Blacks would have been much improved given the low quality of job opportunities available to them in inner-city communities (Kasarda 1989). Moreover, employment opportunities for low-income and/or young workers were severely constrained by inadequate demand for their labor. And since "the human capital policies of the Great Society had no effect on the demand side of the labor market, it is not surprising they had little effect on the earning capacity of the black poor" (Brown and Erie 1981, 314).

Despite the apparent failure of employment and training programs to meet the long-term employment and income needs of the Black poor, liberal antipoverty warriors of the 1960s saw many of the results of their initiatives as critical beginnings in the development of social welfare policy that addressed the broad needs of Black communities in education, employment, housing, health, and welfare. Indeed, they pointed to the success of Black families in increasing their income, which went up to 99.6 percent during the decade of the 1960s, while white family income rose by only 69 percent. Moreover, the ratio of Black to white family income increased from 53 percent in 1961 to 61 percent in 1971—a significant gain considering that during the previous decade no change occurred. In addition, Black gains in education and in professional, managerial, and clerical occupations were also interpreted as evidence of the positive impact of federal initiatives, as were improvements in the housing and health status of poor Blacks (Levitan et al. 1975). Indeed, some observers predicted that if the rate of progress achieved by Blacks over the decade of 1960s persisted, disparities in income, education, and occupational distributions would soon disappear (Wattenberg and Scammon 1973).

But such optimistic assessments of Black progress conveniently ignored evidence of less favorable trends in Black communities and in the larger society that were likely to undermine in the coming decades the real progress made in the 1960s. For example, there were increasing rates of family dissolution, out-of-wedlock births, female-headed families, welfare dependency, and long-term unemployment among Black men and the urban poor, brought about by structural changes in the economy. Early on, such writers as Kenneth Clark (1965), Daniel P. Moynihan (1965), Lee Rainwater (1966), and Bayard Rustin (1965) saw that these problems had far-reaching implications for Black communities and called for a shift in direction of federal policy and programs to attack the structural conditions that contributed to their rise and persistence. Moreover, Moynihan and other scholars such as St. Clair Drake (1966) and Andrew Brimmer (1969) called attention to the growing schism in Black communities between the haves and have-nots—that is, between "a stable middle-class group that is steadily growing stronger and more successful, and an increasingly disorganized and disadvantaged lower-class group" (Moynihan 1965, 5–6). Indeed,

Moynihan warned that the success and increasing visibility of the Black middle class should not be allowed to obscure the ominous trends among poor urban Blacks. However, such warnings went unheeded in the wake of the storm of indignation and controversy aroused by the publication of the "Moynihan Report" (1965), which focused on the breakup of Black families.

By the early 1970s, however, many of the problems identified by Moynihan, Clark, and others had grown worse, despite substantial increases in federal expenditures during this period. For example, the employment situation of young Black males, eighteen to nineteen, continued to deteriorate in the 1970s, even as federal employment and training programs and related efforts became better organized and more extensive (Murray 1984). Moreover, the labor force participation rate of Black males continued its downward trend in the early 1970s, particularly among teenagers, despite a tight labor market. Similarly, the percentage of Black husband-wife households declined between 1968 and 1973 from 72 to 63 percent of all Black families, a precipitous decline in just five years. And after steep declines in Black poverty during the 1960s, the 1970s saw the poverty rate among Black families stabilize at about 30 percent, even as expenditures for federal welfare programs that provided food, shelter, and medical benefits for the poor reached their highest level (Farley 1984).

A variety of explanations were advanced to account for such trends, including the adverse and disproportionate impact of periodic recessions and double-digit inflation on Black employment and family income; the incidence of single-parent households (Hill 1981); the federal policy shift from the human-capital strategy of the Johnson era to an income-maintenance strategy based on cash and in-kind transfers during the Nixon years (Levitan, Johnston, and Taggart 1975); structural changes in the economy; and incompetent management of employment and training programs targeted on disadvantaged Black youth (Levin 1977). However, a growing consensus among some policymakers and scholars was that federal interventions were at best ineffective in addressing many of the deep-rooted problems of poor Blacks, and at worst contributed to the growth and intractability of such problems.

The neoconservative attack on Great Society initiatives, launched in the late 1960s, gained considerable strength in the 1970s with the collapse of the liberal coalition and the election of Richard Nixon. The neoconservatives largely agreed with Richard Nixon's assessment that

> The Great Society's strategy of "throwing money at problems" was ill-conceived and ineffectual, exaggerating the capacity of the government to change institutions and individuals. The nation was pushed too far, too fast, and was unable to afford or digest the overtly ambitious agenda of the Great Society; its legacy was inflation, worker alienation, racial tension, and other lingering ills. (Quoted in Steinfels 1979, 219)

In short, the Great Society had promised far more than it could deliver, raising public expectations about the ability of government to eliminate what were in some cases intractable social problems. From the perspective of some neoconservatives, the condition of the poor, or what had recently been dubbed the "underclass," was just barely amenable to social intervention: "Whether by nature or by nurture, by constitution or culture, the members of this group have been so deeply injured, that they are to a large degree ineducable, unemployable, and alien to middle-class norms of behavior. They are, to boil it all down, 'shiftless' " (Steinfels 1979, 61).

Thus, by the late 1970s, a new analysis of poverty and other social problems besetting Black communities gained ascendancy among intellectuals and policymakers, to wit, that poverty, unemployment, welfare dependency, and female-headed households, among other problems, were less the result of such structural factors as racial discrimination and social isolation than of excessive welfare programs and policies. Such initiatives had destroyed the incentive of the poor to be productive and exacerbated their behavioral deficiencies. Indeed, this was the major theme of presidential candidate Ronald Reagan, who vowed to dismantle much of the Great Society's social legislation and entitlement programs were he to be elected. With his election came drastic cuts in social programs targeted on the poor and the most sweeping policy reversals in the thirty-five years since the New Deal (Orfield 1988).

With the election of Ronald Reagan to the presidency in 1980, federal policy had come full circle, from an emphasis on the structural sources of poverty, unemployment, and related social problems in the 1960s to an emphasis on the behavioral characteristics, norms, and values of the poor, which in the 1980s were seen to produce such problems. The latter focus implies that social programs can do little to correct the behavioral deficiencies of the Black underclass or promote improvements in their social condition. But such a conclusion is based on the faculty assumption that, despite enormous expenditures on social programs targeted on the poor, little was accomplished. In fact, while federal expenditures on "social welfare" programs did increase markedly during the 1960s and 1970s, more than 70 percent of that increase was accounted for by such traditional welfare programs as Medicare, Medicaid, Social Security, veterans' benefits, and aid to the blind, aged, and handicapped (Harrington 1974; Burtless 1986). The remaining 30 percent of federal spending was accounted for by increases in funding for welfare, food stamps, housing subsidies, and students aid. In addition, only a small fraction of these funds were expended on such programs as Job Corps, legal aid, and community action. In short, the fraction of national income distributed to the poor through various federal programs since the mid-1960s was and remains quite modest compared to other programs (Weir, Orloff, and Skocpol 1988).

As to how much such expenditures accomplished, Levitan and Taggart (1976) carefully reassessed the vast data and many analyses generated by evaluation studies of Great Society programs. They reached the general conclusion that "the 1960s programs and policies and their continuation had a massive, overwhelming beneficial impact and that the weight of evidence convincingly supports this view" (pp. vii–viii). Dismissing such programs as failed attempts at social engineering, they noted, had become a fad among "discouraged liberals," "disenchanted proponents," and traditional conservatives. In consequence, "the sweeping and erroneous conclusion that the Great Society failed, continues to hold sway over decisionmakers and the public, generating a timidity and negativism which has retarded needed and possible progress" (p. 9).

Meanwhile, as the erosion of public support, cutbacks and/or dismantling of federal programs targeted on the poor continued, social conditions in many inner cities, and among Black men in particular, grew progressively worse. The deterioration was due in large measure to shifting policy objectives and the failure of such policies to address the underlying structural conditions that promoted the persistence of a variety of social problems in Black communities.

Black Males: Issues, Perspectives, and Social Policy

In the annual report of the National Urban League for 1980, Vernon Jordan (1980) noted that "for black Americans, the decade of the 1970s was a time in which many of their hopes, raised by the civil rights victories of the 1960s withered away; a time in which they saw the loss of much of the momentum that seemed to be propelling the nation along the road to true equality for all its citizens . . . the 1970s . . . brought forth in Black America a mood of disappointment, frustration and bitterness at promises made and promises unkept" (p. i). As Jordan noted, " 'benign neglect' became the battle cry against the War on Poverty, affirmative action, and compensatory programs" (p. ii). Retreat from such issues was evident, not only among policymakers and the larger public, but also among liberal social scientists who shied away from Black issues as a focus of research in response to the notorious sensitivity of such topics and a shortage of funding to pursue such work (Wilson 1984). As a result, the widening gap between Blacks and whites in quality of life, as reflected in such social indicators as employment, income, education, poverty, and health, and the growth of such problems as Black crime, drug abuse, out-of-wedlock births, and family dissolution, received relatively little scholarly attention during the 1970s.

The lack of attention to Black social problems has been especially costly to young Black males, given their high-risk status. On nearly every socioeconomic measure, from infant mortality to life expectancy, Black males are worse off today than they were some two decades ago (Gibbs 1988; Taylor 1987). As Marshall (1988) has noted, because of a complex set of mutually reinforcing factors, Black males start life with serious disadvantages. They are, for instance, more likely to be born to unwed teenage mothers who are poorly educated and more likely to neglect or abuse their children; the children of these mothers are also more likely to be born underweight and to experience injuries or neurological defects that require long-term care. Moreover, such children are more likely to be labelled "slow learners" or "educable mentally retarded," to have learning difficulties in school, to lag behind their peers in basic educational competences or skills, and to drop out of school at an early age. Black boys are also more likely to be institutionalized or placed in foster care (Gibbs 1988).

To be sure, the sources of the problems many Black males experience in education, employment, the criminal justice system, and in other areas of social life can be traced, not only to public and scholarly indifference to such problems, but to recent structural changes in the economy, perverse demographic trends, and intractably high levels of urban poverty, which converged to exacerbate conditions in inner cities across the country and the predicament of Black males in particular (Wacquant and Wilson 1989). With respect to demographic changes, for example, the proportion of Black youth in central cities increased by more than 70 percent during the past two decades. The result may have been a "critical mass" of Black youth which, it has been suggested, is a condition that can set in motion "a self-sustaining chain reaction" that contributes to "an explosive increase in the amount of crime, addiction, and welfare dependency" in the inner cities (Wilson 1977, 20). Under these conditions, community institutions and local labor markets have proved inadequate to meet the needs and cope with the consequences of a substantially enlarged Black youth population. As William Wilson (1983) has observed, "on the basis of these demographic changes alone, one would expect Black youth to account disproportionately for the increasing social problems of the central city" (p. 83).

To such demographic changes must be added continuing problems in education, employment, poverty, and the criminal justice system which diminish the life chances of Black males and imperil the future of Black communities.

Black Males and Education

Data on school enrollment and educational attainment at the precollege level for Black youth and young adults show marked improvements during the past two decades. For example, in 1960, over 77 percent of Black youths ages sixteen and seventeen were attending school, compared to more than 83 percent of white youths in this age group. By 1970, the proportion of sixteen and seventeen year olds in school exceeded 90 percent for whites and 87 percent for Blacks. In 1979, Black sixteen and seventeen year olds were slightly more likely to be enrolled in school than their white counterparts (Taylor 1987). Thus, the gap in median years of schooling between Blacks and whites declined from 2.7 years in 1960 to less than one-half year in 1980: 12.6 years for Blacks and 13.0 years for whites (National Research Council 1989).

These data, however, mask significant differences between Black and white youths in rate of delayed education (i.e., being behind in school) and in nonattendance. For example, Black youth are much more likely to be enrolled below the modal grade for their age group than are white youth, a differential that increases in higher grades. In 1979, more than half (54 percent) of seventeen-year-old Black males who attended school were behind their modal class, compared to 26 percent of their white counterparts (U.S. Bureau of the Census 1981). In fact, at all ages and for both sexes, Black youths are more likely than whites to be enrolled at grade levels below their age group. Among Black males, the delay rate has consistently been twice the rate for white males since 1960 (U.S. Commission on Civil Rights 1978). In consequence, there remains a significant racial difference in the completion of high school: 21 percent of all Blacks eighteen and nineteen years old, and 25 percent of these twenty and twenty-one years old had neither completed nor were enrolled in high school in 1980, compared to 14.9 percent and 14.5 percent, respectively, of white youths in these age groups. The dropout rates for Black males in major cities like New York, Chicago, Philadelphia, and Detroit are considerably higher than the rates for Black youths as a whole, ranging from 40 to 70 percent in these cities. In general, Black males in major cities are about two and one-half times more likely to drop out of school than Black females and have the highest school dropout rate of all gender groups, leaving nearly a quarter of them ill-equipped to enter the job market, military service, or post secondary education (Gibbs 1988).

The difficulties Black youth in general and males in particular experience in public schools are well documented (See, e.g., Grant, 1984; Irvine, 1990; Rist, 1973). Such difficulties are attributed to a combination of factors: parenting deficiencies, poor preparation, peer pressure, and prevailing community attitudes toward public schools (though not toward education per se) on the one hand, and formal and informal policies and practices of public schools on the other (Ogbu 1985; Boykins 1986; Oakes 1985). The latter include "poorly prepared teachers, inadequate educational facilities, low teacher expectations, ineffective administrators, and chronic violence" (Gibbs 1988, 6). These factors interact to produce disastrous educational outcomes for many Black children and have an especially adverse effect on the school performance of Black boys (Hare and Castenell 1985). Thus, Black males are disproportionately enrolled in the lowest ability groups; three times as likely to be in classes for the educable mentally retarded as are white students (Carnegie Corporation of New York 1984/85); more likely to be labeled deviant and described in more negative terms by their teachers and other school personnel; more likely than white males to be sent to the principal or guidance counselor for challenging the teacher or for other misconduct (Grant 1985; Irvine 1990); and two to five times as likely as their white counterparts to have their education interrupted by suspension or expulsion at an early age (Taylor and Foster 1986).

In general, research concerning race and gender differences in the quality of school experiences suggests that the relatively poor scholastic performance, negative attitudes, and high attrition rates of Black males are at least in part a function of the nature of their interactions and treatment in public schools. The implications of such a finding become apparent when viewed in the context of a finding reported in other studies: that limited or negative academic feedback to Black males is related to the tendency among these youth to lower their expectations, degrade their scholastic abilities, and substitute compensatory terms for positive self-regard and sense of achievement (Hunt and Hunt, 1977; Hare and Castenell, 1985, Irvine, 1990).

Whatever the mix and contribution of these factors to the underachievement and failure of Black males in public schools, the consequences are fewer employment possibilities, high rates of joblessness, and long-term limitations on economic and social mobility.

Black Males and Employment

Despite evidence of significant gains in their educational and occupational status during the past twenty years, the labor market position and employment problems of young Black males grew worse during this period, reaching what some analysts describe as "catastrophic" proportions in the 1980s. As recently as 1954 employment rates for young Black and white males were identical (52 percent in each case). By the early 1960s, 59 percent of Black males ages sixteen to twenty-four were employed, compared to 68 percent of white males in these age groups. The startling decline in the employment condition of young Black males between 1970 and 1985 is represented in table 11.1.

As these data reveal, the labor force participation rate of all Black males ages sixteen to twenty-four has declined from its level of twenty-five years ago, with only 44 percent of young Black males in 1985 employed, compared with 59 percent in 1962. In fact, nearly 60 percent of all sixteen to twenty-four-year-old Black men had no work experience at all in 1984 (U.S. Department of Labor 1986).

Thus, although they comprised only about 5 percent of the labor force in 1986, Black males accounted for nearly 12 percent of the 8 million unemployed, and 14 percent of the long-term unemployed (i.e., those without work for fifteen weeks or more). The jobless rate of Black male workers in 1986 remained more

Table 11.1   Black Male Employment, 1970 and 1985

	Percent Employed	
Age	1970	1985
18 and 19	51	36
20 to 24	77	60

Source: Richard B. Freeman, "Cutting Black Youth Unemployment," *New York Times*, July 20, 1986.

than twice the rate for white male workers (14.8 percent versus 6.0 percent). The unemployment rate for Black youth, especially males, remained the highest among all major groups. Black male youths made up 12 percent of all unemployed youth in 1987, about twice their share of the teenage labor force (National Urban League 1988). The employment crisis is particularly severe in the inner cities where, by some estimates, the jobless rate among Black youth approaches 60 percent. As Freeman and Holzer (1986) observed in their analysis of the youth unemployment crisis, the much-heralded problem of teenage joblessness is largely a crisis among inner-city Black youth: "In many respects, the urban unemployment characteristics of Third World countries appears to have taken root among Black youths in the United States" (p. 3).

Various analyses of the Black youth unemployment crisis identify the sources of the problem in deteriorating local economies and functional transformations in urban structures, increased job competition between Black youth and older women in the labor force, increases in minimum wage, discriminatory employer behavior, increased opportunities for criminal activities as alternative sources of employment and income, inadequate education, lack of marketable skills, and low motivation and/or aspiration on the part of Black youth (Kasarda 1989; Thomas and Scott 1979; Freeman 1986). Based on their analysis of extensive surveys and interviews of Black males, ages sixteen to nineteen, in the inner-city poverty areas of Boston, Philadelphia, and Chicago, Freeman and Holzer (1986) found "no single cause" of the decline in employment among these men. Rather, Freeman (1986) observes, "joblessness among young Black men is part-and-parcel of other social pathologies that go beyond the labor market, including youth crime, and drug and alcohol abuse, residual employer discrimination and performance on the job, particularly absenteeism" (p. 2F).

Yet, as Kasarda (1989) has shown, fundamental changes in the structure of city economies (from centers of goods processing to centers of information processing) during the past two decades have severely affected the employment prospects of disadvantaged urban Blacks, particularly males, with less than a high school education. According to Kasarda, "these structural changes led to a substantial reduction of lower-skilled jobs in traditional employing institutions that attracted and economically upgraded previous generations of urban Blacks" (p. 27). Such losses in employment opportunities, Kasarda concludes, have had "devastating effects on Black families, which further exacerbated the problems of the economically displaced" (p. 27). Indeed, between 1973 and 1986, the proportion of employed Black males eighteen to twenty-nine working in a manufacturing job declined by 43 percent, from 36 percent to 20 percent (Sum and Fogg 1989); and between 1970 and 1980, nearly a half million low-skill jobs left the cities of Boston, Chicago, Cleveland, Detroit, New York, and Philadelphia, while nearly 2 million new jobs were added to the suburbs (Kasarda, 1989). Thus, between 1973 and 1986, the average earnings of Black males eighteen to twenty-nine fell by 31 percent, from $10,778 to $7,447, compared to declines of

14 percent and 20 percent respectively, for white and Hispanic males of the same ages (Sum and Fogg 1989).

The consequences of the employment crisis among young Black males are summarized by Freeman (1986, 2F), who writes:

> Lacking skills and facing a desperate shortage of jobs with career prospects, many young Black men consider street life an attractive and rational alternative to the normal working world. Many have serious drug and drinking problems, and are deeply involved in crime . . . many more simply waste their youth hanging around street corners.

In short, conditions that prevent or make it difficult for young men to find work discourage them from trying to obtain economic independence and promote growing disaffection or alienation from society, contributing to a host of social problems and self-destructive behaviors (Taylor 1991).

Crime, Delinquency, and Substance Abuse

Blacks in general and Black males in particular are arrested, convicted, and incarcerated for criminal offenses at rates considerably higher than are whites (National Research Council 1989). Although Black men represent approximately 6 percent of the total population, they constitute nearly 50 percent of the inmates in local, state, and federal jails. The rate of incarceration of Black males was 1,581 per 100,000 population in 1985, compared with 252 per 100,000 for white males. In short, Black males were being imprisoned for criminal offenses at a rate six times the rate for white males. Among youth, Black males are disproportionately represented in arrest statistics on crime and delinquency. While Black youth constituted approximately 14 percent of all youths aged fifteen to nineteen in 1984, they were involved in 69 percent of the robbery arrests, 54 percent of the rape arrests, and 39 percent of the aggravated assaults attributable to persons under eighteen years of age (Federal Bureau of Investigation 1986). In fact, more than half of all arrests for violent crimes and a quarter of all property crimes reported in 1984 involved Black youths. By the time they reach age nineteen, one in six Black males will have been arrested.

Black males are not only more likely to be arrested for violent crimes but are more likely to be the victims of crimes as well. According to a recent report by the U.S. Department of Justice (1985), young Black males have the highest violence/victimization rate of all groups in the United States, including murder, robbery, and aggravated assault. Blacks in general are five times more likely than whites to be homicide victims, and the lifetime risk of being a homicide victim is far greater for Black males than for any other group: only 1 out of 179 white males is likely to be a homicide victim in his lifetime, compared to 1 in 30 Black males, 1 in 495 white females, and 1 in 132 Black females. In almost all cases of

Black male homicide, the offender is another Black male, a fact which in part accounts for the overrepresentation of Black males in correctional institutions. This pattern is true for most crimes of violence and for many property offenses as well (O'Brien 1987).

The overrepresentation of Black youths, especially males, in crime and delinquency has been attributed to a variety of factors, including bias on the part of law enforcement agencies in the treatment and/or disposition of cases involving young Blacks; high rates of joblessness, poverty, and welfare dependency among these youths and their families in inner cities; and a "subculture of violence" created by these conditions, which fosters high levels of interpersonal violence, including homicide (Freeman and Holzer 1985; National Research Council 1989). In addition, the sharp rise in "crack," a form of cocaine, and other drugs in Black communities has contributed to a marked increase in individual and gang violence and crime among Black males during the past decade, with the wider distribution of handguns among Black youth identified as a major contributing factor in the rise of mortality from homicide (National Center for Health Statistics 1989).

The disproportionate involvement of Black males in the criminal justice system entails a variety of costs to these men themselves and to Black communities. For adolescents, arrest and conviction result in "severe limitations on their educational and occupational opportunities . . . creating a vicious cycle of delinquency, incarceration, recidivism, and chronic criminal careers, or unemployment and marginal social adaptation in adulthood" (Gibbs 1984, 9). Moreover, as Hill (1988) observes, the high rates of Black male involvement in crime contribute to the rise in female-headed households. Criminal offenders are less available as marriage partners because "their police records are major barriers to legitimate employment; their low educational skills preclude them from all but the most menial jobs; their periodic court appearances prevent them from obtaining or maintaining steady work, and incarceration at faraway prison facilities keeps them from their wives, girlfriends and children for long periods of time" (p. 12). Finally, the high rate of crime in inner cities drains the limited economic resources of these communities and deters the expansion or location of business enterprises within their neighborhoods, thus accelerating the spread of joblessness, poverty, and other social problems (National Research Council 1989).

Poverty

The growth and concentration of poverty in inner-city communities during the past two decades are perhaps key to understanding some of the changes in other measures of socioeconomic well-being among Black males, since poverty has long been shown to have adverse affects on educational attainment (Rumberger 1983) and employment opportunities (Freeman 1978), and to be positively associated with crime and delinquency (Freeman and Holzer 1985), family disruption (Wilson 1987), and teenage pregnancy (Hogan and Kitagawa, 1985).

In their assessment of poverty in the inner cities, Wacquant and Wilson (1989) conclude that "the urban black poor of today differ both from their counterparts of earlier years and from the white poor in that they are becoming increasingly concentrated in dilapidated territorial enclaves that epitomize acute social and economic marginalization" (p. 9). More specifically, as Wacquant and Wilson have shown, the 1970s saw substantial growth in the proportion of all poor Blacks residing in extreme poverty areas (i.e., census tracts with a poverty population of 40 percent or more). By 1980, "fully 30 percent of all poor blacks in the 10 largest American cities lived in extreme poverty tracts, contrasted with 22 percent a decade before, and with only 6 percent of poor non-Hispanic whites" (p. 10). Hence, as Testa has argued, "simple comparisons between poor whites and poor blacks would be confronted with the fact that poor whites reside in areas that are ecologically and economically very different from poor blacks. Any observed relationship involving race would reflect, to some unknown degree, the relatively superior ecological niche many poor whites occupy with respect to jobs, marriage opportunities, and exposure to conventional role models" (quoted in Wilson 1987, 58).

In recent decades, many inner-city communities have experienced sharp increases in the percentage of poor families, rapid exodus in record numbers of working and middle-income Black families, near collapse of local economies and community institutions, and high levels of unemployment. Moreover, the majority of households in many inner-city neighborhoods are headed by women who are economically worse off than other poor families and are more dependent on public assistance to support their children. In short, the increasing social and spatial concentration of poverty in the inner cities of this country, and the growing predominance of social ills long associated with poverty—family dissolution, school failure, drugs, violent crimes, housing deterioration—have qualitatively and quantitatively altered the psychosocial as well as the material foundations of life for most of their inhabitants, accelerating the process of economic marginality and social isolation (Wilson 1987).

These developments have affected young Black males in the inner cities in a variety of ways. Widespread joblessness, welfare dependency, and social isolation from mainstream institutions have not only deprived many of these young men of opportunities to acquire essential work experience for gainful employment and eventual self-sufficiency, but have discouraged them from marrying and forming families (Testa et al. 1989). In fact, marriage rates of young Black males are at an all-time low. In 1980, for example, 79 percent of Black males, aged 20 to 24, were "never married." By 1989, the percentage increased to 85 percent, compared with 76 percent for white males of the same age (U.S. Bureau of the Census 1990). The percentage of married young Black males was considerably higher in 1960, when 56 percent of young Black males were "never married." As Wilson (1987) and others (Testa et al. 1989) have shown, the sharp rise in Black female-headed families in the inner cities is directly related to increasing Black male joblessness rather than to the availability of welfare to single mothers. Moreover, when joblessness is combined with high Black male mortality and incarceration rates, the proportion of Black men, particularly young men, who are in a position to support a family is significantly diminished. As a result, "Black women, especially young Black women, are facing a shrinking pool of 'marriageable' (i.e., economically stable) men" (Wilson 1987, 91).

The existence of large enclaves of young male adults in the inner cities, mired in poverty and a predatory subculture, without adequate education, marketable skills, or opportunities for earning legitimate incomes, constitutes a genuine crisis in Black communities and a major challenge (and threat) for the larger society.

Breaking the Cycle of Disadvantage

In his appraisal of social policy in the last thirty years, Charles Murray (1984) concludes that government programs designed to eradicate poverty and improve the conditions of life for the poor during this period succeeded in doing more harm than good for their would-be beneficiaries. He contends that increases in unemployment, crime, illegitimacy, female-headed households, and welfare dependency during the past two decades are a direct result of changes that social policy made in the incentive structures (i.e., the rewards and penalties, carrots and sticks) that govern human behavior. The effect of such policy changes, in his view, was to "reward failure and punish success." As he puts it, "once it was assumed that the system is to blame when a person is chronically out of work and that the system is even to blame when a person neglects spouse and family, then moral distinctions were eroded" (p. 180). Among the first casualties of the new emphasis in social policy, Murray notes, was the "moral approbation associated with self-sufficiency," together with the withdrawal of status and support from impoverished but responsible families who struggled to remain self-reliant. The shift in social policy directions, he argues, has been especially disastrous for Black youth, whose values are more plastic than those of their elders, and who tend to respond more quickly to changes in the incentive structure. Thus, it is not surprising that under the new social policy Black youth, particularly males, found it far easier to steal than to work, to survive without the benefit of schooling, to secure drugs to support a drug habit and life-style, and to father children without the benefit of marriage.

If such self-destructive behaviors are to be diminished, Murray argues, the current imbalance between rewards and penalties that inspired them must be redressed, and disadvantaged youth taught the facts of life. "There is this truth," he writes:

The tangible incentives that any society can realistically hold out to the poor youth of average abilities and average industriousness are mostly penalties, mostly disincentives: "Do not study, and we will throw you out; commit crimes, and we will put you in jail; do not work and we will make sure that your existence is so uncomfortable that any job will be preferable to it." To promise more is fraud. (1984, 177)

Perhaps. But Black youth and the underclass are a diverse lot only a small proportion of whom (by some estimates) may be incapable, owing to a combination of behavioral, attitudinal, and environmental factors, of responding to the more positive incentives encompassed by well-conceived social programs designed to increase their level of competence and self-sufficiency through training and legitimate employment opportunities (Taylor 1991). Indeed, as the results from national experiments conducted by the Manpower Demonstration Research Corporation (MDRC) have shown, even among that segment of the underclass hardest to reach, namely, ex-convicts, ex-addicts, school dropouts, delinquent youths, and long-term welfare recipients, the carrot of opportunity is apparently more productive of positive results than the stick of deprivation (Manpower Demonstration Research Corporation 1983; Taylor 1990). But the MDRC experience also revealed the structural and behavioral complexities of the problem which neither liberal nor conservative analyses and policy prescriptions adequately address.

To begin with, the problems of Black males are *cumulative problems* resulting from a complex constellation of mutually reinforcing factors. "Failure to appreciate this reality," as Ray Marshall (1988) correctly observes, "often causes policymakers, the media, and even scholars who should know better to analyze problems such as dropping out of school, teenage pregnancy, high crime rates, unemployment or unemployability as unitary problems with single solutions such as 'better education' or a 'willingness to work' " (p. xiii). Thus any social policy initiative or program intervention that seeks to redress the problems of Black males must focus on the larger social and economic contexts that impact the lives of Black families and shape the environments in which these young men grow up.

In an effort to break the cycle of disadvantage and improve the prospects of young Black males, particularly those in the inner cities, some analysts suggest focusing on the family as the critical point of intervention (Gilder 1981). To be sure, the family is an important starting point in addressing *some* of the problems of Black males, since it is within the family that children and youth learn many of the attitudes and behaviors that shape their lives and program them for success or failure in the larger society. Yet, the structure and functioning of families are greatly influenced by what Ogbu (1985) refers to as the "effective environment" (i.e., level of community resources and knowledge of and degree of access to the economic system) in which they are embedded. For poor families, effective environments are often characterized by widespread joblessness and economic insecurity, physical deterioration and inadequate services, low-quality education and dangerous public schools, which put their children at high risk of exposure to family discord and instability, malnutrition and abuse, drugs, crime, and other social problems associated with material deprivation.

In fact, as Schorr (1988) has noted, persistent and highly concentrated poverty "virtually guarantee the presence of a vast collection of risk factors and their continuing destructive impact over time" (p. 30). For example,

> The child in a poor family who is malnourished and living in an unheated apartment is more susceptible to ear infection; once the ear infection takes hold, inaccessible or inattentive health care may mean it will not be properly treated; hearing loss in the midst of economic stress may go undetected at home, in day care, and by the health system; undetected hearing loss will do long-term damage to a child who needs all the help he can get to cope with a world more complicated than the world of most middle-class children. When this child enters school, his chances of being in an overcrowded classroom with an overwhelmed teacher further compromise his chances of successful learning. Thus risk factors join to shorten the odds of favorable long-term outcomes. (P. 30)

Thus, in order to diminish the high risk of destructive outcomes poor Black males (and females) experience during adulthood, one must focus on the "ecologies of deprivation" to which these youths and their families are exposed. One can reduce the risk to Black children and youth of infant mortality, congenital handicaps, and preventable disease through program interventions that increase their access to broader, enriched, and more effective forms of prenatal care and health services. Similarly, the risk to Black children of malnutrition, neglect, and abuse can be diminished through interventions of flexible, intensive, and comprehensive social and family support services. In combination with health and family support services, greatly expanded preschool programs like Head Start and elementary schools reorganized to better respond to a range of needs of high-risk children and their families can reduce risk of early school failure and related problems (Schorr 1988).

In short, as a number of studies have shown (Rutter 1980; Werner 1982), it is not necessary to eliminate all of the risk factors to which poor children and youth are exposed in order to diminish the destructive outcomes they experience in adulthood. School failure, juvenile crime, drug use and abuse, unwed teenage pregnancy and early parenthood are not the results of a single risk factor, such as being reared in an impoverished single-parent household, but are the products of multiple and interacting risk factors. Premature birth, poor health and nutrition, child abuse, family discord, and the social and economic conditions that are causal to these patterns are all implicated in the production of damaging outcomes for Black males and females, with each multiplying the destructive effects of the others (Taylor 1991). Thus, as Schorr has argued,

It will make a difference if we can reduce the incidence of low birthweight or vision defects, if the isolated mother is helped to respond to her difficult infant, if more children come to school better prepared to succeed in mastering fundamental academic skills, and have reason to look forward to a better future. It will be of value if we can eliminate one risk factor or two, even if others remain. (1988, 28–29)

Although a public policy aimed at reinforcing poor Black families is an essential step toward improvement in the status of Black males, so too are efforts to enhance their employment prospects. While many federally sponsored employment and training programs launched during the 1960s and 1970s were plagued by a variety of administrative, political, and organizational problems, the effectiveness of some of these programs in improving the long-term employment prospects and life chances of disadvantaged Black males has been well documented (Hahn and Lerman 1985; Taylor 1990).

Under these programs, thousands of young Black men received remedial assistance and work experience which enabled them to earn their first steady incomes and to become acquainted with the world of work. As the employment crisis among inner-city Black male youths deepens across the country, such programs may play a decidedly more important role in helping to reduce high levels of joblessness, crime, school truancy, and early parenthood among these men, provided such programs effectively address their personal and educational, as well as their employment needs. Since most of these problems are concentrated among a relatively small subset of young Black males residing in the fifteen to twenty largest U.S. cities (Smith et al. 1987), "a major infusion of resources should be directed to a target group of cities that house these large pools of needy youths . . . the intent would be to build a full program infrastructure at a level of services far closer to the level of need than available resources now permit" (p. 44). In the absence of such a concentrated programing strategy, it is unlikely that the employment or earning prospects of Black males will substantially improve.

In the final analysis, a service strategy must be supplemented with or replaced by an employment strategy designed to create plentiful job opportunities for all if Black males are to find useful and productive roles in a society whose economic institutions are undergoing rapid change. For without the latter, no amount of remediation, employment training, or other social services is likely to improve the job prospects and life chances of Black males. Hence, the key to breaking the cycle of disadvantage among Black males is a federal social policy that seeks to address the employment and familial needs of these men. Indeed, an emphasis on the former may make it less necessary to deal with the problems associated with the latter.

CHAPTER 12

Racial Group Dynamics: Implications for Rearing Black Males

by Chester M. Pierce and Wesley E. Profit

There is a need for theories by Blacks to be tested in research on the Black family, especially about child-rearing practices. Black researchers should examine child-rearing practices to ascertain the ways in which Black children are being prepared to meet the challenge of living in the twenty-first century in America. The theories and research efforts of Blacks should help to illuminate the strengths and weaknesses of the Black family. Greater knowledge of this area will help to facilitate the discovery of better ways to mold and shape Black children for a more hope-filled future based on changing demographics of increased general longevity and increased numbers of colored people. Modification of existing child-rearing practices may prove highly beneficial to the Black community in terms of improving the level of group cohesion and solidarity, while also reducing the incidence of mental illness. Pivotal to any effort in this area is a conceptual model of Black child rearing that is based on quantitative data. The model should promote a greater awareness of those factors that specify indigenousness for Blacks.

The authors completed a study of differences in group problem-solving behavior of Black and white males and females. Graphic, striking, and statistically significant differences were found in the behavior of group members when a problem was kept constant while composition of the group was varied by race and sex. Consideration of the results helped lead us to the belief that the child-rearing practices of Blacks must be very different from those of whites. This paper presents some relevant results from this study of racial group dynamics and what these results imply about rearing Black males. A brief description of the research is warranted prior to presenting the results.

Cohorts of four people, ages eighteen to twenty, some of whom were parents, all without college education and strangers to each other, were given a common problem to solve. They had thirty minutes to decide among themselves how to give away $50 in a legal manner, without keeping it or spending it on themselves. Eighteen groups were videotaped solving this problem. Six groups were all-Black, six groups were all-white, and six groups were composed of Blacks and whites. Of the eighteen groups three groups were composed of all Black males, three were all white males, three were all Black females, and three were all white females. In addition there were also three groups each composed of two Black males, two white males and three groups composed of two Black females and two white females. Interjudgmental reliability on all coded data about a host of verbal and nonverbal measures was at least 90 percent. Chi-square and t-tests were utilized with a significance level set at .05 or better.

The data from this study show clearly and unmistakably that whites behave differently in the presence of Blacks than they do in the presence of other whites. Furthermore, the same can be said of Blacks. Thus the belief, which

Supported by Office of Naval Research Grant # N00014-75-C-0914. The opinions presented in this paper do not represent official views or official endorsement by the U.S. Navy.

frequently appears in the literature, that heteroracial groups are similar to homoracial groups is wrong (Profit 1977).

In thinking about why these differences might obtain, the authors presumed that behavior expressed in the general group situation with respect to problem solving would reflect what the person would do in the parenting situation. For instance, we would think that a young woman who was obsessive about recording all of her cohort's suggestions concerning how to dispose of the money would display a similar obsessiveness in her child rearing. Our chief objective is to present some findings that we think are most teachable to parents or potential parents of Black boys. Some of the lessons may seem obvious. All are chosen because they are derived from experiments reflecting common daily experience and they are teachable.

Black Parent-Child Interactions

Teach the Child That Whites When by Themselves Act Differently

This truism may be obvious, but usually Blacks cannot articulate or describe exactly how whites differ when they are in contact with Blacks. Of utmost importance is the fact that most Blacks are also unable to specify exactly how Blacks differ in front of whites. Therefore, in fact, most Blacks are unable to itemize the features of their lives that constitute racial indigenism and racial discrimination. Our studies help clarify some of these features, which could be passed on to Black children.

White men by themselves will use many suggestions in the negative form, for example, "Can't we do . . ." In front of Blacks, they essentially will not reveal that behavior. By themselves, as compared to being in front of Blacks, this behavior is used at a level of significance that could occur only 8 times in 10,000 by pure chance. Thus the behavior of negative suggestions is deliberately filtered from Blacks. This means white males do not tend to reveal weakness, inferiority, uncertainty, or anxiety in front of Black males. White males and white females offer many other differences in front of Blacks. Naturally a Black never knows that this is distinctive behavior, for he or she is never privy to an all-white group—that is, the presence of a single Black transforms the nonmixed group into a mixed racial group. A Black would not know that white men use fewer words in the presence of Blacks or that white females seem practiced in getting Blacks to say less than flattering things about themselves. Even nonverbal behavior or, perhaps more accurately, especially nonverbal behavior is very different. For instance, white men in the presence of Black men spend many more seconds covering their genitalia than when they are by themselves. We recommend to young Black parents or future parents to teach their children that white behavior differs whenever a Black is present. Further, the Black groups' behavior also differs whenever a white is present.

Teach the Child Not to Overdisclose about Himself

One of the most statistically significant ways Blacks act in white groups is their willingness to share and overexpose information gratuitously. For instance in our study a Black youth, in front of strangers, and in front of a videotape camera, gratuitiously volunteered details of felonious behavior in which he had engaged. There was no need for this confession. Grisly damage might have ensued.

In terms of the definition of our study the quantitative fact was that Black men voluntarily and unnecessarily revealed damaging things about themselves. We believe this behavior can and must be remedied. We suggest that parents focus on this aspect of child rearing. Blacks need not discuss illegal behavior, drug abuse, or facititious events.

One ramification of this factor of overdisclosure by Blacks, in both heteroracial and homoracial settings, is that it may promote excessive reliance on rhetoric and fabrication as the basis for group action or inaction. Regrettably, as inhabitants of extreme mundane environments, Blacks already are handicapped by laboring with insufficient, partial, tardy, delayed and fractionated information (Pierce 1975). When these communication ills are grafted onto the misinformation, distorted information, and audaciously excessive information occasioned by overdisclosure, Blacks may seriously handicap themselves.

Therefore children must be taught to be more discriminating and cagey in what they choose to share with others. In addition children must be shown appropriate places and times where free interchange is useful and needed. It seems especially important to exert some self-censorship as well as group control of levity and publicity in the presence of whites. To fail to do this renders us vulnerable in unnecessary ways, such as diluting the pressure of a petition or appearing overly accommodating and ingratiating, or losing the edge of surprise. We must not collaborate in our degradation in the service of astounding or entertaining or placating whites.

Teach the Child to Look for More Options

The quality of idea in donating money did not seem to vary in mixed or unmixed racial settings. Thus, in three minutes Blacks might suggest a gift to the Red Cross, whereas whites took thirty minutes to decide on a gift to CARE. However, Blacks compared to whites seemed much less prone to look for many moves and opportunities. They spent less time in search of possibilities. This inability to search for alternative possibilities did not seem to reflect a sluggishness of mind but rather a feeling of limitation and resignation about seizing one's destiny. In fact, it is remarkable that the end result was comparable despite such limited examination of the issue. Many pros and cons can be listed about this type of rapid thinkıng. At minimum it suggests the compelling need to capitalize on, as well as to understand, situations where Blacks think much faster than whites.

Parents and teachers of Blacks must do all they can to get Black children to exert options and look for many ways to solve a problem and perhaps to be leisurely and careful as they do so. Perhaps at the base of this issue would be the lack of hope felt by many Blacks. Communicating rigidity and limitation of possibilities to children might be the understandable consequence of lack of hope and an abundance of harsh reality in the lives of Black adults. A solution would involve some confrontation by adults with the unyielding truth that, in order to help descendants, many Black adults may have to live with only a modicum of satisfaction in order to give more to their offspring. Of course, shorn of optimism and goal direction, this situation describes the present plight of most Black parents. Perhaps the difference is that most have not truly recognized, accepted, and incorporated the unhappy likelihood that only immense sacrifice can lead to immense future progress. Even so, the requirement to provide hope when one's own life is scarce in that commodity remains the most elusive of all problems facing the Black parent or potential parent.

Teach the Child to Have More Nonverbal Awareness

It is our view that most racism manifests itself by nonverbal means: "kinetic racism." Because of her presumed superiority of skin color, the clerk disparagingly throws back change to a Black shopper, or a white man waits for a Black man to open a door for him at the airport, or a white audience smiles with ineluctable satisfaction during a play in which a Black man is beating a Black woman.

Almost always, racism in the United States works by putting Blacks on the defensive through microaggressive and/or kinetic racist behavior. Kinetic racism often operates through stunning, cumulative microaggressions delivered as an offense and in an offensive manner to Blacks. The Black remains on the defense. The Black replies, defers, responds, and reacts to the whites' offense mechanisms—for example, he opens the door at the airport, she stalks quietly out of the store, he laughs along with the white playgoer. None of these offensive mechanisms succeed unless Blacks permit or even encourage manipulation of their own time, space, energy, and mobility.

The Black parent must teach his child how and when to take the offense and how and when to counter an offense. In our study Blacks would lean over (using time, space, energy, and mobility) to request, deferentially and defensively, whether a white would accept the Black's suggestion on how to dispose of the money. The nonverbal behavior, in which the white nodded assent, aggravated the Black's tentative position. Simultaneously it verified the white man's hegemony (as decision maker) and the Black man's lack of confidence and esteem (as pleader). In this experimental situation the Blacks could be seen by

Black and white participants as a co-equal. Nevertheless, Blacks awarded decision making to whites without need to do so and without contest. By postural
obsequiousness and hesitancy the Black invited the white to take responsibility
and to make a resolution, regardless of the merit of the idea, in a situation of
overall equality.

The parent must teach how nonverbal posturings, such as deferential
use of time, space, and energy, direct, persuade, and sustain one's thought and
speech. For Blacks this may be more important than the current faddish considerations in "body language" which emphasize how thoughts are reflected in
the body.

We found too that Black women use fewer words than white women. We
wonder if Blacks are reared both with more sensitivity to the nonverbal and with
more concentrated, parsimonious verbalizations. In view of the much greater
survival importance of understanding nonverbal language compared to verbal
language, it would not be surprising if Black child rearing entailed more focus on
nonverbal communications. Nor would it be surprising, given the despair and
frustration in the lives of Black parents, if they resorted to a greater percentage
of angry communications.

Similarly, it is not surprising that Blacks statistically dwelled more on such
nonverbal aspects of life-style as clothing. In another paper we will elaborate our
theory on the meaning of clothes to the Black and how it relates to a competitive
struggle between white females and Black females. It is in female-to-female
competition that we believe most of the racism in the society is generated and
continued. Perhaps one of the greatest research needs in race relations is to discover more about the origins of racial attitudes in white female children, who are
destined to become the true bearers of American culture. As in all race relations
research, a chief deficiency to overcome is to get more balanced views by having
more whites as experimental subjects for Black investigators; nearly all the literature is based on white experimentation on Black subjects. Suffice it to say at
this time that Black males, who statistically talk more about clothes than any
other group, are in many ways the recipients of tremendous indulgence from
their women. Amongst these indulgences is the Black woman's willingness and
insistence that her man be well groomed. In this sense men are "pets" of strong,
independent females. White females, who as a group have less independence
and a different racial strategy, do not shape the sartorial habits of their men in
the same fashion. Their verbal focus on men's clothes is not as insistent as
Blacks'.

Teach the Child to Feel Needed

It is statistically overwhelming that Black men talk about their mothers.
Serious reflection on this finding led us to interpretations revolving around the
difference between feeling wanted and feeling needed.

The indulgence given Black males by Black females might make them feel wanted. However, this is insufficient to ameliorate problems that result from racial hostility. Perhaps universally men must feel needed. We theorize that much of the preoccupation and behavior reported in our investigation demonstrated that the Black male's efforts to please mother were aimed at feeling needed.

Black females, expecting relatively little help from Black males, have made men feel wanted but perhaps not needed. Economically, even for a "welfare mother," a man is not needed though he may be wanted. More ominously, biologically, Black men are not even needed to produce Black babies. That is, a Black woman mated to any color of man will produce a baby who is Black, especially as regards the social attributes the child will be assigned by American society.

As this awesome reality becomes obvious to coming generations, it will have a material impact on Black courtship, marital life, and child rearing. At present America is heading toward having a nonwhite majority in the twenty-first century. Black female children are growing up with the model of women who indulge but don't need men. There may be increasing bitterness as well as competition over available men. Black female children could also feel augmented confidence about their own ability and independence and usefulness vis-à-vis Black men. For the future Black family, the consequences could be tragic.

On the other hand the Black male child, under similar modeling, must suffer anxiety as well as lack of self-esteem. The functional defeatism inherent in this pattern of male-female interaction can be regarded from the vantage point of still another research finding. Before discussing it, however, parents and potential parents must be reminded that repetitive, simple tasks can be found and given to a Black male child in such a way as to make him feel needed and wanted. This may be the paramount parenting objective that could be most easily negotiated without benefit of money or resources. From the child's earliest infancy, these attitudinal communications and behavioral tasks should be a part of every parent's armamentarium.

As an example of what parents could do in this situation, we submit that Black males could be given numerous, planned modules of rapidly progressive responsibility. These assignments would have to be backed by appropriate authority and commensurate with the boy's age, interests, and motor skills. The parent should communicate to the child that the duties are serious, essential, and helpful. Further he should be aware of exercising near complete dominion over the subject and of working without fear of failure or degradation. The results of his work preferably should be tangible, visible, and of benefit to all members of the household unit. The parents, in helping the boy achieve control over such a module, which we dub a Black space/time/energy/movement module, must be willing to relinquish time, space, energy, and mobility to the child. It is important also that the adult must communicate that the module is indeed something that can be done—and that the youth might find even better ways of doing it.

For instance, it is psychologically important for Black boys to understand how to conserve energy (life). In addition, philosophically, Blacks must conserve energy in the effort to help move the world toward peace and supranationalism. Utilizing these views in a longitudinal psychosexual development scheme, a parent might start by asking a toddler to be responsible for indicating when lights and other electrical sources should be turned on or turned off. By pre-school age, the boy should have the responsibility and authority to turn off lights in an effort to conserve family exchequer. As a school-age youth, he could have general responsibility for seeing the bills were paid, for example, watching the check being written and/or carrying the payment to the proper place or worrying about how it can be paid. The family unit should respond to his feedback suggestions for what could be done.

If listened to carefully and if solicited to help in family management of the budget, the boy could gain valuable insights into energy conservation, with all the potential such insight would hold for psychological and philosophical sophistication for Blacks. Innumerable spinoffs such as some familiarity and confidence with budgeting, resource development, and waste control; sensitivity about different demands; concerns about balancing generosity with reality; and understanding of the fear of darkness would be bonus advantages. Such ideas as this are consonant with the research finding that of all tested groups, Black males, when alone, statistically differed by having *more* talk about families. Black male preoccupation with families should be marshalled for its positive potential in racial dynamics.

Parents could make up deliberate, longitudinal, and highly individualized and interrelated sets of space/time/energy/mobility modules. The use of such modules might contribute to strengthening the Black future. The more any individual commands or regains control of space, time, energy, and mobility, the less that person is oppressed or stressed.

Teach the Child to Think of What Can Be Done

This suggestion relates to earlier ones. However, it is presented in terms of the study. It is of statistical significance that Blacks talk more about race. It may be in fact that Blacks should be taught to talk less about race. Or at least when race is talked about, it should be discussed in terms of "what can be done" rather than the more commonplace "what can't be done," as happened in the experiment. In our observations, no matter what is under discussion, Blacks quickly go to the issue of race and immediately are bound by considerations of what can't be done. In contrast it is statistically significant that white males in considering the experimental problem spent much effort examining ways to circumvent the imposed legal proscriptions, even though their final decision met the restrictions of the exercise.

Thus, Blacks are curbed almost immediately by negative, defeatist, demoralized, and less imaginative verbalizations. Therefore it is of extreme importance for Blacks to teach children, when thinking of race, to cogitate always about what can be done to help us. We must banish thinking about what can't be done. "What can't be done" is typical of the most negative aspects of defensive thinking, which whites have been happy to have Blacks accept and perpetuate.

Related to this sort of negative thinking is the concept of inhibited venturesomeness. On our tapes a Black male describes to his peers an interaction with a white policeman. This description is filled with boldness, flamboyance, and bravado on the part of the narrator. However, in actuality, the adventure was probably considerably blunted or inhibited when the speaker talked to the policeman. Therefore at the moment of occurrence the actor was inhibited in his venturesomeness. Later, with the safety of time and space, he is much more expansive, confident—and misleading about the event.

In order to recover from being demeaned and to dilute the unsavoriness of real-life experiences, the Black may overinflate and overdisclose. Perhaps most inhibited venturesomeness is secondary to contacts with whites, which reinforce for Blacks what can't be done.

We believe that Blacks need to encourage children to be adventurous but not to show inhibited venturesomeness. In the ghetto, the latter concept may relate to the word *pirate* from the Greek πειρατή's. This is a person who *attempts* adventurous raids. The risks pirates accepted rather than the immorality of these raids deterred people of more common courage. Thus, the boldness, not the badness, is what enthralled people about pirates. In this way the ghetto community gets assurance, of a fallacious sort, that there are powerful individuals ready, able, and willing to wrestle with adversity. We need to ostracize pirates from our communities and replace them by adventurers. Parents should remember that great adventures—again, without need for resource or outside help—can take place in the very young child's mind. He must be encouraged to be limitless in his undertakings. This also would help to give confidence and hope. Then as opportunities to dare, without piracy or destruction to self or community, are presented to older children, they would be more able to take advantage of such situations. In this way perhaps we may get more Black men brazen enough to venture into competition in areas such as academia, business, and engineering. Parents at the minimum must not thwart hope. At the maximum they must encourage the child to believe that anything can be done, that all problems have solutions which await only dedication, resource deployment, and energy.

The Black boy, perhaps unlike the mainstream youngster, must be motivated by attention to life-style possibilities and advantages prior to the consideration of cognitive preparation for a given life task. For example the child is told all about the good life of an astronaut as seduction to get him to study arithmetic. It is more difficult for the Black boy to do arithmetic first and then be told he can be an astronaut.

The Black boy must be cunning and limitless as he considers options, imagines situations, and fantasizes success in a hostile society in which by analogy he is often a prisoner of war, assigned indefinitely to the ghetto prison. Such options about what can be done are similar to those needed by prisoners of war. Options must be tempered with large doses of knowing what difficulties to expect and how to be undeterred by animosity. Overall the child should believe something always can be done, with proper expenditure of effort, including that needed to overcome racism, which is inherent in almost all situations. Thus the boy can be urged to achieve in areas traditional to Blacks, such as entertainment, athletics, or certain learned professions, and also in positions now untraditional for Blacks.

Parents in the next couple of decades must provide more ingredients so that the child's imagination can range through nontraditional areas. For instance a child can be encouraged in the dream that he can control the weather. Someday perhaps the boy may find ways to energize such dreams into the reality of a career in oceanographic micropaleoclimatology. In this way the person could contribute to the possibility of controlling the weather.

Teach the Child That He Will Live Longer

In our studies whites talked of death with statistical significance. Blacks did not. Perhaps this reflects the demographic situation that Blacks will not live as long as whites, and that Blacks have, on the whole, a greater struggle to survive the here and now without the luxury to speculate about the doom of death. Blacks also, by force of demographic and social lessons, may feel more familiar with, and perhaps more accepting of, death.

We think the Black view of life will change as more Blacks live longer and live better. This will have much impact on the Black future. It will mean at least more consideration of job satisfaction, making long-range community and family plans for the Black future, and saving enough money to retire.

All this may seem pointless when there are such horrendous demographic odds tearing at the Black family. Yet, our view, in terms of teaching hope and options, demands that we present the need to prepare our children for the likelihood of their increased longevity in a world that is rapidly graying and browning and being assaulted by human perturbations to the environment.

For purposes of completion however we would like to end by setting forth some demographic possibilities that must be included in any consideration of the Black family as it deals with Black boys.

Consider that the general population at present has a relative shortage of males between eighteen and forty. For Black women the supply of men is reduced further by the relatively large percentage of men who are in the military or in jail (more young Black men are in jail than in college). The available pool of "choice" men is further reduced by the great unemployment of Blacks (50 percent of some age cohorts in urban areas) or underemployment. The problem is intensified by the fact that relative to white women, Black women are more likely to be educated compared to their men. Issues of AIDS, drug abuse, homicidal violence, and shifts in mothering patterns and childrearing, secondary to increased teenage pregnancy, all compound the demographic impact on the Black future.

The facts don't begin to speak to matters of life-style or psychology. At any rate those interested in the Black family must consider the impact of all these conditions on the way Black men and women will view each other and interact with each other as well as with whites as they continue to define and refine their indigenism.

Conclusion

This chapter has attempted to present some lessons for parenting by Blacks. It is based on observations and data made on young Blacks and whites in a study of group dynamics. It is concerned with the importance of the future of Black males. It calls attention particularly to the need to discover more about specific thinking and behavior.

CHAPTER 13

Intervention Research Methods and the Empowerment of Black Males

by Fabricio E. Balcazar, Yolanda Suarez-Balcazar, and Stephen B. Fawcett

The portrait of young black males in American society is grim. Schools have failed them, so they have dropped out or been pushed out. Without education or skills, employers have rejected them or consigned them to menial dead-end jobs. Without jobs and legitimate income, they have gravitated to the illegitimate world of drugs and delinquency. Without security and stability, they have been unwilling or unable to assume family responsibilities for the children they father.

—Gibbs, 1988, 317

Societal exploitation, bigotry, and neglect have created conditions in which the dream of a good family and a decent job eludes most Black men. The American educational system has consistently failed to offer Black youths the necessary preparation to compete for meaningful, well-paying jobs, and the American labor market has allowed discriminatory hiring and job promotion practices to persist. The plight of African-American men in America is a national tragedy requiring immediate and direct action.

Unfortunately, no simple solutions to these complex problems exist. A combination of direct governmental intervention through policy changes and funding actions as well as legal remedies must occur. In a discussion of the current status of Black men in North America, Gary (1981) concluded that research is crucial for the development of innovative strategies to improve their quality of life. The relevance of research is underscored by repeated instances in which research findings have called the attention of policymakers and the general public to the supposed "negative inherent deficits" of Blacks (Hall 1981).

A radical departure from traditional research practices, however, might be required now. An action-oriented, problem-solving research model that contributes, not only to the study of complex social issues, but also to developing innovative solutions is proposed here. This model calls for involving Black males—and other community members—in efforts to address their own problems. Researchers and practitioners might join with participants in designing interventions that can facilitate personal goal attainment. Such research pursues a goal of empowerment (Fawcett, Seekins et al. 1984; Rappaport 1984), which increases control by groups over consequences that are important to them and their communities. Community-intervention research should enable participants—Black males, in this case—to empower themselves and other community members.

Within the traditional research community, however, intervention research at the present time is not well accepted. It is sometimes equated with activism, and it is also in conflict with the notion that the only legitimate function of research is to prove or disprove theory. The goal of a community-intervention research model is to assist community members in identifying their own problems and to enable them to design their own solutions (Serrano-Garcia

This chapter was supported in part by grant # G0085C3502 from the National Institute on Disability and Rehabilitation Research (NIDRR) to the Research and Training Center on Independent Living at the University of Kansas.

1984). Three guiding questions are useful in this process: (1) Will the research effort enhance the quality of life within a particular community? (2) Will research participants be able to use social interventions and teach others in dissemination efforts? (3) Will community members be able and willing to maintain the social intervention on their own? (Fawcett 1989).

Strategies to promote community organizing, consumer involvement, and leadership development are just a few examples of the types of research that can significantly improve the odds that young Black men can "make it" in this society. Such research could be centered on the change process of participating communities. Yet, our recent review of the psychological research literature conducted with Blacks in areas such as empowerment, advocacy, self-help, mentoring, and social support suggests that Black women are taking the lead as participants in self-help efforts. Examples include projects designed to promote use of self-help groups for Black women's stress (Mays 1985), evaluate a group approach to promote empowerment in young women who are low income (Parsons 1988), promote career counseling for black women (Obleton 1984), and evaluate support networks of low-income women (Ball 1983; Malson 1982). Hall (1981) noted that the majority of studies of African-Americans concentrated on the black family and black women, concluding that the academic literature relegated black men to the position of either villains or phantoms.

This chapter first outlines a method of community-intervention research (Fawcett, Suarez-Balcazar et al., in press) that applied researchers can use to help Black males and other minorities develop the capacity to gain some degree of control over their own environments. A case study is then used to illustrate the research and development process. Details of the experimental procedures used in this case study are described elsewhere (Balcazar, Majors et al. 1991). This study was part of an innovative mentoring project sponsored by an inner-city settlement house. The research model is discussed in terms of its applicability to designing empowering strategies.

A Model of Community-Intervention Research

Community-intervention research should contribute to our understanding of variables that affect attainment of goals—including those of African-American men—and should inform actions designed to address problems important to Black males and their communities. Such research should attempt to provide information on the functional relationships between modifiable environmental variables and behaviors critical to goal attainment (Balcazar, Fawcett, and Seekins 1991).

The emphasis on examining environmental variables and their influence on people's behavior constitutes a departure from more traditional approaches that focus on the cognitive processes of individuals. Many examples of such research could be cited. For instance, Shure and Spivack (1982) developed a cognitive problem-solving program to prevent impulsive and inhibited behaviors among Black low-income children, and Hirsch and Rapkin (1987) assessed changes in self-esteem and psychological well-being—among other variables— in a comparison of psychological adjustment to transition to junior high school among Black and white students.

The emphasis on external rather than internal variables also helps avoid the trap of blaming the victims for their own predicament (Ryan 1971)—a common-place occurrence in the study of minorities in general and Black males in particu-lar. By focusing on environmental and situational factors that affect behavior— rather than intrapsychic factors—research can contribute to the goal of changing people's environments so that they can better support adaptive behaviors.

The primary goals of the community-intervention research paradigm are to develop effective social interventions and to improve understanding of envi-ronmental variables that affect social problems. In this paradigm, theory takes the form of general statements about relationships between features of the social and physical environment—such as social support or availability of services— and socially important behaviors and related outcomes. Theory results from the accumulation of practical and applied knowledge in solving specific problems. This is another departure from traditional theory-driven psychological re-search, in which theory testing, not problem solving, is the principal goal. By contrast, community-intervention research is characterized by "client driven" and "problem oriented" approaches to research (Seekins and Fawcett 1984).

In this research paradigm, independent variables typically involve ante-cedent and consequent events that take the form of instructional procedures (e.g., teaching self-advocacy skills, Balcazar, Seekins et al. 1990), behavior-management methods (e.g., offering incentives to people participating in skills-exchange programs, Fawcett, Mathews et al. 1976), and environmental design interventions (e.g., introducing new handicapped parking signs, Suarez-Balcazar, Fawcett, and Balcazar 1988).

After variables controlling relevant events are identified through func-tional analysis, they may become part of the intervention and be evaluated under field conditions. For example, careful review of the performances of members of advocacy organizations suggested that instructional procedures to assist members to report issues and plan actions during advocacy group meetings were needed (Balcazar, Seekins et al. 1990). New interventions—such as an action-planning guide for advocacy groups—were then disseminated to com-munity leaders, advocates, or other relevant change agents.

This research model has been used by a group of community researchers at the University of Illinois and the University of Kansas to conduct empower-ment research with ethnic minorities and people with physical disabilities. Sev-eral research projects conducted during the last eight years have yielded a num-ber of products. Examples are training materials that communities can use to organize advocacy groups and plan for actions (Seekins, Balcazar, and Fawcett

1986),[1] manuals that people can use to recruit mentors and potential helpers to attain personal goals (Balcazar and Fawcett 1988)[2], as well as materials that community members can use to organize and direct self-help groups (Paine, Suarez-Balcazar, and Fawcett 1990).[3]

Based on an intervention-research model proposed by Rothman and Thomas (in press) and further articulated by Fawcett, Suarez-Balcazar et al. (in press), a research model for the study and development of empowerment interventions for minorities is discussed here. The research process includes five interrelated phases: (1) problem identification and analysis, (2) knowledge acquisition and synthesis, (3) project design and development, (4) field testing and evaluation, and (5) dissemination and adaptation.

Problem Identification and Analysis

The selection of problems for intervention research should be conducted in collaboration with potential participants. Many aspects of community life offer potential areas of research and intervention, particularly in behalf of minorities living in poor inner-city neighborhoods. Whatever the problem selected for study in the context of action-research, a key determinant is to be able to answer the question: Can something actually be done to address the problem, if we can foster support from the community?

Conducting collaborative research has several important implications. Participants should be allowed to help set the research agenda, expressing their satisfaction with the goals of the project. They should also help design the intervention, giving opinions and raising concerns about the various steps or strategies to be used in the project. Researchers should make clear that community members' participation and collaboration is not only desired but a valuable and necessary condition for the success of the project. Collaboration requires using the community's experiences and goals in choosing research questions, research measures, and, if appropriate, social interventions (Fawcett, Mathews, and Fletcher 1980; Kelly 1986).

Intervention-research projects cannot be imposed on a community by an outside researcher. Attempts to do so are likely to result in failure, and such projects are unlikely to be sustained over time. Participants should share the ownership of the project, making it more likely to be maintained and supported.

The following are some specific considerations for conducting problem identification and analysis:

Getting entry to the setting or population. To enter the community, researchers should start by identifying individuals who can introduce them to key community members. They, in turn, can assist researchers to convey their values and credibility to potential research participants. Most researchers attempting to conduct community-intervention research with minorities are neither black nor poor. Interracial research teams are more likely to be accepted by community members and can facilitate the process of gaining participants' confidence. White researchers are more likely to be accepted if they are introduced to community members by someone trusted by the local community.

Researchers themselves—with good reason, based on experience—are often perceived by the people in low-income neighborhoods as being part of the problem, not part of the solution. Although researchers cannot alter the past experiences of people in the community, they can prove to the community that they want to help. Cultural anthropologists have developed effective methods to gain entry into communities by way of gradual approximations, casual observations, and maintaining a continued presence for a period of time (Agar 1980).Taking time to gain the confidence of at least some members of the community is highly beneficial, and it is unfortunate that many researchers do not take the time required to make a gradual entry into a community. In some settings, even this method can fail. Some communities simply are not ready to embark on a change process, regardless of the wishes of outside researchers.

Investigators who want to work with minorities should also do their homework. They should learn to communicate with the community, learn local customs and traditions, and even adopt some of these customs. By gradually gaining community members' confidence, researchers can feel comfortable among them and make local people feel equally comfortable. Avoiding the middle-class intellectual stance and assuming a one-down position of learner of local ways is particularly helpful (Agar 1980).

Identifying concerns. Various methods have been used to identify the concerns of community members, including interviews (Morganstern and Tevlin 1981), informal personal contacts (Biddle and Biddle 1968), door-to-door canvassing (Fawcett, Miller, and Braukmann 1977), and surveys and community forums (Fawcett, Seekins et al. 1982). Conversations with key informants, such as local leaders, service providers, and advocates, can facilitate understanding local issues and problems. Small-group discussions (Wallerstein and Berstein 1988) are also an effective way for community members to identify issues and relevant dimensions of community problems. Specific problems to be addressed should be selected with the active participation of those most affected.

Analyzing the problem(s). Small-group discussion formats can also be used to explore the dimensions of identified problems. Paulo Freire's model of empowering education (Freire 1973) outlines a five-step questioning strategy researchers can use to facilitate dialogue among community members and prompt them to discuss the issues and propose alternative solutions. In this dialogue, people affected by the problem analyze the situation starting from a personal-experiential level, move to an analysis of the social factors influencing the problem, and conclude by identifying specific actions that they could take to correct the situation.

Participants in group discussions are asked to (1) describe what they see and how they feel about the situation, (2) define the different levels of the problem in their community, (3) share with the group how the situation has affected them personally, (4) question why this problem exists, and (5) develop an action plan to address the problem (Wallerstein and Berstein 1988). Of course, such group efforts to raise consciousness about the root causes of social problems initiate a process of change that can have unpredictable results. It is not unusual to face hostility and repression when members of the establishment feel threatened by organized efforts. Despite the risks, involving local people in identifying and analyzing problems that affect them is a necessary aspect of community-intervention research.

Knowledge Acquisition and Synthesis

The purpose of this phase of the community-intervention research process is to review research in related areas to identify useful intervention strategies and avoid repeating previous mistakes. This review should be conducted before developing the intervention.

Using existing information sources. Conducting a literature search involves reviewing books and journal articles from disciplines related to the particular problem area. Looking at newsletters and newspaper reports might also provide some useful ideas about projects being conducted in other cities.

Studying natural examples. It is useful if researchers and community members involved in planning the project have the opportunity to observe and talk to people who have attempted to address the same or a similar problem in the past. Such discussions can help uncover what obstacles other people encountered and what mistakes others made in attempting to deal with similar problems. Studying other projects also helps provide an understanding of the time, effort, and commitment required to implement a project.

Project Design and Development

The objective of a proposed intervention is to solve an identified problem. The project is designed with active participation of community members, and its effectiveness is documented by collecting data.

Developing a prototype or preliminary intervention. It is appropriate to refer to the first intervention program as a prototype, because it is more likely to be modified after implementation. The preliminary intervention is likely to include several procedures or to combine strategies. Potential examples include the use of information and education campaigns, proposed changes or re-arrangement of environmental variables, the introduction of incentives to reward desired performance or ways to punish undesired ones, creation of new services, and elimination or improvement of existing services. For example, Tripi (1984) reported the effectiveness of a welfare rights consumer organization that paired trained and experienced welfare clients with new ones. Organized consumers were able to influence decisions affecting their welfare benefits and modify bureaucratic rules to suit their needs. When designing the intervention, it is useful to include as many strategies as people can manage in order to increase the chances of success.

Developing an observational system. Selected problems should be defined in ways that can be observed and recorded (Bijou, Peterson, and Ault 1968). As mentioned earlier, participants should help identify the relevant dimensions of the problem to be observed and recorded. For example, when discussing peer pressure for using drugs, youths themselves can describe the types of situations and statements that they are confronted with, and those situations are then reenacted to practice assertive responses. Observational systems usually start with an operational definition of the targeted event—a definition that is objective, clear, and complete (Hawkins and Dobes 1975). Then, a procedure to record and score the occurrence of the event using either independent observers, self-monitoring, or self-reports is developed (Kazdin 1981; Hollon and Bemis 1981).

A useful observation system should identify relevant environmental conditions occurring before the targeted event takes place—*antecedents*—and the changes in the environment following the event—*consequences* (Nelson and Hayes 1981). For example, in the case of peer pressure for drug use, some youngsters who are socially isolated might give in to peer pressure easily, hoping to gain acceptance from their peers. The result may be a youngster's association with a peer group that offers social support but also stimulates drug abuse.

Whenever possible, direct observations should be used to collect necessary data, which are then used to design the intervention strategy. Events that occur with very low frequency can be recorded continuously, while events that occur at high frequency might be observed using random samples or interval sampling (see Hersen and Bellack [1981] for a more detailed review of observational systems). Observations are made reliable by having at least two independent observers record the occurrence of the targeted event(s) on several occasions.

Once data are recorded, they can be plotted for public display or for evaluation by project participants. The simplest way to plot data is to have a frequency display of the occurrence of the event(s) over time (see Drew and Hardman [1985] for a detailed explanation of data plotting and graphic display of data).

Selecting an experimental design. Experimental designs allow for a demonstration of causal relationships between the intervention and the behaviors or events it is intending to change. Single-case designs, such as the interrupted time-series designs (Cook and Campbell 1979) or multiple baseline designs (Baer, Wolf, and Risley 1968) are very useful in intervention research. When these designs are used, researchers typically collect repeated measures before and after interventions that are staggered across individuals, groups, or settings. For example Suarez-Balcazar et al. (1988) introduced new parking signs in one site, and after a period of time, new signs were added in a different site. These designs can be used with small samples and control for history, maturation, and other threats to internal validity (Campbell and Stanley 1968).

Field Testing and Evaluation

The field test allows for a preliminary refinement of the intervention, which can then be replicated in other communities.

Conducting a field test. At this point, it is assumed that any training or instructional materials have already been developed. A primary goal of community-intervention research is to generate procedures that can be effective in several settings and with a variety of participants. The field test allows testing the generality of the procedures and might be conducted on a small scale or with involvement of only a few community residents. This process allows researchers to start a project and evaluate its impacts carefully.

Usually, some form of pre-post comparison design is appropriate to evaluate the effects of the intervention under field conditions, with an emphasis on collecting outcome measures. For example, to evaluate the effects of an advocacy training program (Balcazar, Seekins et al. 1990), the number of outcomes or changes in the community resulting from group efforts were compared before and after training. More than fifteen outcomes were identified after training, compared with only one before training. Examples of such outcomes were changes in policy regarding services for people with disabilities, new budget allocations for medical emergency alarm equipment, and improved fire safety procedures at local nursing homes.

Regardless of the strategies selected, researchers should always be open to changing the course of the intervention if it becomes evident that it is not working. There are no fool-proof strategies, and approaches should change according to the specific circumstances of the local community. Being flexible and willing to keep putting the intervention "back on track" are keys to achieving success.

Collecting and analyzing data. During the field test, researchers collect and analyze data. Data are frequently analyzed using some form of statistical or visual analysis. Several computer programs are now available to simplify and speed up the data analysis (e.g., SPSS PC+, SYSTAT). Data-collection procedures allow for evaluation of the effectiveness of the intervention. However, it is also important to evaluate the social significance of goals and effects as well as participants' satisfaction with the intervention. Questionnaires and personal interviews are usually used to collect these data (see Wolf [1978] for a detailed explanation).

Dissemination and Adaptation

After a program or intervention has been tested and revised, it is ready to be disseminated to community agencies, advocacy organizations, coalitions, or other target audiences. Seekins and Fawcett (1984) identified several strategies for marketing social innovations, which include modeling (e.g., asking publicly known people to endorse the program); organizing demonstrations of the program in other settings or communities; advertising the program through fliers, brochures, newspaper releases, and media campaigns whenever appropriate; presenting the program at professional conferences at the local and national levels; and preparing manuscripts for publication.

Encouraging appropriate adaptation. An important consideration when encouraging dissemination of a community intervention is that any replication should be adapted to the particular circumstances of each new setting. Adopters should be free to modify the program in order to fit their local conditions.

Offering technical assistance. Seekins and Fawcett (1984) pointed out that adaptations might result in a loss of effectiveness or other valued attributes of the original intervention. Offering technical assistance and consultation to communities planning to implement the intervention might be the most effective way to overcome such limitations. Such involvement in adoption programs may result in increased cooperation and ownership—critical ingredients in successful dissemination.

Case Study

The Board of Global Ministries of the United Methodist Church invited the Della C. Lamb Neighborhood House to serve as a demonstration site for a "Youth Enterprise Project" involving minority youths. Della C. Lamb—a settlement house in Kansas City, Missouri—provides a variety of services to low-income minority clients, including food distribution to elderly neighbors, day care, and recreation programs for children. The house has been in operation for several years and has already gained recognition and acceptance by community members.

Problem Identification and Analysis

This project was successful in getting access to key members of the Black community of an inner-city neighborhood because of its association with Della C. Lamb Neighborhood House, which gave project members credibility among community members. On the basis of interviews with community leaders, youths, and parents, staff identified key concerns, including scarcity of employment opportunities available to area youths and insufficient support for high school seniors searching for financial aid to attend college.

A group of sixteen black youths—nine women and seven men—participated in this project, which lasted two years. At the start of the project, the youths were sixteen and seventeen years old and attended high schools from the inner-city school district of Kansas City, Missouri. Thanks to the cooperation of inner-city high schools, students were recruited by letters of invitation. Minority students with GPAs of 2.5 or more and living in low-income neighborhoods were invited to participate.

Knowledge Acquisition and Synthesis

In order to obtain sufficient information to initiate the various project components, the project director conducted a search for information regarding scholarships and financial aid available to minority students. The office of minority affairs from a local college was very helpful in this process. Several scholarships and sources of financial aid were identified, and application forms were also collected.

The director also visited employment programs for minority youths operating in the Kansas City area, identifying common elements that make an employment program more likely to succeed. One of the local projects starting at that time—sponsored by the Boys and Girls Club of Kansas City—recruited mentors to provide one-to-one instruction and supervision to twelve- and thirteen-year-old minority youths in managing and operating a small business. The mentoring component of the program was judged to be beneficial, and thus the project director contacted the researchers at the University of Kansas for assistance in developing this particular component.

Mentor programs—connecting youth with business people and others in a position to help them achieve educational and employment goals—are increasingly used as part of efforts to reduce the number of high school dropouts and increase educational achievement. The "Career Beginning Program"—coordinated by the Center for Human Resources at Brandeis University and sponsored by the Commonwealth Fund, the MacArthur Foundation, and the Gannet Foundation—is a widely heralded example. But despite their apparent advantages, traditional mentor programs that arrange contacts for youth might require too much time and effort for widespread adoption and may actually increase dependency on the one mentor to whom the youth has access. It was decided after some discussion to teach students to recruit mentors and to develop support networks that would permit them to access a vast source of potential help, therefore increasing the likelihood of attaining their personal goals.

Project Design and Development

The project was divided into three components: (1) an after-school employment program that provided on-the-job training; (2) technical assistance for finding and filling out applications for financial aid and scholarships; and (3) a social skill development program designed to teach youth how to recruit mentors to attain personal goals. These programs were introduced consecutively, and various local organizations assisted in the process.

The after-school employment program was designed to provide on-the-job training and experience which youths could use for their future employment. Students were paid minimum wage stipends ($3.35 per hour) for two hours of after-school work at Della C. Lamb five days a week. The students participated in a number of job-related activities, including purchasing and distributing food to low-income seniors, serving as teacher aids in the day-care program, entering data in the computer, and substituting for the receptionist at the center. The students recorded the number of hours worked each week.

A functional analysis of the obstacles encountered by minority students looking for financial aid to attend college suggested the following: (1) school counseling offices are understaffed and frequently overwhelmed by the large number of students seeking assistance. (2) There are multiple sources of potential funding with limited guidelines for identifying and choosing among the sources. (3) Some "sources" are dangerous traps, attempting to attract students to technical careers by promises, misrepresenting the debts students acquire and the low marketability of the skills they learn. (4) Some of the scholarship application forms are difficult to fill out. (5) Schools have different guidelines and time lines that must be followed in order to qualify for assistance. (6) Parents are frequently unable to assist financially. Evidence of program success can be measured by the number of financial aid applications sent by each student, the number of positive responses received from funding sources, and the percentage of students receiving at least one acceptable offer of assistance.

The mentor recruiting training program was introduced to improve students' social skills for requesting assistance in attaining employment or educational goals. A functional analysis was conducted to identify typical situations students might encounter where they could ask for help in attaining relevant personal goals. A training manual (Balcazar and Fawcett 1989) was used to teach students how to set goals and plan for action and to provide opportunities to practice skills needed in meeting with potential helpers. The training included clear descriptions of the behaviors that make up the skills, examples, rationales, study guides, situational examples, modeling, role-playing practice, feedback, and criterion performance tests (Borck and Fawcett 1982; Fawcett 1988; Fawcett and Fletcher 1977). Measures of students' help-recruiting skills were collected by observing their performance during role-play analogue situations, such as having students ask a potential employer for a summer job. A simple interrupted time-series design with multiple replications across participants (Cook and Campbell 1979) was used to evaluate the effects of the skills training.

Field Testing and Evaluation

Given budget constraints, it was decided to implement the project as a small-scale field intervention. Eight students participated in the program during the first year. They received assistance with financial aid applications for college and started the after-school employment program. At the end of the first year, two of these students graduated from high school and went to college. During the summer, participants attended business introductory classes at a local college. At the beginning of the second year, eight additional senior students were recruited. They received assistance with financial aid applications and enrolled in academic enrichment classes in such areas as reading, math, English, and business at a local college.

Of the sixteen students participating in the various phases of the project, thirteen (81 percent) started college after graduating from high school, and one enlisted in the Air Force. They submitted a total of sixty applications for financial aid, and all who were attending college were able to secure at least one source of financial aid. For instance, seven students (44 percent) received Pell Grants, and six students (38 percent) received one or more scholarship offers. Three of the students receiving scholarships had the opportunity to choose among several offers they received.

The sixteen students worked a total of 1,120 hours at Della C. Lamb. One of the students was offered a part-time job at the agency after she graduated from high school. Three of the participants were able to find jobs paying more than minimum wage.

The goal-setting and help-recruiting skills training program was started with six students at the end of the second year before high school graduation. This training was completed in two months by four of the six students. (One of the students refused to participate in the training, and another was already involved in a national mentoring program called Inroads.) Direct observations of students' performance during role-playing evaluation sessions showed consistent improvement in help-recruiting skills following training (the baseline average of 37.5 percent increased to an average of 75.3 percent after training). Trained students reported attaining almost all (87 percent) of the short-term goals they set for themselves. Examples of goals attained included being able to find summer employment after graduating from high school and learning to use a microcomputer.

Dissemination and Adaptation

Given the small scale of the project, additional replications of the after-school employment and financial aid components are required before starting large-scale dissemination efforts. Training materials designed to assist students to set goals and recruit help in attaining their goals are now closer to dissemination, however, since these materials have also been evaluated with a group of college students with physical disabilities (Balcazar, Fawcett, and Seekins 1991). In each replication, efforts to adapt the materials to the specific needs of the participants were made, particularly regarding the types of role-play situations that are more likely to represent real-life events.

Discussion

The goals of the proposed model of community-intervention research are to better understand variables controlling important behaviors and community outcomes and to solve client-identified social problems. The model has five elements: problem identification and analysis, knowledge acquisition and synthesis, project design and development, field testing and evaluation, and dissemination and adaptation. Together, these elements result in a design for social innovations, testing under field conditions, and dissemination of acquired knowledge and proven techniques. The model thus provides a pragmatic approach to analyzing some of the most pressing problems confronting Black males in America and offers guidelines for developing interventions that empower people of marginal status (Fawcett, Seekins, et al. 1984).

The results of the mentoring case study suggest that the project improved participants' opportunities to attend college and learn help-recruiting skills. Some of the students described several positive reactions to the training experience. For instance, one commented, "The mentoring program gave me awareness of how to present myself to get favorable results." Another said, "Now I feel like a different person. I am more secure, and [I] can tell what I feel and be more open with people. I used to be very shy, and I was frequently by myself. Now I am with other people and [I] can speak more." The students were empowered by the intervention to the extent that they learned how to get access to potential helpers and mentors who could facilitate attainment of their personal goals. The role playing reportedly improved students' performance when they later applied for summer employment.

The promising findings of the case study have important implications. Results suggest that it is possible to teach help-recruiting skills that can be used by minority youth to meet and interact with adults who might be in a position to provide help. Such social competence is important, since it can facilitate contact with people outside their own social class and minority culture.

In a discussion of the current status of Black men in North America, Gary

(1981) concluded that more research is necessary for developing innovative strategies to improve the quality of life for Black men. He emphasized how important it is that social scientists and practitioners conduct such research in the context of Black families and communities. To corroborate the argument presented here, he also stressed the importance of involving the Black community in the development of strategies designed to strengthen the role and position of Black men in their respective communities. Such efforts should result in the development of social interventions that empower African-American men.

Conditions and opportunities for most Black males in America reflect a long history of racism and oppression for which society as a whole is responsible. But individual actors—including elected and appointed officials, social scientists, and Black males themselves—are not doing enough to remedy the situation. Traditional research and action practices must change if Black leaders and other community members are to be incorporated in the design of solutions to problems they experience. Researchers can play a role in promoting social change by designing interventions that enable communities to take control over those environmental factors that impede development and growth. Each such endeavor is a step in the long march toward freedom and justice.

Notes

Special thanks to Jim Meyer, director of the "Youth Enterprise Project" at Della C. Lamb Neighborhood House, for his invaluable cooperation in the preparation of this manuscript. We also appreciate the useful suggestions of Betty T. Horton, and Vince Francisco, as well as the editorial assistance of Susan Elkins. Correspondence should be addressed to Fabricio E. Blacazar, UAP/DD University of Illinois at Chicago, 1640 West Roosevelt Rd., Chicago, IL 60608.

1. Copies of the four-volume series *Consumer Involvement in Advocacy Organizations: Rehabilitating Communities for Independent Living*, by T. Seekins, F. E. Balcazar, and S. B. Fawcett (1986) may be obtained at cost from the Research and Training Center on Independent Living, 3111 Haworth Hall, University of Kansas, Lawrence, KA 66045.

2. Copies of the training manual *Recruiting Mentors and Potential Helpers: A Guide to Personal Success*, vols. 1 and 2, by F. E. Balcazar, and S. B. Fawcett (1989) may be obtained at cost from the Research and Training Center on Independent Living, 3111 Haworth Hall, University of Kansas, Lawrence, KA 66045.

3. Copies of the training manual *Self-Help Group Leader's Handbook: Leading Effective Meetings* by A. L. Paine, Y. Suarez-Balcazar, S. B. Fawcett, L. Burck-Jemeson and M. G. Embree (1989) are also available at cost upon request from the Research and Training Center on Independent Living, Haworth Hall 3111, University of Kansas, Lawrence, KA 66045.

CHAPTER 14

Empowerment Opportunities for Black Adolescent Fathers and Their Nonparenting Peers

by Edith M. Freeman

According to Chilman (1989), researchers have been able to obtain more information about reproductive behaviors from females than from males. Accordingly, estimates of fatherhood among adolescents range from 7 percent to 40 percent, but these numbers tend to be too low (Marsiglio 1987; Elster and Lamb 1986). Nonmarital intercourse rates for males are considerably higher than the 20 percent to 50 percent reported for females until age twenty, when many unmarried males *and* females are reported to be sexually active. Hays (1987) noted that by age nineteen, three-quarters of white males are sexually active compared to almost all Black males.

These prevailing statistics have not changed society's ambivalence about adolescent sexuality. Concerns about preventing pregnancy in this age group conflict with fears about encouraging early sexual involvement (Freeman 1989). Consequences have included inadequate education about sex and contraceptives and a birthrate among teenaged females of 5.3 percent in 1982, a decline from 9 percent in 1970 (Chilman 1989). The birthrate decreased even more rapidly among Black teens, but the latter are less likely than whites to have marital births. Only 15 percent of Black adolescent males in a recent study married the mothers of their children, compared to 48 percent of Hispanics, 58 percent of disadvantaged whites, and 77 percent of nondisadvantaged whites (Marsiglio 1987).

These racial differences in marital birth rates may occur because a larger percentage of Black teenagers than whites do not have abortions (Chilman 1989). Another factor is that only one-third of Black males under twenty have permanent jobs, compared with two-thirds of young whites (Wilson and Neckerman 1986). Two-thirds of all Black adolescent males live in families with incomes at or below the poverty line (Chilman 1989). Equally important, there are higher rates of homicide, accidents, and incarceration in jails and prisons among young Black males (Farley 1980; Blumstein 1982). These factors reduce the likelihood of marriage and increase the rate of nonmarital births among young Blacks.

In addition to age biases, there are societal biases related to gender and race. It is assumed that Black males will not share responsibility for or help to decrease the high rate of nonmarital births. They have been described as difficult to reach and serve. Consequently, most have been ignored by pregnancy prevention programs (Elster and Lamb 1986; Freeman 1988). This bias "has led to missed opportunities for providing additional resources to the mother-child dyad, and to young fathers in terms of their needs" (Freeman 1989, 114).

Similar biases have led to limited educational, health, employment, housing, and political opportunities for young Black males. Thus discrimination has increased risk factors related to dropping out of school, unemployment, low-

This chapter is a revised version of a paper presented at the First Annual Conference of the National Council of African American Men (NCAAM), Kansas City, MO, July 11–13, 1990.

income jobs, substance abuse, depression, and physical violence. In consequence, fewer Black males become aware of and build on their strengths or experience a sense of empowerment.

This article briefly reviews risk factors and the need for such empowerment experiences by Black parenting and nonparenting males. It describes an exploratory study designed to clarify strengths and barriers to empowerment perceived by this population. Finally, the article discusses implications for future research and some practice considerations regarding the active involvement of the Black community.

Review of Risk Factors

The concept of high-risk youth is now being used in the literature to identify those who experience many interacting factors that render them more vulnerable than the average youngster to negative consequences. Black males may be more vulnerable than males from other races and females in general simply because the effects of institutional racism are weighted more heavily against them (Kunjufu 1985). Risk factors can be a function of the individual as well as a function of the physical, cultural, social, political, and economic environment in which he or she resides. It is not important to identify a direct cause-and-effect relationship between a particular risk factor and a consequence; it is assumed that there is a systematic relationship between various risk factors and combinations of outcomes.

Chilman (1989) summarized research findings on risk factors associated with teenage nonmarital intercourse among males (some are also relevant to females):

1. Lower social class
2. An interaction of racism and poverty
3. Unemployment
4. Peer group pressures
5. Sexually active friends
6. Large family size
7. Early use of tobacco, drugs, and alcohol
8. Low educational goals and poor educational achievement
9. Low tested intelligence
10. Deviant attitudes
11. Steady love partner with permissive attitudes
12. Aggressiveness and a high level of activity
13. Sixteen years of age or older

Some of the risk factors may have a differential effect on Black males. For instance, more Black families live below the poverty line (2 above), while unemployment rates for Black teens are higher than for any other age or racial group (3). In addition, because of poor educational achievement and other factors, Blacks have the highest dropout rates among teens (8). Similarly, they are more likely than others to score low on culturally biased intelligence tests currently used by many psychologists (9) (Kunjufu 1985).

This brief review of risk factors serves to clarify the manner in which they may predispose, but do not predetermine, Black youths' vulnerability to early fatherhood and other negative outcomes. The danger of this focus is that only negative factors are identified, without clarifying individual and environmental conditions that allow teens to overcome risk factors and to thrive. Without such conditions, empowerment experiences are less likely to occur.

The Need for a Sense of Empowerment

The American Heritage Dictionary (1976) defines the word *empower* as follows: "To invest with legal power; to authorize. To enable or permit." It is the aspect of *enabling* that is relevant to youth empowerment. While one person cannot empower another, according to Simon (1990), one can contribute to the conditions under which individuals, groups, and communities empower themselves. These conditions include opportunities to feel good about the self, to feel connected with significant others in meaningful ways, and to act effectively and positively in changing the environment as needed (Freeman 1988). Thus, empowerment involves both a specific consciousness (a sense of efficacy) and skills (a set of behaviors that demonstrate problem solving and lead to further competence).

All individuals seek opportunities for empowerment as an inherent need (Maslow 1967; Towle 1965). Black males who are subjected to many of the risk factors discussed in the previous section generally have few opportunities for feeling good about themselves or for reducing or eliminating these factors. Germain and Gitterman (1984) noted that limited resources have a negative impact on self-image, dignity, and self-esteem; similarly, Chilman (1983) reports that adolescents with hope and aspirations are more likely to postpone parenthood.

While the literature is replete with information about the relationship between risk factors and disempowerment and between the latter and early parenthood, few researchers have clarified how Black males in particular view their lives. Little is known, for example, about what risk factors or barriers these youngsters identify in their situations and whether they also perceive strengths, develop goals for the future, and have problem-solving abilities for overcoming the barriers.

For these reasons, the following questions were developed to guide an exploratory study that focused on some of these issues:

1. What strengths and barriers do Black male adolescents report in terms of themselves and their social networks?
2. What strengths and barriers do these adolescents perceive within their neighborhoods and communities?
3. To what extent are those identified strengths and barriers related to the adolescents' development of future goals?
4. Are there similarities and differences in the reproductive behaviors of adolescent fathers and those teens who are not fathers?
5. Can similarities and differences be identified between fathers and nonfathers in this population in terms of their use and abuse of substances?

An underlying assumption of the study was that risk factors or barriers decrease empowerment opportunities and that exploring the questions listed above could actually provide conditions for helping the participants to empower themselves. For philosophical consistency, a study focused on individuals' strengths should encourage them to use and become more aware of their strengths, both through its contents and through the manner in which it is conducted. Therefore, it was assumed that the interview process should emphasize the importance of the participants and their ideas, provide encouragement for them to discuss those ideas freely, and validate explicitly their points of view when expressed, as well as raise and listen to issues that are meaningful to them now and in the future. The topic of empowerment was not included as a research question, but the participants' reactions to the interview were explored at the end of the process. Those reactions and other empowerment issues will be discussed when the study findings are reported.

Methodology

The study was designed to explore in depth the five questions identified in the previous section. Face-to-face interviews, rather than a written survey, were chosen for that reason. The discussion of methodology includes the sample, the settings, and the research instruments.

The Sample

The purposeful, nonrandom sample consisted of twenty Black adolescent males from a metropolitan area in the Midwest with a population of approximately half a million persons. To be included in the sample, the participants had to be Black males between thirteen and eighteen years of age. As can be seen from table 14.1, the majority of the participants (90 percent) were thirteen to sixteen years old. All of them were in school at the time of the study, and 70 percent were in grades seven through ten. Although all the participants were

Table 14.1 Characteristics of the Sample (N = 20)

Age	Grade in School	Racial Identification	Parental Figure(s) Present in Household	Adolescent Income
13–14 years: 35% (7)	7th–8th grade: 35% (7)	Black or Black American: 70% (14)	Mother: 55% (11)	Unemployed: 20% (4)
15–16 years: 55% (11)	9th–10th grade: 35% (7)	Biracial or mixed Race: 15% (3)	Both parents: 25% (5)	Less than $999 yearly: 55% (11)
17–18 years: 10% (2)	11th–12th grade: 30% (6)	African-American: 5% (1)	One parent and one stepparent: 15% (3)	$1,000–$1,999 yearly: 20% (4)
		Negro: 5% (1)	Other relative: 5% (1)	$2,000–$2,999 yearly: 5% (1)
		Brown: 5% (1)		

Black, they identified themselves with a variety of labels including African-American, brown, Negro, biracial or mixed race, and Black or Black American. One participant indicated that he was of the human race first and then was Black. The three biracial participants all had one Black and one white parent. The majority of the participants had problems understanding the question: How do you identify yourself racially? Responses ranged from a puzzled look to the question, What do you mean? to statements that they had never been asked that question before.

All members of the sample lived at home with family members. Most (55 percent) lived with their mothers, while 40 percent lived with two parents (15 percent with a mother and stepfather). One person lived with his grandmother (table 14.1). Eighty percent of the sample were employed primarily in summer job programs, with the majority of them (55 percent) earning less than $999 yearly.

The Settings

Since access to this population is difficult, settings where they spend free time were chosen as sites for the study. Unfortunately, the decision to utilize those settings excluded current school dropouts, noninvolved youths, and a larger percentage of unemployed teens from the study. All members of the sample were participating in one of two community programs that provide summer employment as one of their services. Some of the findings, therefore, are an artifact of how the sample was selected and the settings from which it was drawn.

Programs in the two settings are similar in many ways, especially in terms of their goals and aims. They focus on self-esteem building, for example, along with providing structured activities for developing social skills and a sense of responsibility. Both also provide educational and tutoring services. The programs are different in some significant ways as well. Setting A is housed in a Black church and has been in existence for approximately twenty years. It places major emphasis on developing cultural awareness and in maintaining Black traditions such as the Juneteenth celebration. It serves 250 Black children and youth from three to eight years of age. It is funded through the church, United Way, and private donations.

Setting B is a privately funded alternative school that is housed in a Boys and Girls Club. Its major emphasis is on improving educational achievement: services include remedial classes, GED classes, a writers' project, day care, survival skills for urban living, a choir, and teen parenting and prevention programs. Each year the program serves 450 youngsters of all races from age twelve to eighteen, but it serves a predominantly Black group of children and youth (87%).

Research Instruments

The instruments developed specifically for this study consisted of a twenty-eight-item semistructured interview schedule and a thirty-item self-assessment inventory. The ethnographic interview was designed to encourage participants to tell their stories in their own language, and to reflect on and discuss freely their current and future lives (Spradley 1979). The tape-recorded interviews required approximately forty-five minutes. The schedule was organized into several major sections including the participants' self-perceptions, their significant relationships, their reproductive behaviors, experiences with substances, future goals, coping and problem-solving patterns in terms of relationships, and demographic information.

Questions within each of these areas involved creative strategies to encourage self-reflection and reduce inaccurate information. An example from each area of the schedule follows (note that each question was related to a series of other questions for further exploration):

1. Has anyone ever asked you about your view of your life? If so, what were some important things the two of you discussed about you?
2. Who is the most important person to you and in what ways is that person important to you?
3. Have you ever been told by a young lady that she is pregnant or has had a child and that you are the father? If so, what kind of relationship did you have with her?
4. Have you used alcohol or other drugs? If so, what happens when you use alcohol (or other drugs)?
5. Let's assume that it is now five years into the future, 1995, tell me what you are doing.
6. I'm going to tell you a story about a young man named Joe and his friend. After I tell you about him, I will ask you to finish telling me his story as though you are Joe.

Following the interview, participants were asked to complete the self-assessment inventory. It included items focused on their attitudes and values and on relationships and environmental factors that influence their lives. Each of the items on the inventory was followed by a Likert rating scale. Table 14.2 contains paraphrases of each item and the rating scale. Participants were provided with a copy of their completed self-assessment inventories for later reflection on their strengths and for linking their goals and any new insights with future behavior.

The inventory was designed to help participants discover the strengths and barriers in their environments and within themselves. It is based on the researcher's concept of resource-enriched and resource-limited urban communities (Freeman

Table 14.2 Most Important Strengths and Barriers Reported by Black Adolescent Males (for self, social networks, community) N = 20

Strengths		Barriers	
Item	Group Mean*	Item	Group Mean
1. Sisters are accepting of me	1.0	1. Community agencies are used for problem solving	4.25
2. Parents encourage independence	1.3	2. Community has positive role models for day-to-day advice	3.45
3. Peers discourage drug use	1.4	3. Community has people with problem-solving skills	3.4
4. School learning relevant to work world	1.45	4. Community is safe	3.0
5. Family helps to feel good about self	1.55	5. Newspapers show positive view of black males	3.0
6. It's okay for males to discuss feelings	1.6	6. Community residents have interesting jobs	2.95
7. Positive male role models in family	1.65	7. Brothers are accepting of me	2.88
8. Have developed positive future goals	1.7	8. Television shows positive role of Black males	2.7
9. Equal opportunity for males and females	1.8	9. Community has positive models for adult responsibility	2.6
10. Peers help to feel good about self	1.8	10. Radio shows positive view of Black males	2.55
11. Peers help to stay in school	1.9		
12. Peers help enjoy free time activities	1.9		
13. Have learned to problem solve	1.95		
14. School helps to plan for career/jobs	1.95		
15. Peers discourage alcohol use	2.0		
16. Peers help with legal free time activities	2.0		
17. Black community helps to feel good about self	2.05		
18. Peers encourage positive attitude toward females	2.1		
19. Community provides opportunities for jobs for teens/preparation for adult work	2.15		
20. Parents understand I will soon be grown up and leave home	2.15		

*Scale for responses:

1	2	3	4	5
Always	Often	Sometimes	Seldom	Never

1989). Items rated 1 and 2 by the participants are considered to be strengths, and those rated from 2.5 to 5 are barriers that make life difficult for them.

To help in designing and interpreting the inventory for this study, strengths were defined as positive qualities that lead to a sense of empowerment, growth, stress management, functional adaptations and coping, and effective problem-solving. Examples of strengths include attitudes, values or belief systems, ways of functioning, supportive relationships, knowledge, competencies as reflected in behavior, the availability of material goods and other services, and access and ability to use those resources. As can be seen from the definition and examples, strengths can be tangible or intangible and they may be an aspect of individuals or of their environments (family, peers, role models, social systems, the community, or society).

Barriers or resource limitations, on the other hand, are risk factors that make life difficult and decrease any sense of empowerment. They may mask or block access to resources (for example, restrictive social or agency policies that limit eligibility), or they may undermine such pathways to those resources as persistence and hope within the individual. As with strengths, barriers can be tangible (e.g., lack of job opportunities) or intangible (e.g., subtle encouragement of drug use or unsafe sex). Barriers can be within the individual (low self-esteem) or within the environment (an unsafe community or racial stereotypes in the media).

Findings and Discussion

Many recurring themes are apparent from reviewing the findings of this study, including those related to strengths and barriers as defined in the previous section. The discussion of findings has been organized in terms of the five research questions that were developed to guide the study.

Individual and Social Network Strengths/Barriers

The participants' identification of individual strengths reflected themes related to feelings, values, and the concept of competence. For instance, they identified the following strengths: beliefs that sharing feelings with someone you trust is "okay," that males and females should have the same opportunities, that they have developed personal goals for the future, and that they have learned to problem solve effectively (see table 14.2 for the mean ratings of these items). Moreover, when asked during the interview to describe themselves, many of them indicated they are nice, friendly, fun to be with, intelligent, strong, and talented in sports.

Strengths identified in regard to their social networks focused on both tangible and intangible aspects of relationships with family members and peers. During the interview, the majority (85 percent) indicated that parents were the most important persons to them because they provided material resources such as food and a place to stay, but also because they listen to problems, are there when the youths are sick, and encourage them when they are "down." As can be seen from table 14.2, mean ratings on the self-assessment inventory indicate that acceptance by sisters was the highest rated strength (in contrast to brothers), while parental encouragement to be independent, the family's ability to make youngsters feel good about themselves, and the family's provision of role models were seen as other strengths.

Peers were viewed as strengths when they helped to resist drugs and increased self-esteem (see table 14.2). In addition, the interviews revealed that peers were supportive in giving advice ("leave before a fight begins") and in listening to problems.

Individual barriers and risk factors were also clarified through the study. Few of the risk factors identified in this study were consistent with those from the literature, which were discussed in a previous section. This may be due to the use of a nonrandom and nonrepresentative sample. When respondents were asked to describe themselves they gave examples of negative qualities or barriers: they talk too much, play jokes on others, are stubborn, do not work hard enough in school, and they "look strange." In discussing what they would be like in the future, many of the participants indicated they would be more mature in terms of these negative qualities (they would think about what they wanted to say first or they would be more serious in the future).

In terms of barriers related to the family, only acceptance by brothers was identified as a factor that makes life difficult for these youths. On this item, 100 percent of the participants rated sisters as always accepting, while only 30 percent rated brothers as always accepting. Gender socialization may be important here, in that females are traditionally socialized to be more caring and accepting than males. Findings related to peers as barriers were equally interesting; none of the responses for peer-related items on the self-assessment inventory could be considered negative, since the mean ratings ranged only from 1.4 to 2.1 (see table 14.2). In comparison, during the interviews only two participants (10 percent) identified peers as the most important persons in their lives, and some (30 percent) indicated that they did not have close friends at the present because they had found they could not trust or talk openly with peers.

Community Strengths and Barriers

Findings related to the community reflected primarily themes related to work in terms of strengths. For instance, table 14.2 indicates that most of the participants viewed what they were learning in school as useful for the work world and that their schools provided helpful information about what they could do after high school graduation. They also perceived that the community provides opportunities for teenagers to work and learn job-related skills (a sample bias perhaps), in contrast to opportunities for adults.

The participants indicated that, as a result, there are few people in their community who have interesting jobs with whom they can talk (see table 14.2). In terms of other barriers, community-related items on the self-assessment inventory had the highest group means, indicating that they make life difficult for the participants. In their neighborhoods, for instance, competence was the major theme as participants noted the lack of positive models for effective problem solving, advice for day-to-day problems, and adult role responsibilities. Table 14.2 indicates that most do not feel their immediate communities are safe, possibly because of the generally high homicide rates for males.

However, the barrier with the highest mean rating was "there are social agencies in my community that I go to if I have problems." This finding indicates a lack of knowledge about or confidence in the social services provided within their communities. It is possible that such services are not present, visible, or viewed as culturally relevant by the respondents, although the study did not explore reasons for this barrier.

Responses for societal-related items were even more revealing; these items focused primarily on the role of the media. As can be seen from table 14.2, newspapers, television, and radio were seen as presenting a negative view of Black males in that order. Radio may have received the most positive mean rating (2.55) of the three media because of the acceptance of "Black cross-over music" on white as well as Black radio stations. Also, less radio time may be devoted to entertainment or news programs that are overtly race related in contrast to newspapers and television. As a consequence, there may be more opportunities for stereotypes and other forms of institutional racism in both the hiring practices and products of the other two media. The Black male images presented by media may have influenced some of the negative self-perceptions of respondents in the study, along with their goals for the future.

Relationship between Strengths, Barriers, and Goals

During the interviews, participants were asked to discuss what they would be doing five years into the future, who they would be with (who would be important to them), and where they would be located. The goals they identified focused primarily on education and employment rather than on personal growth, leisure time, or material goods.

Forty-four percent (eleven) of these teenagers identified education—specifically college—as a goal, while another 44 percent (eleven) focused on employment. Of those who indicated they would be involved in a particular type of employment, their responses often implied that college was an intermediate goal (for work in engineering, for example). Others chose a type of employment that implied vocation training, such as bricklaying, or specialized abilities, such as becoming a musician.

All participants with goals for college said they expected to win athletic scholarships involving basketball or track, but one also indicated he hoped to win a scholarship in debate. This overwhelming choice of college via an athletic scholarship reflects, not only the limited opportunities open to Black males, but also the unrealistic stereotypes of Black athletes as portrayed by the media. Many other avenues to achievement for Black males are neither presented in the media nor reflected in adult employment patterns within their communities, so that youths such as those in the present study can hardly see them as goals. Thus, barriers related to their immediate neighborhoods as well as those involved in the larger environment have influenced the goals chosen by these adolescents.

Many authors indicate that decreasing numbers of Black males are enrolling in college presently (Ekstrom et al. 1986), so it is unlikely that all the participants in this study will attend college *or* win an athletic scholarship leading inevitably to a career in professional athletics. It is not clear whether or how these youngsters will be able to revise and implement their goals once they are confronted with this reality. Several of the barriers they identified in their communities, such as a lack of role models, could make this process difficult.

Most of the participants indicated that family members will continue to be important to them in the future in terms of goals (40 percent). Others noted that having a family of their own is an important goal in the next five years (50 percent); their plans often involved their current girlfriend or the mother of their child. These goals are consistent with the strengths they identified in terms of their current social networks.

A majority indicated that one future goal was to live in some other city (55 percent, or eleven) or another community in the same city (25 percent, or five). This is not surprising since the major barriers identified by participants in this study were community-related. Only two respondents (5 percent) thought that they would be living in the same community, while three (15 percent) indicated they were not certain where they would be located.

Similarities and Differences in Reproductive Behaviors

Equally important as the participants' goals are the reproductive behaviors they described in response to questions asked during the interview. Fathers (N=6) and sexually active nonfathers (N=8) were different in terms of the age at which they had their first sexual experience. The mean age for fathers was thirteen years, with a range from twelve to fifteen, while the mean age for nonfathers was fourteen years, involving a range from thirteen to fifteen.

A number of other similarities and differences were noted across the subgroups of fathers and nonfathers in the sample. It is clear from table 14.3 that fathers do not view abstinence as a pregnancy prevention strategy and that they have a higher frequency of sexual activity than nonfathers. Some of the fathers also are more selective than nonfathers in using condoms, indicating that they

Table 14.3   Reproductive Behaviors of Black Adolescent Fathers and Their
Nonparenting Peers (N = 20)

Subgroups	Mean Frequency of Sexual Activity	Pregnancy Concerns and Prevention	Concerns about Sexually Transmitted Diseases and Prevention
Adolescent Fathers (N = 6)	Once weekly	100% expressed concerns. Prevention: condoms; selectivity in partners; partners use birth control	83% expressed concerns. Prevention: Condoms; one sex partner only
Sexually Active Adolescents (not fathers) (N = 8)	Once monthly	62% expressed concerns. Prevention: Periodic abstinence; condoms; doing nothing; don't know how to prevent	62% expressed concern. Prevention: Periodic abstinence and condoms
Non–sexually Active Adolescents (N = 6)	No sexual activity	100% expressed concerns. Prevention: Abstinence; awareness of condoms	50% expressed concerns. Prevention: Abstinence

often do not use condoms with their girlfriends because they have a strong trusting relationship with them. Fathers and the group of non-sexually-active participants expressed concerns about their role in preventing pregnancy at an equal level (100 percent), but fathers were more concerned about preventing sexually transmitted diseases (STDs) than the other two subgroups. AIDS and gonorrhea were the most frequently identified STDs that all three groups wished to prevent.

Analysis of the self-assessment inventories pinpointed other similarities and differences related to reproductive behaviors and gender values. For instance, the mean rating for peers helping with a positive attitude toward females was similar for fathers (1.8) and nonfathers (1.5). In comparison, fathers have fewer nonsexual friendships with females: the mean rating for fathers was 3.16 while the mean for nonfathers was 2.14. This pattern among fathers in the study may increase the likelihood that their relationships with females will result in pregnancy compared with nonfathers. The pattern may also cause fathers to have a narrow view of females in contrast to the more multidimensional view of nonfathers.

Similarities and Differences in Substance Use or Abuse

Interestingly, there were fewer differences noted between fathers and nonfathers in the study in their use or abuse of substances. Thirty-three percent of the fathers (two) use substances compared with 35 percent of the nonfathers (five). Overall, 35 percent (seven) of the participants across both groups reported using substances. Most use alcohol combined with one or more other substances: marijuana, PCP, or speed.

Although the amounts and frequencies of reported alcohol use fit within the moderate range (a wine cooler every week or so), all who use alcohol indicated that the consequences have been negative. Those consequences include loud talk, fighting, having to call parents in order to get home, and having a hangover. Given these examples of consequences, it is likely that the reports of quantity and frequency are underestimated. Moreover, respondents' pattern of combining substances is consistent with patterns reported in the literature. This could indicate that, while none of the study participants report more significant consequences currently, problems may increase in the future. More important, some research has shown that much teenage sexual activity takes place under the influence of substances (Freeman et al. 1987).

Issues of Empowerment

An interesting finding resulted from responses to the question What was the experience of talking about yourself and your life situation like? The responses fell into three categories after three unclear answers were eliminated. Thirteen of the seventeen remaining responses (76 percent) were positive and contained elements of empowerment as described in a previous section. Examples of participants' comments included the following:

"It was fun because I seldom get to talk about myself."

"It made me think about what I want to do with my life—graduation, college, and sex."

"It was a good experience—allowing me to finish the story and asking me how I see myself in the future."

"I learned more about myself."

"It was good to talk to someone I could trust, and it gave me a chance to get out my feelings."

Three of the responses could be considered neutral. One participant indicated "I don't know, I'm not used to talking about myself," and another said, "It was nothing bad or spectacular." From their responses it can be inferred that a sense of empowerment did not occur, but it is also clear that the experience did not do harm. Only one response indicated a possibly negative experience, since the respondent said, "It felt weird, like talking to a psychiatrist, I didn't learn a thing." This youngster went on to say that his mother had taken him to a psychiatrist during the previous year, but she prepared him by saying he was going to have a physical examination. He was still angry and hurt by the experience. Possibly, going through the interview in spite of that experience was a positive risk on his part, demonstrating his willingness to trust the situation.

In general, the low mean ratings for a number of strengths identified by the participants (see table 14.2) and the positive relationship to their future goals indicates that many empowerment opportunities currently exist in their lives. Increased awareness of such strengths may encourage teens to find more effective ways to use and build upon them in the future.

On the other hand, the high ratings for some risk factors and barriers in the study indicate a potential negative impact on the selection of appropriate goals and their implementation. The negative images of Black males in the media and the lack of adult employed role models in their communities may have caused some teenagers in the study to feel disempowered. Selecting unrealistic goals or giving up hope for the future could be a result. Moreover, fathers in the study revealed additional risk factors in terms of their reproductive behaviors: they were younger than nonfathers when they had their first sexual experiences, had a higher frequency of sexual activity, used condoms selectively, and reported fewer nonsexual friendships with females. The impact of these disempowerment conditions seems significant enough to warrant additional research and practical changes at societal and community levels.

Implications for Future Research

While findings from the present research are useful, they involve an exploratory study which can be expanded in the future. It would be useful, for instance, to utilize a larger random sample and a longitudinal research design. The participants in this study were chosen because they met prescribed criteria for a purposeful sample and represented an unexplored subgroup within the population of young Black males. A random sample would no doubt include a larger percent of unemployed youngsters who do not participant in community programs such as those represented in this study and those who are school dropouts as well.

The advantage of a longitudinal study is that the strengths, barriers, goals, and reproductive behaviors that were the focus of this study could be researched to clarify how they change and interact over a period of four or five years. Strengths and barriers in other types of social networks could be studied in the process, including the role of employers, teachers, and helping professionals. The latter are of particular importance given the attitudes of study participants about not using social agencies in their communities for problem solving. Barriers and risk factors associated with these and other community conditions could be explored in more depth to determine their influence and how they can be changed.

Moreover, the literature has indicated that the reproductive behaviors of teenagers are influenced by the same behaviors of their parents and siblings as teenagers. Future research should focus on the factors listed in table 14.3 for these significant others, as well as whether they were teenage parents and the age of their first sexual experiences. Some of these potential influences were evident in the present study. One participant's father cautioned him about premarital sex by sharing that he had contracted a STD as a teenager. Another youth said his mother warned him about how fatherhood could prevent him from finishing school; she told him he had been born before she and the teenage father were married because they had not thought about preventing the pregnancy.

Practice Considerations and the Black Community

In addition to the research implications discussed in the previous section, a number of practice considerations flow from the study findings. They pertain primarily to Black helping professionals but may be useful also to white professionals who serve Black adolescents and their families. The focus is on the role of the Black community as an active participant in providing empowerment opportunities for Black youth.

Black parents, community leaders, helping professionals, and politicians may need to form coalitions to counteract negative media images of the Black male, improve job opportunities for adults in the Black community, improve safety within communities, and design more comprehensive mentoring programs to help Black adolescents develop and reach a broader range of goals for the future. These programs can provide conditions leading to a variety of empowerment experiences affecting reproductive behavior, drugs, violence, and employment opportunities as follows (most existing programs focus on only one or two of these areas):

1. *Self-Esteem Building:* focused on building self-pride, teaching self-assessment, and using psycho-education in a cognitive behavioral model to emphasize choices—especially in the area of sexuality.
2. *Life Skills Training:* involves teaching competencies and problem solving (urban skills, parenting, Outward Bound activities, college prep, mentoring, leadership training, assertiveness, and entrepreneurial skills).
3. *Cultural Maintenance:* emphasizes cultural awareness, consciousness raising, African and African-American history, rites of passage and other rituals, and the oral tradition.
4. *Job Readiness and Placement:* designed for vocational or job training; interpersonal and communication skills related to applying for and maintaining jobs; tutoring, remedial, or GED classes; job placement services; and creation of new job opportunities for Blacks (especially males) in the public and private sectors.
5. *Community or Political Development:* includes grass roots development beyond the level of individuals for more large-scale changes such as voter registration, tenant organizing, political lobbying and block voting, and neighborhood groups against crime including drug and alcohol abuse, homicide, and other physical or verbal violence.

In summary, a broader approach to changing communities could enhance the life experiences and achievement of future goals for youths such as those participating in the present study. It could also provide needed empowerment opportunities to strengthen Black families, counteracting individual, community, and societal barriers that are currently weakening these families. Growth would be possible, not only for families and their communities, but also for the professionals who provide services in those communities.

Conclusion

Many significant barriers and risk factors have been clarified through this study. Equally important are strengths related to the participants and family members whom the majority viewed as important in their lives. In order to build on these strengths, professionals can help design and implement services that reach out to Black teenage males in their communities and that are culturally relevant to how they perceive themselves and their important relationships.

Helping them to use those social networks as effectively as possible for problem solving, advice, and models of adult role responsibilities is an important strategy. Where these networks do not exist, professionals can help relatives and informal community leaders identified by the families to create such resources and opportunities for empowerment. Black churches, social organizations such as African-American sororities and fraternities, and civic organizations may be sources for these alternative social networks.

When it seems appropriate, practitioners can go beyond providing services to one youth or family and participate in coalition building involving Black parents, community leaders, and politicians. While this may be a new role for some practitioners, its benefits can include an increase in conditions that support empowerment and a reduction of the risk factors that young Black males perceive in their situations.

PART 4

Psychosocial Development and Coping

The Psychosocial Development and Coping of Black Male Adolescents: Clinical Implications

by Vera S. Paster

Gauntlet: 1. Two lines of men facing each other and armed with sticks or other weapons with which they beat a person forced to run between them. 2. A severe trial; an ordeal.   —*American Heritage Dictionary of the English Language*

The gauntlet that Black men run takes its toll at every age, but at nearly every stage of life the toll is very high and the effect is cumulative. . . . Even though Black men run the gauntlet all of their lives, the wonder is not that so many are wounded and crippled during their passage, but that so many survive with their minds healthy and their souls intact.   —McGhee, 1984, iii

The most disastrous of social indicators are disproportionately associated with the lives of African-American males (Gibbs 1984; McGhee 1984). Yet even the highest casualty figures indicate that most Black men not only survive the gauntlet but also cope adequately in the world. For example, by 1986, 15.5 percent of Black youth had dropped out of school (National Center 1989, table 2), but by 1980, 74 percent of Black men had completed high school (Jaynes and Williams 1989), and 28 percent of college enrollees were Black males (Arbeiter 1986). While most Black men were in low paying, menial jobs or were unemployed in 1986, 20 percent were in sales, technical jobs, professions, and managerial positions (U.S. Dept. of Labor 1987). Fifty percent of Black children under eighteen years of age were living in mother-headed families in 1985, but Black men were living with 50 percent of the children and 28 percent of wives (Jaynes and Williams 1989). In 1989 there were 328 mayors (Williams 1990) among 9,500 Black elected officials (Persons 1987). The tragic impact on Black men of this racist society is undeniable. Yet there is also the need to turn the spotlight on those who develop and retain their personal and social competence. Understanding these survivors can help prevent the destruction of self and others by which an alarmingly high proportion of Black males express their frustrations. It can also increase clinical effectiveness with them. These are the concerns of this chapter.

The African-American male youth confronts the formidable challenges of developing a positive identity as a self-directed individual in the context of family, community, and a racist society, while managing the turmoil of adolescence. He is a special object of projection for a white-male-dominated society that focuses on his blackness and his maleness as representations of its disowned self. Irresponsibility, lack of intelligence, unbridled sexuality, dangerous aggression, and other stereotypes thus attributed engender anxiety which the dominant society seeks to bind by its elaborate system of isolation, control, humiliation, and punishment of the rejected-self representation, Black males. Hence the gauntlet.

But the battle is not one-sided. There is energy, choice and power on the Black side of this struggle. The concept of salutogenesis proposed by Antonovsky (1979) applies. He says,

> Given the ubiquity of pathogens—microbiological, chemical, physical, psycho-
> logical, social, and cultural—it seems to me self-evident that everyone should
> succumb to this bombardment and be constantly dying. (P. 13)

According to Antonovsky, the critical difference results from "generalized resistance resources" (p. 99) in the person, the group, or the environment that facilitate
tension management. These resistance resources are not all-or-none phenomena.
They are personality characteristics and external supports that, in varying degrees, fortify against different kinds and intensities of stressors. Stressors are stim-
uli from within or from without that actually do challenge or are perceived to challenge the homeostatic balance necessary for competent internal and external
function. Each factor that strengthens against imbalance is a *salutogen*, or unit of
health. Salutogens combine to form resistance resources that promote the capacity to function adaptively—that is, resist disruption of homeostatic internal and
external positive self-management (Antonovsky 1979).

Competence is used herein to mean the innate drive to understand, to
master, and to influence the world, on a level that is appropriate to the developmental stage and sociocultural context of the youth. This competence depends
on the ability to maintain both internal balance and nondestructive interactions
with the outside world, and to be goal directed and effective (Loasa 1984; White
1984).

The salutogenic approach of this chapter does not explore the person's
illness but places an individual at one point on the health-illness or homeostasis-
disruption continuum at a given time, assuming that stressors are unrelenting.
Thus, the chapter focuses on the resistance resources, that is, the combination
of salutogens that are present and that need to be strengthened or established to
maintain or reach a healthy position on the continuum. Positions are not fixed.
Change is not only possible but constant.

This framework leads to a primary prevention model (Goldston 1977).
Rather than relying on rescue and repair measures for the fallen, the primary
prevention approach directs us to reinforce strength and resistance resources to
obviate breakdown. In addition, the model directs attention to the political, economic, and social changes necessary to ameliorate the assaultive stressors. Obviously the major battle is to realign the society so that African Americans have
equal access to its economic and social bounty as respected, contributing, equal
participants. In the meantime, however, concomitant emphasis must be placed
on preventing and healing the destructive consequences of the current reality.

Some of the elements in the cultural, family, and adaptational life of Black
male youth may be considered resistance resources. These salutogens require
identification, cultivation, and dissemination as a means of reinforcing and restoring Black adolescents' positive self-management. The following sections
will discuss the adolescent stage of development, and the impact of Black cul-

ture, family style, self-esteem, and attitudes toward education that characterize competent Black male youth. The clinical implications will then be addressed.

Adolescence

Adolescence in itself is a stressor (Blos 1983; Giovacchini 1977). The renewed urgency of dependency needs and aggressive impulses, extremes of mood and passion, joined by sexual awakening, underline the youth's need for controls, but controls have become unreliable. The adolescent is often filled with raging self-doubt, alternating with unrealistic omnipotence. His tolerance for fools and enemies is almost nil, and his idealization of heroes, almost boundless. His ability to differentiate between thought, wish, impulse, and action is compromised. He fluctuates from despair to elation, from enthusiastic abandonment to studied indifference to anomie.

The loving support of confirming persons and a sense of belonging are psychological necessities, especially during adolescence. At the same time, the adolescent is impelled to prove his ability to take an independent stand and to thrive on his own. He looks with varying degrees of trepidation to the future when he must achieve both goals. Through all of this he must struggle to develop a sense of identity, to face facts about his assets and limitations, and to decide what he wants to do about them. He must commit himself to the kind of person he wants to be and choose the place in the world that he aims to occupy.

Since the poverty rate for Black people rose to 32.7 percent in 1990 (Pear 1992), and 50 percent of Black children live in poverty (Barringer 1992), many adolescents have grown up poor. The more this is true, the more likely the youth is to have lacked protection from the most devastating of disconfirmations at school, in the streets, and even at home, convincing him to trust no one and to believe that no good lies ahead (Dohrenwend and Dohrenwend 1974). Many, however, in similar circumstances preserve their optimism and confidence. These are the survivors (Garmezy 1987; Rutter 1987; White 1984).

According to Erikson (1963), the adolescent's primary task is to establish his own identity and to avoid confusion about his role. Erikson's epigenetic model asserts that this task is facilitated to the degree that conflicts in the youth's earlier life stages were resolved positively. As an infant, was he able to establish basic trust in the benevolent reliability of the world? Were subsequent tasks well accomplished: autonomy rather than doubt and shame, initiative rather than guilt, capacity for industry and competence rather than a sense of inadequacy and inferiority? The more satisfactorily these developmental issues were managed, the more the youth arrives at adolescence with a sense of continuity and coherence, and the better he will be enabled to handle his adolescent struggles.

But no matter how preoccupied he is with these developmental issues, the African-American youth cannot escape racism. Some develop what Ogbu (1986) describes as a "collective institutional discrimination perspective" (p.28), because, according to Ogbu, Black people in America occupy a "caste-like" position. That perspective is the belief that it is impossible to enter the preferred or middle-class way of life either through one's own initiative or by adapting one's behavior to that of the dominant group. Yet Black youth have not been spared indoctrination into the materialistic and other values of the society, nor with identification with a male sex role that requires them continually to prove a manhood that is defined by both Black and white males to mean provision of economic support and social protection to a family (Cazenave 1984). The Black adolescent's stage-appropriate narcissistic doubts about worth, competence, and identity are combined with his indoctrination with the criteria for respect pushed by an alienating dominant culture and that culture's simultaneous barriers to those perquisites. The resulting dilemmas are indeed severe stressors.

Resistance Resources of Black Male Youth

Black youth can draw on a number of resources in this struggle, including Black culture, family, their own self-esteem, and certain school influences.

Black Culture

Antonovsky (1979) found that survivors of circumstances of dire stress like concentration camps tended to be those who had a strong sense of belonging to a stable subgroup which had predictable, clearly defined expectations and definitions of self held in common with other subgroup members. African-Americans are a cultural subgroup. This subgroup's traditions have made it possible for its members to survive slavery and the ensuing struggles. The more recent attempts to conceptualize Black culture (Boykin and Toms 1985; Jenkins 1982; Nobles 1978; Ogbu 1985) seek to capture the essence of what that culture is—whether it is a poverty-determined variant of the dominant culture (Lewis 1966; Moynihan 1965), a unique African-derived culture (Nobles 1980), or another combination (Boykin and Toms 1985; Sudarkasa 1988). Because of the heterogeneity of African Americans, it is less important to reach agreement about specific cultural origin and content than to affirm the existence of an African-American culture. There is a general consensus, however, about the African-American attributes identified by Hill (1972): strong kinship bonds, achievement orientation, adaptability of family roles, strong religious orientation, and a strong work orientation. Boykin (1986) describes Black culture as a combination of mainstream American values, remnants of West African values, and reaction to racial oppression, the point of view of this chapter.

Practical judgment as well as Antonovsky's findings (1979) lead to the belief that competence among African-American youth would be supported by positive identification with their cultural heritage. Certainly the "Black is beautiful," "Black power" movements are credited with reinforcing Black pride.

Studies of the color preference of Black children, however, have not supported this notion. While most of these studies are problematic in methodology. They have found that the older the child, the greater the preference for Black over white, but that self-esteem is independent of the selection of Black over white (H. McAdoo 1985; J. McAdoo 1985; Ward and Braun 1972). Parham and Helms (1985a) found that the particular level of Black identity (Cross 1978, 1985) was related to whether or not the child's self-esteem was positive. Apparently, it is not necessary to prefer Black as a racial membership group in a racist society to benefit from membership in that group, or to be influenced by the family styles that express its culture.

Family Influence

Black grandmothers' involvement is a salutogen for youth. Their contributions are extensive and, to a large extent, replace absent fathers' contributions. For example, Tolson and Wilson (1990) focused on family composition, using the Family Environment Scale to measure the nature of the interactions within lower- and middle-class Black families. They found a shift to more emphasis on achievement, moral and religious values, and on organization and control when the adult caretakers increased from one to two, regardless of whether the second was a grandmother or the father. Black grandmothers are more active in child-rearing than comparable white grandmothers; they are more likely to be a member of the household of younger children; and they more actively link the family to the larger kinship system (Pearson et al. 1990). In another study, 100 percent of Black females and 91 percent of Black males, as compared to 75 percent of white males and 72 percent of white females, considered their grandmothers as significant, helpful parent figures (Schab 1982). The active participation in child-rearing and family support by grandmothers, as well as other kin, and even nonbiologically related kin-equivalents, is a characteristic of Black culture (Boyd-Franklin 1989; White 1984).

While there are fewer such studies, some effort has been directed to the study of normal Black families (Billingsley 1968; Boyd-Franklin 1989; Clark 1983; Hill 1972; Lewis and Looney 1983). Lewis and Looney carried out a comprehensive examination of well-functioning, two-parent, working-class Black families. Ten years before, they had carried out a similar study of well-functioning, middle-class white families. The most competent Black families were characterized by egalitarian power sharing within a strong parental coalition; recognition and acceptance of each member's individuality; clear and direct expressions of thoughts and feelings with mutual acceptance; empathy, warmth, affection, and optimism; members assuming an individual sense of responsibility; and demonstration of instrumental efficiency with life's tasks. The adolescents were friendly, open, self-confident, active and assertive doers who had average grades, were future oriented, and became active in extracurricular enterprises. They expressed positive regard for their parents. They had a slight inclination to regard their mothers as those with whom they could more readily discuss sensitive issues and to perceive their fathers as the greater disciplinarians. They had no significant conflicts with outside authority. They did have some difficulty in separating their own desires from their perception of parental expectations. Lewis and Looney found that these Black families were similar in almost all respects to the well-functioning, affluent white families who were studied earlier. The least competent working-class Black families, in comparison to the most competent Black families, were described as more rigid, less sharing of power and feelings, and less competent in negotiating or solving problems. There was also a marked difference in the role of religion, which was central in the lives of the most competent families but of less importance to the least competent.

The Lewis and Looney study was restricted to two-parent working-class Black families. Clark (1983) studied both two-parent and one-parent low-income urban Black families. The results of both studies were remarkably similar.

Clark developed in-depth case studies of the families of high and low school achievers. Whether consisting of one or two parents, the families of children who were successful in school shared characteristics that differentiated them from the families of low achievers. The high achievers' families groomed the children for the student role, encouraging academic skill and learning-related activities. There was frequent parent-child dialogue; clear and consistent limits were set; and an atmosphere of warmth, acceptance, and nurturance prevailed. The parents were optimistic about their own effectiveness and empowered themselves to freely intervene in the schools on behalf of their children. Like Lewis and Looney (1983), Clark found that competent youths and their parents struggled together to achieve an optimal position between over-control and independence, while emphasizing the maintenance of the bonds of affection and cohesion within the family. It is important to reiterate that Clark found the same parent-child positive interactions in single-parent as in two-parent families that produced competent high achievers.

Because increasing numbers of Black children are growing up without their fathers, the effects of positive family dynamics are significant. Most studies have attended to deleterious results of father absence, but other studies have found that even when fathers are present, Black boys are more strongly influenced by their mothers. And, as we have seen, single mothers do develop high-functioning children. The picture is mixed.

One employment study revealed that the Black youths who identified with an adult of the same sex were more likely to value jobs that provided independent risk-taking opportunities and secure futures. These youths also internalized the value of work as a means to independence, self-esteem, and autonomy as well as money (Thomas and Shields 1987).

Upwardly mobile, achieving, effective Black males reported stronger attempts to be like their fathers and felt encouraged by their mothers to identify with their fathers. At the same time, they shared their mothers' ideals and values and also were strongly influenced by their mothers' belief in hard work, sacrifice, and the concept that effort is appropriately rewarded (Moulton and Stewart 1971).

Daniels (1986) found that there were "super-achieving" Black males reared in single-parent, mother-headed homes, but they had twice as many years of father presence than those who were underemployed. The men who were chronically unemployed had less than half as many years of father presence (Daniels 1986). Krause (1985) found that Black youth from two-parent families had higher self-esteem than did those from one-parent families.

Taylor (1989) found that parental models were most important for Black youth who had achieved college attendance. Their mothers were most significant, especially during childhood, and were the models chosen for moral values and for emotional support. During adolescence, fathers or father surrogates were significant models if they provided pertinent behavior patterns and value orientations, or if they had made important familial contributions, as judged by the youths themselves.

On the other hand, Taylor (1989) found that less successful inner-city youths had more trouble identifying with any persons who were significant models for them, because they distrusted others too much to invest in them as role models. More identified with their mothers than with their fathers, and many were indifferent or negative toward their fathers.

Self-Esteem

The self-esteem of Black children has been widely studied. The assumption is that those who feel better about themselves will cope more effectively, but this has not been found to be necessarily true. The consensus is that Black children have high self-esteem in the general sense, whether or not they feel successful in particular areas.

Like all persons, Black youth strive for adequacy (White 1984). They turn away from disconfirming areas to those of competency. For the most part, this shift occurs in relation to school. Black children lag academically, and Black males are not well treated in school. But Black children can maintain high self-regard even when faced with school failure (Hare 1988, 1985; Holliday 1985; Spencer 1985). They frequently turn to peers for confirmation. The more academic and social failures accumulate in the school setting, the more absorbed and competent they become in the peer setting.

Thus, there is more than one source of self-esteem for youth (Hare 1985). They construct a general sense of esteem, as well as school self-esteem, home-based self-esteem, peer self-esteem, job self-esteem, sports self-esteem, and esteem pegged to all the other important areas of their functions.

Allen (1978) found that general self-esteem was highest when the mother's socioeconomic status was relatively high, when there was parental approval and closeness within the family, and when the parents exercised strong control over the son's decision making.

Holliday (1985) examined the competencies that Black children demonstrated in three different settings—home, school, and neighborhood. She compared children who were judged to be high and low performers and found that different skills were required in the following different settings: functional life skills in the home, interpersonal skills and academic proficiency at school, and problem solving skills in the neighborhood. She found no consistency between home and neighborhood competency and academic proficiency. Competence in all three situations requires the child to be flexible in using a repertoire of skills appropriately selected. The difference between children who were judged to have high and low competencies was determined according to seven characteristics, including family size, number of persons per room, presence of an adult male, and the giving of responsibilities. High achievers were distinguished by being members of large families, living in more crowded homes, and having greater demands placed on them. These children were also strongly socialized and had high self-esteem.

In general, competent youths feel good about themselves. But so do many who encounter failure. Positive self-esteem is a salutogen, but it appears that it is not a distinguishing characteristic of successful Black youths.

School Function

School achievement is an age-appropriate index of competence. Unfortunately, it is a major stressor that systematically eliminates Black youth, especially young Black males, from equity in entering the competition for economic and social survival. The major emphasis must be on the competence of the school's teaching and interaction with Black children. Dropout and achievement rates indicate the poor job that the schools are doing in that regard (Edelman 1985; Spencer 1985). Hare and Castenell (1985) state that "Black males are probably the most feared, least likely to be identified with, and least likely to be effectively taught group" (p. 211). Yet, 11 percent completed four years of college in 1980–81, 5.8 percent earned M.A. degrees, and 3.9 percent were awarded doctorates during that year (Jaynes and Williams 1989).

Abatso (1985) found that Black community college students who excelled did so, not because of greater aptitude, but as a result of their personality characteristics and coping behavior. She found that high-coping males, in comparison to average and low copers, had higher self-concepts of ability, more internality in their locus of control, more confidence in their academic capability, and a high positive reaction to successful achievement. They used more varied coping strategies more flexibly and were more comfortable in initiating contact with their teachers. They planned their schedules, prepared their work, were persistent, and were active in making choices and decisions.

According to Scanzoni (1985), three factors support Black children's scholastic achievement: their socioeconomic position, the role modeling of the expected behaviors by parent(s), and the nature of the influences provided by kin, peers, school, church, and the media. These outside influences are very difficult to control. Fortunately, many studies have found that the youth is not a passive captive. He makes choices among peers, adult models, and media messages. His selection is largely determined by the basic values with which he identifies (Mussen 1983).

Allen (1978) believes that Black sons' school function is strongly influenced by goals and aspirations that their parents hold for them. These goals and aspirations determine parent(s) child-rearing practices and the way they affectively interact with their sons. He found that adolescents' achievement conformed to the grades expected by the parents, their emphasis on college, and their aspirations concerning the youths' subsequent occupational status. The competent youth expressed warmth for their parents, which interacted with parents' positive approval of them. These approving parents of competent youth also exercised strong control over their sons' decision making.

While other studies have found that students poor in academics were more self-critical, Katz et al. (1976) found that better Black students were more self-critical. They also found a high relationship between positive social reinforcement from parents and teachers and the youths' self-approval.

Fordham (1988) has found that school achievers tend to be "raceless." Since Black culture has a collective view of the world, many Black youth see their lot in terms of how they perceive all Black persons, especially peers, treated. Because the schools are rejectors of both Black male students and Black-style self-presentation, these youth reject school. School achievers, according to this theory, have loyalty to a sense of Blackness, but because of various influences, they have a greater loyalty to education as a means of achieving middle-class success. Since they are also aware that the school rejects Blackness, they minimize their Black identification, assimilate, and become, thereby, raceless, as the price of school success.

Academic success for Black male youth is a complicated matter. While certain styles of parental handling have been found to be associated with such success, neglected or negatively handled youth also can succeed. Their academic facility, the school's instruction and social climate, and one or more significant role models probably contribute more to the school competence of these youth and are therefore more necessary for them than for those whose families are able to provide the required incentives and support.

Summary, Resistance Resources

These findings indicate that the copers among African-American adolescent males come from economically deprived and middle-class backgrounds, from two-parent, one-parent, or multigeneration extended families, or from other family structures. Whatever the composition, the families that develop successful youth share a set of characteristics that include loving support, loyalty, parent direction, protection of the youth, and consistent teaching and modeling of values and competence. As a result, the youth are well prepared to deal with the pressures of adolescence when the time comes. The youth believe in themselves and in their ability to determine their futures. They are not discouraged by the barriers set before them by a society that is stratified by race. Nor have they absorbed the stereotypes that reserve academic achievement, upward mobility, and self-protection for the Euro-American other and construct peer involvement and street culture as the essence of true Blackness. These are the generalized resistance resources with which some Black adolescent males "overcome."

Clinical Application

The salutogenic approach to clinical intervention with Black male adolescents attends to the socioecological forces in the youths' lives as well as to their internalized psychological state. It seeks to stimulate their generalized resistance resources and to reduce the destructive stressors that impinge on the youths. It is a problem-solving approach that uses an isomorphic plan of intervention. Isomorphism assumes that all actions and reactions are mutually dependent and reciprocally linked. A change in one will alter and be altered by each component in the system. The points of clinical intervention, therefore, are selected on the basis of the probable effectiveness of producing change with the resources available to the clinician, since a salutary change in one area will initiate and be reinforced by reactive changes in other areas. This applies to the areas of the youth's representation of his world, his internal accommodations, and the daily realities of his life.

Jones (1985) presents a framework that is useful for guiding this kind of treatment with Black male adolescents. He suggests consideration of four variables: (1) the client's reactions to racial oppression; (2) the influence of the majority culture; (3) the influence of the traditional African-American culture; and (4) his individual and family experiences and endowments. Possible application follows.

Reactions to Racial Oppression

By adolescence Black youth have developed relatively entrenched defensive styles in relation to the discrimination they have experienced, observed, or heard about. Their behavior and attitudes reflect, in part, their reactions. A youth may be guarded, suspicious, belligerent, self-effacing, or ingratiating—all self-protective measures. He may attribute all his troubles to unfair treatment, prejudiced teachers, or to "just the way it is," without considering possible alternative actions on his part. His walk, talk style, dress, and general appearance may be in exaggerated Black youth style as statements of defiance, or on the contrary, nondescript and innocuous. He may be preoccupied with the racist world or deny its occurrence. The clinician should not expect that the adolescent can or will verbalize these attitudes or even have insight about them.

Since many Black people, as well as non-Black people, fear young Black men, the clinician must be aware that harassments, rejections, and casual affronts are probably ongoing, and that the youth may bring his reactions into the sessions.

Competent youth are realistically aware of the discrimination they face and are prepared to deal with it as a problem to be solved. As a result, they neither absorb negative self-appraisals nor are distracted from their own goals.

At an appropriate time, clinicians, Black or non-Black, need to raise questions about the occurrence of racial hurts to encourage communication about this difficult area, to confirm the youth's perception of the reality, and to promote his constructive problem solving about such experiences, where practical.

Influence of the Majority Culture

How isolated has the youth been from exposure to the dominant culture? Has his knowledge of its ways and its members been limited to images conveyed by television and the movies, except for essentially negative contacts with school personnel, strangers, the police? Does he know enough about the ways of the dominant society to be able to protect himself as he moves about in it? Does he actively reject any behavior that he labels white? or Black? Is he intimidated by the belief that all of the "others" are richer, smarter, more powerful, and more beautiful than those with whom he identifies? Is he furious? Or resigned? The clinician should also be aware that if the youth comes from a middle-class background, he may have been reared completely within the dominant society's value system. He also may have been so protected from potentially hostile racial encounters that these issues are remote to him.

Competent Black youth are well aware of the values and expectations of the majority culture. They have a realistic view of white people as fallible individuals with strengths and weaknesses like everyone else, regardless of how segregated their exposure has been. They are confident in their taste and goals and do not worry about whether they are Black enough. They are self-directed, based on values instilled by family members and other significant persons in their lives. Many of these values overlap those of the dominant culture.

Influence of Traditional African-American Culture

There is a relationship between consciousness and content of Black culture and socioeconomic status. The poorest group un-self-consciously identifies with being Black, and during adolescence especially enacts its view of the proper Black attitudes, dress, taste, achievements. The middle class tends to be less restricted to attitudes and behaviors that they define as Black, or at least to be more flexible about what is included. Youth from materially and educationally advantaged families experience Black culture as a social and political agenda which frequently they can articulate. Many of the dysfunctional Black adolescents referred for clinical attention, however, are not aware of an African-American culture, although they benefit from it, and reach for a distinctive Black presence, even as do competent youth. When the understanding of the dysfunctional adolescent is limited to the stereotypes of school dropout, the unemployed street corner lounger, the hustler within the alternative street economy, the sexual adventurer and drug experimenter, and the tough guy, initiated through arrests and jail, he will bring those images into the sessions for status and for attempts to titillate the clinician. Other youth believe there is nothing positive within the Black experience and actively reject it or try to dissociate themselves from it, thereby simultaneously rejecting and dissociating parts of themselves.

The clinician needs to understand the youth's view of his culture and, if possible, to see to his exposure to knowledge about and models of proud conceptualizations of the traditional positives that have characterized Black people. Participation in youth groups and church activities can help toward this purpose for salutogenic effect.

Individual and Family Experiences and Endowments

The likelihood is that Black adolescents referred to agencies for clinical attention will be poor, since almost 33 percent of Black people and 50 percent of Black children are officially classified as below the poverty level (Barringer 1992; Pear 1992). Clinicians tend to pathologize even creative arrangements resorted to by poor Black families that actually have salutogenic as well as problematic effects. For example, absent fathers' roles are assumed by biologically related or non-biologically related males in the kinship system, or by serial involvement with different members of the kinship system. Frequently all of these persons try to exercise authority over the youth, which may cause problems. Mothers on welfare allowances often work off-the-books in order to survive, are secretive about the employment, and sometimes try to please authorities by accepting appointments that they are not able to keep. Some single women endure abusive relationships with the fathers of their children or a male companion in exchange for the financial protection their contributions provide the family. Often poor Black parents try to keep tight control over their sons' behavior because of their fears of the dangers that surround them. Or they give up. The sons react negatively to both extremes.

Clinicians often make another systematic error. Because of the limited repertoire of behavioral expressions of distress displayed by Black male youth, especially the poor, clinicians do not recognize the anxiety and conflict beneath the acting out, the pain and cry for help beneath "oppositional defiant disorder" or "conduct disorder" (DSM-I.11-R). When depression of Black male adolescents is masked in this way, clinicians may not recognize it (Paster 1985; Toolan 1974). The reckless self-endangerment reflected in the extremely high homicide rates among young Black men (Barriers and Opportunities 1989) and the recent triple increase of suicide among them (Gary 1981) express this depression. A study by Lewis and her associates (1979) demonstrates the systematic routing of Black youth to the courts and correctional services, while white youth of equal symptomatology and intrapsychic function were directed to mental health facilities.

Even clinicians do not escape the negative value judgments that the dominant society makes about the coping efforts of Black adolescents. The myriad of intractable problems that beset their lives are daunting to those from relatively protected backgrounds. As a result, clinicians start off, not with hope, but primed for defeat. The prophecy is often fulfilled. Once such a youth is engaged in the treatment enterprise (Paster 1985), however, and adjustments are made to the youth's communication style, the intrapsychic component of his situation is responsive to the same kinds of joining, and analysis of transference and resistance, that is necessary to treat any adolescent.

These variables are areas to be considered in diagnosing and treating the adolescent. Some may not apply at all; others may warrant exclusive focus. Some may be amenable to intervention while others, more significant as stressors, may be inaccessible to intervention. All four variables are likely to be affected, however, by changes in one or more.

Summary and Conclusions

Black males are the scapegoats of this society. Early in life their disadvantaged position in relation to power distribution is dramatically brought to their attention upon their initial encounters with the larger society, usually in school. Yet many Black men escape lasting damage. We learn from these competent survivors that they tend to share in common a supportive, directive upbringing, that they reinforce home-instilled values by their selection of models, that they identify with achievement, generally have high self-esteem, and struggle with their sense of Blackness. There is more that is known and more to learn about the differences between these successful youths and their dysfunctional peers.

The salutogenic, primary-prevention approach calls our attention to the drive for health and competence that Black male adolescents, like all persons, have. They have the ability to withstand even severe distress if there are sufficient strengthening resources. Clinicians can more effectively facilitate this process if they broaden traditional interventions to include, not only intrapsychic and family-centered treatment, but also initiation of salutogenic changes in other areas of the youth's function.

Finally, the salutogenic, primary-prevention approach does not let us forget that human distress results from a mismatch between stress and the ongoing efforts to adapt to the life we have. Any who are seriously committed to reducing the toll on Black males must seek to change the forces that result in their organized abuse. These efforts should aim to make it unnecessary for Black adolescents and men to require heroic efforts to survive with "minds healthy and . . . souls intact" (McGhee 1984).

CHAPTER 16

The Cool Pose:
An Africentric Analysis

by Merlin R. Langley

The purposes of this chapter are: (1) to examine the psychosocial consequences of an Eurocentric socially constructed definition of masculinity on the behavior of African-American males; (2) to define "the cool pose" as a construct and as a phenomenon evidenced by some African-American males as a symbolic expression of their masculinity; (3) to examine and understand the role and function of the "cool pose" as displayed by the African-American male from an Africentric cultural model.

Masculinity: A Eurocentric Perspective

A perusal of the recent literature related to the study of men and masculinity indicates that there are only a few references concerning the etiology of the different types of role behaviors displayed by African-American men in America. In particular, there exists a poverty of literature regarding the etiology, growth, and development of these various roles and their relation to the African-American male's sense of masculinity. The ramifications of this void in the literature are many. There is the lack of understanding in the definition of masculinity across various racial-cultural groups within American society. There is no organized forum to discuss the effects on the African-American male particularly of such negative Eurocentric structural-cultural factors as institutional racism, discrimination, and oppression. The African-American male represents only 7 percent of the U.S. population and has the shortest lifespan among African Americans and whites; he is considered by various governmental agencies to be an "endangered species" (Centers for Disease Control 1983; Department of Health and Human Services 1985). For these reasons, the omissions in the literature appear highly noteworthy.

Historically, the traditional view of masculinity has been based on a sex role model that systematically attributed certain attitudes and behaviors to males on the basis of biology, cultural evolution, or psychological predisposition (Kimmel and Messner 1989, 4–7). However, a major limitation of this model was that it "ignored the extent to which our conceptions of masculinity and femininity . . . [are] relational; that is, the product of gender relations that are historically and socially conditioned" (Kimmel 1987, 12). Furthermore, an examination of research in the fields of sociology and psychology using the above model as a conceptual framework indicated a lack of interest in understanding the effects of culture, race, or ethnicity on males', in particular Black males', view of themselves as men. A countervailing force, beginning in the 1970s, was the "mens movement," a social movement that examined issues (men's anger, domestic violence, war, and peace) pertaining to the roles of men in contemporary American society (Shiffman 1987, 295). A central focus of this social movement concerned the conditions of men's lives that influenced, directly or indirectly, their perception of themselves as men (Feigen-Fasteau 1975; Pleck and Sawyer 1974; Farrel 1975).

The development of the men's movement has been conceptualized as consisting of two distinct historical periods or generations (Kimmel and Messner 1989). Beginning in the mid 1970s, the first generation of researchers in men's issues adopted a feminist-derived framework for critiquing traditional explanations of gender differences. The major contribution of this generation of researchers was the publication of a number of books that challenged the idea that the traditional concepts of masculinity should be the norm against which both men and women were measured. These researchers also began to question the validity and necessity of certain behaviors associated with the traditional concept of masculinity (i.e., the prescribed roles of males in American society), which appeared to have constrained many men's lives and experiences. In other words, this first generation of researchers emphasized in their analyses the limitations inherent in assuming that only one hegemonic definition of masculinity should be the standard by which all men and women should be judged (Brod 1987; Carrigan, Connel, and Lee 1985; Connel 1987; David and Brannon 1976; Farrell 1975; Feigen-Fasteau 1975; Hern 1987; Kimmel 1987; Pleck and Pleck 1980; Pleck and Sawyer 1974).

The women's movement and the gay liberation movement were the historical precursors of the men's movement. The organizational goals of the men's movement have paralleled the political concerns of the prior movements. Attention has been focused on issues related to sexism, and as a result the men's movement has become involved in consciousness raising activities. The men's movement also adopted a number of issues raised by the gay liberation movement, such as the rights of gay men to parent children and more recently the treatment of gay men suffering from AIDS—acquired immunodeficiency syndrome (Shiffman 1987). In addition, the men's movement has raised a number of issues derived directly from the experiences of men in their daily lives and their subjective perception of themselves. Job satisfaction, gender roles, men's health, and fathering are examples of these issues (Pleck 1985, 1987; Thompson and Pleck 1987; Shiffman 1987).

Initially, the challenge to the hegemonic definition of masculinity came from men whose masculinity was seen as significantly deviating from the traditional definition of masculinity (i.e., Black men, gay men, and men representing different cultural and ethnic groups). In this vein, Messner (1989, 11), studying men's issues, stated the following:

> Working class men, men of color, gay men, and younger and older men were all observed as departing in significant ways from the traditional definition of masculinity . . . therefore it was easy to see these men as enacting problematic or deviant versions of masculinity. . . . Black masculinity differs from white masculinity, each further modified by age and class.

The work considered by many experts in the field of men's studies to be the "single most important book" of the men's movement is Pleck's (1981) *The Myth of Masculinity*. This treatise criticized the previously unexamined assumptions underlying the traditional sex role model used to socialize males in contemporary American society. Pleck reviewed the empirical literature and analyzed the elements that are normally assumed to be related to the traditional definition of masculinity. His analysis of the literature yielded no empirical support for these normative features. Pleck concluded that the assumed constituent elements underlying the model of the traditional sex role were wholly incapable of describing men's experiences. In fact, he saw the traditional male sex role model as "problematic, historically specific, and unattainable" and proposed that it be replaced by a "male sex role strain" model. The "male sex role strain" model suggests that the conventional expectations of what it means to be a man within Western culture (e.g., provider, protector, pillar of strength, independent, active and achievement oriented, dominant in interpersonal relationships, level-headed and self-contained, and suppressing emotions) are difficult to achieve and generally lead to self-depreciation (Thompson and Pleck 1987; Pleck 1989).

During the early 1980s, the focus of research on women by feminist scholars reflected a basic interest in the ways in which different women experience femininity as a function of membership in various social groups (class, age, race, sexual orientation, etc.). The focus of research of the second generation of researchers on men and masculinity paralleled the work of feminist researchers and attempted to clarify how variations in men's lives and experiences are central to an understanding of their lives (Kimmel and Messner 1989; Pleck 1989; Shiffman 1987).

Men's movement researchers, similar to feminist scholars, also adopted "social constructionism" as a theoretical framework for understanding how the traditional definition of masculinity is maintained through various social institutions within contemporary American society. The social constructionist model posits that the definition of what it means to be a man is "neither transhistorical nor culturally universal, but rather varies from culture to culture and within any one culture over time," as a result of social processes operating within a given culture at a given time (Kimmel and Messner 1989, 11). That is, different cultural groups (e.g., racial and/or ethnic groups) have various definitions of masculinity.

In sum, a new definition of masculinity (i.e., what it means to be a man) began to emerge in the 1980s as a result of the influence of a group of men who felt they had been "left out," and because of Pleck's (1981) proposed male sex role strain model as an alternative to the traditional sex role model. Essentially, this change in the definition of masculinity denotes a conceptual (paradigm) shift (Pleck 1981, 1983; Gerson and Peiss 1985). However, it remains a limited perspective, because it concerns mainly the kinds of issues and experiences of white males in American society.

This "blind spot" is the result of the Eurocentric socialization process within contemporary American society. According to Kimmel and Messner (1989, 3), "white people rarely think of themselves as 'raced' people, and therefore rarely think of race as a central element in their experience. But people of color, on the other hand, are marginalized by race, and so the centrality of race is both painfully obvious and is in need of further study."

Robert Staples (1989) has attempted to describe the consequences of this benign neglect of the role of race in the research programs of whites relative to the African-American male in American society. He asserts that social science literature has perpetuated many negative stereotypes about African-American men as a result of applying white American norms to Black behavior. The social science literature fails to convey an understanding of the meaning and form of masculinity expressed in African-American culture (Staples 1989, 74). In addition, he states that in the case of "Black men, their subordination as a racial minority has more than cancelled out their advantages as males in the larger American society" (p. 73). He concludes that, generally speaking, African-American men have been ascribed a marginal status in American society.

Recent research has documented the physical and psychological consequences resulting from the marginal status imposed and maintained by Eurocentric culturally derived definitions of the role and function of the African-American male. For example, chronic unemployment and/or underemployment are experienced by many African-American men as a result of their race and membership in a minority group in American society. These kinds of frequently occurring events can and often do endanger African-American men's psychological health. Again, government reports, articles in the social science literature, and the mass media suggest that African-American males between the ages of fifteen and twenty-four are an "endangered species" (Ball 1989; Gibbs 1988; Morris 1989; Moses 1989; Parham and McDavis 1987; Staples 1989).

Additionally, daily encounters with racism and overt discrimination in American society no doubt negatively affect the lives of African Americans in general and African-American men in particular. The frequency of these daily encounters has helped to propel many Black men into significant stress-related health problems. Some literature suggests that "stress for the African American is perhaps more varied, more intense, and more sustained than almost any other cultural group" (Hilliard 1985, 74).

According to Pierce (1970), an African-American psychiatrist at Harvard Medical School, the concept of microaggression has been useful in understanding the degree of psychological distress experienced by Blacks in the larger white society. He argues that inner-city youth are reminded daily of their disadvantaged marginal status in American society. Pierce suggests that the following types of daily reminders constitute acts of microaggression and are unconsciously anticipated by Black youth (and Black adults) when they interact with members of the majority culture:

> Teacher calls him stupid, a white stranger gets up and walks away when he sits next to him on a crowded bus or subway; a bank teller reacts suspiciously when he

tries to cash a check; an employer refuses to interview him for a job, a clerk ignores him in a department store; a cab driver ignores him or refuses to take him to
a "Black" neighborhood; a police officer stops to question him in a white neighborhood. (1970, p. 10)

Pierce suggests that as a result of these many and varied microaggressions, many
Black youth are faced with a psychological dilemma. If they do not respond to
the assaults and insults, they can (1) internalize their anger and become depressed, or (2) convert these angry feelings into such psychosomatic symptoms
as hypertension and ulcers, and/or (3) reduce their level of frustration through
alcohol or drug use and abuse. Regardless of the choice, he concluded "these
daily interactions take an enormous toll on the mental health of Black youth in
America, driving many of them to the depths of despair and the brink of mad-
ness." Other clinical researchers (Gibbs 1988) have noted that the entry of many
African Americans, in particular African-American male youth, into the ranks
of the homeless has made them more vulnerable to severe physical and mental
health problems stemming from a lack of housing, inadequate health care, and
the vicissitudes of survival on the streets.

Recent epidemiological findings suggest that psychological disorders
have increased among African-American males. Beyond this, homicide now
represents the leading cause of death for African-American males, accidents
represent their second leading cause of death, and suicide rates, having tripled
since 1960, represent their third leading cause of death. These three categories,
called the "new morbidity," account for 75 percent of the fatalities in the fifteen
to twenty-four age group among African-American males (Centers for Disease
Control 1983). The concept of "new morbidity," coined by the Centers for Disease Control (CDC), was designed to describe the "interrelationship of these
self-destructive and life threatening behaviors among American youth, in particular, young Black males" (Gibbs 1984, 1985).

Clearly, based on the review of the above literature, the work of white
social scientists focusing on masculinity seems not to address the experience of
the African-American male and his conception of masculinity. The relationship
between displays of masculinity among African-American males and their relation to cultural, economic, social and political oppression in American society,
resulting in physical and psychological distress, has not been examined. Consequently, there are gaps in the empirical literature regarding how the African-
American male's internalized view of masculinity influences his personality and
the quality of his interpersonal relationships with significant others.

Black Masculinity: A Social Psychological Perspective

Majors (1983, 1986, 1987, 1989, 1990; Majors and Billson 1992), an African-
American social scientist, has attempted through his research to address this

"blind spot" or gap in the social science literature. Specifically, he has focused his attention on describing and understanding how the contemporary African-American male makes use of different masculine "cool" behaviors as psychological defenses or coping mechanisms (Majors 1990, 5). Very few social scientists have conducted research focusing on the role and function of cool behaviors as an important social and historical aspect of the psychological reality of the African-American male in American society (Peterman 1986; Tunsil 1987). We would like to emphasize that this virtual absence of scientific research related to study of cool behaviors is important given that historically, according to Janzen (1989), the phenomenon of cool in Africa dates back to at least 2000–3000 B.C. He believes that coolness was expressed in oral culture, character building, artwork, linguistics, dance, initiation rituals, warriors cults, mating rituals, and the concept of health.

A cursory review of poetry and prose literature (e.g., short stories, novels, plays) written by and for African Americans indicates that coolness is seen as a fundamental character trait of the African-American male in his struggle to assert his masculinity (Ellison 1952; Malcolm X and Haley 1964; Wright 1945). These works tend to depict the African-American male constantly in a struggle to establish, maintain, or enhance his masculinity. For example, the African-American feminist writer Michele Wallace (1987) describes, within the context of the Black movement of the 1960s, the struggle of the African-American male to assert his masculinity. She states the following:

> The Black man of the 1960 found himself wondering why it had taken him so long
> . . . yes, he wanted freedom, equality, all of that. But what he really wanted was to
> be a man. . . . Out of his sense of urgency came a struggle, the Black Movement,
> which was nothing more or less than the Black man's struggle to attain his pre-
> sumably lost manhood. (1987, 32)

Clearly, many African-American observers view cool behaviors as an important phenomenon and a very real element in the African-American community, especially with regard to the psychological and social reality of the African-American male. Thus, it appears that our description of the African-American male and his manhood would be incomplete without an understanding of the phenomenon of coolness.

In this developing literature, Majors (1983, 1986, 1987, 1989, 1990, 1992) and others (Doyle 1989; Larrabee 1986; Mcleod 1986; Messner 1987; 1989; Page, 1986; Ridley 1984; Sariola and Naukkarinen 1989), working within an Eurocentric (white) conceptual framework, have employed the term "cool pose" to describe the various psychological defenses or coping behaviors displayed by the African-American male to cope with stress. In particular, the "cool pose" as a social psychological construct is posited to explain and describe both positive and dysfunctional behavior in the lower socioeconomic status (SES) African-

American male (Majors 1983, 1987; Majors and Billson 1992). Majors argues that the adoption of these "cool poses or postures" arises from the mistrust that the Black male feels toward the dominant society and is designed to offset an externally imposed "zero" image (Majors 1986, 84). In other words, the use of cool behaviors by an African-American male represents attitudinal and behavioral reactions to an oppressive cultural milieu designed to keep him invisible (Ellison 1947; Majors 1986, 1987, 1990; Majors and Billson 1992). He contends that, in addition, the cool pose is a form of "masculine self-expression adopted by the African-American male as a result of the denial of access to the dominant culture's acceptable avenues of expressing masculinity" (Majors 1986, 84).

Majors's (1992) current working definition and analysis of the underlying dynamic structure of the cool behavior rests primarily upon the work of Erving Goffman (1959), a social scientist who has conducted seminal work in the area of self-presentation sociology. Self-presentation theory suggests that "actors attempt to control their interactions with others by expressing themselves in ways that lead targets to act voluntarily in accordance with the actor's own plan" (Goffman 1959).

Other social scientists have suggested that an individual exhibits various types of self-presentations relative to certain self-beliefs and idiosyncratic predetermined goals in a given situation (Baumeister 1982; Schlenker and Leary 1982). To say it another way, they believe that, consciously or unconsciously, in social interaction individuals attempt to manipulate others to perform in a manner commensurate with either their self-beliefs (i.e., how they see and feel about themselves) or their desired goals.

In addition, some advocates of self-presentation theory have suggested that there are two important psychological motives for engaging in self-presentational behavior: (1) to obtain rewards and to avoid punishment; (2) as a means of self-fulfillment (i.e., the self-construction of a public self that is congruent to one's private [ideal] self). Several social scientists have defined "the more or less intentional control of appearances in order to guide and control the responses made by others as strategic self-presentations" (Weary and Arkin 1981, 225).

Recently, some social scientists (Jones and Pittman 1982; Tedeschi and Norman 1985; Tedeschi and Reiss 1981) have proposed a framework for understanding specific strategic self-presentations as a function of different types of social situations. They argue that "people adopt different strategies depending on whether a situation is perceived as identity threatening or identity enhancing and whether the focus is on responsibility or consequences."

Another social scientist, B. R. Schlenker (1980), has suggested that an individual will tend to perceive a situation as identity threatening when a "real or imagined event casts aspersions on the lineage (e.g., race), character, conduct, skills, or motives of the actor [individual]." Further, he contends that the individual will tend to respond to this threat in a defensive or protective manner as a means to avoid blame or social disapproval.

Thus, drawing upon self-presentation theory, Majors (1990, 5) has defined the cool pose as a behavioral response to cultural oppression that is psychologically "entrenched as established performances and rituals (e.g., roles, facades, etc.) that serve to express social competencies (e.g., self-respect, inner strength, stability, control, and manhood) as their goal."

Recently, Majors (personal communication, May 1990) has stated that the use of the "dramaturgic approach" can also enhance our understanding of the types and function of various self-presentations displayed by the African-American male. The dramaturgic approach, a mode of analysis that is used increasingly within social psychology, is presumed to increase our understanding of the actor's perspective (i.e., how the actor views his life and the types of roles he displays) (Messinger et al. 1962). Messinger, Sampson, and Towne (1962), advocates of the dramaturgic approach, tend to use the analogy of "life as a theater" as a conceptual framework to describe and understand the social interaction occurring between the actor and the target. For instance, they think that life is the theater (i.e., context) whereby the self is provided the opportunity to stage (i.e.,express) its roles, self-presentations, and other symbolic behaviors. Essentially, the dramaturgic approach attempts to describe the configurations of the self as functions of the ever-changing cultural context. Within this perspective, the individual's behavior is determined by whether or not he perceives himself to be "on" or "off" the world stage, depending on certain situational factors (e.g., the presence or absence of important others, the kinds of people present—Black or white—etc.).

Particularly relevant to our discussion is the fact that the dramaturgic approach has been used to describe the social reality of the African-American male. For example, Wolfe (1950) attempted to describe how "Negroes" tended to act when outside the sight of whites: "Negroes in our culture spend most of their lives 'on.' . . . Every Negro is to some extent a performer. . . . At other times, relaxing among themselves, Negroes will mock the 'type' of personalities they are obliged to assume when they're 'on' " (p. 203).

The above description of "Negroes" performance "on stage" can be conceptualized as an instance of playing it cool. More specifically, the cool performance(s) displayed by "Negroes" when they are "on stage" can be considered an attempt to communicate to a white audience (via various cool postures) an explicit message that has meaning only within the context of a previously negotiated but not openly acknowledged contract. The contract is based on a historical understanding of the nature of race relations within the dominant American society.

In summary, a review of the most recent work of Majors (1983, 1987, 1990, 1991; Majors and Billson, 1992) indicates a primary reliance on sociological self-presentation theory in general and the dramaturgic approach of social psychology in particular as conceptual frameworks to describe and understand how the contemporary African-American male has come to adopt at times a dysfunctional behavioral stance called the "cool pose." In particular, it is important to keep in mind that the "cool pose" is presumed to describe the psychologically entrenched and ritualized behavior or performance that is used primarily by the low-SES African-American male to manage social perceptions of self and to serve as a vehicle for the construction, affirmation, and expression of Black manhood (i.e., Black masculinity).

Although, I believe that Majors's (1986, 1987, 1990, 1991; Majors and Billson 1992) concept of the cool pose has historical significance and heuristic value, it is important to be aware of the following:

First, the kind of coolness, cool behavior, or "cool pose" exhibited by African-Americans in contemporary society is not the same kind of coolness displayed by our African ancestors. We submit that the coolness that was integral to the culture of many ancient African civilizations was transformed (as a result of the experience of the middle passage, slavery, institutional racism, discrimination and cultural oppression) by African Americans into a style of self-presentation that shares only a superficial similarity to the coolness displayed in African society.

Second, although the phenomenon of the "cool pose" is not exclusive to the lower-socioeconomic-status (SES) African-American male, we speculate that the cool pose is more likely to be a salient behavioral response pattern of the lower-SES African-American male because he is more vulnerable to social stressors (e.g., poverty, poor education, unemployment, institutional racism, discrimination, etc.). Consequently, he may be more likely to adopt the cool pose as a symbolic vehicle to express and validate his sense of self and masculinity.

The Cool Pose: An Africentric Perspective

Again, a major limitation of the men's studies literature is that there appears to be only a few references concerned with examining and understanding cultural and structural factors operating in American society that influence the development and growth of African-American male culture, in particular, those structural cultural factors that influence the functional and dysfunctional displays of masculinity among African-American men. Several social scientists have described how most institutions (e.g., family, schools, churches, social organizations, etc.) in American society are structured to psychologically empower and inculcate a sense of masculinity exclusively in white males (Doyle 1983; Pleck and Sawyer 1974).

Other social scientists have focused their research efforts on describing the cultural and structural forces throughout American history that have conspired to undermine some African-American men and keep them from developing healthy and functional masculine identities and roles (Staples 1983; Wilkinson and Taylor 1977).

The concept of the "cool pose" as posited by Majors (1986, 1987, 1990, 1991; Majors and Billson 1992) represents another significant theoretical contribution because it is an attempt to address the "blind spot" or gap in the existing men's studies literature as it relates to the African-American male and his perception of his masculinity. More precisely, Majors's concept of the cool pose has pedagogical value, because it denotes, within the scientific community, a scholarly attempt at increasing our understanding of various behavioral presentations (postures) evidenced by some African-American males in their effort to affirm their masculinity, that is, their manhood.

We will attempt to contribute to this growing literature by offering an Africentric conceptualization and reinterpretation of the role and function of the "cool pose" as a behavioral style of some African-American males. Specifically, it is suggested here that an analysis of underlying cultural factors that contribute to some African-American males adoption of the cool pose role would broaden our understanding of their conception of themselves as men.

A number of social scientists have posited that African Americans display beliefs, attitudes, values, and behaviors that are cultural carryovers from Africa. Furthermore, they argue that an understanding and respect for the above remnants of an African worldview is integral to an understanding of African Americans in general and African-American men in particular (Baldwin 1981; Langley 1990, 1992; Myers 1988; Nobles 1974; Staples 1989).

In addition, several social scientists have argued that there is a significant difference between Africentric and Eurocentric worldviews regarding: (1) their conception of the nature of reality; (2) values orientation toward the world; (3) relationship to nature; (4) nature of knowledge; (5) nature of time; (6) nature of logic; and (7) nature of process (Baldwin 1985).

An African-American male who tended to display the cool pose as a salient aspect of his personality or character would most likely be diagnosed as being a psychologically "misoriented" individual (Azibo 1983a, 1983b, 1989; Baldwin 1980a, 1980b, 1989). According to Baldwin, a psychologically "misoriented" person is

> one who in his own mind is neither necessarily confused about his/her identity, nor dysfunctional in his/her behavior, according to the standard prescribed by Euro-American culture. For the black person operates (thinks, feels, acts) in the manner of a European. Clearly, then, such an individual is certainly not "disoriented" in the sense of consciously experiencing confusion and its attendant anxiety. The social cues in Euro-American society reinforce acting in such a manner. As a point of fact, however (that is, in view of the fact that he or she is actually an African), the black person is indeed "misoriented" because he or she can achieve at best only a pseudo form of European existence. (1980a, 109)

To say it another way, Baldwin (1980a) is suggesting that an African-American would be considered culturally and psychologically "misoriented" if he or she accepted the European system perception (beliefs, attitudes, and values orientation) of social reality as an exclusive guide for his or her behavior and life.

Similarly, Nobles (1974) has also attempted to describe the psychological effects of African Americans' uncritical adoption of the European definitional system of social reality. He refers to this process as the "conceptual incarceration" of Black people. He states:

> The natural consciousness of black people is forced to relate to a reality defined by white consciousness. That is, contemporary black people in the United States live in a psychological reality consistent [with] and supportive of white mental functioning. Such a situation is tantamount to black people living in [what for black people must be] white insanity. (1974, p. 26)

Akbar's (1976), Baldwin's (1980a), and Nobles's (1974) scholarly works have attempted to describe the effects of the process of cultural oppression on African Americans, and their works have relevance to Majors's (1992) notion of the "cool pose." From an Africentric perspective, Majors's concept of the cool pose could be reconceptualized as the psychological tendency of Americans of African descent, especially the male, to internalize the beliefs, attitudes, and values of a Eurocentric imposed definitional system of social reality under conditions of cultural oppression.

Majors's concept of the cool pose, from an Africentric perspective, could be operationally defined as overt behavior displayed by African Americans, in particular the African-American male in response to environmental pressure to adapt to or at the very least assimilate into American society. In other words, the adoption (consciously or unconsciously) of the cool pose by an African-American male can be thought of as a behavioral manifestation of the degree to which some African-American males have become "psychologically misoriented or conceptually incarcerated" as a function of their struggle to affirm themselves as men in a culturally oppressive and race-conscious society.

Akbar (1981) has posited that many African Americans experience racial oppression and, as a result, experience great stress resulting in three kinds of cultural specific maladaptative response patterns (mental disorders): (1) alien-self disorders are characterized by a denial or rejection of one's own cultural values in attempting to assimilate into the majority white American culture; (2) anti-self disorders are characterized by a tendency to over identify with the anti-Black hostility in the dominant white American culture; and (3) self-destructive disorders are characterized by acts of self-destruction that result from the faulty attempt of the person to cope with frustration associated with the many impediments to growth and development and to feelings of security and well-being under racially oppressive social conditions.

We suggest that under conditions of cultural, economic, social, and political oppression some African-American men will perceive the "cool pose" as a *functional* behavioral response (i.e., an act of self-affirmation) designed to express and embellish their manhood, although they may be psychologically "misoriented or conceptually incarcerated." In other words, from the Africentric perspective, the "cool pose" at a societal level may be conceived of as serving a functional rather than a dysfunctional purpose; however, at the level of the individual, it indicates that the person is psychologically "misoriented" or conceptually incarcerated (Azibo 1983a, 1983b, 1989; Baldwin 1980a; Nobles 1974).

Given the above Africentric analysis of the role and function of the "cool pose," what can be done to foster and facilitate the development and functioning of culturally healthy African-American males? Particularly relevant to this question is the increasing recognition by several social scientists that the adoption of the cool pose by some African-American males represents the *sole* means of masculine expression for a class of men who have been defeated by a Eurocentric patriarchal social structure (Majors and Billson 1992; Oliver 1990; Tunsil 1987).

Should institutions (churches, schools, colleges, universities) or programs (pre-school, head start, or after-school activities) designed to address the above situation of many young African-American men focus on adaptation (encourage African-American males to live with the way things are), assimilation (encourage African-American males to accommodate or join the status quo at the expense of self-affirmation), or self-affirmation (encourage and support African-American males to reject societal dictates or prescriptions when they are in conflict with a concept of self that is culturally congruent with the Black experience)?

Within the last ten years, several African-American scholars in response to the documented plight of many young black males in contemporary American society have developed manhood training programs (Hare and Hare 1985; Karenga 1977; Oliver 1984). The manhood training programs are based on African values and customs and "incorporate African-style rites of passage for the socialization of young Black boys" (Majors and Billson 1992). According to Hare and Hare (1985), the purpose of manhood training for young black males is to teach them a sense of responsibility, personal mastery, and a commitment to family, race, community, and country.

I believe that manhood training programs provide relatively safe, caring and culturally compatible environments where young Black males can become involved in therapeutic group experiences that could provide them with an opportunity to critically examine the role and function of the masculine "cool pose" in their lives.

Summary

In conclusion, the physical and psychological costs that African-American males continue to pay in order to be perceived as Black men are enormously high, due to individual racism, institutionalized discrimination, and cultural oppression. The problem is well documented (Centers for Disease Control 1983; Gibbs

1984, 1985). The concept of the "cool pose" represents a move toward identifying culturally specific process variables involved in the various roles enacted by African-American males for the sole purpose of expressing some aspect of their masculinity. Cool pose can also serve as a conceptual framework to begin to understand the nature and relationship of structural cultural factors relevant to the African-American male's conscious or unconscious decision to accept an Eurocentric, culturally imposed definition of self.

Finally, but most importantly, the incorporation of the concept of the cool pose as a strategic self-presentation and the use of the dramaturgic approach within the Africentric conceptual framework has some heuristic value. Specifically, from the perspective of the Africentric model, the cool pose symbolizes a gambit utilized by some African-American males with an implicit goal of disarming the other fellow, to get him to reveal himself before you disclose yourself to him. That is, it is a behavioral style adopted by some African-American men that is functional and has adaptive (i.e., survival) value within a culturally oppressive society (Comer 1969; Pinderhughes 1969). It is a functional strategy designed to negotiate a social reality that has historically been unwilling to acknowledge the African American as a man.

CHAPTER 17

Cool Pose: A Symbolic Mechanism for Masculine Role Enactment and Coping by Black Males

by Richard Majors, Richard Tyler, Blaine Peden, and Ron Hall

Being cool is not a way of life for teenagers, it is life.
                                        —Stanislaw and Peshkin, 1988

The African-American Black male has been characterized as enigmatic, mysterious, and someone to fear. As a result of these misconceptions and stereotypes,
harsh socioeconomic sanctions have contributed to the maltreatment of Black
males. Such unfair characterizations and treatment have produced a unique way
of responding to adverse conditions that has been largely overlooked by researchers. To promote the study and understanding of Black males, the first
author has termed their different masculine roles and coping behaviors as "cool
pose" (Majors 1986, 1989, 1990, 1991b; Majors and Billson 1992).

This chapter discusses the origins, functions, consequences, and remediation of maladaptive cool pose behaviors. In brief, cool pose originated as a coping mechanism for the "invisibility," frustration, discrimination, and educational and employment inequities faced by Black males. In response to these
obstacles, many of these individuals have channeled their creative talents and
energies into the construction of masculine symbols and into the use of conspic-
uous nonverbal behaviors (e.g., demeanors, gestures, clothing, hairstyles, walks,
stances, and handshakes). For many other African Americans, these unique, expressive, colorful, stylish and theatrical behaviors are ways to act "cool," gain
visibility, and demonstrate pride.

Acting cool, or cool pose, is an essential concept in understanding how
many Black males use, create, and manage their self-presentation to others.
Cool pose is both structurally and functionally dynamic. Moreover, cool pose
entails diverse functions such as roles, values, presentation of self, situationally
constructed and performance-oriented behaviors, scripts, and physical posturing. Uncovering the cultural context in which Black males enact these various
culture-specific and ritualized masculine "cool" roles reveals various negative
consequences for those who become a "gang-banger," tough-guy, drug-dealer,
lady's man, street hustler, or pimp.

In this chapter, we review the historical origins and cultural importance of
cool pose and then articulate a conceptual framework for understanding it. Sub-
sequently, we demonstrate that cool pose constitutes a compulsive masculine
alternative and that a historical imperative to defend one's manhood often produces problematical consequences for those Black males who adopt and enact
cool pose in social, sexual, and educational settings. The chapter ends with a
discussion about some intervention and prevention strategies that may promote
the welfare of Black males.

An Historical Review of Cool Behavior

Cool behaviors by Black males have historical origins and cultural importance.
Coolness was central to many ancient African civilizations. For example, cul-

tural anthropologist John Janzen (personal communication, May 4, 1989) dates the concept of coolness to at least 2000–3000 B.C. According to Janzen, traditional African societies expressed coolness in their oral tradition, character building, artwork, language, dance, initiation rituals, warrior cults, and rituals for acquiring a mate.

Robert Farris Thompson, an art historican (1973), discusses the aesthetic of cool. Thompson dates the origins of the concept of cool to Nigeria in the first half of the fifteenth century, where Ewuare (which means "it is cool") was king of the Nigerian empire, Benin. In the same century, a Yoruba ruler from Ilobi, in what today is southern Egabado, took the name *Oba tio tutu bi asun*, which means "Cool-and-Peaceful-as-the-Native-Herb-Osun." In the sixteenth century, the same name was awarded to an Ijebu Yoruba king.

The most recent documentation of the historical and cultural importance of coolness to the Black male comes from autobiographies and ethnographies by Black men who were formerly pimps, street hustlers, and drug dealers (e.g., Beck 1969; Brown 1965; Goines 1972, 1973; Haley and Malcolm X 1964; Thomas 1967). Such indigenous books provide insight into Black males and cool behaviors (e.g., in regard to street-life activities, walking, and "rapping" to women).

Contemporary social conditions generate and support cool behaviors among Black males. For example, in 1989, both the National Research Council report "A Common Destiny: Blacks and American Society" and the Trotter Report documented that racism and other forms of discrimination by the dominant white culture have inflicted harsh sociopolitical and socioeconomic sanctions on Black people. Hardest hit, however, are Black males, many of whom have become frustrated, angry, embittered, alienated, impatient, and mistrustful of the words and actions of the dominant culture. To ease the frustration and pain from restricted opportunities to express legitimate patterns of masculinity, Black males have constructed a symbolic universe and adopted unique postures to overcome an externally imposed "invisibility" (Ellison 1947). To many Black males, demeanor, mannerisms, speech, gestures, clothing, stance, hairstyles, and walking styles are ways to act cool and show the dominant culture that they are strong, proud, and capable of survival despite their low status in society.

A Conceptual Framework for Understanding Cool Pose

Cool pose, then, is a term that describes the ways Black males use coolness as a coping mechanism. These ways of coping are symbolically expressed by acting cool. These various postures have become firmly entrenched in the psyche of such males as established performances and rituals that seek social competence as their goal.

Historically, Black people have used humor, shucking and jiving, "playing the dozens," and "inversion" as ways to "play it cool." These postures and poses convey power and control, alleviate anxiety, give the impression that one is suave and charming, make white people uncertain about their intentions, entertain, display pride, express anger, and hide real feelings and emotions.

In sports and other contemporary activities, Black males have used various poses and postures to accentuate themselves and promote their attractiveness and social significance. For example, Black athletes stylishly dunk a basketball, spike a football, and dance in the end zone after a touchdown, wear tassels on boxing shoes, and perform unique handshakes. Cool pose is a dynamic rather than static model of expression, and new forms continuously emerge. Rap talking, break dancing, the "cabbage patch," and "electric boogie" dances constitute recent examples of innovative modes of cool self-expression adopted by Black males.

Structurally, the modern expression of cool pose may best be understood in the context of "impression management" or performance-oriented behaviors. Sociologist Erving Goffman (1959) introduced the concept of dramaturgical roles to analyze both impression management and performance-oriented behaviors. According to Haas and Shaffir (1982), "The dramaturgical approach to understanding human behavior takes as a given the idea that conduct can be viewed as a performance in which the script has to be enacted in such a way as to make the performance of a role credible to an audience" (p. 1). Snowe, Zurcher, and Peters (1981) also argue that "dramaturgy views social action as the consequence of the adjustments interactants make to the impressions they formulate about each other in specific situations. Behavior is seen as situationally constructed action" (p. 136).

Dramaturgy shares the basic assumption of symbolic interaction that meaning is not inherent in social interaction but rather, meaning must be "negotiated" by individuals in a given situation. The symbolic interactionist perspective, then, focuses on the products of communications. That is to say, symbolic interaction focuses on how an individual interprets his own and others' behavior, how he defines his interaction with others, and consequently, how he shapes his behavior toward others to provide for the most satisfying outcome (Mancini 1981). Symbolically, then, cool pose for Black males communicates adherence to particular roles, ideas, values, or norms.

Social conditions have encouraged many Black males to learn how to use dramaturgical roles. For Black males with limited control or access to any real power or resources, dramaturgical roles empower Black males by helping them to satisfy mainstream norms and expectations, appear competent, and survive. Even though dramaturgical roles are often used for manipulative purposes, many Black males nevertheless view them as necessary for their continued existence (Majors 1991a). Cool pose is often understood in the context of performance-oriented behaviors. However, cool pose also has a negative side. The negative side of cool pose is often expressed by the compulsive masculine alternative. That is discussed in the next section.

Cool Pose and the Compulsive Masculine Alternative

Although cool pose has the positive function of enhancing self-esteem, it can lead to health problems and violence. Cool pose behaviors or facades often advertise one's willingness to resort to violence and to resolve interpersonal conflicts violently. Cool pose behaviors and facades may also prevent males from expressing their concern or guilt when they are involved in violent incidents with others:

> To be cool, in terms of presenting one's self as tough, requires that males structure their behavior to give the impression that they are independent, always in control and emotionally detached. . . . Typically [then] adherence to the toughness norm is symbolically displayed by appearing and remaining cool in social situations perceived as potentially threatening to one's self-image or physical safety. (Oliver 1988)

According to Lyman and Scott (1970), "Coolness is defined as poise under pressure. . . . [It] refers to the capacity to execute physical acts, including conversation, in a concerted, smooth, self-controlled fashion in risky situations, or to maintain affective detachment during the course of encounters involving considerable emotion" (p. 45). Therefore, in addition to walk, stance, gestures, etc., Black males symbolically use demeanor and various facades to communicate adherence to the toughness norm. Hence, various cool pose behaviors facilitate and/or legitimize toughness and violence.

Symbolic displays of toughness defend or promote an individual's identity (Oliver 1988) and garner respect from others. Furthermore, symbolic displays of toughness promote a sense of camaraderie and solidarity among Black males. Unfortunately, Black males who refuse or are unable to express toughness often are labeled "punks" and may become outcasts in the Black community. In addition, punks are easy targets for Black males who choose or seek to enhance their status at the expense of weaker individuals (Hannerz 1969). The risk-taking and self-destructive aspects of cool pose then are often symbolically expressed as part of one's masculine presentation. Black males accept Eurocentric definitions of masculinity; however, unlike most white males, they lack the means to enact these traditional roles (Parker and Kleiner 1969). To compensate for an inability to enact traditional roles, many Black males acquire values and norms that Hannerz (1969) and Oliver (1984) refer to as the "compulsive masculine alternative." Olvier argues that many Black males have redefined manhood to compensate for feelings of shame, guilt, lack of self-esteem, etc. However, the compulsive masculinity alternative is a dysfunctional cultural adaptation.

According to Oliver (1984), the compulsive masculine alternative refers to the unique ways in which many lower-class males demonstrate masculinity. This masculine behavior overtly emphasizes values and norms that portray or demonstrate toughness, sexual promiscuity, manipulation, thrill-seeking, and a willing use of violence to resolve interpersonal conflict. These values constitute an alternative to traditional definitions of manhood that prescribe and reinforce the notion that men must be tough, emotionally unexpressive, detached, responsible, and occupationally successful and always provide for and protect their family. Therefore, cool pose is an exaggerated or ritualistic form of masculinity. As stated above, Black males accept the traditional values of masculinity but because successful enactment of masculinity is dependent on sociopolitical factors, many Black males have been unable to enact traditional masculine roles. In fact, in 1939, Franklin Frazier stated that a Black man's family role and responsibilities depended on his ability to provide for his family. Frazier also believed that Black men both embraced the traditional values of American patriarchy and often overconformed to them. Cazenave (1979) interviewed fifty-four Black fathers employed as letter carriers regarding the importance of family responsibility and the provider role. The findings support Frazier's position. One of the questions respondents were asked was, "What do you think it means to be a man today?" Forty-one percent of the respondents felt "responsibility" to be the major characteristic. Other major categories indicated were hard work, ambition, and firm guiding principles. The most prominent masculine role for them was the role of economic provider. Being a man meant taking care of one's family (see Cazenave and Leon's 1987 study also). Such themes of family responsibility remain central to the understanding of Black men (Casenave 1981, 1984; Cazenave and Leon 1987; Staples 1982). In the next section we will discuss how culture and historic factors shape masculinity development.

The History of Black Masculine Roles

The Black male's ability to conform to traditional masculine values is affected by socioeconomic conditions. However, the strong emphasis on masculinity among Black males may have cultural and historical derivations. As Milner (1972) notes, the existence of the masculine role of the "bad nigga" or the "bad man" as a folk hero has been well documented by folklorists and ethnographers for years. The bad nigga was known for his physical strength, courage, pride, and ability to overcome hardships. He was also known as someone who was willing to confront the white man at any time about his subservient position in society without fear or apprehension. In other words, the bad nigga refused to allow anyone to determine his place in society or to determine how he should live. There have been a variety of bad niggas celebrated in Black folklore. For example, John Henry Stagalee and Shine are two historical figures who performed feats of great physical endurance with style and courage. What is basic to the various types of bad nigga is physical and mental strength. There is a need to prove that one can "dish it out" and "take it." The bottom line, then, for the bad nigga is to have pride in himself and to command respect from others (Folb 1980; Wiggins 1971). The Black male today still fights to defend his manhood constantly, on a day-to-day basis. In various activities and events, "Black males remain through-out most of their lives manqué" (Keil 1962). This persistent quest for masculine identity is referred to as masculine attainment (Cazaneve 1981) or "masculine protest" (Majors 1987); it often produces unfavorable consequences, as illustrated in the next section.

Problematic Consequences of Cool Pose

Cool pose is related to violent behavior, on the streets and at home, to sexual promiscuity, and to problems at school.

Violence

Many Black males often emphasize masculine values or norms that contribute to violence. Turner (1970) reported that Black males' two most common responses to threats toward masculine attainment are rigidity and aggressiveness. In American society, the primary means by which Black males can demonstrate their masculinity is to exert violence, toughness, and control over others (Cazenave 1981). Historically, our society has not provided many Black males with legitimate channels or resources to demonstrate their masculinity and command respect. Thus, for many Black males, violence is perceived as the only tool for achieving a sense of masculinity, respect, and status. In fact, violence can be a form of social achievement (Cazenave 1981). Sociologists refer to this phenomenon as the "resource theory of violence" (Goode 1974). This theory suggests that violence is viewed as a resource that can be used to achieve a desired goal when other resources are unavailable or limited.

In this country, most middle-class white males have the benefits of social status, money, prestige, and the respect that comes from work, and so they do not have the desire or need to look elsewhere for something to provide them with self-esteem and confidence. On the other hand, for many Black males who lack jobs, money, or status, the only real way to feel good about themselves or to gain respect is through the use of superior physical force—the only resource they feel truly works for them (Cazenave 1981).

Janet Mancini's book *Strategic Styles: Coping in the Inner City* (1981) identifies five distinct coping styles that Black males often use to help deal with social, family, and environmental pressures. One is an overemphasis on masculinity and "toughness." Her character "Leroy" illustrates the "tough guy" character, a role that is masculine, delinquent, and violent. Mancini argues that some Black males are socialized to show both affection and disapproval, especially toward their fathers, brothers, and other male relatives, by hitting each other, wrestling, fighting, playing, and punching. She noted that in Leroy's family, violence was prevalent. For example, when Leroy failed at something or disobeyed his parents, he often got "yelled at and pushed around." Thus, Leroy's family frequently modeled both verbal and physical violence as a means to show disapproval. Mancini concludes that families such as Leroy's use force as a normal means to resolve interpersonal relationships; however, these attitudes and behaviors may cause conflict and problems with others outside the family.

Even though the compulsive masculinity alternative can serve as an ego defense mechanism to help an individual cope with anxiety, it is a dysfunctional compensatory adaptation that often leads to violence (Oliver 1984). According to Majors and Billson (1992), homicide is the leading cause of death of Black men and women between the ages of twenty-five and thirty-four (Hampton 1987). According to the Centers for Disease Control (1985), homicide for Black males aged fifteen to twenty-four is the leading cause of death. Overall, the rate of homicide for Blacks is 5.6 times higher than it is for whites (Hampton 1987). Most national and local studies have found that the majority of Black victims were relatives, friends, or acquaintances of the offenders. The majority of those crimes were caused by males under twenty-four years of age (Gibbs 1988). The prevalence of violence among Black males is also reflected in arrest and criminal data. Blacks comprise 13 percent of the population but are disproportionately represented among both perpetrators and victims of violent crime and incarceration.

There are other cool pose behavioral patterns that convey a predisposition for violence but do not necessarily lead to physical violence. For example, a Black cultural masculine identity behavior referred to as "woofing" (Folb 1980; Kochman 1981; Oliver 1988) is "a style of bragging and boasting about how bad one is" (Cooke 1972, 44). Woofing is a form of communication, consistent with the oral nature of Black culture (Abrahams 1970; Boykin 1983; Oliver 1988). This behavioral style that many Black males manifest often does not lead to violence but promotes their masculine identity (Cooke 1972; Kochman 1981). More often than not, a young Black male will mitigate the impact of a challenge to his manhood by ridiculing or "sounding" on the person who made the remark rather than fighting. Hence, Black males regard woofing as a ritualized manhood contest, entertainment oriented rather than violence oriented. Kochman (1981) argues that woofing gains respect and fear from others without violence, but its success depends on an aura of fearlessness and toughness. Oliver (1988) notes that even though woofing is a symbolic act, it is only one step short of violence.

As Abrahams (1970), Boykin (1983), and others have noted, because of the emphasis West Africans and Black Americans place on verbal skills and storytelling, Black culture has been referred to as an oral culture. Sociolinguistic research clearly shows that Blacks are very sensitive to the power of words to sexually arouse, to insult, to comfort, and to enhance social status (Oliver 1988).

To show adherence to masculinity and toughness, storytelling among young Black males usually involves accounts of having successfully managed a conflict-ridden situation. The story is often highlighted by the storyteller's portrayal of what he claims to have said to be an antagonist, how he managed his demeanor, or how he used verbal threats or violence to handle a situation that was potentially threatening to his self-image or physical well-being (Oliver 1988).

Domestic Abuse

Domestic abuse is prevalent among Blacks. Straus (1980) found that wife abuse was almost 400 percent more common among Black families than in white families. Also, Cazenave and Straus (1979) reported that Black husbands were three times more likely than white husbands to have hit their wives or engaged in violence. Oliver (1989b) indicated that Black male-female conflict leads to assault and murder of Black females at a greater frequency than in any other racial or ethnic group in the United States. According to Hampton (1987), Black females also murder Black males at very high rates.

It is much more difficult for Black males to successfully enact traditional roles than it is for Black females. A Black female can successfully enact the traditional female role by having a child and making the decision to take care of that child. However, Black men, like most men in this society, define social esteem and manhood by their ability to work and to support their family (Oliver 1988). Thus, due to social and economic limitations, most Black males are sensitive to role failure. To compensate for role failure, many Black males define masculinity in terms of impregnating women and producing children (especially sons who are extensions of themselves) and having multiple relationship and sexual partners (Staples 1978). As Staples (1978) argued, for Black males there is an inseparable link between their self-esteem as men and their ability to have sex with women to produce children.

Many Black males are very sensitive about challenges to their manhood and may inflict harm or injury on threatening women. Often, male-female conflict develops when a female criticizes a male for his inability or failure to support the family, when she raises her voice at him, or, even worse, when she raises her voice at him around "the guys." Many Black males feel that any of these criticisms are a direct insult to their manhood. Because they feel that such remarks display disloyalty and disrespect, these males often become violent to "save face." Essentially, many Black men feel that, even though they may not be able to control how the white man or society treats them, they at the very least should be able to control their women.

Cool Pose, Symbolic Behaviors, Gang Formation, and Violence

Black gang members manifest masculinity and toughness physically through murder, violence, crime, and assault. Masculinity and toughness are expressed in the symbolic behaviors of gang members as well. To counter their invisibility as Black men, gang members use symbolic behavior as a way to make themselves "visible" to society. In addition to gaining visibility for the gang member, symbolic behaviors also express anger, defiance, pride, protest power, solidarity, and entertainment.

Black gang members have their own rules and culture and are obsessed with the symbols that identify and promote their masculine-oriented culture. The ways that gang members symbolically convey masculinity include provocative walking styles, handshakes, hairstyles, stances, use of various colors, clothes (e.g., baseball caps, jackets, warm-up suits), bandannas, hairnets, "battle scars" (from turf wars with other gang members), jewelry (e.g., gold chains, earrings), hand signals, language, nicknames (Majors 1991b).

Black gang members also promote their adherence to masculinity through ritualistic activities. For example, to gain membership in one Los Angeles gang, an individual must complete a masculine initiation ritual called "jump-in." According to Stewart (1989), an individual must buy a pair of khaki pants, "sag" the waist, and "put on the look." Next the individual has to "jump-in" and fight three gang members all at once. If the individual still stands after ten minutes, he is considered "tough" and thus is accepted into the gang. Hence, fighting and being tough are a means to gain membership in a gang, and they are also a way to gain respect, prestige, and status.

Unfortunately, Black gang members advertise their propensity for violence through masculine symbolic behaviors. Particular ways in which Black gang members use masculine symbolic behaviors violently are drive-by shootings, the placing of a black wreath on an individual's door (to serve notice that they want to execute the person in question), the displaying of a "Columbia necktie" on a corpse (i.e., after someone is killed the throat is cut and the tongue is pulled through the slit of the cut) (Della Cava 1989), and painting graffiti to communicate death threats. For example, when a gang in Los Angeles paints the police murder code, "187," on a building, it means the gang has placed a death threat on someone (Stewart 1989).

The Black gang member epitomizes the frustrated Black male in this country. The basis of a Black gang member's frustration derives from a history of social and economic neglect common to many Blacks. In addition to high Black teenage unemployment rates (Gibbs 1988), urban areas in the United States in which many Black males live lack recreation centers, educational opportunities, and health-care services. Angered and embittered by this social isolation and neglect, Black gang members have become obsessed with symbols and behavior that promote their masculine-oriented culture. This is to say, because of group emasculation, many Black males become obsessed with masculinity as demonstrated by their involvement in self-destructive and risk-taking behaviors (e.g., emphasis on violence, aggression, promiscuity, fighting, toughness, drinking) as a way to enhance self-esteem, power, control, and social competence. Hence, Black gang members' obsession with masculinity is, in a sense, exaggerated traditional masculinity. Gang membership provides a way to organize one's world, direct anger, create stimulation, and entertain. Also, gang membership provides the gang member with a sense of family and belonging, affiliation, respect, status, and empowerment—all things his own society has not provided him. For a gang member, belonging to a gang may be a way of saying, "I may not be able to depend on you, society, but I can depend on this bunch of guys."

Sexual Promiscuity and Masculine Behaviors

Sexual promiscuity is one of the primary ways in which Black males demonstrate their masculinity. Sexual promiscuity can cause male-female conflict, which often leads to domestic violence. In addition, sexual promiscuity contributes to various social problems such as the spread of venereal disease and AIDS. The Centers for Disease Control (1986) reported that AIDS occurs 2.6 times more often among Black males than it does among white males. Although the use of condoms can prevent the spread of venereal disease and AIDS, some authors (Jimenez 1987) have suggested that some Latino and Black males view the use of condoms as "unmacho."

Cool Pose and the Schools

According to the cool pose hypothesis, young Black males adopt and display certain behaviors, attitudes, demeanors, and dress that they perceive and intend to convey their coolness, individual self-esteem, pride, and adherence to their culture. However, there is often conflict between white teachers and Black males because teachers misunderstand the intent of culture-specific behaviors. Quite simply, white middle-class teachers and school authorities often perceive provocative walking styles, "rapping," use of slang, expressive hairstyles, excessive use of jewelry, wearing hats (and wearing hats backwards), wearing the belt unbuckled, untied sneakers, and so on as arrogant, rude, defiant, aggressive, intimidating, threatening, and, in general, behaviors not conducive to learning (Foster 1986).

Because teachers tend to misinterpret, overreact to, and become frightened of Black males' culture-specific behaviors, Black males are not only physically punished and suspended by teachers more than any other group, but they are also more often recommended by teachers for remedial classes, special education, and classes for the emotionally disturbed. They are labeled mildly mentally handicapped more than any other group (Foster 1986).

Although many Black males are suspended from school for discipline and conduct problems, a considerable number are suspended for what can be classified as culture-specific behaviors. Since 1976, the percentage of Black high school graduates and especially Black males enrolling in higher education insti-

tutions has been on the decline. The high suspension rate and drop-out rate of
Black males may help to explain why there are fewer Black males enrolling in
colleges across the country.

Intervention and Prevention Strategies

Various organizations and institutions have sponsored intervention and prevention programs for delinquent and emotionally troubled Black youths who experience lack of impulse control and show exaggerated forms of masculinity associated with cool pose. These programs provide impulse management, life skills,
social skills, values and vocational training, placement, remedial education, and
counseling.

Some successful and innovative intervention and prevention programs for
Black youths include the National Urban League's Black Male Responsibility
Program, City Lights, The Door, and the Junior Citizens Corp (Gibbs 1988).
New intervention and prevention programs developed for Black youths include
mentoring (see Balcazar et al. 1991), conflict-resolution (see Spivak et al. 1989),
and De La Cancela's Dialectical Therapy Model (1986). However, the present
discussion centers on the Afrocentric Socialization model that has been used
successfully with both delinquent and nondelinquent Black youths. The Afrocentric Socialization model is particularly appropriate for those Black youths
who have experienced a lack of impulse control and exaggerated forms of masculinity that have often led to violent behavior (e.g., compulsive masculinity,
self-destructive behaviors, the "tough guy" role). Oliver (1989) noted that compulsive masculinity, self-destructive behaviors, the "tough guy" role, and violence among Black males form a dysfunctional adaptation to racism and discrimination. Oliver (1989a) argues that Blacks, and especially Black males, have
failed to develop an Afrocentric cultural ideology or world view that could help
them to mitigate the adverse effects of racism, discrimination, compulsive masculinity, self-destructive behaviors, and violence.

The Afrocentric cultural ideology is based on African civilization and philosophy. The Afrocentric cultural ideology is not antiwhite, but it is a cultural
ideology that encourages Black Americans to transcend various problems by reclaiming traditional African values such as mankind's "oneness with nature,"
"spirituality," and "collectivism" (Oliver 1989a). The Afrocentric perspective
contrasts with the Eurocentric world view, which encourages "controlling nature," materialism, and individualism (Mbiti 1969). That is to say, Afrocentric
cultural ideology develops the necessary collective philosophy, cultural traditions, and institutions that other American racial and ethnic groups have established to make themselves successful and competitive in this country. Even
more important, Afrocentric socialization encourages Black parents and adults
to structure their behavior and institutions to teach their children and youth val-

ues that emphasize cooperation, mutual respect, commitment, and love of family, race, community, and nation.

Hence, Afrocentric socialization encourages Blacks to define self- and group-destructive behavior as counterproductive to themselves and the Black community. The failure of Blacks to develop an Afrocentric culture ideology and world view, then, has made Blacks vulnerable to structural pressures that ultimately cause social problems and violence in the Black community.

Many Blacks feel that the Eurocentric value system's emphasis on individualism and materialism is one of the primary reasons for the decay in the Black community. That is to say, constant exposure to the Eurocentric value system of individualism and materialism has led many Black Americans to develop an interest in and desire for material goods. The emphasis on individualism and materialism naturally neutralizes values like unity, cooperation, and mutual respect—whereas the Afrocentric cultural ideology socializes or resocializes values that elevate the interests of the community over those of the individual. According to Mbiti (1969), native-born Africans view themselves in the context of their relationship and social obligations to their community. The Afrocentric cultural ideology socializes children and youths to view themselves in terms of "I am because we are; and since we are, therefore I am" (Oliver 1989). Therefore, the emphasis on individualism and materialism may also help to explain how some Black Americans have become involved in self-destructive behaviors. Therefore, socializing Black children and Black youths to value the Afrocentric perspective could substantially reduce their involvement in self- and group-destructive behaviors.

Many Black males make the passage from boyhood to manhood under the tutelage of the "streets" and peer influences that often define manhood in terms of toughness, sexual conquest, and thrill seeking. To counteract this kind of socialization among Black youths, the Afrocentric cultural movement in the 1980s incorporated African-style rites of passage into the socialization of young boys (Fair 1977; Hare and Hare 1985; Kunjufu 1983, 1986; Perkins 1986). Oliver (1989a) feels that these African-style rites-of-passage ceremonies help Black boys internalize definitions of manhood that contribute to the survival and progress of the Black community. Various rites-of-passage ceremonies have different content depending on the age of the initiates and the specific objectives of manhood training. Nonetheless, all of these ceremonies promote Afrocentric values and commitment to community (Oliver 1989a). Oliver (1989a) writes that the rites-of-passage ceremony for young Black boys should contain some of the following components: training in the importance of enacting appropriate roles for son, husband, and father; Black history and cultural enrichment; sex education; educational reinforcement; political awareness; community service; and life-skills management. Hare and Hare (1985) report that the purpose of manhood training for young Black boys is to teach them a sense of responsibility, personal mastery, and a commitment to one's family, race, community, and country.

Taking a different emphasis, Oliver (1989a) and Karenga (1986) argue that manhood training should emphasize the principles of *Nguzo Saba*, which could considerably reduce the high rates of social problems and violence among Blacks. The Afrocentric value system of *Nguzo Saba* encompasses seven core values: *Umoja* ("unity")—striving for unity in family, race, community, and nation; *Kujichagulia* ("self-determination")—defining ourselves, naming ourselves, instead of allowing our culture to be defined by others; *Ujima* ("collective work and responsibility")—emphasizing the interests of the community over the individual; *Ujama* ("cooperative economics")—developing and maintaining business in the Black community); *Nia* ("purpose")—desiring to understand how the dominant society uses racism and discrimination to oppress Blacks, so as to prevent problems in the future; *Kuumba* ("creativity")—desiring and needing to contribute to the aesthetic quality of the Black community; and *Imani* ("faith")—internalizing the values and roles of the Afrocentric world view. Karenga (1977) notes that these seven core values that comprise *Nguzo Saba* are the necessary core and the moral minimum of values needed to rescue and reconstruct the Black community. In sum, then, the African-style rites of passage and *Nguzo Saba* teach Black youths that manhood is not inseparable from actions that contribute to the development of the family, community, and one's nation (Oliver 1989a).

Conclusion

The thesis of this chapter is that historical and cultural factors force Black males to accept the traditional definition of masculinity but, unlike most White males, Black males lack the means to enact traditional roles of masculinity. Many Black males have adopted cool pose as a way to demonstrate their masculinity and "visibility" (Ellison 1947). Masculinity is symbolically expressed in cool pose, but cool pose can directly or indirectly contribute to disproportionate rates of marital and female abuse, crime, alcohol and drug abuse, and violence.

However, the consequences of Black males' cool behaviors will continue to plague our society and the Black community unless scientists and public policy analysts begin to do the kind of research that attempts to understand and analyze masculinity. The present cool pose analysis is a serious attempt to understand and study compulsive masculinity among Black males. This kind of research should help us to overcome the stereotype of the Black male as someone who is mysterious and enigmatic and perpetuates the current problems.

The full impact of cool pose must be addressed in the context of masculinity; however, most research on Black males and masculinity has focused on Moynihan's (1968) concept of the "pathological" and antisocial nature of the Black matriarchal family, father absences, and the so-called negative effects of such Black family patterns on the ego development of Black males (Silverman and Dinitz 1974).

Instead of this kind of approach, more studies are needed to address the ways in which race, class, gender, and socioeconomic forces help to shape and define masculinity among Black males. Also, very little is known about the cultural context in which Black males learn and act out masculinity, roles, norms, and values that later lead to high levels of problematic behaviors or that help Black males to cope. If we are to correct many of the societal problems discussed in this chapter, much more research is needed on how Black males use masculinity as a coping strategy.

PART 5

The Future

CHAPTER 18

Black Males in the Work Force in the Twenty-First Century

by William C. Brooks

One of my responsibilities at the Department of Labor is the Office of Federal Contract Compliance Programs—the OFCCP—which enforces nondiscrimination and affirmative action laws in the federal contractor community. This year OFCCP will celebrate its silver anniversary—it has been in existence for twenty-five years. The year 1990 is also the silver anniversary of the Civil Rights Act, which paved the way into the American education and economic mainstream for many Black Americans.

These twenty-five years frame my remarks this morning. They have brought us both progress, and decline.

Twenty-five years does not seem like a long time to me. Our progress seems momentous, and yet paradoxically, almost commonplace in 1990. And yet I know what the job and education statistics I'm going to share with you today mean to those who are *not* represented in our employment tables and our salary charts. To them, twenty-five years may as well be forever, because the starting gate is getting farther away, and the rest of the pack is rounding the curve and coming into the home stretch. And I know that unless we find a way to get them in the race, these twenty-five years might as well not have existed for any of us. This morning I'm going to talk to you about:

- The status of Black males in the work force, and the current trend in affirmative action and multicultural diversity.
- What I think makes or breaks Blacks' careers and job aspirations.
- Giving back to our community, especially the Black community, and not getting so comfortable individually that we forget about the collective struggle, and about the necessary relationship between individual achievement and collective progress.

An objective picture of the current status of Black males in the work force is not pretty. We are losing ground. Nonwhites currently comprise 13.6 percent of the labor force. By the year 2000, native nonwhites and immigrants will constitute 42 percent of the new labor force entrants. The unemployment rate for Black Americans is more than twice as high as the rate for whites. The number of minorities employed or looking for work has been steadily declining. While 81.6 percent of all young Black males were employed in 1965, the figure had declined to 58 percent in 1984. Worse yet, if current trends continue, the problems will worsen, because Blacks are overrepresented in occupations and heavily concentrated in urban areas that will likely lose the greatest number of jobs over the next decade. Adding to this are the cultural, social and often physical isolation of the economically disadvantaged from job opportunities. Indeed,

Speech given by the Honorable William C. Brooks, Assistant Secretary for Employment Standards, U.S. Department of Labor, at the First Annual National Black Male Conference, Kansas City, MO, July 12, 1990.

teenage Blacks are only half as likely to be employed as their white counterparts. This has been true for the last two decades and is not improving.

Our problems are not race specific, any more than drugs, unemployment and homelessness are. However, Blacks are disproportionately affected by the impediments that separate those with jobs skills from those without them.

And what happens once we get in the door? The progress of Blacks in U.S. corporations has been disappointing, as you here in this room know too well. Only one Black American heads a Fortune 1000 company.

Frankly, too few of us have enjoyed the education that corporations most need: degrees in business administration, engineering, and hard sciences. In 1985, Black Americans earned only about 3 percent of the doctorates, master's or bachelor's degrees in engineering, computer programming, or the hard sciences. This percentage is essentially unchanged since 1977. MBAs from the top schools earned by minorities comprised only 7 percent of the 1987 class. And I'm here to tell you, straight from my "Workforce 2000" speeches, that tomorrow's jobs are going to need increasingly higher skills.

The Urban League's "Report on Black America—1989" noted that the "fight at the back of the bus thirty years ago is now centered over much more powerful issues—education, jobs, values, and money." The Urban League report includes an updated "Racial Parity Index"—a number of comparative measurements of the relative standing of whites and Blacks in key areas of life. With 100 RPI measuring full parity, the scale measures only 47 today. The scale was 51.2 in 1967.

Of the things that are measured—housing, health, employment, career advancement, earnings, family income, poverty, education—only education is closing the gap. If we continue to improve our high school graduation rates at the same pace that held between 1967 and 1985, in sixteen years Black and white high school graduation rates will be equal. However, for college completion rates, it will take forty years. We obviously do not have sixteen years to waste, nor forty: We clearly need to get Black youngsters with the education program.

Besides education and job training, and besides computer literacy, there is another skill set that I think we all need to cultivate. And those skills relate to being a Black in the corporate world. These are some personal, hard-earned observations about who gets ahead and who doesn't. Both formal corporate organizations and informal networks are deeply ingrained social systems, resistant to change, and part of the unconscious psyche of the business community. Predictably, they are tailored to suburban, anglo males.

Most Blacks, however, grow up in predominantly Black, often urban, communities. We live in Black neighborhoods and go to Black schools. Our social and cultural reactions are formed by that environment, that experience. Therefore, in my view, the major problem Black Americans have in entering and staying in the traditional corporate world is one of socialization. When we move into the corporate world, a second, anglo-specific lens is layered onto our original viewpoint. Since these worlds are very different, new experiences tend to feel incongruous to us, and often cause us some duality of perception and reaction, some double vision.

Traditional organizations enhance that feeling by tending to react schizophrenically to us—gladly acknowledging our presence on the one hand, but not accepting us as "one of the boys" on the other. This can play out by way of heightened scrutiny of our work, in missed opportunities, and in young Blacks not finding and forming mentor relationships with entrenched executives.

The baseline reality is that the Anglo corporate structure and the Black community are two powerful, discrete entities in the United States that have often engaged in profound ideological conflict. This would seem to pose a natural, unresolvable conflict for those of us who have one foot in each world. Indeed, how can Black Americans who possess business talents and aspirations, who have supplemented those talents with solid formal education, and who have attained significant management posts in large corporate organizations, pursue satisfying, productive careers in corporate America?

By both proudly retaining our special strengths and perspective, and by being agents for changing a hard corporate structure. In other words, by both demonstrating individual achievement, and fostering collective progress. Let me give you a specific example. When racial and related social issues are debated in business or corporate circles, Black Americans should not be so integrated with the corporate structure that we hesitate or refuse to contribute our true insights—business and personal—into the discussion or the formulation of corporate policy.

Black Americans have the great advantage of instinctively questioning whether what is, is necessarily right. Our heritage conditions us to be more ready to see reality and to "tell it like it is." In business terms, we're more conversant with risk—identifying it, analyzing it, and taking it. Because attitudes do not change over night, I have tended to make my contributions by trying to influence behavior rather than attitudes. This is a matter of honest moderation, borne of genuine, disclosed double-identity.

And there's something else to be said for developing these skills. Your effectiveness along these lines will, I believe, make you recognize the obligation to "give something back," to strengthen the collective group. First, on giving back to the *Black* community, a longstanding issue between the Black community and its members in corporate America is that many of us too quickly isolate ourselves from the concerns and institutions we came from. Among other things, I'd suggest that this isolation can create a very unhappy personal identity crisis, especially in a predominantly white world.

Another issue is that isolation suggests ingratitude to the Black community. Ingratitude is inexcusable. It is a hard fact that the entry of sizeable numbers of Black Americans into high-level positions, and into educational programs such as business schools to prepare for these posts, is a direct result of tireless, often dangerous, and sometimes fatal struggle by lots of Black American individuals and organizations. *The way to combat actual or perceived ingratitude is to make time, as a matter of discipline, to give something back.*

Let me tell you a personal story. Early in my career at General Motors I sat next to Mrs. Rosa Parks at an awards banquet in Pittsburgh. During dinner she leaned over to me and said, "Make sure you always work to enable other Blacks to get where you are." Mrs. Parks's gentle command—to give back—has motivated me ever since.

"Giving back" can mean a lot of things. It can mean offering expertise and financial support to promising, deserving community organizations. It should mean, for all of us, being a role model to others coming up behind us. it might mean, where possible, an effort to direct "establishment resources" to programs that serve constructive ends. And, especially, it may mean a hand-in-hand relationship with the Black business community, and with our schools.

I believe we also have an obligation to give back *to America.* Public service is a high calling, whether you're in the government or in the private sector. I've gone back and forth several times, gaining knowledge and insight each time. There's a deep responsibility for all of us who succeed to help others. Moreover, you don't have a right to complain about the system unless you're willing to get in and change it.

That's why I took this job. With Labor Secretary Elizabeth Dole, I'm trying to wipe out the last vestiges of discrimination from our workplaces. One of my ambitions is to "break the glass ceiling"—to make sure that minorities are not only getting into the stockroom and the conference room, but into the boardroom. This is one of the mandates of the Office of Federal Contract Compliance Programs, a particularly fitting mandate as OFCCP celebrates its achievements in this silver anniversary year.

I say it's particularly fitting, because the whole concept of affirmative action is evolving. The demographic and sociological trends that we hear about and can see every day tell me that businesses simply cannot afford to waste talent, or America will become an economic colony of Asia and the European community, a third-rate has-been that cannot support its obligations or fund its dreams. Consequently, I believe very passionately that affirmative action by the year 2000 will be less an enforcement issue than a management issue.

It might have been nicer if there were a little less self-interest in this phenomenon, but I believe that the bottom-line profitability of American businesses is dependent on empowering employees, no matter who, or what, they are. As Dr. Roosevelt Thomas of Morehouse College told my people at a recent Enforcement Conference in Washington, the issue is not affirmative action goals, although the laws must continue to be enforced. The issue is not valuing diversity, because that is not in itself productive.

The bottom line is helping people to manage diversity in their work forces. It is empowering people to make their full contribution. In other words, it's making the most of what you've got.

Dr. Thomas tells a very funny story about affirmative action programs that try to graft peach tree branches onto old established corporate oak trees. As he put it, they get little, teeny, hard peaches. The people posing as peaches are bitter. And the people doing the grafting can't figure out what's wrong.

What's wrong is that managing diversity has to supplement, to complement, affirmative action. It's the sequel: Affirmative Action II. It's the care and feeding of affirmative action, so that we continue to move forward.

Affirmative action gives you diversity, but it does not cut to the roots of inequality and discrimination, nor does it nurture potential growth. Managing diversity tells us that performance is the key to success and that changing the root structure of corporate organizations by empowering all employees is going to boost productivity and enhance the corporate bottom line.

And incidentally, part of that empowerment for us is not using the crutch of racism. There is racism, no question. Indeed, 95 percent of Black business-people in a recent poll thought their career advancement had been hindered because of race. But you can't think about it or let it color your activities.

Performance is the only thing that counts. Even if it's twice as much performance as the guy at the next desk, for the same reward. Martin Luther King, Jr., used to say that "the only way to get ahead is to run faster than the man in front of you." Performance, not racism—that's not a paradox, that's reality. You've got to get up in the morning. You've got to get up and get out there. That's pure Booker T. Washington. It hasn't changed in all these years. I have many more thoughts on self-help and community support, on reaching back, and giving back. One I'd really like to focus on is mentoring.

I noted a little earlier that we don't have forty or even sixteen years to achieve education parity. Right now, 40 percent of adult Black males are functionally illiterate. Our high school drop-out rates, although improving overall, approach 50 percent in some inner city areas. And as you and I know, if you can't read, you can't get a job—even today, in the dark ages before Workforce 2000.

I give a lot of speeches to schoolchildren, and I talk to a lot of teachers and school administrators, going around spreading the gospel of Workforce 2000. I rarely meet a Black male teacher, especially in elementary schools. Teachers and administrators tell me that the absence of Black male role models is the single greatest cause of young Black males' educational failure.

So I say to you today, if you're worried about being an endangered species: Volunteer one day a month in a city school. Fight the failure syndrome. Mentoring a youngster in your community who is at risk of dropping out of school is probably the most important contribution you can make to our collective future.

Mentoring is one of our top priorities at the Labor Department. We are going around the country asking each American business to give 10 percent of its workforce the job flexibility to serve as mentors—to provide encouragement, tutoring, knowledge of the world of work, and wisdom to help students understand the importance of staying in school and helping them achieve their goals. There is also mentoring that takes place in the corporate world, and it, too, is invaluable.

Participating is so important. Every leader I have admired, of whatever race, has been a participant, not an observer. The best have participated in organizations that enriched the community, especially schools and churches. I read an article last week in the *New York Times* that said there were no Black men in our community's churches. None. Now why is that? The church has been the cornerstone, the foundation, of our culture. We have to get back to the things that give us strength. Church is where Black men belong. Churches need us, to be role models, to bring stability to families. And we need the faith in things bigger than we are which only churches can give us.

We are not an endangered species. The end of our story, the story of Black males, has not been written. Indeed, we will write it, by our own actions in the next twenty-five years, and by our children's and our grandchildren's in the generations that follow. If we have to choose between despair and hope, between dying out and thriving, and I do believe it is a choice, I will choose hope and thriving every time.

Look around us today. Walls are falling, people are coming together, the barriers separating nations and nationalities are disappearing. The most obvious example of this to us in this room today is Nelson Mandela. Clearly, if we are in need of role models, or the old-fashioned kind of hero to fill our children's imaginations with dreams and convictions, Nelson Mandela will do just fine. He is a hero of our times: Has anyone here been imprisoned for twenty-seven years and remained unbowed?

Yet Mandela is not the only hero, by far. Growing up, my heroes were Jackie Robinson, Ralph Bunche of the United Nations, my parents, and my teachers. Today, I can choose my heroes from among politicians, businessmen, athletes, artists, scholars. I count so many Black friends in public service:

- Connie Newman, director of the Office of Personnel Management
- Condoleezza Rice, director of Soviet and East European Affairs, National Security Council
- Gwendolyn King, commissioner of the Social Security Administration
- Louis Sullivan, secretary of Health and Human Services
- Arthur Fletcher, chairman of the Civil Rights Commission
- Colin Powell, chairman of the Joint Chiefs of Staff
- Dorothy Height, president, National Council of Negro Women
- Douglas Wilder, governor of Virginia
- Guy Buford, astronaut

But even as we admire these men and women, and seek to emulate them, we must remember that there cannot be individual achievement without collective progress. We must remember that we cannot get too comfortable with our heroes' achievements, or our own, and forget about the 600,000 Black males under thirty-five who are incarcerated—who outnumber the 400,000 in college.

Or forget about the almost half of our young men who are unemployed and on the road to becoming unemployable. Or forget about the half of our teenagers in urban areas who drop out of high school, and thus drop out of their futures, or who give in to drugs, to teenage parenthood, or to despair.

We must never think that those who are not in the mainstream are somehow different from us. They're no different at all. And we have to keep our end of the collective deal. We have to reach out our hands and our hard won success and most of all our compassion—or we truly will become an endangered species.

Those in the so-called ghettos will kill themselves with homicides or hypertension or crack; and we, sitting safely away from those dangers of the inner city will lose ourselves because we will have walked away from the very things that gave us strength to begin with: our identity as Black Americans, our culture of self-help, and our affirmation of the values that have enabled us to overcome hardship—family, church, community, education, and productive work.

It is up to us—each of us, and all of us—to carry that message home, and to carry it to the mountaintop: individual achievement, collective progress.

CHAPTER 19

Ain't I a Man? The Efficacy of Black Masculinities for Men's Studies in the 1990s

by Clyde W. Franklin, II

Michael Kimmel and Michael Messner (1989) asked a very simple question and yet a very complicated one, in the introduction to their edited work *Men's Lives*. They query, "But what does it mean to examine 'men as men?' " "Most courses in a college curriculum are about men, aren't they?" Kimmel and Messner continue. Still, because such courses seem only to deal with men in their public roles, Kimmel and Messner conclude that "rarely, if ever, are men understood through the prism of gender." Catherine Stimpson (1987), founding editor of *Signs: Journal of Women in Culture and Society*, was confronted with this reality when she wrote the foreword to philosopher Harry Brod's edited volume *The Making of Masculinities* (1987). Stimpson said about the volume, "It's dogged, imaginative scholarship, sticking to its task, in rewriting that deceptively simple word 'man.' " Brod (1987, 39), in an initial attempt to make a case for men's studies, proposed a general theory of men's studies as an academic field, gave illustrative examples of men's studies research endeavors, and compared and contrasted several political perspectives on men's studies. The underlying and persistent theme of Brod's arguments was, "while seemingly about men, traditional scholarship's treatment of generic man as the human norm in fact systematically excludes from consideration what is unique to men qua men." Precluded from traditional scholarship about men, according to Brod, is "the study of masculinity as a *specific male* experience, rather than a universal paradigm for human experience" (p. 40).

But . . . "Ain't I a Man?"—Including Black Men

But what "man" is being studied? It is 1992, and 140 years since Sojourner Truth stood before the second annual convention of the women's rights movement in Akron, Ohio, in 1852 (hooks 1981, 160). In an impassioned plea for Black women's rights, she spoke of the fact that (white) men in the audience were talking about helping (white) women into carriages and over ditches and making sure they had the best places. Yet, Sojourner Truth felt, "Well, children, whar dar is so much racket dar must be something out o'kilter. But what's all dis here talkin' about?" Baring her breast, she asked, "Ain't I a woman? Look at me! Look at my arm! I have plowed and planted, and gathered into barns and no man could hold me—and ain't I a woman? I could work as hard as any man and bear de leash as well . . . and ain't I a woman. . . ?"

What Sojourner Truth does, according to bell hooks, unlike most white women's rights advocates, is refer to her own personal life experience as evidence of women's ability to function as parent; to be the work equal of men; to undergo persecution, physical abuse, rape, torture; and to not only survive but emerge triumphant (hooks 1981, 160).

Presented at the 1st Annual Conference of the National Council of African American Men (NCAAM), Kansas City, MO, July 11-13, 1990.

In 1981, bell hooks repeated Sojourner Truth's cry in her volume *Ain't I a Woman: Black Women and Feminism*, because 129 years later America still had not responded to Black women. The popular Black singer James Brown croons, "It's a Man's World" . . . but is it a Black man's world? Are Black males "men" in America? After all, the concept "man" is socially constructed and for that reason, the question must be raised, *"Are Black males "men" in America?* Let us explore briefly this question.

Early Black Masculinity in America: In the Beginning

Uprooted from their culture, land, and loved ones, the twenty Black slaves who were brought to Jamestown, Virginia, in 1619 had no idea what awaited them. They could not have imagined that they would be separated from their fellow tribespersons, placed with Blacks from different tribes who spoke different languages, auctioned off like cattle, and beaten and killed culturally and physically. It was during this time period that Black males and white males began to construct masculine identities for Black males. These social constructions have connoted many things over the decades, but all too often they did not signify "man" in the early beginning. This was so because Black males had to live within a social system imposed by plantation owners. Yet slave men often attempted to be providers by supplementing their meager food supplied by plantation owners by hunting and trapping game. This, however, was not the hegemonic definition of masculinity in early America. Black males were not human, and thus it was impossible for them to be masculine.

Characteristics of the Black Male Sex Role: In the Beginning

Characteristics of the Black male sex role constructed and assigned to male slaves were varied. Kitano (1985) notes that the status of Blacks initially was clearly undefined. In the seventeenth century, Blacks were indentured servants with rights to freedom after fulfilling contractual obligations (pp. 104–5). But, Kitano feels, because Blacks were easily identifiable, a racial caste system evolved. This system has been said to be the single most important experience for the Black person in the United States. It was a system that classified people into human/subhuman, master/servant, adult/child, owner/owned—and meant, essentially, the degradation of a human being to the status of property (p. 106). What did this mean for the Black male's sex role? It meant development of several dimensions of the Black male sex role, some of which are discussed below.

Dimensions of the Black Male Sex Role

The Black man as property. Central to the treatment of the Black male in early America was the notion that he was "property." Actually, not only was he property, but also those persons closest to him were "property." This is a critical point that we will return to later. Succinctly, in the beginning, one critical dimension of Black masculinity—what it means to be a man—was "you were property, owned, could be brought, sold, bartered, given, or eliminated."

The Black man as submissive. Slave masters quickly perceived a very real problem: slaves did not want to comply with their wishes. As a result, discipline became a central feature of socializing Black male slaves. Generally, slaves had come from extended families, but now they were thrown into diverse African groups. Violence had to be used to make slaves fearful, compliant, and submissive.

The Black male as nonprotective. Being slaves, Black males could not exert any protective control over the lives of family members. Black women were used to breed slaves for slave masters. Families could be destroyed at any time in the slave community. The male slave was taught that his proper role was to assume a nonprotective stance regarding the people he loved most.

The Black male as powerless. In America during slavery, a patriarchal system existed. The male was the head of the home. This was the model Black males saw. But Black male slaves could not be heads of families. They had little voice in running their families, telling their children what they could or could not do, beyond what the slave master wanted. Black male slaves were powerless within their families and in the outside world. Still, Gutman found that marriages occurred and endured. They were legitimized often by rituals such as jumping over a broomstick, and fidelity was expected from both males and females after marriage (Gutman 1976).

The Black male as stud supreme. By now it is probably obvious that the Black male slave role was a contradictory and peculiar one. Black male slaves were considered subhuman and expected to behave only marginally as human. Most of the rights and privileges accorded "men" in America were denied this subhuman male. But, the black male slave *was* expected to be healthy and strong, to work hard, and to be a good breeder. Ironically, the very system that mandated nonbinding, intensive, and frequent sexual relationships between Black males and Black females (for breeding purposes) also defined Black males as hypersexual subhumans. A plethora of sexual myths surrounded the Black male slave. The myths ranged from the unusual enormity of the Black male slave's penis to his spectacular feats and endeavors in the sexual arena. Indeed, the Black male slave *was* an animal—a subhuman who was fit only for working and breeding. The perception of Black male slaves as studs supreme meant that white women had to be protected from the potentially sexually aggressive subhumans. This perception of the Black male slave as stud supreme, along with a resulting paranoia that Black male slaves would rape white women led to numerous lynchings of and other heinous crimes against Black male slaves. The perception of the sexual prowess of Black males persists to this very day. Black families, too, were sexually stereotyped, but, as sociologist Robert Staples notes, it was the Black male who was most sexually demeaned. Staples writes:

> Although the sexual stereotypes apply equally to Black men and women, it is the Black male who has suffered the most because of the white notions of his hypersexuality. Between 1884 and 1900 more than 2,500 Black men were lynched, the majority of whom were accused of sexual interest in white women. The Black man, it was said, had a larger penis, a great sexual capacity, and an insatiable sexual appetite. These stereotypes depicted Black men as primitive sexual beasts without the white man's love for home and family. (Staples 1986, 58)

In summary, during slavery and for a period afterward, the Black male sex role had the following dimensions: property, submissive, nonprotective, powerless, and stud supreme.

Of all the aforementioned sex-role dimensions, perhaps none was more important to the Black male than society's refusal to extend him "manhood." As John O. Killens concluded in his novel, *And Then We Heard the Thunder*, "The only thing they [white society] will not stand for is for a Black man to be a man. And everything else is worthless if a man can't be a man." But how does one become a man? I submit that becoming a generic man with a particular kind of masculinity is a process of social construction. Becoming a Black man with a particular kind of masculinity is an even more difficult and tedious social construction because of the numerous adaptations that must be made in a racist society.

The Black Male as a Unit of Analysis: Being a Black Man

Understanding Black men means recognizing that in America adult Black males have been Black "men" for only about twenty years. In addition, even during this time Black males have not been recognized as "societally approved" men. While there has been gradual recognition of Black males as "men," there has been concomitant understanding of Black men as aberrant and not quite capable of assuming the "masculine role." How else is it possible to explain white society's reluctance to extend male power and privilege to Black men? Could it be that Black men still are perceived as subhuman, animalistic sexual perverts?

Seeing the Black male as an object of study means understanding Black males' diversity. Black males, like males of all races, ethnicities, and nationalities, come in all statures, dispositions, attitudes, sexualities, and so forth. Yet, there is a thread of commonality linking Black men in America. This thread of commonality is the experience of oppression. Even so, hooks (1981) suggests that "enslaved Black men were stripped of the patriarchal status that had characterized their social situation in Africa but they were not stripped of their masculinity" (p. 21).

Hooks argues that the white slave owners sought to exploit the masculinity of the African male. Defining masculinity in terms of such attributes as strength, virility, vigor, and physical prowess, hooks contends that young, strong, healthy African males were prime targets. She says:

> That white people recognized the masculinity of the Black male is evident by the tasks assigned the majority of Black male slaves. No annals of history record that masses of Black slave men were forced to execute roles traditionally performed exclusively by women. Evidence to the contrary exists, documenting the fact that there were many tasks enslaved African men would not perform because they regarded them as female tasks. . . . If white women and men had really been obsessed by the idea of destroying Black masculinity, they could easily have physically castrated all Black men aboard slave ships or they could have forced Black men to assume feminine attire or perform so-called feminine tasks. (1981, 21)

It is apparent in the above statement that hooks feels maintaining Black male slaves' physical strength, virility, and vigor while not making them perform traditional female roles can be equated with maintaining their masculinity. I take issue with hooks on this point because my perception of masculinity is that it is socially constructed. Black male slaves, by definition, were subhuman nonmen. Certainly, if healthy, vigorous, strong, and virile, they were expected to perform tedious tasks for long hours, sire children, obey the master. But this did not mean preserving Black male slave masculinity—in fact, it meant the opposite. Black male slaves had no gender; they did have a sex—but no gender. In order for the Black male slave to have had a gender, he would have had to be recognized as a human being. To the contrary, numerous myths about the Black male during slavery were constructed and perpetuated—all supporting the idea of Black male slave subhumanity.

In a very real sense, the ambiguity surrounding the Black male sex role today may be due in part to the legacy of a nondefinition of the Black male slave sex role, and continued reluctance to perceive the Black male as a man—at least in the hegemonic sense of the word.

The Truth about Masculinity: A Men's Studies Perspective

Men's studies literature in the 1980s recognized an important fact about masculinity in America. The culturally exalted form of masculinity, the hegemonic model, corresponds to the actual character of a small number of men (Carrigan et al. 1987). As Carrigan, Connell, and Lee elaborate, "There is a distance and a tension between collective ideal and actual lives" (p. 92). Few, if any males' ac-

tual lives fit the hegemonic model. Still, a critical division exists between hegemonic masculinity and various subordinated masculinities. There are groups of
men who possess power and wealth and who legitimate and reproduce social
relationships that generate and sustain the hegemonic model. The way Black
males fit into this overall power framework, and how Black males construct their
various forms of masculinity, are problematic concerns in men's studies. The
processes of constructing Black masculinities are difficult ones. They are difficult because the societal institutions are headed by white males who have vested
interests in supporting the hegemonic model. This means, as Carrigan, Connell,
and Lee imply, Black males continually are negotiating their masculinities from
positions of powerlessness.

The results are obvious—many forms of Black masculinities are seen as
falling outside of culturally prescribed masculinities. This is not surprising because America has yet to recognize large numbers of Black males as men/mas-
culine. This is so despite the fact that thousands of Black males keep trying to be
men.

Ontological and Epistemological Assumptions Underlying the Study of Black Masculinities

Studying Black masculinities before the late 1960s was a rather static process.
Black males had participated in various masculinity constructions; however,
those masculinities departing from society's conception of the Black male role
were considered anomalies—something out of the ordinary. George W. Carver,
Marcus Garvey, Elijah Mohammad, Booker T. Washington, E. Franklin Frazier, W. E. B. Du Bois, Langston Hughes, Paul Robeson, Bayard Rustin, A.
Phillip Randolph, all were seen as enigmas, and society was ambivalent toward
them. These Black males certainly were different from society's prescribed role
for Black males. Thus, society really had no response for them and often treated
them awkwardly (Rustin 1971).

Actually, American society's treatment of Black men who depart significantly from societal expectations, but do so in a socially acceptable manner, reflects the inadequacy of using sex role models to study Black men. Men's studies
scholars point to the fact that "there is variation in masculinity arising from individual experiences that produces a range of personalities . . . the male role is
unduly restrictive because hegemonic masculinity does not reflect the true nature of men" (Carrigan et al. 1987, 78). This may be an especially acute problem
when studying the lives of *Black males* who reluctantly were extended the label
"man" only during the modern day civil-rights movement in the late 1960s.
Ironically, the label "man" was extended only when Black males in sufficient
numbers threatened to use a mainstay male trait, violence, to accomplish what
cooperation and negotiation had *not* been able to accomplish. Just as ironic was
the fact that buttressing the extension of the label was not only threatened vio-

lence but also frequent objectification and exploitation of white women. The rationale for this aspect of the revolution, according to bell hooks, was that success means little for Black males if they cannot also possess that human object white patriarchal culture offers to men as the supreme reward for masculine achievement (hooks 1981, 113). About Black men hooks writes:

> In their eagerness to gain access to the bodies of white women, many Black men have shown that they were far more concerned with exerting masculine privilege than challenging racism. Their behavior is not unlike that of white male patriarchs who, on one hand, claimed to be white supremacists, but who could not forego sexual contact with the women of the very race they claimed to hate. (Pp. 113–14)

Quite simply, adult Black males became "men" when they publicly incorporated violence and actively sought sexual liaisons with white women—all with the permission of those powerful white males in charge of maintaining hegemonic definitions of masculinity.

Ontological Assumptions Underlying the Study of Black Masculinities: A Proposal

When Black males became "men" in America it had little to do with accepting a static male sex role; it had much to do with actual and perceived alterations in power relations between the supporters of hegemonic masculinities and subordinated masculinities. For a few brief moments, Black-male-led riots in major American cities, kidnappings, and general racial unrest produced novel and different forms of Black masculinity. Challenges to the traditional power holders actually called into question static definitions of masculinity which had implied that there was something called a "male sex role."

Challenging the power holders meant *freeing Black males to become Black men.* It connoted allowing the construction of Black masculinity. Put simply, the "male sex role" did not exist. It is impossible to isolate a "role" that constructs masculinity (Carrigan et al. 1987, 80). There is no reality of a sex role out there that gives us the basis for masculinity. *Masculinities are constructed.* Black masculinities, in particular, are constructed under the cloud of oppression.

For Black males historically it was not a matter of having subordinated masculinities because, as stated repeatedly, Black males were not perceived as "men." To reiterate, through *violence* and *sexism* Black males and white males began to construct masculinities for Black males during the modern-day Black-male-led movement in the late 1960s (Staples 1986, 80). When Black males became Black men through these social constructions, various forms of Black masculinities emerged: traditionally heterosexual masculinity, androgynous Black masculinity, homosexual Black masculinity, and ambisexual Black masculinity. But these social constructions all developed simultaneously with societal conditions that produced the following characteristics of Black males in America in the 1980s:

> Suicide [was] the third leading cause of death among Black males ages 18–29.
>
> Black-on-Black homicide [was] the leading cause of death for Black males ages 15–34.
>
> The incidence of drug-related disease for Black males under 35 [was] 12 times higher than for any comparable group.
>
> Black males [had] ten times the incidence of heart attacks and prostate cancer as white males.
>
> From 1950–1985 the life expectancy for white males increased from 63 to 74.6 years, while for Black males it increased only from 59 to 65 years over the same period of time.
>
> Between 1973 and 1986 the real earnings of Black males age 18–29 declined 31%, the percentage of young Black males in the full-time work force fell by 20%, and the number who [had] dropped out of the labor force doubled from 13% to 25%.
>
> From 1973–1987, real earnings of Black males ages 20 to 29 decreased by 27.7%.
>
> In 1987, 31.5% of Black males ages 16–19 were unemployed compared to 16% of white males within the same age group.
>
> Blacks [comprised] 48% of the U.S. prison population, yet [comprised] only 12% of the general population.
>
> Black males [comprised] 89% of the Black prison population.
>
> Of the Black male population in large metropolitan areas, 51% [had] been arrested compared to only 14% of white males.
>
> Eighteen percent of all Black males [had served] time in prison compared to only 3% of white males. (*Ohio's African-American Males* 1990).

Certainly these are heinous, difficult, and debilitating experiences for Black men in America. Still, they form the bases for new Black masculinities produced by a society that still seems ambivalent about extending male privileges and statuses to Black men. But aren't adult Black males "men"? Don't Black males work at some of the most menial tasks which support this country? Don't Black males overwhelmingly protect America in the armed forces? Despite rejections, don't the majority of Black males continue to believe in the American dream? Aren't Black males "men"? Understanding the processes Black men in America use to construct their masculinities in the face of great odds and obstacles is a major task for academicians interested in men's studies. Key ideas here are the ontological assumptions that Black masculinities *are not biological*; they are *socially constructed within a framework of power relations or dynamics often dominated by powerful white males and subordinated minority males.*

Many Black males in America perceive American society to be permeated with normlessness and incapable of controlling individual behavior. This view of society suggests that there is a perceived lack of socially imposed restrictions on individual needs and desires. From this perspective society does not have sufficient resources for its members and thus, the emergence and persistence of anomie (Farley 1990, 218).

Sociologist Robert K. Merton (1968) feels that anomie results when individuals in a society internalize certain needs and desires through societal inculcation but face structural impediments to the realization of these needs and desires. He proposes several modes of individual adaptation that may be used to construct "ideal" types of Black masculinities.

I submit that Black men, more than others in America, experience anomic situations in society. The experience for many Black males results in the gradual recognition that they, indeed, are destined to be excluded from mainstream society, and that their situation is futile. This is the state of countless Black men in America today. Feelings of futility and internalized desires for success generate modes of individual adaptations that define generally various forms of Black masculinities: (1) conforming Black masculinity, (2) ritualistic Black masculinity, (3) innovative Black masculinity, (4) retreatist Black masculinity, and (5) rebellious Black masculinity.

Conforming Black masculinity. Contrary to some opinions, Black males in America overwhelmingly are conforming in the sense that they continue to accept mainstream society's prescriptions and proscriptions for heterosexual males. They do so despite the fact that, when society teaches men to work hard, set high goals, and strive for success, it does not teach Black men simultaneously that their probability of failure is high because blocked opportunities for Black males are endemic to American society. Historically, this strategy paid off quite well for American society—especially white society—because social dislocation characterizing Black males did not reach catastrophic proportions until the mid-1970s, as noted by William J. Wilson (1987). According to Wilson, the increasing rate of social dislocation has been due more to changes in the social organization of inner-city areas than social psychological sources of nonconformity (p. 3). Succinctly, a large proportion of the Black male population chooses the conforming mode of individual adaptation to American society's dictates.

Ritualistic Black masculinity. Because of certain experiences, another group of Black men comes to realize that American societal goals and their individual goals are not coterminous. That is, regardless of whether they accept or reject the goals, America will decide how successful they will be in life. Such men may gradually develop cynical attitudes about the goals of individual success and realizing the American dream. Frequently, these Black men construct uncanny abilities to "follow the rules," giving little thought to any reasons for doing so. They participate in societal institutions, "playing the game" without purpose or commitment. Black men of this genre appear to be conforming but in actuality are ritualistic in their actions—*performing* without rhyme or reason. In one sense, this form of Black masculinity remains highly functional for American society, since it closely resembles conformity. But in another sense, the individual Black male suffers because he becomes a social zombie, following societal dictates regardless of consequences to himself and those close to him.

Innovative Black masculinity. The most publicized, feared, and reviled Black men in America today are those who have constructed innovative Black masculinity forms. The innovative forms of masculinity constructed may be relatively nonthreatening physically but somewhat socially distasteful to many. For example, it may exaggerate one aspect of traditional masculinity which *can* be achieved in order to receive desired responses. An example that comes to mind is 2 Live Crew's recording, "As Nasty As They Wanna Be." The recording emphasizes sexual explicitness and debases women—two aspects of masculinity most American men are very familiar with. Simultaneously, the recording also achieves the societally desired goal of materialistic success. It is very doubtful that rapping about the contempt held for Black women, Black religion, Black parents, and, in essence, the Black culture would have been used as a means for attaining success in America if blocked opportunities did not characterize these Black men's experiences. It is common to find Black men in such circumstances, and it is becoming increasingly common to see similar consequences of such circumstances.

Strikingly different from the aforementioned relatively mild innovative Black masculine form is a much more lethal form of Black masculinity. It is the type of Black masculinity that responds to blocked opportunities by developing and glorifying heinous means of achieving materialistic success, including Black-on-Black homicide, drug dealing, theft, and various other forms of deviance. This is the form of Black masculinity that has resulted in a growing crisis for Black males in America (Strickland 1989; Tiff 1990). What has to be remembered, however, is that it is not lack of resources or poverty that results in the construction of this form of Black masculinity. Rather, it is the fact that one lacks the ability to fulfill the societal masculine role while being surrounded by those not so disabled, in a society that keeps emphasizing that fulfilling the role should be the goal of every American man.

Retreatist Black masculinity. There is an alarmingly growing number of Black men in America who are constructing and nurturing a kind of Black masculinity signifying withdrawal from American society. These Black men may be characterized by high rates of joblessness, welfare dependency, drug addiction, alcoholism, and homelessness. Essentially, having grown weary of participating in a system that denies them the means for achieving common goals most members of society achieve, these men have opted to leave the system—withdraw.

Rebellious Black masculinity. By and large Black males in America today do not adopt societal anomie by simultaneously rejecting America's *goals* and *means* of achieving the goals. They may reject one or the other as suggested earlier, but rarely do Black men reject both. If sizeable members of Black men were to reject both, it is likely that they would construct rebellious forms of Black masculinity similar to or more intense than what occurred during the late 1960s and early 1970s. The new men's studies could be used by Black men as a framework in which to construct new goals and means more compatible with the interests and welfare of Black men. Similarly, Black masculinities could be integrated with the new men's studies in order to further demystify the lives of men in America. In essence, this is the efficacy of Black masculinities for men's studies and vice versa in the 1990s.

Epistemological Assumptions Underlying the Study of Black Masculinities: A Proposal

William J. Wilson (1987, 18) argues that it is not sufficient to rely solely on census data and other secondary data when studying the recent rise in rates of social dislocation in the underclass. This is especially relevant for studying Black men who have disproportionate rates of Black social dislocation.

Also important for Black men's studies in Wilson's view is that the aforementioned methodologies should be augmented with empirical data on both the ghetto underclass experience and conditions in the broader society that have shaped and continue to shape that experience. This calls for a number of different research strategies ranging from survey to ethnography to historical work.

It is clear that little about Black men in America can be gleaned from sterile statistics alone. Without adequate accompanying explanations, knowledgeable interpretations from informed perspectives, and other methodologies, Black men will remain an enigma in the 1990s. Surely the necessity for understanding the everyday experience of Black men is apparent as an appropriate empirical tool in Black men's studies. Correlational and regression analyses certainly have their places in Black masculinity studies. Alone, however, they are not sufficient substitutes for qualitative methodologies that can produce knowledge with human depth and richness of dimension.

It is also possible, with certain qualitative methodologies, to attenuate the problem of reification in Black men's studies. Black men are viewed in many ways, as we have seen. Depending on one's political persuasion, ethnic affiliation, racial group membership, and sex, Black men's intelligence, power, sexuality, compassion, and other traits will vary. To be sure, this is to be expected. But because Black men are relatively isolated in America, dangerous misconceptions, myths, and unsupported conjectures about them abound. Also, these simply are mental constructions. They are abstractions. Yet, with media bombardment supporting myths, research reports without adequate interpretation, and prevailing racism in America, abstractions or mental constructions related to Black men are converted into real, living beings. This is the danger of acquiring knowledge about Black men using only quantitative methodologies. The knowledge obtained may be socially constructed and then may be responded to as though it is real. During slavery Black men were mentally constructed as subhuman, not quite men, and legacies of this abstraction remain today. This is precisely why there is a need for Black men's studies. Without Black men's studies and an appropriate epistemology, it is indeed possible that in the year 2000, many Black men will still be asking the question, "Ain't I a man?"

CHAPTER 20

The African-American Father's Roles within the Family

*by John Lewis McAdoo
and Julia B. McAdoo*

The study of the father's roles in the family is a relatively new phenomenon. In the past, the father's main contributions were assumed to be those of provider, protector, disciplinarian, and representative of the family to the wider community. This paper focuses on some of the contributions African-American scholars have made to the understanding of the father's role in the family.

The African-American father always seems to be either absent in family studies or dominated by the mother in mainstream literature. Even when he was observed to respond in the same way as white fathers, his behavior was interpreted negatively and sometimes even pejoratively (J. McAdoo 1988a, 1988b, 1990).

In reviewing the literature on fathers' participation in the family, the contributions of African-American scholars have been virtually ignored. This omission has led some scholars to feel that the disciplines of family studies, developmental psychology, and family sociology are ethnocentrically biased.

Several African-American researchers (H. McAdoo 1988; J. McAdoo 1988a, 1988b, 1991; Gary et al. 1983; Hill 1981; and Billingsley 1968) have reviewed the social science literature and noted that the following traits are crucial in any analysis and definition of African-American family strength and stability.

1. Economic sufficiency: stable employment, adequate income, property ownership, and a strong work orientation
2. Religiosity: positive ethical values and a positive religious orientation
3. Future orientation or achievement orientation: educational attainment, educational expectations and aspirations
4. Flexibility of family roles: the presence of a leader in a family, ability to deal with crisis in a positive manner, good communication patterns, and consistent rules
5. Strong kinship bonds: a high degree of commitment, appreciation, mutual obligations, helping networks and exchanges, and spending time together
6. Positive friendship relationships: reciprocal sharing and reaching out and support in times of crisis
7. A realistic attitude toward work: an ability to compartmentalize negative racial stereotypes, an ability to get along with others, and balancing work and family time

Theoretical Perspectives

Mainstream researchers on family life development have offered several theories to explain the functioning of African-American families in American society. The major theories include the cultural deprivation theory, matriarchy theory, conflict theory, domestic colonialism theory, exchange theory, Black nationalism theory, and ecological theory.

African-American researchers sometimes adopted these theories, sometimes criticized the various theories, and sometimes modified the theories to control for weaknesses in their explanatory power.

Weaknesses of some of the major theories have been identified by African-American writers: cultural deprivation/deficiency (Peters 1988; White and Parham 1990), Black matriarchy (Staples 1978; White and Parham 1990); conflict, historical materialism, and domestic colonialism (Staples 1978); exchange theory, and ecological systems (Peters 1988).

Billingsley (1968) reacted to the negative evaluations of African Americans as pathological or culturally deprived by Eurocentric researchers and clearly presented the notion that the African-American family was a viable system. Peters (1988) provided an excellent critique of the research approaches and conceptual frameworks used in studying parenting roles in African-American families. She discussed the descriptive, comparative deficit and ecological approaches to studying the African-American family. From the comparative deficit perspective, families who experienced the ravages of enslavement lack the cultural background to fulfill the various family roles expected of those living in Western society. This cultural deprivation has led to a number of social psychological problems in the adjustment of African-American men in the performance of their provider, nurturer, and protective roles in the family.

Other theories seem to involve a value judgement of cultural deprivation that hinders objective observation in the real world. Peters suggested that these theories do not adequately take into account the demands, the extreme pressures, and the social constraints placed on African-American fathers.

White and Parham's (1990) analysis of the deprivation/deficiency theoretical models provided some further explanations of Peters's comparative deficit model. They feel that theorists from the deprivation/deficiency school assumed that the effects of years of racism and discrimination had deprived most African Americans of the strength to develop a healthy self-esteem (Kardner and Ovessey 1951) as well as legitimate family structures (Moynihan 1965). They noted that this model led to the concept of cultural deprivation that has been used to differentiate African Americans from others in the society. Cultural deprivation theory assumed that, due to inadequate exposure to European-American values, norms, customs, and life-styles, African Americans were culturally deprived and required cultural enrichment to be accepted by the dominant society.

While White and Parham suggested that white middle-class culture established the norms of society, their analysis of the Black matriarchy model as a variant of the deprivation/deficiency model may be of more interest here because it provides some of the social theorist's assumptions about the roles of African-American men in the family. Staples (1978) noted that matriarchy was seen as a pathological form of family life where the wife dominated the family members. The proponents of the matriarchy hypothesis suggest that the African-American male lacks the masculine role behaviors characterized by log-

ical thinking, willingness to take responsibility for others, assertiveness, managerial skills, achievement orientation, and occupational mastery (White and
Parham 1990).

The African-American female became the matriarch, from this point of
view, because American society was unwilling to permit the African-American
male to assume the legal, psychological, and social positions necessary to become a dominant force within his family. The African-American female was
also seen, from this perspective, as unwilling to share the power she gained by
default even in situations where the male was present and willing to take family
responsibility. An analysis of mainstream and African-American empirical
studies by the National Research Council (1989) testing this hypothesis found
no evidence to support the theory of the Black matriarch. In a review of studies
of power and decision making, the African American husband was found to
share equally with his wife (J. McAdoo 1986, 1988b).

Staples (1978), while agreeing with much of Peters's analysis, noted that
African-American researchers could utilize a Black nationalist orientation. He
suggested that pan-Africanism has become a dominant conceptual model
among African-American researchers in studying African-American families.
Among the many tenets of this approach is that people of African descent have a
common culture as well as a common history of racist oppression that has culmi-
nated in a shared destiny. An important ingredient of this model is its focus on
the comparative study of African and African-American culture. Staples (1976)
found some difficulties with this model. First, Africa has a diversity of cultures,
cultural values, languages, and behavioral patterns. Another problem is the difficulty in translating cultural forms from Africa to the African-American experience. Staples felt that those who use this model tend to emphasize the study of
cultural forms rather than political and economic analysis. The major weakness
of this approach is that it focuses on cultural subjugation rather than the political
and economic oppression that he feels affects African Americans. A basic assumption of this perspective is that a cultural group never loses its cultural heritage; it simply fuses it into another form.

In sociological research, the conflict theory provides some support for understanding the universal experiences of people of African descent, but Staples
does not demonstrate its utility in understanding current research approaches.
Instead, he sketchily presents two related approaches, domestic colonialism and
historical materialism. Domestic colonialism seems to be a variant on the Marx-
ist theme that all societies were divided into two groups—the oppressors and
the oppressed. Domestic colonialist societies were divided along racial lines into
groups of superior and inferior status. Domestic colonialism defines the rules
governing the relationships between European Americans, the exploiters and
African Americans, the exploited (Staples 1978).

Historical materialism suggests that the economic influences on African
American family life may play an important part in the destabilization and

breakup of many families. From this perspective, the father's role in the family is heavily influenced by outside sources that control his access to economic resources and limit his capacity to fulfill the provider role. Those who see some utility in this approach point to racial economic disparities, segregated housing and schooling patterns, high unemployment and incarceration rates, and the predominance of African Americans in the underclass (Glasgow 1980).

Choice and exchange theory also has been suggested as a conceptual framework to understand the context in which the African-American male makes choices and participates within the family processes (J. McAdoo 1990). This theory shows how African American fathers make choices in the operations of their roles within the family. Fathers will choose negative roles or refuse to play some roles within the family when access to economic and social resources is perceived by them to be unavailable. The theoretical propositions were expanded to take into account the economic, political, residential, and educational barriers to the father's ability to carry out important roles within the family and the community. The assumption of this theory is that these can operate as barriers that limit the father's choices and options in his exchanges within the family.

Ecological theory presents family roles and functioning from an Afrocentric perspective. This perspective allows us to predict alternative outcomes to the racial barriers to employment, experiences of social isolation on the job and in the mainstream community, and the development of roles that African-American men play in their families. Ecological theory allows us to describe and explain the many roles fathers may play in their families. It allows us to test the assumptions of female dominance in the home and the lack of father involvement in the family. It helps us to better understand the historical, societal, political, and social influences on the roles African-American fathers play in the family. Peters (1988) sees the ecological framework as a move to understand African-American family functioning in a less ethnocentrically biased manner.

The assumption of ecological theory is that fathers may play a variety of roles in the family and community that can lead to positive family outcomes. Fathers may use a variety of coping strategies to control negative outside influences in the performance of their nurturing, support, disciplining, provider, and other family roles. Ecological theory allows us to explore the differential choices that working-, middle-, and upper-class fathers use to develop stability and positive growth in African American family life. The theory allows us to explore the positive and negative father roles and their effects within the family.

The Provider Role

In American society, a man is defined by his ability to provide for his family. Ecological theory allows us to understand how structural dissonance at the societal level may have profound influences on ethnic minority communities. As

Duster (1988) has shown, at the structural level the extraordinarily high and sustained unemployment rates among African-American adults and youth are the results of such converging factors as moving of capital to foreign soil, from cities to suburbs, and from northern cities to selected areas of the Sun Belt. He also pointed to the decline in manufacturing and the increase in the advanced service sector occupations in major cities, where the majority of African Americans live, and the changing patterns of immigration that produce competition for scarce jobs.

Malveaux (1989) noted that finding and keeping a job is synonymous with being accepted into society for many Americans. This ability to provide for self and family has a great deal of impact on how a man perceives himself in a variety of family roles. From an ecological perspective, it might be suggested that an African-American man's ability to successfully fulfill the provider role depends upon other community systems over which he has little control. Several writers (J. McAdoo 1990; Gibbs 1988; Billingsley 1968) have discussed the historical, political, and social barriers that influence his ability to perform that role.

In an analysis of the work force participation of African-American youth, Malveaux suggested that the labor force may be a hostile place for them. These youths appear to suffer from the same employment and economic barriers faced by their fathers, grandfathers, and great-grandfathers before them. Wilson (1987) reviewed the national labor statistics for 1954–87 and found the unemployment rate for African Americans sixteen and over to be twice the national average during that period. He also provided empirical evidence that employed African-American males earned 57 percent of the wages earned by their European-American counterparts with the same experience and job classifications. African-American males experience a glass-ceiling effect when it comes to occupational and economic opportunities.

Gibbs (1988) eloquently discussed the educational and other structural barriers that influence the African-American male in participating in provider and community roles. Leshore (1981) noted that African-American males have been coerced by public social agencies and ignored by the private service sector.

Very few studies have been found that evaluated the family's ability to cope when, because of racial prejudice or severe economic depression, the father was unable adequately to fulfill the provider role. There needs to be some understanding of the father's reactions to sharing this role with his wife and sometimes his children. The role of the extended family (H. McAdoo 1988) in providing some support to the provider role could add another level to our understanding of the utilization of family resources. Provider role stress has been the major focus of our research efforts.

African-American men may experience stress related to their inability to fulfill their provider role in the family. Bowman (in press) found a link between unemployment and family estrangement in a national study of African-American fathers. His summary of the literature on the impact of massive deindustrialization in the urban communities noted that the loss of jobs and employment opportunities creates vulnerabilities in some fathers' personal lives and leads to a succession of provider role strains within some families. He discussed the impact of joblessness and job search discouragement, which can intensify provider role strain and lead to vulnerability to drugs, crime, family estrangement, and other psychological problems.

Bowman suggested that we need to evaluate existing research to determine how the harmful psychological and social effects of provider role strain might be reversed by extended family networks, religious orientation, and reality-based attributional patterns. We might begin by studying how some fathers are able to successfully reduce their provider role strain, maintain a positive feeling of self-esteem, and continue positive family relationships in spite of adversity.

Structural factors within society have both a direct and an indirect effect on how the provider's role is handled by fathers. J. McAdoo's (1988a) research with economically sufficient men in their role as providers found no significant differences across ethnic groups and races in the way they carried out that function. They were able to provide the necessary social and economic resources for their wives and children. Cazenave (1979), in a study of fifty-four mailmen, found that the greater their economic security, the more active these fathers became in their child-rearing functions.

Decision-making Roles

African-American family decision making has been described from a resource and choice exchange perspective (J. McAdoo 1991). This perspective suggests that the father's role in the family depends upon how he and his spouse perceive the resources that each brings. Fathers who bring in the greater resources make the greater decisions from this perspective. Blood and Wolfe (1969), utilizing resource theory, suggested from the responses of spouses that African-American families were mother-dominated because mothers made all the decisions. This led many mainstream researchers to conclude that the structure of the decision-making process was different for African Americans than for European Americans. A reanalysis of the original Blood and Wolfe data revealed that the responses of African and European Americans were similar. Both groups reported they shared equally in family decision making with their spouses.

Our review of the African-American research on this issue provides support for a more ecological approach to studying the decision-making process within the family. This approach would allow us to consider the responses of both husband and wife before we reach conclusions about who was the dominant decision maker in the family. Fathers across a number of studies reported that they shared equally with their wives the major decision making in child rearing, important purchases, health care, transportation, and employment of either spouse (TenHouten 1970; Mack 1978; Grey-Little 1982; Hammond and Enoch 1976; Willie and Greenblatt 1978). Mack (1978) suggested that socio-economic status may make a difference in the decision role African-American men perceive themselves as playing in the family. However, Jackson (1974), TenHouten (1970), Hammond and Enoch (1976), and Willie and Greenblatt (1978) reported few if any social class differences in the fathers' responses.

Jackson (1974), in a study of working- and middle-class fathers, noted that both groups reported being involved equally in the family decision making regarding disciplining children, grocery shopping, insurance, selection of a physician, and residential location. Middle-class fathers reported being more significantly ($p < .05$) involved than working-class fathers in shopping, vacationing, engaging in family recreation or commercial recreation, visiting relatives jointly, or engaging in other activities. She found that employed fathers were more likely to report attending church, shopping, vacationing, family and commercial recreation, and other activities with their spouses. They also reported visiting relatives with their spouses.

The Jackson study explored a wider range of father role behaviors than is usually found in the literature. While one may criticize the smallness of her sample size, her findings do suggest that African-American fathers play a variety of important roles within the family. Our summary of the decision-making literature found African-American fathers' responses to be similar across social classes to that of fathers of other ethnic groups. Future research on fathers who experience severe role strain as the result of unemployment or racial discrimination on the job is needed to clarify the impact on their psychological well-being and their decision-making capacity in the family. We need to examine the impact of extended family and community resources on family functioning related to family power relationships. Again, we need to evaluate differential responses across social economic statuses and to evaluate both positive and negative responses.

Child-rearing Roles

Mainstream researchers have debated the issue of the roles fathers play within the family related to child-rearing activity. Most of these studies have been theoretical, with little recognition given to the context in which the fathers relate to their children. There has been little systematic attempt to evaluate father-child relationships across age levels or in other than family systems. Research is needed to evaluate these relationships in church, school, and other settings as well as the family.

Cazenave (1979), in a study of fathering roles across two generations, noted that middle-income fathers reported being involved in child-care activities more than their fathers. These fathers reported being very actively involved in baby-sitting, changing baby diapers, and playing with their children. They reported that they were spending more time with their children and punishing them less often than their fathers punished them.

One (H. McAdoo 1988) observational study of African-American fathers noted that these economically sufficient fathers were warm and loving toward their children. While they perceived themselves to be strict, expecting their children to obey right away and not allowing any display of temper or bad behavior, their verbal and nonverbal interactions with their children were observed as nurturant. These fathers would interrupt the interview process to answer their children's questions. When they reprimanded their children, they would provide explanations regarding the unacceptable behavior and sometimes express their expectations about future child behaviors.

There is a need for more observational studies of fathers and their children in a variety of age and system contexts. An ecological approach would allow us to study fathers who are experiencing severe role strains and fathers who have been able to cope successfully with external threats to their personal and family systems. We would begin to develop normative adjustment patterns of reactions to external and internal pressures or role strains in terms of fathers' relationships with their children. This would lead to the possibility of discovering natural mediating factors in both role strains and child development. For example, in our research we found that nurturant fathers had little direct influence on the high self-esteem of their children. We also found that the father's nurturance of the mother led her to provide the support the children needed to feel good about themselves, their fathers, mothers, siblings, peers, and teachers.

Many young African-American fathers have been observed positively interacting with their young sons and daughters. Some fathers were unemployed; others were underemployed. However, their employment status did not seem to interfere with their ability to show love and affection to their children. Fathers have been observed working together on household chores with their teenagers in Washington, D.C., Los Angeles, Detroit, and other places by this researcher. However, public and private funds have not been made available to systematically study these occurrences. Funds have been more forthcoming to study the most problematic families, and there has been a proliferation of studies outlining the effects of disrupted families. An ecological perspective would allow researchers to describe, explain, and predict the effects of differing fathering roles and attitudes on child and adolescent development.

Family and Marital Influences

Many researchers seem to study the father's roles from a static linear perspective. The roles do not seem to change over time, and the father alone seems to be responsible for how those roles are played out in the family. An ecological perspective allows us to see that all family members are responsible for the family organizational climate, decision making, nurturance, and protection of the family. In all families, fathers play both positive and negative roles; however, little research has been found on the way the family develops rules that both regulate behaviors and provide support for positive development. What are the internal and external ingredients that allow for stability and positive change in the father's roles in the family?

It has been pointed out that the African-American father's nurturance of his wife leads to a positive self-evaluation in their children (H. McAdoo 1988). However, the literature on the subject seems to focus more on marital disruptions than on the way husbands and wives work cooperatively together in the mutual development of satisfactory marital roles. Future research should explore more fully the impact of the above ingredients on marital well-being and satisfaction within the family.

The Future

From an ecological perspective, our historical presence and the unity and integration of the patrilineal and matrilineal (Sudarkasa 1988) heritage within a capitalist society have led to changes and conflicts within our community and with the larger society to which we belong. The African-American community needs to return to the visions developed in the pre-enslavement era, and sustained during the enslavement period, to develop the kinds of institutions that will provide nurturance for positive growth for everyone in the community. Future visionaries may need to consider how we can maintain our values, namely, collective community responsibility, within a changing world economic community. How do we answer the question, What kind of world view should the African-American community develop that will lead to survival, growth, and positive relationships with communities that are not African American?

African-American fathers, mothers, and communities, if they are to have a future, must see how their problems relate to those of the larger world community. Our communities have been allowed to suffer from high crime rates, unemployment, homelessness, deadly diseases, and the movement of economic institutions out of our communities in much the same manner as what seems to be happening in third-world countries. We need to see the relationship between the flow of economic resources out the African-American community, which is sometimes described as one of the ten wealthiest countries in the world, and the inability of members of this community to find gainful employment, obtain meaningful education for their young, or receive competent protective and social services.

Finally, the survival of fathers'/husbands' roles within the family will depend upon the collective wisdom and courage of the African-American community to reject the divisive strategies represented by the terms "endangered species," "feminization of poverty," and "Black underclasses." The strategies have been fomented by other ethnic groups to blame the victims and force the victims to blame themselves. We must learn the lessons of our civil rights leaders and shun the retreatism of the 1980s and the me-isms of some of our current leaders. We must return to the basic understanding that in unity there is strength.

The future should bring a more balanced evaluation of the roles African-American men play in their families. There needs to be a shift from the focus on the most problematic families so as to study fathers in all socioeconomic groups. Future studies should focus more on what internal and external resources help fathers to help build successful families. Racial prejudices and racism have been a part of the experience of African Americans since they arrived on America's shores. There is no indication that things are going to be any different in the immediate future, and socioeconomic conditions may be getting worse for some families. However, some African-American men and women have been able to survive, and this again will be no different in the future.

Concluding Comments

The debate about family relationships in some African-American professional circles seems to be around the wrong issues. It should not focus on whether we will survive—we will—but rather on what can be done to help more African-American men, women and their families to survive, thrive, and provide positive nurturance, motivation, and support to their children and community. The discussion should not center around whether or not we have an underclass—not because the term relates to something real for us and many more European-American ethnics, but because it is a counterproductive, divisive discussion. It does not help us focus on what should be done to help African-American fathers who are in the lower socioeconomic stratum of our societies find ways to support and nurture their families.

Some of these so-called scholars need to spend a little less time in labeling and placing blame when family and community relationships are deteriorating and spend more time finding positive solutions for positive role functioning in families. Less research emphasis should be placed on evaluating African-American families from a European-American middle-class perspective, and more emphasis should be placed on developing a multicultural perspective (White and Parham 1990). We need to foster understanding of positive multi-class perspectives in trying to understand African-American father's roles and other ethnic group fathers' roles.

Arguments that the male is an endangered species have offered us little new or helpful information since the period of African-American enslavement in this country. African-American men have always been vulnerable in this society. The many chapters in this volume offer conclusive evidence that too many African-American men experience high arrest and incarceration rates, drop out of school at a high rate, and experience violence and deaths related to crime in their community. Some African-American men also experience significant and prolonged unemployment, and some are forced to rely on the drug trade for their economic survival when they and their family members are denied meaningful employment. The simple truth is that they have survived and they will survive and thrive as long as the African-American family and community survives. Professional literature might be better served by our collectively developing mechanisms for helping men in problematic economic, psychological, and social situations to become part of an economically stable family.

Fathers in African-American families seemed from the studies reported in this paper to perform their roles in the family about as well as their non-African-American counterparts within different social classes. The major causes for the diminution of these roles are related to stress around the father's ability to provide for his family. This ability is related to his educational and economic opportunities as well as his ability to handle and overcome racial prejudice and racism. While these are not fully within their control, many of these fathers throughout the postenslavement experience have found ways to mitigate the negative consequences of occupational and educational discrimination on the positive roles they play within their family and community.

Future analysts of the father's role within the family may need to evaluate some of the internal and external influences that help him to remain a provider, nurturer, motivator, stimulator, and protector of his wife and children. Learning what role the wife plays in this interaction is vitally important to the understanding of successfully coping fathers. As Bowman and Sanders (1988) suggested, provider role strain is a complex component of the equation and could lead to severe problems related to the psychological well-being of unmarried fathers. However, we suggest that in families where both spouses are working to provide economic support to the family, these strains may be reduced. American society is moving to a dual provider perspective, since it is becoming increasingly difficult for families to survive on one income. Dual role perspectives allow for a lessening of the pressure on the male to be the sole provider.

The survival of positive fathering/husbanding roles in the family may depend on how well African Americans are able to provide or obtain from outside resources the kinds of community services that may enhance the development of families in trouble. Role development in these fathers may depend upon how well we come together as a community to develop and utilize our political and economic clout so as to influence the broader American community to provide greater employment opportunities, including the ownership of major corporations, heading major franchises in the private service sector, and receiving equal wages for the same employment.

Father role development will depend even more on our ability to educate our children about the ingredients of positive family functioning and to provide community control and support for families who are in trouble. There is a need to develop strategies for educating children of all ethnic groups in our society about the rich heritage of African-American culture shared by the men in these communities. Father roles need to be seen from a perspective that takes in the community values for such roles. Finally, we will be able to provide more realistic family-role assessment when we are able to understand how differential spiritual values influence a father's ability to perform these roles. A more balanced approach to the evaluation of the influences on the different roles an African-American father plays in his family and community may lead to a realistic reassessment of the same influences on the European-American father's role and position in his family and community.

Conclusion and Recommendations: A Reason for Hope?—An Overview of the New Black Male Movement in the United States

by Richard Majors

The preceding chapters have attempted to understand Black males in the context of their marginality and limited opportunities. For the purpose of intervening in and empowering the lives of Black males, the following topics, among others, have been discussed and analyzed: social and health issues, poverty, unemployment, single-parent families, violence, drug prevention, the criminal justice system, racism, AIDS, coping mechanisms, homelessness, mentoring, and social and public policies. The major theme linking these chapters is that Black males cannot be understood or helped without considering the environment and the institutions that shape and influence their lives (Bowser 1991).

The portrait painted in the preceding chapters is grim. Since the 1950s and 1960s, the quality of life for Black males in America has deteriorated markedly. For example, according to the Center for the Study of Social Policy, the number of unemployed Black men doubled between 1960 and 1984. In 1960, almost three-fourths of all Black men included in the census were working; in 1986, only 57 percent were working (Wilkins 1991). Moreover, a recent study in the *New England Journal of Medicine* (McCord and Freeman 1990) reported that the life expectancy of Black men in Harlem was lower than it was for men in the third-world country of Bangladesh. Furthermore, in 1991, the Sentencing Report found that one out of every four Black men between the ages of twenty and twenty-nine are either incarcerated, on probation, or on parole.

In a 1991 article, "Raising Black Boys in America," Keith Thomas cited a report estimating that in twenty years, 70 percent of the Black males now in second grade will be unqualified to work—they will be addicted to drugs, in jail, on parole, unemployed, or dead. The sad fact is, we may not have to wait twenty years—we may have lost a generation of Black males already.

In viewing the Black male as an endangered species, we might also consider the following statistics:

- In 1991, the Black-male unemployment rate was 12.9 percent, more than double the white-male rate of 6.4 percent (African American Task Force 1990).
- Over 30 percent of black males (but only about 15 percent of white males) were not in the work force because they were unemployed or unaccounted for (Newport 1991).
- Although 54 percent of the Black men are married, for every 100 unmarried Black women, there are only 63 marriageable Black men (Newport 1991).
- Homicide is the leading cause of death for Black males between the ages of fifteen and thirty-four (Thomas 1991).

I would like to thank Allen Curtis, English Department, University of Wisconsin—Eau Claire, and Tara Huebner for their editorial comments on an earlier draft.

- A young Black male has a 1 in 21 chance of being a victim of homicide, six times the rate of white males (Kazi-Ferrouillet 1991).
- African-American males are the only segment of the U.S. population with a decreasing life expectancy—65.1 years in 1987 as opposed to 65.6 years in 1984.
- One-third of all Blacks live in poverty.
- One-half of all Black children live in poverty.
- African Americans now account for 28.8 percent of U.S. AIDS cases.
- Forty-four percent of all Black males are functionally illiterate.
- There are more Black males in prison than in college.
- The infant mortality rate for African Americans—17.7 deaths per 1,000 births—is more than double that of whites. The infant mortality rate for African Americans is higher than it is in Malaysia.

Given these appalling statistics, it is not surprising that Jewelle Taylor-Gibbs, in *Young, Black and Male in America* (1988), stated that Black males are an "endangered species." While some people may view this term as ambivalent or exaggerated, it serves to call attention to the alarming social and economic conditions of Black males in our society today.

To help Black males to get off the endangered species list, we must provide them with access to quality education, adequate health care, job training, better employment opportunities, higher minimum wages, and more alcohol and drug treatment centers.

A Reason for Hope: An Overview of the New Black Male Movement in the United States

During the last four years, a movement has been growing to determine ways to understand and solve the problems that Black males must cope with. In the spirit of this movement, a number of organizations, conferences, commissions, and research centers have sponsored events and publications, providing education as well as leadership. Together, these efforts have helped shape a new Black-male movement in the United States. Following discussion of these initiatives, I will analyze specific programs that, along with the above activities, will help to solve the crisis of the Black male.

Unlike the National Council of Negro Women, founded in 1937 by Mary McCleod Bethune, there was no national *umbrella* organization for Black males in the United States until 1990.* In 1990, the National Council of African

*While the 100 Black Men of America was the first national Black men's organization in the United States, it is not viewed as the first umbrella group for Black men. The word *umbrella* as used here is defined as having as its primary purpose the representation of Black men nationally (rather than developing programs and activities for Black men who live in a given state or community). While 100 Black Men is a national organization, concerned about Black males nation-

American Men (NCAAM) was founded by Richard Majors and Jacob Gordon. NCAAM was founded on the premise that if we as Black men were ever going to be able to control our own future and the future and destiny of young Black boys and men, it was crucial that we develop some kind of "infrastructure" to provide long-term solutions and change. Many great civil rights organizations such as the NAACP, the Urban League, and the Southern Leadership Conference have been responsible for creating and developing successful Black male programs (e.g., The Urban League's Male Responsibility program). In spite of the good intentions of these civil rights organizations, however, their efforts have not been enough. Given the many problems and issues needing immediate attention within the Black community, it is nearly impossible for our civil rights groups to dedicate staff, money, time, and resources to Black-male issues exclusively. Thus, most civil rights groups at any given time are able to maintain only a limited number of Black-male programs. Hence, Gordon and I felt that if we were serious about saving Black men and boys from poverty, unemployment, crime, a lack of education, and racial stereotypes—in short, saving them from being endangered—we needed an organization like NCAAM, one whose sole vision was to serve Black males exclusively. We felt that by developing such an organization, we could begin providing Black men and boys with the necessary person-power, money, expertise, leadership, time, and resources to educate, fight, advocate, inform, and lobby on their behalf. NCAAM, we believe, will provide us with more control over the institutions we rely on for survival.

NCAAM is a nonprofit organization whose primary purpose is to give Black males a national voice in developing social and economic policies affecting the Black community as a whole and Black males in particular. It seeks to empower Black males to assume responsibility for their own lives and the destinies of their families and communities, pursuing these goals through self-help initiatives, community-based programs, coalition building, advocacy participation in social, political, and economic decision making, and research. NCAAM has developed the *Journal of African American Male Studies (JAAMS)*, the first academic journal in the United States for Black males. NCAAM has also created the *Annual State of Black Male America*, the first document of its kind in America. Both of these documents will provide much needed information and guidance in such crucial areas as: poverty, unemployment, education, intervention-prevention, and social policy.

---

ally, its primary purpose is to develop programs, provide services and resources, and raise money for state and local communities. On the other hand, the National Council of African American Men (NCAAM) is a national Black male organization that, while interested in state and local communities, is primarily concerned with developing national programs, initiatives, and policies that affect Black men nationally. Also, NCAAM is more research and policy oriented. That is to say, one of the goals of the organization is to develop research programs, collect data, and publish material that will influence and shape social policy towards Black males.

Because of the importance of investing in our future—young Black children and youth—NCAAM has developed a Youth Affairs Division. Black male adults in NCAAM will provide leadership and be role models for Black youth and children, something that has been missing in the Black community.

The Youth Affairs Division of NCAAM, because of its success, has developed or is developing other programs in the following areas: mentoring (i.e., "Boys of Character" program) and manhood training, among others. These programs will be discussed later.

Established prior to 1988, 100 Black Men of America has had a major impact on the Black community and on the Black male movement. The organization was founded in New York in 1963 by a group of concerned Black public officials, businessmen, lawyers, retailers, and government employees. Today, 100 Black Men of America is composed of Black businessmen, attorneys, physicians, dentists, corporate leaders and other professionals with twenty-eight active chapters and a national membership of about 3,300. Its purpose is to facilitate the economic and social mobility of Blacks in such areas as education, employment, housing, and health services. 100 Black Men of America is actively involved in such areas as drug abuse, teenage pregnancy, and violence prevention. Hence, it is not a social club, but a civic organization.

100 Black Men of America has chapters across the country, two of the most active being the New York and New Jersey chapters. Under the influence of presidents Roscoe Brown and William Giles, these chapters have made outstanding contributions, providing the necessary leadership, services, and resources to help empower their respective Black communities. Both chapters sponsor various activities and events each year to raise money for scholarships for Black youths—mentoring programs, a golf tournament, an annual dance (to raise money for scholarships), and an annual track festival, among other things.

To help save our young Black boys, several research centers have been created in the past four years. One center in particular, the Center for Educating African American Males, developed by Dr. Spencer Holland and 100 Concerned Black Men and housed at Morgan State University, has been especially successful in developing a program that stimulates Black boys to excel in the classroom. Called Project 2000, the main goal of this program is to increase the number of Black male role models in the classroom (e.g., volunteers, tutors, and mentors). The program is primarily designed for young school-age boys in grades one through three.

Other programs of the center include teacher recruitment, training, and curriculum development. Currently, there are three elementary schools participating in the Baltimore area. Because of the success of these programs, others are being developed across the country.

In 1988, the Albany State Center for the Study of the Black Male was established—the first center in the United States dedicated to the study of the Black male. One of the center's most successful programs, a Saturday morning academics program, provides education for young Black boys. Future plans include research projects and annual conferences.

Another institute involved in the study of black males, the Morehouse Institute for Research, was established in 1990. Much like the Albany State Center for the Study of the Black Male, its goal is to sponsor research projects and hold conferences.

In recent years, many commissions, committees, and forums have studied and analyzed Black males and offered recommendations. In 1989, Ohio's Governor Richard Celeste formed the Governor's Commission on Socially Disadvantaged Black Males, the first of its kind in the United States. Chaired by Senator William F. Bowen, this commission is comprised of 41 appointed commissioners and 106 subcommittee volunteers. The Commission will study such Black-male issues as education, unemployment, crime, and health, as well as other issues. Public hearings have been held throughout the state; data from these hearings, after being studied and analyzed, will be formulated as recommendations to be presented to the governor's office, helping to shape social and public policy in the state of Ohio. Since the formation of the Ohio Governor's Commission on Socially Disadvantaged Black Males in 1989, a number of commissions devoted to studying the status of Black males have been formed. For example, Illinois, California, and Maryland are states that have recently developed commissions to study the status of Black males.

Representative Major Owens (New York) has been one of the most active Congressmen in the fight to help save young Black boys. At least since 1990, Representative Owens has chaired the Congressional Black Caucus Foundation's Higher Education Braintrust Symposium: Endangered African American Males—Agenda for Research and Development, at their annual conference. The purpose of this symposium is to discuss and analyze educational policies affecting at-risk Black boys in our schools. The symposia have been very well attended during the past two years. But Representative Owens, sincerely committed to saving our young Black boys, has not stopped there; he has developed one of the first commissions in the United States to study Black children and their education—the National Citizens Commission on African American Children. Established in September 1991, this commission—a national advocacy group of one hundred African-American professional educators, parents, elected officials, and foundation executives—is primarily concerned with Black children in urban and poor rural schools, analyzing and developing current educational policies and strategies that will benefit Black children in our public schools. A Seven-Point Plan has been developed to insure that Black children have a fair chance of accomplishing the commission's goals. A number of additional projects are planned for the future.

The Committee to Study the Status of the Black Male in the New Orleans Public Schools was another noteworthy educational initiative. This committee, formed in 1987, was made up primarily of school and college educators appointed by the New Orleans Parish School Board. Its major goal was to develop recommendations to improve the low educational performance of young Black boys. Rather than merely analyze data, discuss the problem, or blame Black boys for their poor school performance, the committee chose instead to interview students, parents, teachers, school personnel, and individuals in the community about such issues. As a result, some very useful recommendations were developed that could go a long way to improve black boys' school performance (see *Committee to Study the Status of the Black Male* 1988).

The 21st Century Commission on African American Males, one of the first congressional commissions on Black males in the United States, held a conference in May 1991 in Washington, D.C. The conference was convened and co-chaired by Virginia Governor Douglas Wilder; North Carolina Senator Terry Sanford; Dr. Dorothy Height, president of the National Council of Negro Women; New York City Mayor David Dinkins; Arthur Fletcher, chairman, U.S. Commission on Civil Rights; and John Jacobs, president and CEO, National Urban League. The commission, consisting of elected officials, corporate leaders, foundation presidents, and civil leaders brought elected officials, scholars, corporate leaders, and Black community leaders together to discuss solutions to the critical problems confronting Black males. During the three-day conference, twelve panels discussed such issues as education, health care, the Black family, employment, substance abuse, and crime.

Despite its good intentions, this conference had some shortcomings. A prevailing opinion among the participants was that those most in need of the commission's help—poor Black males—were largely left out and uninvolved. In addition, the commission was criticized for what was perceived as a failure to propose solutions or make recommendations that would have a long-term effect on the lives of Black males.

Finally, during the last four years, the Urban Institute has been one of the most active organizations in the country in focusing its energies on understanding and helping young Black males (developing social-policy initiatives, publishing documents, and conferences). Most of these projects have been spearheaded and published under the supervision of Ronald Mincy, a senior research associate at the Urban Institute.

The dedication of the Urban Institute in calling attention to the plight of Black males has sparked interest in the development of a new program—the "underclass research project." Based on a six-year policy study, the focus of this project will be (1) teenage parents, (2) high school drop-outs, (3) female-headed, welfare-dependent families, (4) males detached from the labor force, and (5) young Black males involved in violent, criminal, drug-related activities.

One of the interests of the Urban Institute is to discover what programs serve Black boys as well as how many Black boys they serve. What are the goals of these programs? Their staffing needs? Their funding? The expected outcomes for the boys served by such programs? To find answers to such questions, the Urban Institute sponsored a conference in July 1992 on "Nurturing Young Black Males: Challenges to Agencies, Programs, and Social Policy." A book by the same title is planned, analyzing the problems and making recommendations.

Since 1988, there have also been a great number of academic projects (books, journal articles, monographs, research documents, and special feature stories) contributing to our growing national concern to study, understand, and help Black males.

While a number of books on Black males (e.g., Wilkinson and Taylor 1977; Gary 1981; Lee 1992; Madhubuti 1990; Bowser 1991) have made impressive contributions; Jewelle Taylor-Gibbs' 1988 book, *Young, Black and Male in America: An Endangered Species*, has to be considered one of the best. Her book is a comprehensive and interdisciplinary study of social and economic factors affecting Black males in America. Overall, despite a few shortcomings, the book achieves its goal. The sheer number of statistics that Gibbs presents on education, employment, health, fatherhood, drug abuse, and so on is nearly overwhelming. In her concluding chapter, Gibbs offers a variety of social policy initiatives that have proven effective with Black males.

The most recent book on Black males is Majors and Billson's *Cool Pose: The Dilemmas of Black Manhood in America* (1992). This book offers some useful analyses of gender roles, macho attitudes, stylish behaviors, and coping mechanisms among Black males. The term "cool pose," coined by Majors (1986), seeks to understand how many Black males *use*, *create*, and *manage* the impressions they make on others. Thus, cool pose is concerned with roles, values, self-presentation, situationally constructed and performance-oriented behaviors, scripts, and physical posturing. Masculinity is symbolically expressed in cool pose behaviors. Cool pose is thus a ritualized form of masculinity. Black males who use cool pose behaviors are like chameleons—capable of changing their roles or behaviors at any time.

Cool pose roles enhance self-esteem and pride, providing Black males with a sense of power and control, as defined by their ability to scrutinize, calculate, and manage behaviors (what they say, what they do, how they act). Thus, for the Black male who has limited control or access to any real power or resources, cool-pose roles empower him by helping him to appear competent to satisfy mainstream norms and expectations and to simply survive. Because of the lack of research on gender roles, "macho" attitudes, coping mechanisms, and performance-oriented behaviors, this book goes a long way in helping us to understand how and why Black males become involved in risk-taking and self-destructive behaviors.

Another interesting book on Black males (forthcoming) is Lawrence Carter's *Crisis of the African American Males: Dangers and Opportunities*. This book analyzes the current state of the Black male in America and makes recommendations.

A monograph recently published by Na'im Akbar, *Visions for Black Men*

(1991), has also contributed to the current debate. Although Jawanza Kunjufu's *Countering the Conspiracy to Destroy Black Boys* (Vol. 1, 1985; Vol. 2, 1986) were published prior to 1988, they provide us with valuable information and insights on Black males.

Even such academic organizations as the American Psychological Association have become involved in researching and studying the Black male within the last four years. For example, in 1988, Brenda Evans and James Whitfield compiled a bibliography on black males, *Black Males in the United States: An Annotated Bibliography from 1967–1987*. This bibliography does an excellent job of reviewing the empirical literature focusing on Black males. It should not only serve as a handy reference guide but also stimulate research.

Other publications that have provided invaluable information, insights, and recommendations on young Black males are *Long-term Investments in Youth: The Need for Comprehensive Programs for Disadvantaged Young Men in Urban Areas* and *A Structural Impediment to Success: A Look at Disadvantaged Young Men in Urban Areas*. Both are published by the Union Institute (1990).

Recommendations: What Specific Programs Help Black Males?

Over the years a number of institutions, colleges, and individual scholars have conducted crucial research on Black males. Although much remains to be done, this research has provided us with enough insights, ideas, and facts to allow us to act on behalf of Black males. Yet, given the availability of this material, the real question becomes, Do we have the conviction, resolve, and commitment to solve the problems and save our Black males? The following is a description of selected programs that either have proved to be, or that have the potential for being, effective with the Black male population. Also described are programs needed to educate our society about the problems of Black males.

With the recent proliferation of programs in Afrocentric education, such as all-Black boys' schools and manhood training and mentoring, Blacks are exploring avenues that will advance and empower Black males in the future. In 1991, because of such problems as low academic performance and low test scores, truancy, over-tracking to low ability classes, dropping out of school, discipline problems, over-representation in special education and remedial classes, and, especially school suspensions, the Milwaukee Public School District approved a plan for all-Black boys' schools, the first of its kind. The term "all-Black boys' school" is somewhat misleading, because the Milwaukee schools are open to all children regardless of race or gender. However, the Afrocentric curriculum of the all-Black boys' schools will be designed specifically to meet the needs of Black boys.

What are some of the more pressing problems that give rise to Milwaukee's all-Black boys' schools? One is the unacceptably high suspension rates. Between 1978 and 1985, for example, 94.4 percent of all students expelled from Milwaukee Public Schools were Black. Although Black boys make up only 27.6 percent of Milwaukee's school population, they accounted for 50 percent of the students suspended (African American Male Task Force 1990). Nor are school suspensions just a Milwaukee problem. Herbert Foster (1986), Jewelle Taylor-Gibbs (1988), as well as a Children's Defense Fund report (1975) document the fact that, in elementary school, Black students were suspended three times more often than white students; in secondary school, they were suspended twice as often. In both elementary and secondary schools, these sources reveal that Black boys have higher suspension rates and the highest "drop-out" rates.

These sources conclude that Black students get suspended (a) more often, (b) for longer periods of time, and (c) with greater repetition than anyone else. Since 1976, the percentage of Black high school graduates (and especially Black males) enrolling in higher education institutions has been on the decline. Obviously, these data help to explain why there are fewer Black males enrolling in our colleges and universities across the country.

Further analysis of these drastic statistics has provided us with some interesting findings. While many Black boys are suspended for conduct problems, they are suspended with greater frequency for nonviolent behaviors. For example, Poda (1992) reported that 85 percent of the school suspensions in the Milwaukee Public Schools were not for fighting or assault, but for such offenses as not having books, refusing to do work, not following instructions, and so on. On the other hand, only 11 percent of the suspensions were for physical safety regulations (e.g., harassment, verbal abuse, assaults, and threats). The remaining 4 percent of the school suspensions were for vandalism and property-related violations.

Also, a considerable number of Black boys get suspended for what can be classified as culture-specific behaviors: rapping, using slang, "playing the dozens," woofing (bragging or boasting about how tough one is), using certain kinds of clothing, strutting, wearing sneakers with shoelaces untied, wearing hats backwards or cocked to the side, wearing belts unbuttoned, and being overly physical. However, research shows that Black boys tend to be more physical and expressive (e.g., they move around more in their seats and tend to wrestle more) than white boys (Foster 1986; Hanna 1984; Mancini 1981). When teachers observe Black boys exhibiting what they perceive as overly physical behaviors, they often over-react and punish them. Black boys are also suspended for other behaviors exhibited less frequently by white boys. For example, Black boys will challenge a teacher if they feel they have been spoken to in an inappropriate manner (yelled at or talked down to), if they perceive their masculinity to be threatened, or if they feel they have been embarrassed in front of their peers. Such behaviors on the part of teachers are considered to be disrespectful or condescending by many Black boys. When Black boys sense that they are being treated with disrespect, they feel they must "save face," which often results in challenging the teacher. Culturally, Black children (as opposed to white children) learn at a young age to be more confrontational, to speak what is on their minds, and to challenge things they perceive as being unfair (Kochman 1981).

White teachers use a middle-class lens when observing Black boys' behaviors; consequently, when a challenge is perceived by a Black boy, or if he demands a clarification, white teachers often characterize such behaviors as "having an attitude" or "talking back." Significantly, Herbert Foster, in his 1986 book *Ribbin', Jivin' and Playin' the Dozens*, says that teachers view such behaviors as negative, rude, arrogant, intimidating, aggressive, sexually provocative, and threatening—in short, not conducive to learning. Consequently, Black males are not only suspended by their teachers more than any single group but also recommended more often for special education classes, classes for the emotionally disturbed, and remedial classes; they are also more frequently labeled mildly mentally handicapped than are female students or males of other groups. While we do not always condone these behaviors, we do not see these behaviors as disruptive or necessitating punitive responses. The fact is that when teachers observe Black males in school exhibiting certain culture-specific behaviors and attitudes, they are likely to misinterpret them, since most schools and the teachers within them operate in terms of white middle-class norms and expectations (Hall 1992). Most white teachers simply lack the cultural insight, training, and sensitivity to interpret (let alone understand) Black culture. Their failure to do so is a major reason why Black students are disproportionately recommended for remediation, special treatment, or punishment.

The irony here is that the more Black boys engage in behaviors that their teachers dislike and misunderstand, the more they are "turned off" by those teachers' attitudes and behaviors. When they sense their teachers' negative attitudes and low expectations, they respond negatively toward them and become uninterested in school and indifferent to schoolwork. Even worse, more often than not, such experiences lead to disproportionate levels of low self-esteem among Black boys. As a consequence, to enhance their self-esteem, Black boys often engage in culture-specific behaviors, behaviors that provide them with a sense of visibility, pride, status, identity, control, social competence, and show adherence to cultural norms. Moreover, as a result of having had negative experiences in the classroom, Black boys oftentimes seek recognition in nonacademic areas in order to enhance their self-esteem.

In sum, teachers too often fail to understand the culture-specific behaviors of Black boys simply because they use a middle-class lens to interpret such behaviors. Their non-middle-class students' experiences, behavior, dress, style, and ways of expressing their sexuality do not fit teachers' own class norms and sensibilities. Most educators feel secure working with middle-class students, while they tend to perceive students with non-middle-class ways as "problems." Moreover, in trying to understand and solve problems such as school suspensions among Black boys, we tend to evaluate the boys' behavior and ignore the teachers' behavior. The fact is, of course, that before Black boys can change their behaviors, the teachers will have to change theirs. Once they understand the behavior of Black boys, they will be less likely to over-react and to intervene in ways that invite negative responses. In particular, teachers need to find ways to talk to and relate to Black boys without putting them down or demeaning them.

Black boys, as suggested earlier, have lower achievement rates and higher drop-out rates than members of any other group. During the 1986–1987 school year, Milwaukee's Black students had an average grade-point average of 1.46. A Milwaukee Public School report revealed that when sex and race are controlled for, 80 percent of Black male students in grades 9–12 were doing less than "C" work (a 2.0 grade-point average). Only 17 percent had a cumulative grade-point average between 2.0 and 2.9 and only 2 percent had a cumulative grade-point average between 3.0 and 4.0 (African American Male Task Force 1990). Unfortunately, the dismal prospect for young Black boys in the Milwaukee Public Schools is symbolic of their situation in other urban cities across the country.

A specific problem that the Milwaukee Public Schools share with other schools nationally is the problem of lower expectations for young Black boys. For example, Herbert Foster's research on teachers' expectations (personal communication, 1991) of Black boys reveals that teachers have more stereotypical as well as more negative views of Black boys than of either females or members of other races. In 1988, for example, a New Orleans Public School study showed that 56 percent of the teachers in the New Orleans School District predicted that Black boys in their district would not go on to college (Committee to Study the Status of the Black Male 1988). These statistics are consistent with teacher expectations nationally. Moreover, teachers' behaviors and attitudes in the classroom cause other problems. Because of racial stereotypes, a lack of cultural sensitivity, and a generalized socio-economic status bias toward young Black boys, teachers are less likely to provide verbal and nonverbal feedback, less likely to respond to their questions or interact with them, and, on the other hand, are *more* likely to demand less of them, criticize them more frequently, give them less praise, and seat them further away from themselves (Thomas 1991).

There are also social and cultural concerns among young Black boys that need to be addressed. Black boys are socialized to see females more sexually than are white boys; this socialization creates conflicts when females are in authority roles. Thus, at or around fourth grade (age eight or nine), many young Black boys begin to have trouble with female authority figures. Also, many Black boys come from fatherless homes; they need opportunities to see, touch, and talk to adult Black male role models in order to develop appropriate masculine roles. Young Black boys need to "bond" with older Black males in order to learn the values and behaviors that will later become civic virtues.

Because of a host of factors—a lack of Black adult male role models, discipline problems, low academic performance, high drop-out and suspension rates, teachers' negative attitudes, the absence of cultural awareness on the part of teachers, the presence of low expectations for Black boys—there is an urgent need for an alternative school model for the nation's Black boys. We recommend the creation of all-Black boys' schools, including an Afrocentric curriculum, as an alternative to traditional schools. If the present experience of Black boys in our schools is not a sufficient argument for alternative schooling, consider again a statement quoted earlier: "Some sociologists estimate that twenty years from now, 70 percent of Black males now in the second grade will be unqualified to work—[they will either be] addicted to drugs or alcohol, in jail, on parole, unemployed, or dead" (Thomas 1991, 4).

The idea of an all-Black boys' school has already been tried. For example, the Toussaint Institute, founded in 1988, an historically Black, independent school for Black boys in New York City, has been very successful in stimulating their interest and in providing them with sound educational opportunities. After identifying elementary-age Black boys who have had repeated academic and behavioral problems, the Institute provides them with need-based scholarships, Afrocentric instruction, role-models, quality educational experiences, cultural enrichment programs, and then closely monitors their progress.

Another example of alternative schooling for Black boys is the Milwaukee all-Black boys' school, now in its first year. The Milwaukee Public Schools' proposal has gained a lot of national interest and support, representing a serious effort to revolutionize education for Black boys. To achieve this goal, the Milwaukee All-Black Boys' School Plan will use an Afrocentric curriculum, which has been drawing attention in the Black community as a means to educate and motivate Black boys. Firmly grounded in African and African-American culture and history, Afrocentric education inspires Black boys to structure their behavior, attitudes, and values in new ways. They are encouraged to learn values that emphasize cooperation, mutual respect, commitment, and love of family, race, community, and nation. The Afrocentric ideology is a value system based on African civilization and philosophy. It is not antiwhite; rather, it is an ideology that encourages Black boys to transcend their problems by reclaiming traditional African values. This perspective is in direct contrast to the Eurocentric world view, which encourages efforts to control nature, materialism, and individualism (Majors and Billson 1992). Some argue that the failure of Blacks to develop such a view before now has made them vulnerable to structural pressures that lead inevitably to academic and social problems. For example, Eurocentric modes of socialization have had an adverse affect on how Black boys perceive themselves and their contributions to the world. Black boys often use a Eurocentric mode of assessing self, and this promotes low self-esteem and self-hatred. Therefore, such socialization oftentimes contributes to poor academic performance, low aspirations, antisocial behaviors, violence, crime, drug abuse, and gang behavior, among other things. The Afrocentric ideology attempts to socialize children (or resocializes adults) toward values that elevate the interests of the community over those of the individual. Therefore, Black boys who are exposed to an Afrocentric curriculum would be less likely to be self-destructive, bored, "turned off," or disinterested in school and therefore more likely to do better in school.

Eurocentric education has ignored the accomplishments of Black people, thus most Black boys have no knowledge of Black people, for example, who were well-known inventors or who otherwise made outstanding contributions to this country. Black boys who have been given neither a sense of purpose nor information about their own history can hardly be blamed for exhibiting self-destructive behavior. They need to be informed not just that their ancestors were slaves but also that their African history included tribes with kings and queens and complex societies. The Afrocentric curriculum helps to inform Black boys about their history, their homeland, and their culture, restoring racial pride and instilling in them a sense of responsibility, self-esteem, family values, and mutual respect.

In its effort to educate, stimulate, and motivate Black boys, the Afrocentric curriculum of Milwaukee's all-Black boys' schools will emphasize both African and African-American history and culture. The schools will incorporate Black adult, male role models and require the boys to develop close relationships with these mentors. In addition to stressing the important roles of parents, business, and the community in their lives, the schools will require the boys to wear uniforms and to adhere to strict codes of conduct. In the final analysis, Afrocentric education has the potential not only to save Black boys from lives made tragic by ignorance and self-hatred but also to reduce racial stereotypes and to promote better race relations between Blacks and whites.

Manhood training—designed to facilitate the development of prosocial values among Black boys—is yet another outstanding program that has proliferated in recent years. Among the social problems such programs seek to address are the absence of fathers in the homes to provide positive masculine role models; the breakdown of traditional institutions such as family, church, and school; the often dominant role of peer-influence among youths; and the proliferation of violence (along with the concomitant increase in the availability of guns, alcohol and drug abuse, crime, and divorce).

Because of the lack of fathers in the home and the impact of peer influence, Black boys oftentimes learn and become involved in negative masculine roles. Keith Thomas's portrayal of one Black man's "growing up" years ("Raising Black Boys in America" 1991) puts into perspective the effects of peer influence on masculine development and identity among Black boys. "When I was growing up [he says], I always thought before you can become a man, you have to have a big car, fine clothes, women fighting over you, a baby here, a baby there, and the reason I thought that was because all the men I was supposed to look up to were in that group." Thus, it was precisely to subvert such a pattern—

of Black boys making the passage from boyhood to manhood under the tutelage of the streets and peers who define manhood in terms of toughness, sexual promiscuity, material possessions, and thrill-seeking—that the Afrocentric movement in the 1980s incorporated African-style rites of passage (manhood training) into programs for socializing young Black boys (Majors and Billson 1992).

Alex Haley in his book *Roots* (1976) provided a description of "manhood training" as a traditional African ritual. During adolescence, boys were separated from their families for an extended period of time and put through rigorous physical and mental training. This experience was viewed as essential to becoming a man. The training was conducted by "elders"—respected older males in the tribe. The purpose was to develop the attitudes, behaviors and skills necessary to become responsible and productive men (i.e., fathers, husbands, brothers, uncles) in the tribe (Lee 1987).

Much like the past, manhood training programs today provide ways to help Black boys make the transition from boyhood to manhood (traditionally referred to as "rites of passage" or "initiation rituals"). Today there are a number of such programs in the United States that teach Black boys some or all of the following: African history and culture; appropriate roles of fathers, husbands, brothers, and sons; respect for older people; how to develop positive male/female relationships and adopt appropriate sexual roles; how to make positive contributions to one's family and community; and how to resist peer pressure and to make personal decisions.

Black boys who participate in Black manhood training programs develop pride, respect for others, self-esteem, and a sense of community. These experiences in turn promote attitudes, behaviors, skills, and values that are associated with a healthy and positive African-American masculine identity.

After boys in manhood training programs have completed the assigned activities, exercises, and tasks, they attend graduation ceremonies that may properly be called "African style rites of passage." Although these ceremonies vary in substance and style, the one at Browne Junior High School in Washington, D.C., is unique. Trotter (1991) describes this ceremony: While youth clad in African costumes pound on drums, boys in African garb and hats called "kufis" walk toward the front of the auditorium. Once on stage, one by one they step across a symbolic threshold and accept a kinte cloth around their shoulders from the school's "elders" (teachers and administrators who are also dressed in African garb). The transition from boyhood to manhood is complete once the boys have accepted the kinte cloth from the elders.

Many other such mentoring programs have sprung up around the country. All share a common goal—to save Black boys from the negative influences produced by father absence, negative role models, antisocial pressure, dysfunctional educational systems, poverty, violent crime, and so on. Such programs are needed today more than ever before.

In "Raising Black Boys in America," Keith Thomas notes the importance of Black boys receiving time, love, and attention if they are to thrive. Citing the pain and hurt of growing up without a father, he describes how the birth of his own son eased the pain of his father's absence, while at the same time the birth made him question his own preparedness to be a responsible father. He goes on to say that he remembers all the things he needed as a child but never received from his father:

> I wanted someone to hug me. Someone to play catch with me. Someone to tell stories about brave knights and dragons. Someone to tell me the hurt would go away after scraping my knee. Someone to fix broken toys. Someone to carry me on their back. Someone to chase all the ghosts from my room late at night. Someone to say "I love you, son."
>
> . . . I know too many of our sons and daughters never get the simplest of things. No hugs. No kisses. No discipline. No "I love you. . . ."
>
> I talked to an 8-year old boy who told me he had never had a birthday party. Never. Not even a little gathering. I guarantee he will if I'm around when he turns nine.
>
> But what really hurts is, I know he's not alone. There are too many black boys just like him out there—small souls with sad eyes in desperate need of attention, especially from concerned black male role models.
>
> And it doesn't take a Michael Jordan or a Magic Johnson to make a difference in their lives.
>
> Every black man in America—from sports hero to corporate executive to blue-collar worker—should try to help at least one boy reach manhood. . . .
>
> Be that one man willing to take time—as little as two to four hours a week—can make a difference. One man willing to take an active interest in one boy's life. One man willing to read to him. To ask how he's doing in school. To take him to a ballgame on his birthday. To call him now and then just to say "hello."
>
> One man, human enough, to teach him how to be. (Thomas 1991, 4)

As Thomas notes so eloquently, Black boys need time, attention, and love if they are to develop appropriate masculine roles and prosocial behaviors—to become responsible citizens. And one of the best ways to provide such things is through mentoring and role-modeling (Balcazar, Majors, Blanchard, et al. 1991). Two of the more successful programs are the "Boys of Character,'" sponsored by The National Council of African American Men (NCAAM), and Paul Quinn's College First and Ten program.

The Reverend James Kendricks, president and founder of NCAAM's Memphis Chapter, started the Boys of Character program in June 1991. Sixty-three boys, ranging from nine to seventeen and representing over twelve city schools, meet with their mentors every Saturday for two to four hours. The program features field trips, assertive-skill training, African-American classes, and manhood training classes to develop self-esteem and concepts of responsibility among their participants. After the boys complete the prescribed activities, they are invited to an official graduation ceremony, referred to as the NCAAM "Men of Action" Appreciation/Bonding Banquet, to be held annually. The first banquet was held on March 28, 1992. One hundred black boys, ages nine to eighteen, were special guests at the banquet. Fourteen boys were honored as "Boys of Character."

Paul Quinn's College First and Ten mentoring program was founded in 1990 by Oliver Spencer. In this program, 125 boys, age twelve to fourteen, meet with their mentors once a week. The program's purpose is to improve reading skills and self-esteem. College students from Paul Quinn College act as mentors. "Rap" sessions are held each week, during which the boys are free to discuss peer pressure, gangs, school problems, and so on. Professional athletes are brought in often to discuss such things as peer pressure, drugs, and violence. A major reason for the success of the First and Ten Programs is that the college students monitor their mentorees during the week, calling parents to make sure the boys are completing their reading assignments, helping out around the house, and so on.

With the growing interest in mentoring programs in the United States, a number of resource materials, guides, and directories have been produced. Two of the more helpful resources are *Recruiting Mentors and Potential Helpers: Vol. 1. A Road Map to Success* (Balcazar and Fawcett 1988) and *Recruiting Mentors and Potential Helpers: Vol. 2. A Meeting with Success* (Balcazar and Fawcett 1989). Another is the directory, *A Mentor Peer Group: An Incentive Model for Helping Underclass Youth* (United Way of America 1990).

To empower and save Black males in this country, we must begin in earnest to develop comprehensive policies and programs designed to address causes rather than symptoms. These policies and programs must focus on social, economic, and political forces that shape the lives of Black males. To ensure that Black males have a future, we must develop long-term policies and programs that are sustainable over generations. If we can find over $500 million a day for a questionable hundred-day war in the Persian Gulf, we can find enough money to save our people at home.

The fact is, we do have the capability, people power, resources, technology, and money to save Black males in our society. The question is: Do we have the desire and commitment to do so?

At the 1990 conference of the National Council of African American Men (NCAAM), held in Kansas City, Missouri, Ronald Taylor, author of *The Black Male in America*, spoke of the dire consequences of choosing to ignore the issues discussed above: Should we fail to meet this great challenge, he said, we will have forgone an opportunity to save an entire generation of young Black males who could have grown up to be productive members of society, responsible husbands, and loving fathers.

REFERENCES

Introduction

Bowser, B. 1991. *Black Male Adolescents: Parenting and Education in a Community Context.* Washington, DC: University Press of America.

Bulhan, H. 1985. "Black Americans and Psychopathology: An Overview of Research and Theory." *Psychotherapy* 22: 370–78.

Cazenave, N. 1984. "Race, Socioeconomic Status and Age: The Social Context of American Masculinity." *Sex Roles* 11 (7–8): 639–56.

Cheatham, H. E., and Stewart, J. B. 1990. *Black Families.* New Brunswick, NJ: Transaction Publishers.

Cordes, C. 1985. "Black Males at Risk in America." *APA Monitor* (January): 9–10, 27–28.

Gary, L. 1984. *Black Men.* Beverly Hills, CA: Sage Publications.

Gibbs, J. T. 1988. *Young, Black, and Male in America: An Endangered Species.* Dover, MA: Auburn Publishing House.

Gite, L. 1985. "Black Men and Stress." *Essence Magazine* (November): 25–26, 130.

Hall, R. E. 1993. "Clowns, Buffoons and Gladiators: Media Portrayal of African-American Men." *The Journal of Men's Studies* 1: 239–51.

Hatter, D., and Wright, J. 1993. "Health and the African-American Man: A Selective Review of the Literature." *The Journal of Men's Studies* 1: 267–76.

Heckler, M. 1985. *Report of the Secretary's Task Force on Black and Minority Health.* Washington, DC: U.S. Department of Health and Human Services.

Lee, C. 1992. *Empowering Young Black Males.* Ann Arbor, MI: ERIC Counseling and Personnel Services Clearinghouse.

Madhubuti, H. 1990. *Black Men: Obsolete, Single, Dangerous?* Chicago: Third World Press.

Majors, R., and Billson, J. 1992. *Cool Pose: The Dilemmas of Black Manhood in America.* New York: Lexington Books.

Mauer, M. 1990. *Young Black Men and the Criminal Justice System: A Growing National Problem.* Washington, DC: The Sentencing Project.

_____. 1991. *Americans Behind Bars: A Comparison of International Rates of Incarcerations.* Washington, DC: The Sentencing Project.

Mincy, Ronald B., ed. 1994. *Nurturing Young Black Males: Challenges to Agencies, Programs and Social Policy.* Washington, DC: The Urban Institute Press.

Robinson, J., Bailey, W., and Smith, J. 1985. "Self-perception of the Husband/Father in the Intact Lower Class Black Family." *Phylon* 46: 136–47.

Staples, R. 1994. *The Black Family: Essays and Studies.* Belmont, CA: Wadsworth Publishing Company.

Wilkinson, D., and Taylor, R. 1977. *The Black Male in America.* Chicago: Nelson-Hall.

Chapter 1: Men's Studies, the Men's Movement, and the Study of Black Masculinities

August, E. R. 1982. "Modern Man, or Men's Studies in the '80s." *College English* 44(5):585.

Brod, H. 1986. "New Perspectives on Masculinity: A Case for Men's Studies." In M. Kimmel (ed.), *Changing Men: New Directions in Research on Men and Masculinity.* Beverly Hills, CA: Sage.

_____. 1987. "The Case for Men's Studies." In H. Brod (ed.), *The Making of Masculinities.* Boston: Allan & Unwin.

Carrigan, T., B. Connell, and J. Lee. 1987. "Toward a New Sociology of Masculinity." In H. Brod (Ed.), *The Making of Masculinities: The New Men's Studies*, pp. 63–100. Winchester, MA; Allen & Unwin.

Davis, T. 1985. "Men's Studies: Defining Its Contents and Boundaries." Paper presented at the Ninth National Conference on Men and Masculinity, St. Louis, June 1985.

Doyle, J. A. 1983. *The Male Experience.* Dubuque, IA: W. C. Brown.

Franklin, Clyde W., II. 1984. *The Changing Definition of Masculinity.* New York: Plenum Press.

Gibbs, J. T., ed. 1988. *Young, Black, and Male in America: An Endangered Species.* New York: Auburn House.

Grier, William H. and Price M. Cobbs. 1968. *Black Page.* New York: Basic Books.

Gutman, Herbert. 1976. *The Black in Slavery and Freedom, 1750–1925.* New York: Pantheon.

Hare, N. 1971. "The Frustrated Masculinity of the Negro Male." In R. Staples (ed.), *The Black Family.* Belmont, CA: Wadsworth.

Harris, W. 1990. "Why Most Black Men Won't Go to Church." *Upscale* April/May, pp. 22–23.

Killens, J. O. 1983. *And Then We Heard the Thunder.* Washington, DC: Howard University Press.

Kitano, H. H. L. 1985. *Race Relations*, 3d ed. Englewood Cliffs, NJ: Prentice-Hall.

Kluegal, J. R., and E. R. Smith. 1986. *Beliefs about Inequality: American Views of What Is and What Ought to Be.* New York: Aldine de Gruyter.

Ladner, J. A. 1972. *Tomorrow's Tomorrow: The Black Woman.* Garden City, NY: Doubleday.

Larson, T. E. 1988. "Employment and Unemployment of Young Black Males." In J. T. Gibbs (ed.), *Young, Black, and Male in America: An Endangered Species*, pp. 97–120. New York: Auburn House.

Levinson, D. J.; C. Darrow; E. B. Klein; M. H. Levinson; and B. McKee. 1978. *The Seasons of a Man's Life.* New York: Ballantine.

Mead, G. H. 1934. *Mind, Self, and Society.* C. W. Morris (ed.). Chicago: University of Chicago Press.

Merton, R. 1968. *Social Theory and Social Structure*, rev. ed. New York: Free Press.

Morgan, D. 1981. "Men, Masculinity, and the Process of Sociological Enquiry." In H. Roberts (ed.), *Doing Feminist Research.* London: Routledge & Kegan Paul.

Pleck, E. H., and J. H. Pleck. 1980. *The American Man.* Englewood Cliffs, NJ: Prentice-Hall.

Pleck, J. H. 1981. *The Myth of Masculinity.* Cambridge, MA: M.I.T. Press.

Reed, Ishmael. 1992. Telephone conversation between Professor Reed in Berkeley, CA, and Professor Clyde Franklin in Columbus, OH, Sept. 3.

Richards, M. P. M. 1982. "How Should We Approach the Study of Fathers?" In L. McKee and M. O'Brien (eds.), *The Father Figure*. London: Tavistock.

Spender, D., ed. 1981. *Men's Studies Modified; The Impact of Feminism on the Academic Discipline.* Elmsford, NY: Pergamon.

Strickland, W. 1989. "Our Men in Crisis." *Essence*, Nov., pp. 49–52, 109–15.

Stryker, S. 1980. *Symbolic Interactionism*. Menlo Park, CA: Benjamin/Cummings Pub. Co.

Tiff, S. 1990. "Fighting the Failure Syndrome." *Time*, May 21, pp. 83–84.

William, R. M. 1970. *American Society: A Sociological Interpretation*, 3d ed. New York: Knopf.

Wilson, William J. 1987. *The Truly Disadvantaged: The Inner City, the Underclass, and Public Policy.* Chicago: University of Chicago Press.

Chapter 2: Klansmen, Nazis, and Skinheads: Vigilante Repression

Anderson, S., and J. L. Anderson. 1986. *Inside the League*. New York: Dodd, Mead.

Anti-Defamation League. 1987. *Shaved for Battle*. New York: ADL.

Bermanzohn, P. C., and S. A. Bermanzohn. 1980. *The True Story of the Greensboro Massacre*. New York: Cesar Cauce.

Carlson, J. R. (Derounian, A. B.). 1943. *Under Cover: My Four Years in the Nazi Underworld of America*. New York: Dutton.

_____. 1946. *The Plotters*. New York: Dutton.

Chalmers, D. M. 1981. *Hooded Americanism: The History of the Ku Klux Klan*. New York: Franklin Watts.

Christie, S. 1984. *Stefano Delle Chiaie: Portrait of a "Black" Terrorist*. London: Anarchy/Refract.

Committee for Action/Research on the Intelligence Community. 1973. "The FBI and the Paramilitary Right: Partners in Terror." *CounterSpy* 1 (4–5): 4–12.

Cook County Grand Jury. 1975. *Improper Police Intelligence Activities: A Report by the extended March 1975 Cook County Grand Jury*. Chicago: Grand Jury Print.

Edgar, D. 1982. "The International Face of Fascism." *Urgent Tasks* 14: 1–7.

Forster, A., and B. R. Epstein. 1964. *Danger on the Right*. New York: Random House.

Ford, Henry. 1920. *The International Jew: The World's Foremost Problem*. Dearborn, MI: Dearborn Pub. Co.

Huie, W. B. 1968. *Three Lives for Mississippi*. New York: Signet.

Gearino, D. 1980. "Klan's Blueprint for Revolution, Takeover of Nation Is Revealed." *Chicago Sun-Times*, Aug. 5.

Janson, D., and B. Eismann. 1963. *The Far Right*. New York: McGraw-Hill.

James T. 1983. "Mike Brown, Patriot, Energy Expert, Explains UN Episode." *Spotlight*, Nov. 7, pp. 30–31.

Kahn, H., M. Ryter, and R. Bellant. 1977. "NCLC: America's Largest Political Intelligence Agency." *The Public Eye* 1: 3–37.

King, D. 1989. *Lyndon LaRouche and the New American Fascism*. New York: Doubleday.

Langer, E. 1990. "The American Neo-Nazi Movement Today." *The Nation* 251 (3): 82–107.

Lawrence, K. 1981. "Fighting the New Ku Klux Klan/Nazi Threat." In K. Lawrence (ed.), *Fighting the Klan*, pp. 1–18. Chicago: Sojourner Truth Org.

_____. 1982. "The Ku Klux Klan and Fascism." *Urgent Tasks* 14: 12–16.

_____. 1985. "The New State Repression." *CovertAction Information Bulletin* 25: 3–11.

_____. 1989. "Klansmen, Nazis, and Skinheads: Vigilante Repression." *CovertAction Information Bulletin* 31: 29–33.

Liberation News Service. 1973. "Who's Behind NCLC?" *CounterSpy* 1 (1): 15–19.

Lipset, S. M., and E. Raab. 1970. *The Politics of Unreason: Right-Wing Extremism in America 1790–1970*. New York: Harper and Row.

Macdonald, A. (Pierce, W. L.). 1978/1980. *The Turner Diaries*. Washington, DC: National Alliance.

National Socialist Vanguard Report. 1984. Vol. 2, no. 2 (Oct.-Dec.).

New York Times. 1935. Nov. 14, Dec. 26, and Dec. 28.

New York Times. 1945. May 22, May 31, June 15, June 18, and Aug. 12.

New York Times. 1954. Nov. 15.

New York Times. 1955. March 16.

Reaper, The. 1984. Vol. 8, no. 40 (Nov. 1).

Seldes, G. 1943. *Facts and Fascism*. New York: In Fact.

Senate Select Committee on Intelligence. 1976a. *Final Report of the Select Committee to Study Government Activities with respect to Intelligence Activities of the United States Senate, 3, Supplementary Detailed Staff Reports on Intelligence Activities and the Rights of Americans*. Washington, D.C.: U.S. Government Printing Office.

Senate Select Committee on Intelligence. 1976b. *Hearings before the Select Committee to Study Governmental Activities With Respect to Intelligence Activities, 6, Federal Bureau of Investigation*. Washington, D.C.: U.S. Government Printing Office.

Singular, S. 1989. *Talked to Death: The Murder of Alan Berg and the Rise of the Neo-Nazis*. New York: Berkley Books.

Stern, D. J. 1976. *Security Agency Activities in Chicago, Illinois*. Chicago: Repression Research Group.

Terrorism Information Project. 1976a. "National Caucus of Labor Committees: Brownshirts of the Seventies." *CounterSpy* 2 (4): 40–41.

Terrorism Information Project. 1976b. *NCLC: Brownshirts of the Seventies*. Arlington: TIP.

Zinn, H. 1965. *SNCC: The New Abolitionists*. Boston: Beacon Press.

Besides the listed references, portions of this chapter are informed by unpublished background material (not for specific attribution, for security reasons), furnished by the Center for Constitutional Rights, the Center for Democratic Renewal (formerly the National Anti-Klan Network), the John Brown Anti-Klan Committee, the Klanwatch Project of the Southern Poverty Law Center, Political Research Associates, Russ Bellant, Chip Berlet, Jason Berry, Daniel Gearino, Lance Hill, Dennis King, Jonathan Mozzocchi, Sheila O'Donnell, Daniel J. Stern, Lyn Wells, Randall Williams, and Louis Wolf.

Chapter 3: Neoconservative Attacks on Black Families and the Black Male

Balkin, S. 1989. *Self-Employment for Low-Income People*. New York: Praeger.

Blassingame, J. 1972. *The Slave Community: Plantation Life in the Antebellum South*. New York: Oxford University Press.

Boston, T. D. 1988. *Race, Class and Conservatism*. Winchester, MA: Unwin Hyman.

Brunswick, A. 1988. "Young Black Males and Substance Abuse." In Jewell Taylor Gibbs (ed.), *Young, Black and Male in America: An Endangered Species*, pp. 166–87. Dover, MA: Auburn House.

Cain, G., and R. Finnie. 1990. "The Black-White Difference in Youth Employment: Evidence for Demand-Side Factors." *Journal of Labor Economics* 8 (1), Pt. 2: S364–S395.

Cogan, J. F. 1982. "The Decline in Black Teenage Employment." *American Economic Review* 72: 621–38.

Curry, L. 1981. *The Free Black in Urban America, 1800–1850: The Shadow of the Dream.* Chicago: University of Chicago Press.

Darity, W. A., and S. L. Myers, Jr. "Review of *Losing Ground: American Social Policy, 1950–1980.*" In Margaret C. Simms and Julianne Malveaux (eds.), *Slipping Through the Cracks: The Status of Black Women.* New Brunswick, NJ: Transaction Books.

Du Bois, W. E. B. 1908. *The Negro American Family.* Atlanta, GA: Atlanta University Press. (Report of a social study made principally by the college class of 1909 and 1910 of Atlanta University, under the patronage of the trustees of the John F. Slater Fund; together with the *Proceedings of the 13th Annual Conference for the Study of the Negro Problems.*)

_____. 1924. *The Gift of Black Folk: The Negro in the Making of America.* New York: Washington Square Press, 1970. (Reprint)

Farley, J. 1987. "Disproportionate Black and Hispanic Unemployment in U.S. Metropolitan Areas: The Roles of Racial Inequality, Segregation and Discrimination in Male Joblessness." *American Journal of Economics and Sociology* 46 (2): 129–50.

Frazier, E. F. 1926. "Three Scourges of the Negro Family." *Opportunity* 4: 210–13, 234.

_____. 1927. "Is the Negro Family a Unique Sociological Unit?" *Opportunity* 5 (June): 165–68.

_____. 1966 [1939]. *The Negro Family in the United States.* Chicago: University of Chicago Press. (Revised and abridged edition)

Georges-Abeyie, D. 1981. "Studying Black Crime: A Realistic Approach." In P. J. Brantingham and P. L. Brantingham (eds.), *Environmental Criminology.* Beverly Hills, CA: Sage.

_____. 1989. "Race, Ethnicity, and the Spatial Dynamic: Toward a Realistic Study of Black Crime, Crime Victimization, and Criminal Processing of Blacks." *Social Justice* 16 (4): 35–54.

Genovese, E. 1974. *Roll, Jordan, Roll: The World the Slaves Made.* New York: Pantheon Books.

Gibbs, J. T., ed. *Young, Black and Male in America: An Endangered Species.* Dover, MA: Auburn House.

Gilder, G. 1981. *Wealth and Poverty.* New York: Basic Books.

Gutman, H. 1976. *The Black Family in Slavery and Freedom, 1750–1925.* New York: Pantheon Books.

Harrison, B. 1977. "Education and Underemployment in the Urban Ghetto." In A. Ross and H. Hill (eds.), *Problems in Political Economy: An Urban Perspective.* Lexington, MA: D. C. Heath.

Herskovits, M. 1958. *The Myth of the Negro Past.* Boston: Beacon Press.

Hughes, M., and J. Madden. 1991. "Residential Segregation and the Economic Status of Black Workers: New Evidence for an Old Debate." *Journal of Urban Economics* 29: 28–49.

Ihanfeldt, K., and D. Sjoquist. "The Impact of Job Decentralization on the Economic Welfare of Central City Blacks." *Journal of Urban Economics* 26: 110–30.

Jaynes, G., and R. M. Williams, eds. 1989. *A Common Destiny: Blacks and American Society.* Washington, DC: National Academy Press.

Killingsworth, C. 1967. "Negroes in a Changing Labor Market." In A. Ross and H. Hill (eds.), *Employment, Race and Poverty.* New York: Harcourt Brace and World.

Leonard, J. 1987. "The Interaction of Residential Segregation and Employment Discrimination." *Journal of Urban Economics* 21: 323–46.

Murray, Charles A. 1984. *Losing Ground: American Social Policy, 1950–1980.* New York: Basic Books.

Myrdal, G. 1962. *An American Dilemma: The Negro Problem and Modern Democracy.* 20th anniversary ed. New York: Harper and Row.

Macpherson, D., and J. Stewart. 1991. "Racial Difference in Married Female Labor Force Participation Behavior: An Analysis Using Inter-Racial Marriages." *Review of Black Political Economy* (forthcoming).

Nisbet, R. 1986. *Conservatism, Dream and Reality.* Minneapolis: University of Minnesota Press.

Patterson, O. 1972. "Toward a Future That Has No Past: Reflections on the Fate of Blacks in the Americas." *The Public Interest,* No. 27, pp. 25–62.

Piven, F. F., and R. Cloward. *Regulating the Poor: The Function of Public Welfare.* New York: Pantheon.

Rose, A. 1962. "Postscript: Twenty Years Later—Social Change and the Negro Problem." In G. Myrdal, *An American Dilemma: The Negro Problem and Modern Democracy.* 20th Anniversary Ed. New York: Harper and Row.

Scott, J., and J. Stewart. "The Pimp-Whore Complex in Everyday Black Life." *Black Male/Female Relationships* 1(2): 11–15.

Solomon, B. 1988. "The Impact of Public Policy on the Status of Young Black Males." In J. T. Gibbs (ed.), *Young, Black and Male in America: An Endangered Species.* Dover, MA: Auburn House.

Sowell, T. 1975. *Race and Economics.* New York: David McKay.

————. 1981. *Markets and Minorities.* New York: Basic Books.

————. 1984. *Civil Rights: Rhetoric or Reality?* New York: Morrow.

Stewart, J. B. 1984. "Economic Policy and Black America." In Mitchell F. Rice and Woodrow Jones (eds.), *Contemporary Public Policy Perspectives and Black Americans: Issues in an Era of Retrenchment Politics.* Westport, CN: Greenwood Press.

————. 1990. "Back to Basics: The Significance of Du Bois' and Frazier's Contributions for Contemporary Research on Black Families." In Harold Cheatham and James Stewart (eds.), *Black Families: Interdisciplinary Perspectives.* New Brunswick, NJ: Transaction Consortium.

Stewart, J. B. and J. Scott. 1978. "The Institutional Decimation of Black American Males." *Western Journal of Black Studies* 2: 82–92.

————. 1979. "The Institutional Decimation of Black American Males." *Western Journal of Black Studies* 3: 186–96.

Sudarkasa, N. 1981. "Interpreting the African Heritage in Afro-American Family Organization." In H. McAdoo (ed.), *Black Families.* Beverly Hills, CA: Sage.

Thompson, J., and J. Cataldo. 1986. "Comment." In R. Freeman and H. Holzer (eds.), *The Black Youth Employment Crisis.* Chicago: University of Chicago Press.

Vicusi, W. K. 1986. "Market Incentives for Criminal Behavior." In R. Freeman and H. Holzer (eds.), *The Black Youth Employment Crisis.* Chicago: University of Chicago Press.

Willhelm, S. 1970. *Who Needs the Negro?* Cambridge, MA: Schenkman.

Williams, W. 1982. *The State Against Blacks.* New York: New Press.

Wilson, W. 1987. *The Truly Disadvantaged: The Inner City, the Underclass, and Public Policy.* Chicago: University of Chicago Press.

Yette, S. 1971. *The Choice.* New York: Putnam.

Chapter 4: The Black Male in American Literature

Baldwin, J. 1968 [1949]. "Everybody's Protest Novel." *Notes of a Native Son.* New York: Bantam.

Bradley, D. 1982 [1981]. *The Chaneysville Incident.* New York: Avon.

Chase, R. 1957. *The American Novel and Its Tradition.* Garden City, NY: Anchor.

Clemens, S. L. 1977 [1884]. *Adventures of Huckleberry Finn.* New York: W. W. Norton.

Crane, S. 1960 [1899]. "The Monster." *The Red Badge of Courage and Other Writings.* Cambridge, MA: Houghton, Mifflin.

Douglass, F. 1982 [1845]. *Narrative of the Life of Frederick Douglass, An American Slave.* New York: Penguin.

Ellison, R. 1972 [1952]. *Invisible Man.* New York: Vintage.

Faulkner, W. 1972 [1932]. *Light in August.* New York: Vintage.

_____. 1972 [1936]. *Absalom, Absalom*. New York: Vintage.

Haley, A. 1977 [1976]. *Roots*. New York: Dell.

Harding, V. 1968. "You've Taken My Nat and Gone." In John H. Clarke (ed.), *William Styron's Nat Turner: Ten Black Writers Respond*. Boston: Beacon.

Henson, J. 1849. *The Life of Josiah Henson*. Boston: A. D. Phelps.

Kinney, J. 1985. *Amalgamation! Race, Sex, and Rhetoric in the Nineteenth-Century American Novel*. Westport, CT: Greenwood.

Levine, L. W. 1977. *Black Culture and Black Consciousness*. New York: Oxford University Press.

Lewis, S. 1947. *Kingsblood Royal*. New York: Grosset and Dunlap.

Morrison, T. 1977. *Song of Solomon*. New York: New American Library.

Reed, I. 1973. *Mumbo-Jumbo*. New York: Bantam.

Stowe, H. B. 1965 [1852]. *Uncle Tom's Cabin*. New York: Harper and Row.

_____. 1853. *The Key to Uncle Tom's Cabin*. Boston: J. P. Jewett.

Styron, W. 1968 [1967]. *The Confessions of Nat Turner*. New York: New American Library.

Chapter 5: The Black Male: Searching beyond Stereotypes

Davis, A. Y. 1981. *Women, Race and Class*. New York: Random House.

Billingsley, A. 1968. *Black Families in White America*. Englewood Cliffs, NJ: Prentice-Hall.

Lincoln, C. E. 1965. "The Absent Father Haunts the Negro Family." *New York Times Magazine*, Nov. 28.

Clark, K. 1965. *Dark Ghetto*. New York: Harper and Row.

Marable, M. 1983. *How Capitalism Underdeveloped Black America*. Boston: South End Press.

Chapter 6: A Generation behind Bars

Amnesty International. 1987. "USA: The Death Penalty." London: AI.

Austin, J., and J. Irwin. 1987. "It's About Time." National Council on Crime and Delinquency.

Bearak, B. 1990. "Big Catch: Drug War's Little Fish." *Los Angeles Times*, May 6, p. A36.

Blumstein, A. 1982. "On the Racial Disproportionality of United States Prison Populations." *Journal of Criminal Law and Criminology* 73(3).

"Correctional Populations in the United States." 1989. Washington, DC: U.S. Department of Justice, Bureau of Justice Statistics.

Criminal Victimization in the United States, 1990. 1992. Washington, DC: U.S. Department of Justice, Bureau of Justice Statistics.

Currie, E. 1985. *Confronting Crime: An American Challenge*. New York: Pantheon.

Drugs and Crime Facts, 1990. 1991. Washington, DC: U.S. Department of Justice, Bureau of Justice Statistics.

Federal Bureau of Investigation. 1991. *Crime in the United States, 1990*. Washington, DC.

Fundis, J.; L. Greenfield; P. A. Langan; and V. W. Schneider. 1990. *Historical Statistics on Prisoners in State and Federal Institutions, Yearend 1925–86*. U.S. Department of Justice, Bureau of Justice Statistics.

Greenfeld, L. 1992. *Prisons and Prisoners in the United States*. U.S. Department of Justice, Bureau of Justice Statistics.

Isikoff, M. 1991. "Number of Imprisoned Drug Offenders Up Sharply." *Washington Post*, April 25.

Klein, S.; J. Petersilia; and S. Turner. 1990. "Race and Imprisonment Decisions in California." *Science*, Feb. 16.

Manditory Minimum Penalties in the Federal Criminal Justice System. 1991. Washington, DC: U.S. Sentencing Commission.

Mauer, M. 1990. *Young Black Men and the Criminal Justice System.* Washington, DC: The Sentencing Project.

―――――. 1992. "Americans Behind Bars: One Year Later." Washington, DC: The Sentencing Project.

Meddis, S. 1989. "Whites, Not Blacks, at the Core of Drug Crisis." *USA Today,* Dec. 20.

Meddis, S., and M. Suides. 1990. "Drug War 'Focused' on Blacks." *USA Today,* Dec. 20.

Morton, D. C., and T. L. Snell. 1992. "Prisoners in 1991." U.S. Department of Justice, Bureau of Justice Statistics.

Mitchell, E. J. 1990. "Cops Burst In, You Feel Violated." *Detroit News,* April 26.

Overcrowded Time. 1982. New York: Edna McConnell Clark Foundation.

Rich, S. 1990. "Report Says Children Under 6 Have Highest Poverty Rate." *Washington Post,* April 15.

Report to the Nation on Crime and Justice, 2d ed. 1988. U.S. Department of Justice, Bureau of Justice Statistics.

Chapter 7: The Case Against NCAA Proposition 48

American Council on Education. 1989. *Minorities on Campus.* Washington, DC: ACE.

American Institutes for Research. 1988. *Report No. 1: Results from the 1987–88 National Study of Intercollegiate Athletes.* Washington, DC: AIR.

―――――. 1989a. *Report No. 6: Comments from Students in the 1987–88 National Study of Intercollegiate Athletics.* Washington, DC: AIR.

―――――. 1989b. *Report No. 3: The Experience of Black Intercollegiate Athletes at NCAA Division I Institutions.* Washington, DC: AIR.

―――――. 1989c. *Report No. 5: Analysis of Academic Transcripts of Intercollegiate Athletes at NCAA Division I Institutions.* Washington, DC: AIR.

Crouse, J., and D. Trusheim. 1988. *The Case Against the SAT.* Chicago: University of Chicago Press.

Fleming, J. 1988. *Blacks in College.* San Francisco, CA: Jossey-Bass.

Knight Commission on Intercollegiate Athletics. 1991. *Keeping Faith with the Student Athlete: A New Model for Intercollegiate Athletics.* Miami, FL: Knight Com.

Walter, T.; D. Smith; G. Hoey; R. Wilhelm; and S. Miller. 1987. "Predicting the Academic Success of College Athletes." *Research Quarterly for Exercise and Sport* 58(2):273–79.

Women's Sports Foundation. 1989. *Minorities in Sports.* New York: WSF.

USA Today. 1987. "Fewer Athletes Are Getting Benched by Proposal 48." Sept. 8.

Chapter 8: African-American Males and Homelessness

Baxter, E., and K. Hopper. 1981. *Private Lives/Public Spaces: Homeless Adults on the Streets of New York City.* New York: Community Services Society, Institute for Social Welfare Research.

Caton, C. L. M. 1990. *Homeless in America.* New York: Oxford University Press.

Centers for Disease Control, U.S. Department of Health and Human Services. 1990. *Morbidity and Mortality Weekly Report,* Dec., p. 879.

Christmas, V. P., and M. Douglas. 1989. *CSS Homeless Client Residential Placement Quarterly Report.* New York City Department of Mental Health, Mental Retardation and Alcoholism Services, Residential Development Unit.

Fischer, P. J. 1990. "Criminal Behavior and Victimization in the Homeless: A Review of the Literature." In R. Jahiel (ed.), *Homelessness: A Prevention Oriented Approach*. Baltimore, MD: Johns Hopkins University Press.

Institute of Medicine. 1989. *Homelessness, Health, and Human Needs*. Washington, DC: National Academy Press.

Jaynes, G. D., and R. M. Williams. 1989. *A Common Destiny: Blacks and American Society*. New York: National Academy Press.

Lamb, H. R., and D. M. Lamb. 1988. "Factors Contributing to Homelessness among the Chronically and Severely Mentally Ill." *Hospital and Community Psychiatry* 41: 301–5.

New York City Department of Mental Health, Mental Retardation and Alcoholism Services. 1990a. *Levels of Service Trend Report*.

_____. 1990b. *Monthly Report*, Nov.

_____. 1990c. *Residential Development Unit Homeless Client Contact/Placement Information*, Dec.

New York City Human Resources Administration. 1990. *Monthly Shelter Report*, Dec.

Quaison-Sackey, E. 1986. "Homicide in the Black Community: Prevention and Intervention Strategies." *BPA Quarterly* 15: 3–4.

Struening, E. L. 1986. *A Study of Residents of the New York City Shelter System: Report to the New York City Department of Mental Health, Mental Retardation and Alcoholism Services*. New York: New York Psychiatric Institute.

U.S. Department of Housing and Urban Development. 1984. *A Report to the Secretary on the Homeless and Emergency Shelters*. Washington, DC: Office of Policy Development.

Wright, B. *Black Robes, White Justice*. 1987. Secaucus, NJ: Carol Pub. Group.

Wright, J. D.; J. W. Knight; E. Weber-Burdin; and J. Lam. 1987. "Ailments and Alcohol: Health Status among the Drinking Homeless." *Alcohol Health World*, pp. 22–27.

Chapter 9: Black Men and AIDS

Aborampah, O. 1989. "Black Male-Female Relationships: Some Observations." *Journal of Black Studies* 19(3): 320–42.

Bernard, J. 1966. *Marriage and Family among Negroes*. Englewood Cliffs, NJ: Prentice-Hall.

Biernecki, P. 1986. *Pathways to Heroin Addiction*. Philadelphia, PA: Temple University Press.

Bluestone B., and B. Harrison. 1982. *The Deindustrialization of America*. New York: Basic Books.

Bouknight, R., and L. Bouknight. 1988. "Acquired Immunodeficiency Syndrome in the Black Community: Focusing on Education and the Black Male." *New York State Journal of Medicine* 88 (Dec.): 638–41.

Center for the Study of Social Policy. 1986. "The Flip-Side of Black Families Headed by Women: The Economic Status of Black Men." In R. Staples (ed.), *The Black Family: Essays and Studies*. Belmont, CA.: Wadsworth.

Centers for Disease Control. 1987. "Human Immunodeficiency Virus Infection in the United States: A Review of Current Knowledge." *Morbidity and Mortality Weekly Report* 36 (Suppl. 3–6).

_____. 1989. *HIV/AIDS Surveillance Report*, June, pp. 1–16.

_____. 1990. *HIV/AIDS Surveillance Report*, May.

Coates, T. 1990. "Strategies for Modifying Sexual Behavior for Primary and Secondary Prevention of HIV Disease." *Journal of Consulting and Clinical Psychology* 58(1): 57–69.

Dalton, H. 1989. "AIDS in Blackface." *Daedalus* 118(3): 204–27.

Dawson, D., and A. Hardy. 1989. "AIDS Knowledge and Attitudes of Black Americans." *Vital and Health Statistics of the National Center for Health Statistics*, no. 165 (March 30): 1–24.

Drake. St. C. 1989. "Studies of the African Diaspora: The Work and Reflections of St. Clair Drake." *Sage Race Relations Abstracts* 14(3): 1–15.

Drake, St. C., and H. Cayton. 1944. *Black Metropolis.* New York: Harper and Row.

Franklin, C. 1984. "Black Male-Black Female Conflict: Individually Caused or Culturally Nurtured." *Journal of Black Studies* 15 (Dec.): 139–54.

Fullilove, Mindy; Meryle Weinstein; Robert Fullilove, III; Eugene Crayton, Jr.; Richard Goodjoin; Benjamin Bowser; and Shirley Gross. 1990. "Race/Gender Issues in the Sexual Transmission of AIDS." In P. Volberding and M. Jacobsson, *AIDS Clinical Review 1990.* New York: Marcel Dekker.

Fullilove, Robert; Mindy Fullilove; Benjamin Bowser; and Shirley Gross. 1990. "Risk of Sexually Transmitted Disease among Black Adolescent Crack Users in Oakland and San Francisco, Calif." *Journal of the American Medical Association* 263 (6): 851–55.

Furstenberg, F., et al. 1987. "Race Differences in the Timing of Adolescent Intercourse." *American Sociological Review* 52:511–18.

Harris, M. 1968. *The Rise of Anthropological Theory.* New York: T. Y. Crowell.

Icard, L. 1985–86. "Black Gay Men and Conflicting Social Identities: Sexual Orientation versus Racial Identity." *Journal of Social Work and Human Sexuality* 4(1–2): 83–93.

Institute of Medicine, National Academy of Science. 1988. *Confronting AIDS: Update 1988.* Washington, DC: National Academy Press.

Karenga, M. 1982. "Black Male/Female Relationships." In M. Karenga (ed.), *Introduction to Black Studies.* Los Angeles, CA: Kawaida.

Morrison, D. 1985. "Adolescent Contraceptive Behavior: A Review." *Psychological Bulletin* 98: 538–68.

Redfield, R., and D. Burke. 1988. "HIV Infection: The Clinical Picture." *Scientific American* 259(4): 90–98.

Rivara, F., et al. 1985. "A Study of Low Socioeconomic Status: Black Teenage Fathers and their Nonfather Peers." *Pediatrics* 75: 648–56.

Robinson, I., et al. 1985. "Self-Perception of the Husband/Father in the Intact Lower Class Black Family." *Phylon* 46(2): 136–47.

Ryan, W. 1976. *Blaming the Victim.* New York: Vintage Books.

Tanfer, K., and Horn. 1985. "Contraceptive Use, Pregnancy and Fertility Patterns among Single American Women in their 20s." *Family Planning Perspectives* 17: 10–19.

Valentine, C. 1968. *Culture and Poverty.* Chicago: University of Chicago Press.

Weinberg, M., and C. Williams. 1988. "Black Sexuality: A Test of Two Theories." *Journal of Sex Research* 25(2): 197–218.

Weinstein, M., et al. 1990. "Black Sexuality: A Bibliography." Sage Race Relations Abstracts.

Chapter 10: Anger in Young Black Males: Victims or Victimizers?

American College Dictionary. 1969. New York: Random House.

Bandura, A. 1978. "Learning and Behavioral Theories of Aggression." In I. L. Kutash, and B. Schlesinger (eds.). *Violence.* San Francisco, CA: Jossey-Bass.

Brunswick, A. 1988. "Young Black Males and Substance Abuse." In J. T. Gibbs (ed.), *Young, Black and Male in America: An Endangered Species.* Dover, MA: Auburn House.

Children's Defense Fund. 1986. *A Children's Defense Budget.* Washington, DC: CDF.

Clark, K. B. 1965. *Dark Ghetto: Dilemmas of Social Power.* New York: Harper and Row.

Committee for Economic Development. 1987. *Children in Need: Investment Strategies for the Educationally Disadvantaged.* New York: CED.

Dennis, R. E. 1980. Homicide among Black Males. *Public Health Reports* 95: 549–61.

Dollard, J. R.; L. W. Doob; N. E. Miller; and R. Sears. 1939. *Frustration and Aggression.* New Haven, CT: Yale University Press.

Drake, St. C., and H. R. Cayton. 1946. *Black Metropolis.* New York: Harper and Row.

Edelman, M. W. 1987. *Families in Peril: An Agenda for Social Change.* Cambridge, MA: Harvard University Press.

Federal Bureau of Investigation. 1986. "Crime in the United States 1985." In *Uniform Crime Reports.* Washington, DC: U.S. Government Printing Office.

Frazier, E. F. 1967. *The Negro Family in the United States.* Rev. ed. Chicago: University of Chicago Press.

Freud, S. 1961. *A General Introduction to Psychoanalysis.* New York: Washington Square Press.

Gary, L. E. 1980. "The Role of Alcohol and Drug Abuse in Homicide." *Public Health Reports* 95, 553–54.

Gelles, R. J. 1979. *Family Violence.* Beverly Hills, CA: Sage.

Gibbs, J. T. 1988a. "Conceptual, Methodological and Sociocultural Issues in Black Youth Suicide: Implications for Assessment and Early Intervention." *Suicide and Life-Threatening Behavior* 18: 73–89.

_____, ed. 1988b. *Young, Black and Male in America: An Endangered Species.* Dover, MA: Auburn House.

Gibbs, J. T., and A. M. Hines. 1989. "Factors Related to Sex Differences in Suicidal Behavior among Black Youth: Implications for Intervention and Research." *Journal of Adolescent Research* 4, 152–72.

Gibbs, J. T., and L. N. Huang. 1989. *Children of Color: Psychological Interventions with Minority Youth.* San Francisco, CA: Jossey-Bass.

Glasgow, D. 1981. *The Black Underclass.* New York: Vintage Books.

Grier, W., and P. Cobbs. 1968. *Black Rage.* New York: Basic Books.

Hampton, R. L. 1986. "Family Violence and Homicide in the Black Community: Are They Linked?" In *Report of the Secretary's Task Force on Black and Minority Health.* Vol. 5. Washington, DC: Department of Health and Human Services.

Harburg, E.; J. C. Efult; L. S. Hauenstein; C. Chape; W. J. Schull; and M. A. Schock. 1973. "Socio-Ecological Stress, Suppressed Hostility, Skin-Color, and Black-White Male Blood Pressure." *Psychosomatic Medicine* 35: 276–96.

Hawkins, D. F. 1986. "Longitudinal-Situational Approaches to Understanding Black-on-Black Homicide." In *Report of the Secretary's Task Force on Black and Minority Health.* Vol. 5. Washington, DC: Department of Health and Human Services.

Hendin, H. 1969. "Black Suicide." *Archives of General Psychiatry* 21, 407–22.

Jenkins, A. 1982. *The Psychology of the Afro-American.* New York: Pergamon Press.

Jones, E. E., and S. J. Korchin, eds. 1982. *Minority Mental Health.* New York: Praeger.

Liebow, E. 1967. *Tally's corner.* Boston, MA: Little, Brown.

Madhubuti, H. R. 1990. *Black Men: Obsolete, Single, Dangerous?* Chicago: Third World Press.

Mauer, M. 1990. *Young Black Men and the Criminal Justice System.* Washington, DC: The Sentencing Project.

Monroe, S., and P. Goldman. 1988. *Brothers, Black and Poor: A True Story of Courage and Survival.* New York: Morrow.

Morrison, T. 1987. *Beloved: A Novel.* New York: Knopf.

Myers, B. C. 1990. "Hypertension as a Manifestation of the Stress Experienced by Black Families." In H. E. Cheatham and J. B. Stewart (eds.), *Black Families: Interdisciplinary Perspectives.* New Brunswick, NJ: Transaction.

National Center for Health Statistics. 1990. *Homicide in the United States: 1960–1988.* Washington, DC: U.S. Dept. of Health and Human Services.

Peters, M. F. 1981. "Parenting in Black Families with Young Children: A Historical Perspective." In H. McAdoo (ed.), *Black Families.* Beverly Hills, CA: Sage.

Pierce, C. M. 1970. "Offense Mechanisms." In F. Barbour (ed.), *The Black 70s.* Boston, MA: Porter Sargent.

Poussaint, A. 1983. Black-on-Black Homicide: A Psychological-Political Perspective. *Victimology* 8: 161–69.

Rainwater, L. 1970. *Behind Ghetto Walls: Black Families in a Federal Slum.* Chicago: Aldine.

Randolph, L. B. 1990. "The Widening Gap Between Women Who Are Making It and Men Who Aren't." *Ebony Magazine,* Aug., pp. 52–54.

Reed. R. 1988. "Education and Achievement of Young Black Males." In J. T. Gibbs (ed.), *Young, Black and Male in America: An Endangered Species.* Dover, MA: Auburn House.

Report of the National Advisory Commission on Civil Disorders. 1968. Washington, DC: U.S. Government Printing Office.

Rose, H. M. 1986. "Can We Substantially Lower Homicide Risk in the Nation's Larger Black Communities?" In *Report of the Secretary's Task Force on Black and Minority Health.* Vol. 5. Washington, DC: Department of Health and Human Services.

Santa Cruz Sentinel. 1990. "No More Watts Riots, But Despair Remains." Aug. 10, p. A-8.

Schorr, A. 1986. *Common Decency: Domestic Policies after Reagan.* New Haven, CT: Yale University Press.

Schulz, D. 1969. *Coming Up Black: Patterns of Ghetto Socialization.* Englewood Cliffs, NJ: Prentice-Hall.

Shapiro, W.; T. McCall; and J. D. Hull. 1987. "The Ghetto: From Bad to Worse." *Time,* Aug. 24, pp. 18–22.

Smitherman, G. 1977. *Talkin' and Testifyin': The Language of Black America.* Boston, MA: Houghton Mifflin.

Staggers, B. 1989. "Health Care Issues of Black Adolescents." In R. L. Jones (ed.), *Black adolescents.* Berkeley, CA: Cobb and Henry.

Stampp, K. 1956. *The Peculiar Institution: Slavery in the Ante-Bellum South.* New York: Knopf.

Staples, R. 1982. *Black Masculinity: The Black Man's Role in American Society.* San Francisco, CA: Black Scholar Press.

Sue, S., and T. Moore. 1984. *The Pluralistic Society: A Community Mental Health Perspective.* New York: Human Sciences Press.

Sullivan, H. S. 1953. *The Interpersonal Theory of Psychiatry.* New York: Norton.

Tarvis, C. 1989. *Anger: The Misunderstood Emotion.* Rev. ed. New York: Simon and Schuster.

U.S. Bureau of the Census. 1990. *Statistical Abstract of the United States: 1990.* 110th ed. Washington, DC: U.S. Department of Commerce.

U.S. Department of Health and Human Services. 1985. *Report of the Secretary's Task Force on Black and Minority Health.* Vol. 1. Washington, DC: U.S. Government Printing Office.

_____. 1986. *Report of the Secretary's Task Force on Black and Minority Health.* Vol. 5. Washington, DC: U.S. Government Printing Office.

Wicker, T. 1991. "The Punitive Society." *New York Times,* Jan. 12, p. 16.

Williams, R. B., Jr.; J. C. Baufort; and R. B. Shekelle. 1985. "The Health Consequences of Hostility." In M. Chesney and R. Rosenman (eds.), *Anger and Hostility in Cardiovascular and Behavioral Disorders.* Washington, DC: Hemisphere.

Wilson, W. J. 1987. *The Truly Disadvantaged.* Chicago: University of Chicago Press.

Wilson, W. J., and K. M Neckerman. 1984. "Poverty and Family Structure: The Widening Gap Between Evidence and Public Policy Issues." Paper prepared for the conference on Poverty and Policy: Retrospect and Prospects, Dec. 6–8, Williamsburg, VA.

Chapter 11: Black Males and Social Policy

Ashenfelter, O. 1978. "Estimating the Effect of Training Programs on Earnings." *Review of Economics and Statistics* 60: 47–57.

Bassi, L, and O. Ashenfelter. 1986. "The Effect of Direct Job Creation and Training Programs on Low-Skilled Workers." In S. Danziger and D. Weinberg (eds.), *Fighting Poverty: What Works and What Doesn't.* Cambridge, MA: Harvard University Press.

Boykins, A. 1986. "The Triple Quandary and the Schooling of Afro-American Children." In U. Neisser (ed.), *The School Achievement of Minority Children.* Hillsdale, NJ: Erlbaum.

Brimmer, A. 1969. "The Black Revolution and the Economic Future of Negroes in the United States." *American Scholar* 38 (Autumn): 629–43.

Brown, M., and S. Erie. 1981. "Blacks and the Legacy of the Great Society: The Economic and Political Impact of Federal Social Policy." *Public Policy* 29: 299–330.

Burtless, G. 1986. "Public Spending for the Poor: Trends, Prospects, and Economic Limits." In S. Danziger and D. Weinberg (eds.), *Fighting Poverty: What Works and What Doesn't.* Cambridge, MA: Harvard University Press.

Carnegie Corporation of New York. 1984/85. "Renegotiating Society's Contract with the Public Schools." *Carnegie Quarterly* 29/30: 1–11.

Center on Budget and Policy Priorities. 1984. *Falling Behind: A Report on How Blacks Have Fared under the Reagan Policies.* Washington, DC: CBPP.

Clark, K. 1965. *Dark Ghetto.* New York: Harper and Row.

Danziger, S.; R. Haveman; and R. Plotnick. 1986. "Antipoverty Policy: Effects on the Poor and the Nonpoor." In S. Danziger and D. Weinberg (eds.), *Fighting Poverty.* Cambridge, MA: Harvard University Press.

Davis, K. 1977. "A Decade of Policy Developments in Providing Health Care for Low-Income Families." In R. Haveman (ed.), *A Decade of Federal Antipoverty Programs: Achievements, Failures, and Lessons.* New York: Academic Press.

Drake, S. C. 1965. "The Social and Economic Status of the Negro in the United States." *Daedalus* 94: 771–814.

Farley, R. 1984. *Blacks and Whites: Narrowing the Gap?* Cambridge, MA: Harvard University Press.

Federal Bureau of Investigation. 1986. *Crime in the United States, 1985, Uniform Crime Reports.* Washington, DC: U.S. Dept. of Justice.

Freeman, R. 1978. "Black Economic Progress since 1964." *The Public Interest* 52: 52–68.

_____. 1986. "Cutting Black Youth Unemployment." *New York Times,* July 20.

Freeman, R., and N. Holzer. 1986. *The Black Youth Employment Crisis.* Chicago: University of Chicago Press.

Gibbs, J. T. 1984. "Black Adolescents and Youth: An Endangered Species." *American Journal of Orthopsychiatry* 54: 6–21.

_____., ed. 1988. *Young, Black, and Male in America.* Dover, MA: Auburn.

Gilder, G. 1981. *Wealth and Poverty.* New York: Basic Books.

Grant, L. 1984. "Black Females 'Place' in Desegregated Classrooms." *Sociology of Education* 57: 98–111.

Grant, L. 1985. "Race-Gender Status, Classroom Interaction, and Children's Socialization in Elementary School." In L. Wilkerson and C. Marrett (eds.), *Gender and Classroom Interaction.* Orlando, FL: Academic Press.

Hahn, A., and R. Lerman. 1985. *What Works in Youth Employment Policy.* Washington, DC: Committee on New American Realities.

Hare, B., and L. Castenell. 1985. "No Place to Run, No Place to Hide: Comparative Status and Future Prospects of Black Boys. In M. Spencer; G. Brookins; and W. Allen (eds.), *Beginnings: The Social and Affective Development of Black Children.* Hillsdale, NJ: Erlbaum.

Harrington, M. 1974. "The Welfare State and Its Neoconservative Critics." In L. Coser and I. Howe (eds.), *The New Conservatives.* New York: Quadrangle.

Hill, R. 1981. *Economic Policies and Black Progress: Myths and Realities.* Washington, DC: National Urban League.

_____. 1988. "Adolescent Male Responsibility in African-American Families." Paper presented at the National Urban League Conference on Manhood and Fatherhood, Atlanta, GA, March.

Hogan, D.; and E. Kitagawa. 1985. "The Impact of Social Status, Family Strucutre, and Neighborhood on the Fertility of Black Adolescents." *American Journal of Sociology* 90: 825–55.

Hunt, J., and L. Hunt. 1977. "Racial Inequality and Self-Image: Identity Maintenance as Identity Diffusion." *Sociology and Social Research* 61: 539–59.

Irvine, J. 1990. *Black Students and School Failure*. New York: Greenwood Press.

Jordan, V. 1980. "Introduction." In J. Williams (ed.), *The State of Black America, 1980*. Washington, DC: National Urban League.

Kasarda, J. 1989. "Urban Industrial Transition and the Underclass." *The Annals* 501: 26–47.

Levin, H. 1977. "A Decade of Developments in Improving Education and Training for Low-income Populations." In R. Haveman (ed.), *A Decade of Federal Antipoverty Programs: Achievements, Failures, and Lessons*. New York: Academic Press.

Levitan, S.; W. Johnston; and R. Taggart. 1975. *Still a Dream: The Changing Status of Blacks since 1960*. Cambridge, MA: Harvard University Press.

Levitan, S., and R. Taggart. 1976. *The Promise of Greatness*. Cambridge, MA: Harvard University Press.

Levitan, S., and K. Wurzburg. 1979. *Evaluating Federal Social Programs*. Kalamazoo, MI: Upjohn Institute for Employment Research.

Mallar, C.; S. Kerachsky; C. Thornton; M. Donihue; C. Jones; D. Long; E. Noggoh; and J. Schore. 1980. *Evaluation of the Economic Impact of the Job Corps Program: Second Follow-up Report*. Princeton, NJ: Mathematica Policy Research.

Manpower Demonstration Research Corporation. 1983. *Findings on Youth Employment: Lessons from MDRC Research*. New York: MDRC.

Marshall, R. 1988. "Foreword." In J. Gibbs (ed.), *Young, Black, and Male in America*. Dover, MA: Auburn House.

Moynihan, D. 1965. *The Negro Family: The Case for National Action*. Washington, DC: U.S. Department of Labor, Office of Planning and Research.

Murray, C. 1984. *Losing Ground: American Social Policy, 1950–1980*. New York: Basic Books.

National Center for Health Statistics. 1989. "Firearm Mortality among Children and Youth" (advance data). Hyattsville, MD.: U.S. Department of Health and Human Services.

National Research Council. 1989. *A Common Destiny: Blacks and American Society*. Washington, DC: National Academy Press.

National Urban League. 1988. *Fact Sheet: The Black Teen Male*. Washington, DC: National Urban League Research Department.

Oakes, J. 1985. *Keeping Track: How Schools Structure Inequality*. New Haven, CT: Yale University Press.

O'Brien, R. 1987. "The Interracial Nature of Violent Crimes: A Reexamination." *American Journal of Sociology* 92: 817–35.

Ogbu, J. 1985. "A Cultural Ecology of Competence among Inner-city Blacks." In M. Spencer; G. Brookins; and W. Allen (eds.), *Beginnings: The Social and Affective Development of Black Children*. Hillsdale, NJ: Erlbaum.

Orfield, G. 1988. "Race and the Liberal Agenda: The Loss of the Integrationist Dream, 1965–1974." In M. Weir, A. Orloff, and T. Skocpol (eds.), *The Politics of Social Policy in the United States*. Princeton, NJ: Princeton University Press.

Patterson, J. 1981. *America's Struggle against Poverty, 1900–1980*. Cambridge, MA: Harvard University Press.

Piven, F., and R. Cloward. 1971. *Regulating the Poor: The Functions of Public Welfare*. New York: Pantheon.

Plotnick, R., and F. Skidmore. 1975. *Progress Against Poverty: A Review of the 1964–1974 Decade*. New York: Academic Press.

Rainwater, L. 1966. "Crucible of Identity: The Negro Lower-Class Family." *Daedalus* 95: 172–216.

Rist, R. 1973. *The Urban School: A Factory for Failure*. Cambridge, MA: MIT Press.

Rumberger, R. 1983. "Dropping Out of High School: The Influence of Race, Sex, and Family Background." *American Educational Research Journal* 20: 199–220.

Rustin, B. 1965. "From Protest to Politics: The Future of the Civil Rights Movement." *Commentary* 39: 25–31.

Rutter, M. 1980. *Changing Youth in a Changing Society: Patterns of Adolescent Development and Disorder*. Cambridge, MA: Harvard University Press.

Schorr, L. 1988. *Within Our Reach: Breaking the Cycle of Disadvantage*. New York: Doubleday.

Solomon, B. 1988. "The Impact of Public Policy on the Status of Young Black Males." In J. Gibbs (ed.), *Young, Black, and Male in America*. Dover, MA: Auburn House.

Smith, T.; C. Walker; and R. Baker. 1987. *Youth and the Work-Place: Second-Chance Programs and the Hard-to-Serve*. New York: Wm. T. Grant Foundation.

Steinfels, P. 1979. *The Neoconservatives*. New York: Touchstone Books.

Sum, A., and N. Fogg. 1989. *The Changing Economic Fortunes of Young Black Men in the New American Economy*. Paper prepared for U.S. Congress, House Committee on Children, Youth, and Families, Washington, DC.

Sundquist, J. 1968. *Politics and Policy: The Eisenhower, Kennedy, and Johnson Years*. Washington, DC: Brookings Institution.

Taylor, R. 1977. "Black Workers in 'Post-Industrial' Society." In D. Wilkinson and R. Taylor (eds.), *The Black Male in America*. Chicago: Nelson-Hall.

_____. 1987. "Black Youth in Crisis." *Humboldt Journal of Social Relations* 14: 106–33.

_____. 1990. "Improving the Status of Black Youth: Some Lessons from Recent National Experiments." *Youth and Society* 22: 85–107.

_____. 1991. "Poverty and Adolescent Black Males." In P. Edelman and J. Ladner (eds.), *Adolescence and Poverty: Challenge for the 1990s*. Washington, DC: Center for National Policy.

Taylor, M., and G. Foster. 1986. "Bad Boys and School Suspension: Public Policy Implications for Black Males." *Sociological Inquiry*. 56: 498–506.

Testa, M.; N. Astone; M. Krogh; and K. Neckerman. 1989. "Employment and Marriage among Inner-City Fathers." *The Annals* 501: 79–91.

Thomas, G., and W. Scott. 1979. "Black Youth and the Labor Market: The Unemployment Dilemma." *Youth and Society* 11: 163–89.

U.S. Bureau of the Census. 1990. *Marital Status and Living Arrangements: March 1989*. Current Population Reports, Series P. 20, No. 445. Washington, DC: U.S. Government Printing Office.

U.S. Commission on Civil Rights. 1978. *Social Indicators of Equality for Minorities and Women*. Washington, DC: U.S. Government Printing Office.

U.S. Council of Economic Advisers. 1964. *Economic Report of the President, 1964*. Washington, DC: U.S. Government Printing Office.

U.S. Department of Justice. 1985. *Criminal Victimization in the United States, 1983*. Washington, DC: U.S. Government Printing Office.

U.S. Department of Labor. 1986. *Employment and Earnings*. Bureau of Labor Statistics. Washington, DC: U.S. Government Printing Office.

Wacquant, L., and W. Wilson. 1989. The Cost of Racial and Class Exclusion in the Inner City. *The Annals* 501: 8–25.

Wattenberg, B., and R. Scammon. 1973. "Black Progress and Liberal Rhetoric." *Commentary* 55 (April): 35–44.

Weir, M.; A. Orloff; and T. Skocpol, eds. 1988. *The Politics of Social Policy in the United States*. Princeton, NJ: Princeton University Press.

Werner, E. 1982. *Vulnerable But Invincible: A Longitudinal Study of Resilient Children and Youth*. New York: McGraw-Hill.

Wilson, J. 1977. *Thinking about Crime*. New York: Vintage.

Wilson, W. 1983. Inner-City Dislocations. *Society* 21: 80–86.

_____. 1984. "The Urban Underclass." In W. Dunbar (ed.), *Minority Report*. New York: Pantheon.

_____. 1987. *The Truly Disadvantaged: The Inner City, the Underclass and Public Policy*. Chicago: University of Chicago Press.

Chapter 12: Racial Group Dynamics

Pierce, C. M. 1975. "The Mundane Extreme Environment and Its Effects on Learning." In S. G. Brainard (ed.), *Learning Disabilities: Issues and Recommendations for Research*. Washington, DC: National Institute of Education, Department of Health, Education and Welfare.

Profit, W. E. 1977. "Blacks in Homogeneous and Heterogeneous Groups: The Effects of Racism and the Mundane Extreme Environment." Ph.D. diss., Harvard University.

Chapter 13: Intervention Research Methods and the Empowerment of Black Males

Agar, M. H. 1980. *The Professional Stranger: An Informal Introduction to Ethnography*. New York: Academic Press.

Baer, D. M.; M. M. Wolf; and T. R. Risley. 1968. "Some Current Dimensions of Applied Behavior Analysis." *Journal of Applied Behavior Analysis* 1, 91–97.

Balcazar, F. E.; S. B. Fawcett; and T. Seekins. 1991. "Teaching People with Disabilities to Recruit Help to Attain Personal Goals." *Rehabilitation Psychology* 36(1): 31–42.

Balcazar, F. E.; R. Majors; K. A. Blanchard; A. Paine; Y. Suarez-Balcazar; S. B. Fawcett; R. Murphy; and J. Meyer. 1991. "Teaching Minority High School Students to Recruit Helpers to Attain Personal and Educational Goals." *Journal of Behavioral Education* 1: 445–54.

Balcazar, F. E.; T. Seekins; S. B. Fawcett; and B. L. Hopkins. 1990. "Empowering People with Physical Disabilities Through Advocacy Skills Training." *American Journal of Community Psychology* 18(2): 281–96.

Ball, R. E. 1983. "Family and Friends: A Supportive Network for Low-Income American Black Families." *Journal of Comparative Family Studies* 14(1): 51–65.

Biddle, W. W., and L. J. Biddle. 1968. *Encouraging Community Development*. New York: Holt, Rinehart, and Winston.

Bijou, S. W.; R. F. Peterson; and M. H. Ault. 1968. "A Method to Integrate Descriptive and Experimental Field Studies at the Level of Data and Empirical Concepts." *Journal of Applied Behavior Analysis* 1: 175–91.

Borck, L. E., and S. B. Fawcett. 1982. *Learning Counseling and Problem Solving Skills*. New York: Haworth.

Campbell, D. T., and J. C. Stanley. 1966. *Experimental and Quasi-Experimental Designs for Research*. Boston: Houghton Mifflin.

Cook, T., and D. T. Campbell. 1979. *Quasi-Experimentation: Design and Analysis Issues for Field Settings*. Chicago: Rand McNally.

Drew, C. J., and M. L. Hardman. 1985. *Designing and Conducting Behavioral Research*. New York: Pergamon.

Fawcett, S. B. 1988. "Role-Playing Assessment Instruments." In M. Hersen and A. S. Bellack (eds.), *Dictionary of Behavioral Assessment Instruments*. New York: Pergamon.

_____. 1989. "Some Emerging Standards for Community Research and Action." Invited address to the working conference on "Researching Community Psychology: Integrating Theories and Methodologies," De Paul University, Chicago, IL, Sept.

Fawcett, S. B., and R. K. Fletcher. 1977. "Community Applications of Instructional Technology: Teaching Writers of Instructional Packages." *Journal of Applied Behavior Analysis* 10: 739–46.

Fawcett, S. B.; R. M. Mathews; and R. K. Fletcher. 1980. "Some Promising Dimensions for Behavioral Community Psychology." *Journal of Applied Behavior Analysis* 3: 319–42.

Fawcett, S. B.; R. M. Mathews; R. K. Fletcher; R. Morrow; and R. F. Stokes. 1976. "Personalized Instruction in the Community: Teaching Helping Skills to Low-Income Neighborhood Residents." *Journal of Personalized Instruction* 1, 86–90.

Fawcett, S. B.; L. K. Miller; and C. J. Braukmann. 1977. An Evaluation of a Training Package for Community Canvassing Behaviors." *Journal of Applied Behavior Analysis* 10: 504.

Fawcett, S. B.; T. Seekins; P. W. Whang; C. Muiu; and Y. Suarez de Balcazar. 1982. "Involving Consumers in Decision Making." *Social Policy* 13: 36–41.

_____. 1984. "Creating and Using Social Technologies for Community Empowerment." In J. Rappaport, C. Swift, and R. Hess (eds.), "Studies in Empowerment: Steps toward Understanding and Action." *Prevention in Human Services* 3(2/3): 145–73.

Fawcett, S. B.; Y. Suarez-Balcazar; F. Balcazar; G. White; A. Paine; M. G. Embree; and K. A. Blanchard. In press. "Intervention Research Process: Methods and Issues." In J. Rothman, and E. J. Thomas (eds.), *Intervention Research: Creating Effective Methods for Professional Practice.* Chicago: University of Chicago Press.

Freire, P. 1973. *Education for Critical Consciousness.* New York: Seabury Press.

Gary, L. E. 1981. *Black Men.* Newbury Park, PA: Sage.

Gibbs, J. T., ed. 1988. *Young, Black, and Male in America.* Dover, MA: Auburn House.

Hall, L. K. 1981. "Support Systems and Coping Patterns." In L. E. Gary (ed.), *Black Men.* Newbury Park, PA: Sage.

Hawkins, R. P., and R. W. Dobes. 1975. "Behavioral Definitions in Applied Behavior Analysis: Explicit or Implicit." In B. C. Etzel, J. M. LeBlanc, and D. M. Baer (eds.), *New Developments in Behavioral Research: Theory, Methods, and Applications: In Honor of Sidney Bijou.* Hillsdale, NJ: Lawrence Erlbaum.

Hersen, M., and A. S. Bellack. 1981. *Behavioral Assessment: A Practical Handbook.* New York: Pergamon.

Hirsch, B. J., and B. D. Rapkin. 1987. "The Transition to Junior High School: A Longitudinal Study of Self-Esteem, Psychological Symptomatology, School Life, and Social Support." *Child Development* 58: 1235–43.

Hollon, S. D., and K. M. Bemis. 1981. "Self-Report and the Assessment of Cognitive Functions." In M. Hersen and A. S. Bellack (eds.), *Behavioral Assessment: A Practical Handbook.* New York: Pergamon.

Kazdin, A. E. 1981. "Behavioral Observations." In M. Hersen and A. S. Bellack (eds.), *Behavioral Assessment: A Practical Handbook.* New York: Pergamon.

Kelly, J. G. 1986. An Ecological Paradigm: Defining Mental Health Consultation as a Preventive Service." *Prevention in Human Services* 4: 1–36.

Malson, M. 1982. "The Social-Support System of Black Families." *Marriage and Family Review* 5(4): 37–57.

Mays, V. M. 1985. "Black Women and Stress: Utilization of Self-Help Groups for Stress Reduction." *Women and Therapy* 4(4): 67–79.

Morganstern, K. P., and H. E. Tevlin. 1981. "Behavioral Interviewing." In M. Hersen and A. S. Bellack (eds.), *Behavioral Assessment: A Practical Handbook.* New York: Pergamon.

Nelson, R. O., and S. C. Hayes. 1981. "Nature of Behavioral Assessment." In M. Hersen and A. S. Bellack (eds.), *Behavioral Assessment: A Practical Handbook.* New York: Pergamon.

Obleton, N. B. 1984. "Career Counseling Black Women in a Predominantly White Co-Educational University." *Personnel and Guidance Journal* 62(6): 365–68.

Paine, A. L.; Y. Suarez-Balcazar; and S. B. Fawcett. 1990. "Supportive Transactions: Their Measurement and Enhancement in Two Mutual-Aid Groups." Manuscript submitted for publication.

Parsons, R. J. 1988. "Empowerment for Role Alternatives for Low Income Minority Girls: A Group Work Approach." *Social Work with Groups* 11(4): 27–45.

Rappaport, J. 1984. "Studies in Empowerment: Introduction to the Issue." In J. Rappaport, C. Swift, and R. Hess (eds.), "Studies in Empowerment: Steps toward Understanding and Action." *Prevention in Human Services* 3(2/3): 145–73.

Rothman, J., and E. J. Thomas. In press. *Intervention Research: Creating Effective Methods for Professional Practice*. Chicago: University of Chicago Press.

Ryan, W. 1971. *Blaming the Victim*. New York: Random House.

Seekins, T., and S. B. Fawcett. 1984. "Planned Diffusion of Social Technologies for Community Groups." In S. C. Paine, G. T. Bellamy, and E. Wilcox (eds.), *Human Services That Work: From Innovation to Standard Practice*. Baltimore, MD: Paul H. Brooks.

Serrano-Garcia, I. 1984. "The Illusion of Empowerment: Community Development within a Colonial Context." In J. Rappaport, C. Swift, and R. Hess (eds.), "Studies in Empowerment: Steps toward Understanding and Action." *Prevention in Human Services* 3(2/3): 145–73.

Shure, M. B., and G. Spivack. 1982. "Interpersonal Problem-Solving in Young Children: A Cognitive Approach to Prevention." *American Journal of Community Psychology* 10(3): 341–56.

Suarez-Balcazar, Y.; S. B. Fawcett; and F. E. Balcazar. 1988. "Effects of Environmental Design and Police Enforcement on Violation of a Handicapped Parking Ordinance." *Journal of Applied Behavior Analysis* 21: 291–98.

Tripi, F. J. 1984. "Client Control in Organizational Settings." *Journal of Applied Behavioral Science* 20: 39–47.

Wallerstein, N., and E. Berstein. 1988. "Empowerment Education: Freire's Ideas Adapted to Health Education." *Health Education Quarterly* 15(4): 379–94.

Wolf, M. M. 1978. "Social Validity: The Case for Subjective Measurement or How Applied Behavior Analysis Is Finding Its Heart." *Journal of Applied Behavior Analysis* 11: 203–14.

Chapter 14: Empowerment Opportunities for Black Adolescent Fathers

Amerian Heritage Dictionary. 1976. Boston, MA: Houghton Mifflin. S. v. "empower."

Blumstein, A. 1982. "On the Racial Disproportion of United States Prison Populations." *Journal of Criminal Law and Criminology* 73: 1259–81.

Chilman, C. 1983. "Adolescent Sexuality in a Changing American Society: Social and Psychological Perspectives for the Human Services Professions. New York: Wiley.

_____. 1989. "Some Major Issues Regarding Adolescent Sexuality and Childbearing in the United States." *Journal of Social Work and Human Sexuality* 8: 3–26.

Ekstrom, R.; M. Goertz; J. Pollack; and D. Rock. 1986. "Who Drops Out of High School and Why: Findings from a National Study." *Teachers College Record* 87: 357–62.

Elster, A. B., and M. E. Lamb. 1986. "Adolescent Fathers: The Understudied Side of Adolescent Pregnancy." In J. B. Alexander and B. A. Hamburg (eds.), *School-Age Pregnancy and Parenthood*. New York: Aldine.

Farley, R. 1980. "Homicide Trends in the United States." *Demography*. 17: 177–88.

Freeman, E. M. 1988. "Teenage Fathers and the Problem of Teenage Pregnancy." *Social Work in Education* 11: 36–52.

_____. 1989. "Adolescent Fathers in Urban Communities: Exploring their Needs and Role in Preventing Pregnancy." *Journal of Social Work and Human Sexuality* 8: 113–32.

Freeman, E. M., R. McRoy, and S. Logan. 1987. "Teenage Drinking Problems: Survey of Mental Health Agencies." *Arete* 12: 21–23.

Germain, C., and A. Gitterman. 1984. "Education for Practice: Teaching about the Environment." New York: Columbia University School of Social Work. Mimeo.

Hayes, C., ed. 1987. "Risking the Future: Adolescent Sexuality, Pregnancy and Childbearing." Washington, DC: National Academy Press.

Kunjufu, J. 1985. *Countering the Conspiracy to Destroy Black Boys*. Vol. 1. Chicago: African American Images.

Marsiglio, W. 1987. "Adolescent Fathers in the United States: Their Initial Living Arrangements, Marital Experience and Educational Outcomes." *Family Planning Perspectives* 19: 240–51.

Maslow, A. A. 1967. Self-Actualization and Beyond." In J. F. Bugental (ed.), *Challenges of Humanistic Psychology*. New York: McGraw-Hill.

Simon, B. 1990. "Women's Empowerment: Past and Future." Paper presented at the conference "Building on Women's Strengths: A Social Work Agenda for the 21st Century." University of Kansas School of Social Welfare, Lawrence.

Spradley, J. 1979. *The Ethnographic Interview*. New York: Holt, Rinehart and Winston.

Towle, C. 1965. *Common Human Needs*. New York: National Association of Social Workers.

Wilson, W., and K. Neckerman. 1986. "Poverty and Family Structure." In S. Danziger and D. Weingerg (eds.), *Fighting Poverty*. Cambridge, MA: Harvard University Press.

Chapter 15: The Psychosocial Development and Coping of Black Male Adolescents

Abatso, Y. 1985. "The Coping Personality: A Study of Black Community College Students. In M. Perkins, G. Brookins, and W. Allen (eds.), *Beginnings: The Social and Affective Development of Black Children*. Hillsdale, NJ: Lawrence Erlbaum.

Allen, W. R. 1978. "Race, Family Setting, and Adolescent Achievement Orientation." *Journal of Negro Education* 47: 230–43.

_____. 1985. "Race, Income, and Family Dynamics: A Study of Adolescent Male Socialization Processes and Outcomes." In M. B. Spencer, G. K. Brookins, and W. R. Allen (eds.), *Beginnings: The Social and Affective Development of Black Children*. Hillsdale, NJ: Lawrence Erlbaum.

American Psychiatric Association. 1987. *Diagnostic and Statistical Manual of Mental Disorders*. 3d ed., rev. Washington, DC: APA.

Antonovsky, A. 1979. *Health, Stress and Coping*. San Francisco, CA: Jossey-Bass.

Arbeiter, S. 1986. "Minority Enrollment in Higher Education Institutions: A Chronological View." *Research and Development Update*. New York: College Board.

Barriers and Opportunities for America's Young Black Men: Fact Sheet. 1989. Washington, DC: Select Committee on Children, Youth, and Families, U.S. House of Representatives.

Barringer, F. 1992. "New Census Data Reveal Redistribution of Poverty." *New York Times*, May 29, p. A14.

Billingsley, A. 1968. *Black Families in White America*. Englewood Cliffs, NJ: Prentice-Hall.

Blos, R. 1983. "The Contribution of Psychoanalysis to the Psychotherapy of Adolescents." In A. J. Solnit, R. S. Eissler, and P. B. Neubauer (eds.), *The Psychoanalytic Study of the Child*. Vol. 38. New Haven, CT: Yale University Press.

Boyd-Franklin, N. 1989. *Black Families in Therapy: A Multisystems Approach*. New York: Guilford Press.

Boykin, A. W. 1986. "The Triple Quandry and the Schooling of Afro-American Children." In U. Neisser (ed.), *The School Achievement of Minority Children: New Perspectives*. Hillsdale, NJ: Lawrence Erlbaum.

Boykin, A. W., and Toms, F. D. 1985. "Black Child Socialization." In H. McAdoo and J. McAdoo (eds.), *Black Children: Social, Educational, and Parental Environments*. Beverly Hills, CA: Sage.

Cazenave, N. 1984. "Race, Socioeconomic Status, and Age: The Context of American Masculinity." *Sex Roles* 11 (7-8): 639–56.

Clark, R. M. 1983. *Family Life and School Achievement: Why Poor Black Children Succeed or Fail.* Chicago: University of Chicago Press.

Cross, W. 1978. "The Thomas and Cross Models of Psychological Nigrescence: A Review." *Journal of Black Psychology* 5(1): 13–31.

Cross, W. E., Jr. 1985. "Black Identity: Rediscovering the Distinction Between Personal Identity and Reference Group Orientation." In M. B. Spencer, G. K. Brookins, and W. R. Allen (eds.), *Beginnings: The Social and Affective Development of Black Children.* Hillsdale, NJ: Lawrence Erlbaum.

Daniels, S. 1986. "Relationship of Employment Status to Mental Health and Family Variables in Black Men from Single-Parent Families." *Journal of Applied Psychology* 71(3): 386–91.

Dohrenwend, B., and B. Dohrenwend, eds. 1974. *Stressful Life Events: Their Nature and Effects.* New York: Wiley.

Edelman, M. W. 1985. "The Sea Is So Wide and My Boat Is So Small: Problems Facing Black Children Today." In H. McAdoo and J. McAdoo (eds.), *Black Children: Social, Educational, and Parental Environments.* Beverly Hills, CA: Sage.

Erikson, E. H. 1963. *Childhood and Society.* 3rd ed. New York: Norton.

Fordham, S. 1988. "Racelessness as a Factor in Black Students' School Success: Pragmatic Strategy or Pyrrhic Victory." *Harvard Educational Review* 58: 54–84.

Garmezy, N. 1987. "Stress, Competence, and Development: Continuities in the Study of Schizophrenic Adults, Children Vulnerable to Psychopathology, and the Search for Stress-Resistant Children." *American Journal of Orthopsychiatry* 57(2): 159–74.

Gary, L. E. 1981. "Health Status." In L. E. Gary (ed.), *Black Men.* Beverly Hills, CA: Sage.

Gibbs, J. T. 1984. "Black Adolescents and Youth: An Endangered Species." *American Journal of Orthopsychiatry* 54: 6–22.

Giovacchini, P. 1977. "Psychoanalytic Perspectives on Adolescence, Psychic Development, and Narcissism." In S. Feinstein and P. Giovachinni (eds.), *Adolescent Psychiatry.* Vol. 5, *Developmental and Clinical Studies.* New York: Jason Aronson.

Goldston, S. 1977. "Defining Primary Prevention." In G. Albee and J. Joffe (eds.), *Primary Prevention of Psychopathology.* Vol. 1, *The Issues.* Hanover, NH: University Press of New England.

Hare, B. 1985. "Re-Examining the Achievement of Central Tendency: Sex Differences within Race and Race Differences within Sex." In H. McAdoo and J. McAdoo (eds.), *Black Children: Social, Educational and Parental Environments.* Beverly Hills, CA: Sage.

_____. 1988. *Black Youth at Risk: The State of Black America, 1988.* Washington, DC: National Urban League.

Hare, B. R., and Castenell, L. A., Jr. 1985. "No Place to Run, No Place to Hide; Comparative Status and Future Prospects of Black Boys." In M. B. Spencer, G. K. Brookins, and W. R. Allen (eds.), *Beginnings: The Social and Affective Development of Black Children.* Hillsdale, NJ: Lawrence Erlbaum.

Hill, R. 1972. *The Strengths of Black Families.* New York: Emerson-Hall.

Holliday, B. G. 1985. "Towards a Model of Teacher-Child Transactional Processes Affecting Black Children's Academic Achievement." In M. B. Spencer, B. K. Brookins, and W. R. Allen (eds.), *Beginnings: The Social and Affective Development of Black Children.* Hillsdale, NJ: Lawrence Erlbaum.

Jaynes, G. D., and R. Williams, Jr. 1989. *A Common Destiny: Blacks and American Society.* Washington, DC: National Academy Press.

Jenkins, A. H. 1982. *The Psychology of the Afro American: A Humanistic Approach.* New York: Pergamon.

Jones, A. C. 1985. "Psychological Functioning in Black Americans: A Conceptual Guide for Use in Psychotherapy." *Psychotherapy* 22(25): 363–69.

Katz, I.; O. J. Cole; and R. M. Baron. 1976. "Self-Evaluation, Social Reinforcement, and Academic Achievement in Black and White School Children." *Child Development* 47: 368–74.

Krause, N. 1985. "Interracial Contact in Schools and Black Children's Self-Esteem." In H. McAdoo and J. McAdoo (eds.), *Black Children: Social, Environmental, and Parental Environments*. Beverly Hills, CA: Sage.

Laosa, L. M. 1984. "Social Competence in Childhood: Toward a Developmental, Socioculturally Relativistic Paradigm." In J. M. Joffe, G. W. Albee, and L. D. Kelly (eds.), *Readings in Primary Prevention of Psychopathology: Basic Concepts*. Hanover, NH: University Press of New England.

Lewis, D.; D. Balla; and S. Shanok. 1979. "Some Evidence of Race Bias in the Diagnosis and Treatment of the Juvenile Offender." *American Journal of Orthopsychiatry* 49: 53–61.

Lewis, J. M., and L. G. Looney. 1983. *The Long Struggle: Well-Functioning Working-Class Black Families*. New York: Brunner/Mazel.

Lewis, O. 1966. *La Vida*. New York: Random House.

McAdoo, H. 1985. "Racial Attitude and Self-Concept of Young Black Children Over Time." In H. McAdoo and J. McAdoo (eds.), *Black Children: Social, Educational, and Parental Environments*. Beverly Hills, CA: Sage.

McAdoo, J. 1985. "Modification of Racial Attitudes and Preferences in Young Black Children." In H. McAdoo and J. McAdoo (eds.), *Black Children: Social, Educational, and Parental Environments*. Beverly Hills, CA: Sage.

McGhee, J. 1984. *"Running the Gauntlet: Black Men in America."* Washington, DC: National Urban League.

Moulton, R. W., and L. H. Stewart. 1971. "Parents as Models for Mobile and Low-Mobile Black Males." *Vocational Guidance Quarterly* 19(4): 247–53.

Moynihan, D. P. 1965. *The Negro Family: The Case for National Action*. Washington, DC: U.S. Department of Labor.

Mussen, P. H. 1983. "Socialization in the Context of the Family: Parent-Child Interactions." In E. E. Maccoby and J. A. Martin (eds.), *A Handbook of Child Psychology*. Vol. 4, *Socializations, Personality, and Social Development*, edited by E. M. Hetherington. New York: Wiley.

National Center for Education Statistics. 1989. *Digest of Education Statistics 1989*. 25th ed. (NCES 89-643), table 92. Washington, DC: U.S. Department of Education, Office of Educational Research and Improvement.

Nobles, W. 1978. "Toward an Empirical and Theoretical Framework for Defining Black Families." *Journal of Marriage and the Family* 40: 679–88.

_____. 1980. "African Philosophy: Foundations for Black Psychology." In R. Jones (ed.), *Black Psychology*. 2nd ed. New York: Harper and Row.

Ogbu, J. U. 1985. "A Cultural Ecology of Competence among Inner-City Blacks." In M. B. Spencer, G. K. Brookins, and W. R. Allen (eds.), *Beginnings: The Social and Affective Development of Black Children*. Hillsdale, NJ: Lawrence Erlbaum.

_____. 1986. "The Consequences of the American Caste System." In U. Neisser (ed.), *School Achievement in Minority Children*. Hillsdale, NJ: Lawrence Erlbaum.

Parham, T. A., and J. Helms. 1985. "Attitudes of Racial Identity and Self-Esteem of Black Students: An Exploratory Investigation." *Journal of College Student Personnel* (March): 143–47.

Paster, V. 1985. "Adapting Psychotherapy for the Depressed, Unacculturated, Acting-Out, Black Male Adolescent." *Psychotherapy* 22(25): 408–17.

Pear, R. 1992. "Ranks of the Poor Swell, Hitting 35.7 Million, the Most since '64. *New York Times*, Sept. 5, pp. 1, A14.

Pearson, J.; A. Hunter; M. Ensminger; and S. Kellum. 1990. "Black Grandmothers in Multigenerational Households: Diversity in Family Structure and Parenting Involvement in the Woodlawn Community." *Child Development* 161(2): 434–42.

Persons, G. 1987. "Blacks in State and Local Government: Progress and Constraints." In J. Dewart (ed.), *State of Black America 1987*. Washington, DC: National Urban League.

Rutter, M. 1987. "Psychosocial Resilience and Protective Mechanisms." *American Journal of Orthopsychiatry* 57(3): 316–31.

Scanzoni, J. 1985. "Black Parental Roles and Expectations of Children's Occupational and Educational Success: Theoretical Implications." In H. McAdoo and J. McAdoo (eds.), *Black Children: Social, Educational, and Parental Environments.* Beverly Hills, CA: Sage.

Schab, F. 1982. "Early Adolescence in the South: Attitudes Regarding the Home and Religion." *Adolescence* 17(67): 605–12.

Spencer, M. B. 1985. "Cultural Cognition and Social Cognition as Identity Correlates of Black Children's Personal-Social Development." In M. B. Spencer, G. K. Brookins, and W. R. Allen (eds.), *Beginnings: The Social and Affective Development of Black Children.* Hillsdale, NJ: Lawrence Erlbaum.

Sudarkasa, N. 1988. "Interpreting the African Heritage in African-American Family Organizations. In H. P. McAdoo (ed.), *Black Families.* Newbury Park, CA: Sage.

Swinton, D. H. 1988. "Economic Status of Blacks, 1987." In J. Dewart (ed.), *The State of Black America 1988.* Washington, DC: National Urban League.

Taylor, R. L. 1989. "Black Youth, Role Models, and Social Construction of Identity." In R. L. Jones (ed.), *Black Adolescents.* Berkeley, CA: Cobb and Henry.

Thomas, V. G., and L. C. Shields. 1987. "Gender Influencers on Work Values of Black Adolescents." *Adolescence* 22(85): 37–43.

Tolson, T., and M. Wilson. 1990. "The Impact of Two- and Three-Generational Black Family Structure on Perceived Family Climate." *Child Development* 61(2): 416–28.

Toolan, J. 1974. "Masked Depression in Children and Adolescents." In S. Lesse (ed.), *Masked Depression.* New York: Jason Aronson.

U.S. Department of Labor, Bureau of Labor Statistics. 1987. *Employment and Earnings.* Jan., Table 21.

Ward, S., and J. Braun. 1972. "Self-Esteem and Racial Preference in Black Children." *American Journal of Orthopsychiatry* 42(4): 64–74.

White, R. W. 1984. "Competence as an Aspect of Personal Growth." In J. M. Joffe, G. W. Albee, and L. D. Kelly (eds.), *Readings in Primary Prevention of Psychopathology: Basic Concepts.* Hanover, NH: University Press of New England.

Williams, L. 1990. "Black Americans Sense a New Patriotism." *New York Times,* July 4, pp. 1, 12.

Chapter 16: The Cool Pose: An Africentric Analysis

Akbar, N. 1976. *Chains and Images of Psychological Slavery.* Jersey City, NJ: New Mind Productions.

_____. 1981. "Mental Disorders among African-Americans." *Black Bulletin* 7(2): 18–25.

Azibo, D. A. 1983a. "Menticide, Misorientation, and the Destruction of Black Consciousness via Popular Culture: Towards a Learning Theory Analysis." In R. Hayles (ed.), *Abstracts: The Sixteenth Annual Convention of the Association of Black Psychologists,* pp. 6–7. (Robert Hayles, Human Resources Management, Defense Systems Management College, Fort Belvoir, VA 22060.)

_____. 1983b. "Theological Misorientation as an African Personality Disorder. In R. Hayles (ed.), *Abstracts: The Sixteenth Annual Convention of the Association of Black Psychologists,* p. 8.

_____. 1989. "African-Centered Theses on Mental Health and a Nosology of Black/African Personality Disorders." *Journal of Black Psychology* 15(2): 173–214.

Baldwin, J. A. 1980a. "An Africentric Theory of Black Personality." *Proceedings of the 14th Annual Convention of the Association of Black Psychologists.* Washington, DC: Association of Black Psychologists.

_____. 1980b. "The Psychology of Oppression." In M. Asante and A. Vandi (eds.), *Contemporary Black Thought.* Beverly Hills, CA: Sage.

_____. 1981. "Notes on an Africentric Theory of Black Personality." *Western Journal of Black Studies* 5(3): 172–79.

_____. 1984. African Self-Consciousness and the Mental Health of African-Americans. *Journal of Black Studies* 15(2): 177–94.

_____. 1985. "Psychological Aspects of European Cosmology in American Society." *Western Journal of Black Studies* 9: 177–94.

_____. 1989. "The Role of Black Psychologists in Black Liberation." *Journal of Black Psychology* 16: 67–76.

Ball, J. 1989. "Is the Black Male an Endangered Species? *Boston Globe,* Oct. 20, pp. 1B–4B.

Baumeister, R. F. 1982. "A Self-Presentation View of Social Phenomena." *Psychological Bulletin* 91: 3–26.

Brannon, R. 1985. "A Scale for Measuring Attitudes about Masculinity." In A. Sargent (ed.), *Beyond Sex Roles.* St. Paul, MN: West.

Brod, H. 1987. *The Making of Masculinities.* Boston: Allen and Unwin.

Carrigan, T.; B. Connell; and J. Lee. 1985. "Toward a New Sociology of Masculinity. *In Theory and Society* 5: 14.

Centers for Disease Control. 1983. "Fire and Burn Associated Deaths—Georgia, 1979–1981." *Morbidity and Mortality Weekly Report* 32 (Dec. 9): 625–34.

Comer, J. P. 1969. "White Racism: Its Roots, Form and Function. *American Journal of Psychiatry* 126: 802–6.

Connel, B. 1987. *Gender and Power.* Stanford, CA: Stanford Univeristy Press.

David, D., and R. Brannon. 1976. *The Forty-Nine Percent Majority.* Reading, MA: Addison-Wesley.

Department of Health and Human Services (DHHS). 1985. *Report of the Secretary's Task Force on Black and Minority Health.* Vol. 1. Washington, DC: DHHS.

Doyle, J. A. 1989. *The Male Experience,* 2nd ed. Dubuque, IA: Wm. C. Brown.

Ellison, R. 1947. *Invisible Man.* New York: Vintage Books.

Farrel, W. 1975. *The Liberated Man.* New York: Random House.

Feigen-Fasteau, M. 1975. *The Male Machine.* New York: McGraw-Hill.

Gerson, J., and K. Peiss. 1985. "Boundaries, Negotiation, Consciousness: Reconceptualizing Gender Relations." *Social Problems* 32.

Gibbs, J. T. 1984. "Black Adolescents and Youth: An Endangered Species." *American Journal of Orthopsychiatry* 54: 6–21.

_____. 1985. "Can We Continue to Be Color-Bound and Class-Bound?" *Counseling Psychologist* 13: 426–35.

_____. 1988. "Young Black Males in America: Endangered, Embittered, and Embattled." In J. T. Gibbs (ed.), *Young, Black, and Male in America: An Endangered Species.* Dover, MA: Auburn House.

Goffman, E. 1959. *The Presentation of Self in Everyday Life.* Garden City, NY: Doubleday.

Hare, N., and J. Hare. 1985. *Bringing the Black Boy to Manhood: The Passage.* San Francisco, CA: The Black Think Tank.

Hern, J. 1987. *The Gender of Oppression.* New York: St. Martin's.

Hilliard, A. G., III. 1985. "A Framework for Focused Counseling on the African-American Man." *Journal of Non-White Concerns,* pp. 72–78.

Janzen, J. 1989. Personal communication, May.

Jones, E. E., and T. S. Pittman. 1982. "Toward a General Theory of Strategic Self-Preservation." In J. Suls (ed.), *Psychological Perspectives on the Self.* Vol. 1. Hillsdale, NJ: Erlbaum.

Karenga, R. 1977. *Kwanzza: Origins, Concepts, Practice.* Los Angeles, CA: Kawaida.

Kimmel, M. 1987. *Changing Men: New Directions in Research on Men and Masculinity.* Newbury Park, CA: Sage.

Kimmel, M. S., and M. A. Messner. 1989. "Men as 'Gendered Beings.' " In M. S. Kimmel and M. A. Messner (eds.), *Men's Lives.* New York: Macmillan.

Langley, M. R. 1990. "The Effects of Culture, Gender, and Race on the Potential Psychological Treatment of Men: A Critical Review." Florida State University, Tallahassee, FL.

_____. 1992. Effects of Cultural/Racial Identity, Cultural Commitment and Counseling Approach on African-American Males' Perceptions of Therapist Credibility and Utility. Ph.D. diss., Florida State University, Tallahassee, FL.

Larabee, M. 1986. "Helping Reluctant Black Males: An Affirmation Approach." *Journal of Multicultural Counseling and Development* 14: 25–37.

Malcolm X and A. Haley. 1965. *The Autobiography of Malcolm X*. New York: Grove Press.

Majors, R. 1983. "Cool Pose: A New Hypothesis in Understanding Anti-Social Behavior in Lower Socioeconomic Status Black Males." University of Illinois, Urbana-Champaign.

_____. 1986. "Cool Pose: The Proud Signature of Black Survival." *Changing Men: Issues in Gender, Sex, and Politics* 17: 5–6.

_____. 1987. "Cool Pose: A New Approach toward a Systematic Understanding and Studying of Black Male Behavior." University of Illinois, Urbana, IL.

_____. 1989. "Cool Pose: The Proud Signature of Black Survival." In M. Messner and M. Kimmel (eds.), *Men's Lives*. New York: Macmillan.

_____. 1990. "Cool Pose: A Symbolic Mechanism for Masculine Role Enactment and Coping among Black Males." Paper presented at the American Orthopsychiatric Association meeting.

_____. 1991. "Nonverbal Behaviors and Communication Styles among African-Americans." *Black Psychology*. 3rd ed. Berkeley, CA: Cobb and Henry.

Majors, R., and J. M. Billson. 1992. *Cool Pose: The Dilemmas of Black Manhood in America*. New York: Lexington.

Mcleod, M. 1986. "Psychologist Examines Black Males' Cool Mystique." *Orlando Sentinel*, Sept. 18.

Messinger, S. L.; H. Sampson; and R. D. Towne. 1962. "Life as Theater: Some Notes on the Dramaturgic Approach to Social Reality." *Sociometry* 25(1): 98–110.

Messner, M. 1987. "Masculinity, Ethnicity, and the Athletic Career: A Comparative Analysis of the Motivation and Experience of White Men and Men of Color." Paper presented at the meeting of the American Sociological Association.

_____. 1989. "Masculinities and Athletic Careers." *Gender and Society* 3: 71–86.

Morris, E. 1989. "Black Men Battle for Survival." *Tallahassee Democrat*, Dec. 31, Sec. C, pp. 1C–2C.

Moses, S. 1989. "Economic Progress of Blacks Has Stalled." *APA Monitor*, p. 18.

Myers, L. J. 1988. *Understanding an Afrocentric Worldview: Introduction to an Optimal Psychology*. Dubuque, IA: Kendell/Hunt.

Nobles, W. 1974. "African Root and American Fruit: The Black Family." *Journal of Social and Behavioral Sciences* 20: 52–64.

Oliver, W. 1984. "Black Males and the Tough Guy Image: A Dysfunctional Compensatory Adaptation. *Western Journal of Black Studies* 8: 201–2.

Page, C. 1986. "Here's Some Hot Dope on Being Cool." *Chicago Tribune*, Nov. 30.

Parham, T. A., and R. J. McDavis. 1987. "Black Men, an Endangered Species: Who's Really Pulling the Trigger? *Journal of Counseling and Development* 66: 24–27.

Peterman, A. F. 1986. "The Cool Look." *St. Petersburg Times*, Jan. 4, p. 1.

Pierce, C. 1970. "Offense Mechanisms." In F. Barbour (ed.), *The Black 70's*. Boston: Porter Sargent.

Pinderhughes, C. 1969. "The Origin of Racism." *International Journal of Psychiatry* 8: 929–33.

Pleck, E. H., and J. H. Pleck. 1980. *The American Man*. Englewood Cliffs, NJ: Prentice-Hall.

Pleck, J. H. 1981. *The Myth of Masculinity*. Cambridge, MA: MIT Press.

_____. 1983. "The Theory of Male Sex Role Identity: Its Rise and Fall, 1936–Present." In M. Lewin (ed.), *In the Shadow of the Past: Psychology Portrays the Sexes*. New York: Columbia University Press.

_____. 1985. "American Fatherhood: A Historical Perspective." *American Behavioral Scientist* 29(1): 7–13.

_____. 1987. "American Fathering in Historical Perspective." In M. S. Kimmel (ed.)., *Changing Men: New Directions in Research on Men and Masculinity.* Newbury, CA: Sage.

_____. 1989. "Men's Power with Women, Other Men, and Society: A Men's Movement Analysis. In M. S. Kimmel and M. A. Messner (eds.), *Men's Lives.* New York: Macmillan.

_____. 1989. "Prisoners of Manliness." M. S. Kimmel and M. A. Messner (eds.), *Men's Lives.* New York: Macmillan.

Pleck, J. H., and J. Sawyer. 1974. *Men and Masculinity.* Englewood Cliffs, NJ: Prentice-Hall.

Ridley, C. 1984. "Clinical Treatment of the Non-Disclosing Black Clients: A Therapeutic Paradox." *American Psychologist* 39: 1234–44.

Sariola, S., and P. Naukkarinen. 1989. "Cool Pose—Rokote Alkoholismia Vastaan?" *Tiimi-a-Klin Ikkassaatio* (Finland), pp. 22–23.

Schlenker, B. R. 1980. *Impression Management: The Self-Concept, Social Identity and Interpersonal Relations.* Monterey, CA: Brooks/Cole.

Schlenker, B. R., and M. R. Leary. 1982. "Social Anxiety and Self-Presentation: A Conceptualization and Model. *Psychological Bulletin* 92: 641–69.

Shiffman, M. 1987. "The Men's Movement: An Exploratory Empirical Investigation." In M. S. Kimmel (ed.), *Changing Men: New Directions in Research on Men and Masculinity.* Newbury, CA: Sage.

Staples, R. 1989. "Masculinity and Race." In M. S. Kimmel and M. A. Messner (eds.), *Men's Lives.* New York: Macmillan.

Tedeschi, J. T., and N. Norman. 1985. "Social Power, Self-Presentation, and the Self." In B. R. Schlenker (ed.), *Self and Identity.* New York: McGraw-Hill.

Tedeschi, J. T., and M. Reiss. 1981. "Identities, the Phenomenal Self, and Laboratory Research." In J. T. Tedeschi (ed.), *Impression Management Theory and Social Psychological Research.* New York: Academic Press.

Thompson, Jr., E. H., and J. H. Pleck. 1987. "Reformulating the Male Role: The Structure of Male Role Norms." In M. S. Kimmel (ed.), *Changing Men: New Directions in Research on Men and Masculinity.* Newbury, CA: Sage.

Tunsil, L. 1987. "Black Men Suffer from Cool." *Tallahassee Flambeau,* pp. 4 and 9.

Wallace, M. 1987. *Black Macho and the Myth of the Super Woman.* New York: Dial.

Weary, G., and R. M. Arkin. 1981. "Attributional Self-Presentation." In J. H. Harvey, W. Ickes, and R. F. Kidd (eds.), *New Directions in Attribution Research,* Vol. 2. Hillsdale, NJ: Erlbaum.

Wilkinson, D., and R. Taylor. 1977. *The Black Male in America: Perspectives on His Status in Contemporary Society.* Chicago: Nelson-Hall.

Wolfe, B. 1950. "Ecstatic in Blackface: The Negro as a Song and Dance Man." *Modern Review* 111: 196–208.

Wright, R. 1945. *Black Boy.* New York: Signet.

Chapter 17: Cool Pose: A Symbolic Mechanism

Abrahams, R. 1970. *Positively Black.* Englewood Cliffs, NJ: Prentice-Hall.

Balcazar, F. E.; R. G. Majors; K. A. Blanchard; S. B. Fawcett; A. Paine; Y. Suarez; R. Murphy; and J. Meyer. 1991. "Promoting Access to Opportunity: Teaching Minority High School Students to Recruit Help in Attaining Personal Goals." *Journal of Behavioral Education* 1(4): 445–54.

Beck, R. 1969. *Pimp: The Story of My Life.* Los Angeles, CA: Holloway House.

Boykin, W. 1983. "The Academic Performance of Afro-American Children." In J. T. Spence (ed.), *Achievement and Achievement Motives.* San Francisco, CA: Freeman.

Brown, C. 1965. *Manchild in the Promised Land*. New York: Macmillan.

Cazenave, G., and G. H. Leon. 1987. "Men's Work and Family Roles and Characteristics: Race, Gender, and Class Perceptions of College Students." In M. S. Kimmel (ed.), *Changing Men: Directions in Research on Men and Masculinity*. Newbury Park, CA: Sage.

Cazenave, N. 1979. "Middle-Income Black Fathers: An Analysis of the Provider Role." *Family Co-ordinator* 28: 583–93.

_____. 1981. "Black Men in America: The Quest for Manhood." In H. McAdoo (ed.), *Black Families*. Beverly Hills, CA: Sage.

_____. 1984. "Race, Socioeconomic Status, and Age: The Social Context of American Mascu-linity." *Sex Roles* 11: 639–57.

Cazenave, N., and M. Straus. 1979. "Race, Class, Network Embeddedness and Family Violence: A Search for Potent Systems." *Journal of Comparative Family Studies* 10: 281–300.

Centers for Disease Control. 1985. "Homicide among Young Black Males—United States, 1970–1982." *Morbidity and Mortality Weekly Report* 34: 629–33.

_____. 1986. "Summary of Notifiable Diseases—United States." *Morbidity and Mortality Weekly Report* 35: 1–57.

Cooke, B. 1980. "Nonverbal Communication among Afro-Americans: An Initial Classification." R. L. Jones (ed.), *Black Psychology*, 2nd ed. New York: Harper and Row.

De La Cancela, V. 1986. "A Critical Analysis of Puerto Rican Machismo: Implications for Clinical Practice." *Psychotherapy* 23: 291–96.

Della Cava, M. 1989. "L. A. Fights Back." *USA Today*, Dec. 8.

Ellison, R. 1947. *Invisible Man*. New York: Vintage Books.

Fair, F. 1977. *"Orita for Black Youth: An Invitation into Christian Adulthood."* Valley Forge, PA: Judson.

Folb, E. 1980. *"Runnin' Down Some Lines: The Language and Culture of Black Teenagers."* Cam-bridge, MA: Harvard University Press.

Foster, H. L. 1986. *Ribbin', Jivin' and Playin' the Dozens: The Unrecognized Dilemma of Inner City Schools*. Cambridge, MA: Ballinger.

Frazier, E. F. 1939. *The Negro Family in the United States*. Chicago: University of Chicago Press.

Gibbs, J. T., ed. 1988. *Young, Black, and Male in America: An Endangered Species*. Dover, MA: Au-burn House.

Goffman, E. 1959. *The Presentation of Self in Everyday Life*. Garden City, NY: Doubleday.

Goines, D. 1972. *Whoreson: The Story of a Ghetto Pimp*. Los Angeles, CA: Holloway House.

_____. 1973. *Street Player*. Los Angeles, CA: Holloway House.

Goode, W. J. 1974. "Force and Violence in the Family." In S. K. Steinmetz and M. A. Straus (eds.), *Violence in the Family*. New York: Harper and Row.

Haas, J., and W. Shaffir. 1982. "Taking on the Role of Doctor: A Dramaturgical Analysis of Profes-sionalization." *Symbolic Interaction* 5: 187–205.

Hampton, R. L. 1987. *Violence in the Black Family: Correlates and Consequences*. Lexington, MA: Lexington Books.

Hannerz, U. 1969. *Soulside: Inquiries into Ghetto Culture and Community*. New York: Columbia Uni-versity Press.

Hare, N., and J. Hare. 1985. *Bringing the Black Boy to Manhood: The Passage*. San Francisco, CA: The Black Think Tank.

Jimenez, E. 1987. *Pricing Policy in the Social Sectors: Cost Recovery for Education and Health in Devel-oping Countries*. Baltimore, MD: Johns Hopkins University Press.

Karenga, M. 1977. *Kwanzaa: Origin, Concepts, Practice*. Los Angeles, CA: Kawaida Productions.

_____. 1986. Social Ethics and the Black Family. *The Black Scholar* 17: 41–54.

Keil, C. 1966. *Urban Blues*. Chicago: University of Chicago Press.

Kochman, T. 1981. *Black and White Styles in Conflict*. Chicago: University of Chicago Press.

Kunjufu, J. 1983. *Countering the Conspiracy to Destroy Black Boys*. Vol. 1. Chicago: African American Images.

——————. 1986. *Countering the Conspiracy to Destroy Black Boys*. Vol. 2. Chicago: African American Images.

Lyman, S., and M. Scott. 1970. *A Sociology of the Absurd*. New York: Appleton-Century-Crofts.

Majors, R. G. 1986. "Cool Pose: The Proud Signature of Black Survival." *Changing Men: Issues in Gender, Sex, and Politics* 17: 5–6.

——————. 1987. "Cool Pose: A New Approach toward a Systematic Understanding and Studying of Black Male Behavior." Ph.D. diss., University of Illinois, Urbana.

——————. 1989. " 'Cool pose': The Proud Signature of Black Survival." In M. Kimmel and M. Messner (eds.), *Men's Lives: Readings in the Sociology of Men and Masculinity*. New York: Macmillan.

——————. 1990. "Cool Pose: Black Masculinity and Sport." In M. A. Messner and D. Sabo (eds.), *Critical Perspectives on Sport, Men and Masculinity*. Champaign, IL: Human Kinetics.

——————. 1991a. "Nonverbal Behaviors and Communication Styles among African Americans." In R. L. Jones (ed.), *Black Psychology*, 3rd ed. Berkeley, CA: Cobb and Henry.

——————. 1991b. "Cool Pose: Black Masculinity and Sports." In M. Messner and D. Sabo (eds.), *Sport, Men and Gender Order: Critical Feminist Perspectives*. Champaign, IL: Human Kinetics.

Majors, R. G., and J. Billson. 1992. *Cool Pose: The Dilemmas of Black Manhood in America*. New York: Lexington Books (Macmillan).

Malcolm X and A. Haley. 1964. *The Autobiography of Malcolm X*. New York: Grove Press.

Mancini, J. K. 1981. *Strategic Styles: Coping in the Inner City*. Hanover, NH: University Press of New England.

Mbiti, J. S. 1969. *African Religion and Philosophy*. New York: Praeger.

Milner, R. 1972. "The Trickster, the Bad Nigger, and the New Urban Ethnography: An Initial Report and Editorial Coda." *Urban Life and Culture* 1:109–17.

Moynihan, D. 1968. "The President and the Negro: Moments Lost." In R. Perracci and M. Pilisuk (eds.), *The Triple Revolution: Social Problems in Depth*. Boston: Little, Brown.

National Research Council. 1989. *A Common Destiny: Blacks and American Society*. Washington, DC: National Academy Press.

Oliver, W. 1984. "Black Males and the Tough Guy Image: A Dysfunctional Compensatory Adaptation." *Western Journal of Black Studies* 8: 199–202.

——————. 1988. "The Symbolic Display of Compulsive Masculinity in the Lower Class Black Bar." University of Delaware, Newark.

——————. 1989a. "Black Males and Social Problems: Prevention Through Afrocentric Socialization. *Journal of Black Studies* 20: 15–39.

——————. 1989b. "Sexual Conquest and Patterns of Black-on-Black Violence: A Structural-Cultural Perspective." *Violence and Victims* 4: 4.

Parker, S., and R. J. Kleiner. 1969. "Social and Psychological Dimensions of the Family Role Performance of the Negro Male." *Journal of Marriage and the Family* 31: 500–506.

Perkins, U. E. 1986. *Harvesting New Generations: The Positive Development of Black Youth*. Chicago: Third World Press.

Silverman, I. J., and S. Dinitz. 1974. "Compulsive Masculinity and Delinquency: An Empirical Investigation. *Criminology* 11: 498–515.

Snow, D. A.; L. A. Zurcher; and R. Peters. 1981. "Victory Celebrations as Theater: A Dramaturgical Approach to Crowd Behavior." *Symbolic Interactions* 4: 21–41.

Spivak, H.; A. J. Hausman; and D. Prothrow-Stith. 1989. "Practitioner's Forum: Public Health and the Primary Prevention of Adolescent Violence—The Violence Prevention Project." *Violence and Victims* 4: 203–11.

Staples, R. 1978. "Masculinity and Race: The Dual Dilemma of Black Men." *Journal of Social Issues* 34: 169–83.

Staples, R. 1982. *Black Masculinity: The Black Male's Role in American Society.* San Francisco, CA: Scholar Press.

Stewart, S. A. 1989. "For Drug Dealing PBGs, Gang Is 'Better Than Family.'" *USA Today,* Dec. 7.

Straus, M. 1980. *Behind Closed Doors: Violence in the American Family.* Garden City, NY: Anchor.

Thomas, P. 1967. *Down Those Mean Streets.* New York: Knopf.

Thompson, R. F. 1973. An Aesthetic of the Cool. *African Art* 7: 41–43, 64–67.

Turner, R. H. 1970. *Family Interaction.* New York: Wiley.

Walker, L. 1984. *The Battered Woman Syndrome.* New York: Springer.

Wiggins, W. 1971. "Jack Jackson as Bad Nigger: The Folklore of His Life." *Black Scholar* 2: 35–46.

Chapter 19: "Ain't I a Man?" The Efficacy of Black Masculinities for Men's Studies in the 1990s

Brod, H., ed. 1987. *The Making of Masculinities: The New Men's Studies.* Winchester, MA: Allen and Unwin.

_____. 1987. "The Case for Men's Studies." In H. Brod (ed.), *The Making of Masculinities: The New Men's Studies.* Winchester, MA: Allen and Unwin.

Carrigan, T.; B. Connell; and J. Lee. 1987. "Toward A New Sociology of Masculinity." In H. Brod (ed.), *The Making of Masculinities: The New Men's Studies.* Winchester, MA: Allen and Unwin.

Farley, J. E. 1990. *Sociology.* Englewood Cliffs, NJ: Prentice-Hall.

Franklin, C. W., II. 1984. *The Changing Definition of Masculinity.* New York: Plenum.

_____. 1988. *Men and Society.* Chicago: Nelson-Hall.

Gutman, H. 1976. *The Black in Slavery and Freedom, 1750–1925.* New York: Pantheon.

hooks, b. 1981. *Ain't I a Woman: Black Women and Feminism.* Boston: South End Press.

_____. 1984. *Feminist Theory: From Margin to Center.* Boston: South End Press.

Killens, J. O. 1983. *And Then We Heard the Thunder.* Washington, DC: Howard University Press.

Kimmel, M. S., and M. A. Messner, eds. 1989. *Men's Lives.* New York: Macmillan.

Kitano, H. H. L. 1985. *Race Relations,* 3rd ed. Englewood Cliffs, NJ: Prentice-Hall.

Ladner, J. A. 1972. *Tomorrow's Tomorrow: The Black Woman.* Garden City, NY: Doubleday.

Merton, R. 1968. *Social Theory and Social Structure,* rev. ed. New York: Free Press.

"Ohio's African-American Males: A Call to Action." 1990. *Report of the Governor's Commission on Socially Disadvantaged Black Males.* Vol. 1, *Executive Summary.* Columbus, OH: Office of Black Affairs.

Rustin, B. 1971. *Down the Line.* Chicago: Quadrangle Books.

Staples, R. 1986. *The Black Family: Essays and Studies,* 3rd ed. "Black Masculinity, Hypersexuality, and Sexual Aggression." Belmont City, CA: Wadsworth.

_____. 1989. "Masculinity and Race: The Dual Dilemma of Black Men." In M. Kimmel and M. Messner, *Men's Lives.* New York: Macmillan. (Reprinted from *Journal of Social Issues* 34(1).)

Stimpson, C. R. 1987. "Foreword." In H. Brod (ed.), *The Making of Masculinities: The New Men's Studies.* Winchester, MA: Allen and Unwin.

Strickland, W. 1989. "Our Men in Crisis." *Essence,* Nov. 1989, pp. 49–52, 109–15.

Tiff, S. 1990. "Fighting the Failure Syndrome." *Time,* May 21, pp. 83–84.

Wilson, W. J. 1987. *The Truly Disadvantaged: The Inner City, the Underclass and Public Policy.* Chicago: University of Chicago Press.

Chapter 20: The African-American Father's Roles within the Family

American Council on Education. 1988. *One-Third of a Nation*. Washington, DC: ACE, Commission on Minority Participation in Education and American Life.

Billingsley, A. 1968. *Black Families in White America*. Englewood Cliffs, NJ: Prentice-Hall.

Blood, R. O., and D. M. Wolfe. 1969. "Negro-White Differences in Blue-Collar Marriages." *Social Forces* 48: 59–64.

Bowman, P. J. 1991. "Post-Industrial Displacement and Family Role Strains: Challenges to the Black Family. In P. Voydanof and L. C. Majka (eds.), *Families and Economic Distress*. Newbury Park, CA: Sage.

Bowman, P. J., and R. Sanders. 1988. "Black Fathers Across the Life Cycle: Providers Role Strain and Psychological Well-Being." Paper presented at the 12th Empirical Conference on Black Psychology, Ann Arbor, MI.

Cazenave, N. 1979. "Middle Income Black Fathers: An Analysis of the Provider Role." *Family Coordinator* 28(4): 583–93.

Connor, M. E. 1986. "Some Parenting Attitudes of Young Black Fathers." In R. A. Lewis and M. B. Sussman (eds.), *Men's Changing Roles in the Family*. New York: Hayworth Press.

Duster, T. 1988. "Social Implications of the New Underclass." *Black scholar* 19: 2–9.

Gary, L. E. 1981. "A Social Profile." In L. E. Gary (ed.), *Black Men*. Beverly Hills, CA: Sage.

_____. 1986. "Family Life Events, Depression, and Black Men." In R. A. Lewis and M. B. Sussman (eds.), *Men's Changing Roles in the Family*. New York: Hayworth Press.

Gary, L. E.: L. Beaty; G. Berry; and M. D. Price. 1983. Stable Black Families: Final Report. Washington, DC: Howard University, Institute for Urban Affairs and Research.

Gibbs, J. T., ed. 1988. *Young, Black and Male in America: An Endangered Species*. Dover, MA: Auburn House.

Glasgow, D. 1980. *The Black Underclass: Poverty, Unemployment, and Entrapment of Ghetto Youth*. New York: Vintage Books.

Grey-Little, B. 1982. "Marital Quality and Power Processes among Black Couples." *Journal of Marriage and the Family* 44: 633–45.

Hammond, J., and J. R. Enoch. 1976. "Conjugal Power Relations among Black Working-Class Families." *Journal of Black Studies* 7(1): 107–33.

Hill, R. 1981. *The Strengths of Black Families*. New York: Emerson-Hall.

Jackson, J. J. 1974. "Ordinary Black Husbands: The Truly Hidden Men." *Journal of Social and Behavioral Science* 20: 19–27.

Jaynes, G. D., and R. M. Williams, Jr., eds. 1989. *A Common Destiny: Blacks and American Society*. Washington, DC: National Academy Press.

Kardner, A., and L. Ovessey. 1951. *The Mark of Oppression*. New York: Norton.

Leshore, B. 1981. "Social Services and Black Men." In L. Gary (ed.), *Black Men*. Beverly Hills, CA: Sage.

Mack, D. 1978. "The Power Relationship in Black and White Families." In R. Staples (ed.), *The Black Family: Essays and Studies*. Belmont, CA: Wadsworth.

Malveaux, J. 1989. "Transitions: The Black Adolescent and the Labor Market." In R. E. Jones (ed.), *Black Adolescents*. Berkeley, CA: Cobb and Henry.

McAdoo, H. P. 1988. "Transgenerational Patterns of Upward Mobility in African-American Families." In H. P. McAdoo (ed.), *Black Families*. Newbury Park, CA: Sage.

McAdoo, J. L. 1986a. "Black Fathers' Relationships with Their Preschool Children and the Children's Ethnic Identity." In R. A. Lewis and R. E. Salt (eds.), *Men in Families*. Newbury Park, CA: Sage.

_____. 1986b. "A Black Perspective on the Father's Role in Child Development." In R. A. Lewis and M. B. Sussman (eds.), *Men's Changing Roles in the Family*. New York: Hayworth Press.

_____. 1988a. "Changing Perspectives on the Role of the Black Father." In P. Bronstein and C. P. Cowan (eds.), *Fatherhood Today: Men's Changing Role in the Family.* New York: Wiley.

_____. 1988b. "The Roles of Black fathers in the Socialization of Black Children." In H. P. McAdoo (ed.), *Black Families.* Newbury Park, CA: Sage.

_____. 1990. "Understanding African-American Teen Fathers." In P. E. Leone (ed.), *Understanding Troubled and Troubling Youth.* Newbury Park, CA: Sage.

_____. 1991. "Urban African-American Youth: Problems and Solutions." In R. Lang (ed.), *Contemporary Urban America: Problems, Issues and Alternatives.* Boston: University Press of America.

Middleton, R., and S. Putney. 1960. "Dominance in Decisions in the Family: Race and Class Differences." In C. V. Willie (ed.), *The Family Life of Black People.* Columbus, OH: Merrill.

Moynihan, D. 1965. *The Negro Family: The Case for National Action.* Washington, DC: U.S. Department of Labor, Office of Planning Research.

Peters, M. F. 1988. "Parenting in Black Families with Young Children: A Historical Perspective." In H. P. McAdoo (ed.), *Black Families.* Newbury Park, CA: Sage.

Staples, R. 1976. *Introduction to Black Sociology.* New York: McGraw-Hill.

_____. 1978. "The Black Family Revisited." In R. Staples (ed.), *The Black Family: Essays and Studies.* Belmont, CA: Wadsworth.

Sudarkasa, N. 1988. "Interpreting the African American Heritage in Afro-American Family Organization." In H. P. McAdoo (ed.), *Black Families.* Newbury Park, CA: Sage.

TenHouten, W. D. 1970. "The Black Family: Myth and Reality." *Psychiatry* 23: 145–73.

White, J. L., and T. A. Parham. 1990. *The Psychology of Blacks: An African-American Perspective.* Englewood Cliffs, NJ: Prentice-Hall.

Willie, C. V., and S. Greenblatt. 1978. "Four Classic Studies of Power Relationships in Black Families: A Review and Look to the Future. *Journal of Marriage and the Family* 40(4): 691–96.

Wilson, W. J. 1987. *The Truly Disadvantaged: The Inner City, the Under Class, and Public Policy.* Chicago: University of Chicago Press.

Chapter 21: Conclusion and Recommendations

African American Male Task Force. 1990. *Educating African American Males: A Dream Deferred.* Milwaukee, WI: Milwaukee Public Schools.

Akbar, N. (1991). *Visions for Black Men.* Nashville, TN: Winston-Derek.

Balcazar, F.; R. Majors; K. Blanchard; et al. 1991. "Teaching Minority High School Students to Recruit Helpers to Attain Personal and Educational Goals." *Journal of Behavioral Education* 1(4), 445–54.

Balcazar, F., and S. Fawcett. 1988. *Recruiting Mentors and Potential Helpers.* Vol. 1, *A Road Map to Personal Success.* Lawrence, KS: Research and Training Center for Independent Living.

_____. 1989. *Recruiting Mentors and Potential Helpers.* Vol. 2, *A Meeting with Success.* Lawrence, KS: Research and Training Center on Independent Living.

Bowser, B. P., ed. 1991. *Black Male Adolescents: Parenting and Education in Community Context.* Lanham, MD: University Press of America.

Carter, L. (In press). *Crisis of the African American Males: Dangers and Opportunities.* Atlanta, GA: Morehouse College Press.

Children's Defense Fund. 1975. *School Suspensions: Are They Helping Children?* Cambridge, MA: Children's Defense Fund.

Committee to Study the Status of the Black Male in the New Orleans Public Schools. 1988. *Educating Black Male Youth: A Moral and Civic Imperative.* New Orleans, LA: New Orleans Public Schools.

Evans, B. J., and J. R. Whitfield, eds. 1988. *Black Males in the United States: An Annotated Bibliography from 1967 to 1987.* Washington, DC: American Psychological Association.

Foster, H. L. 1986. *Ribbin', Jivin' and Playin' the Dozens: The Unrecognized Dilemma of Inner City Schools.* Cambridge, MA: Ballinger.

Gary, L., ed. 1981. *Black Men.* Newbury Park, CA: Sage.

Gibbs, J. T., ed. 1988. *Young, Black, and Male in America.* Dover, MA: Auburn House.

Haley, Alex. 1976. *Roots.* Garden City, NY: Doubleday.

Hall, R. E. 1992. African American Male Stereotypes: Obstacles to Social Work in a Multicultural Society. *Journal of Multicultural Social Work* 1(4): 7–89.

Hanna, J. L. 1984. "Black/White Nonverbal Differences, Dance and Dissonance: Implications for Desegregation." In A. Wolfgang (ed.), *Nonverbal Behavior: Perspectives, Applications, Intercultural Insights.* Lewiston, NY: Hogrefe.

Kazi-Ferrouillet, K. 1991. "The 21st Century Commission on African American Males: New Realities, a New Initiative." *The Black Collegian,* Sept./Oct.

Kochman, T. 1981. *Black and White Styles in Conflict.* Chicago: University of Chicago Press.

Kunjufu, J. 1985. *Countering the Conspiracy to Destroy Black Boys.* Vol. 1. Chicago: African American Images.

———. 1986. *Countering the Conspiracy to Destroy Black Boys.* Vol. 2. Chicago: African American Images.

Lee, C. 1987. "Black Manhood Training: Group Counseling for Male Blacks in Grades 7–12." *Journal for Specialists in Group Work,* pp. 18–25.

Lee, C. L. 1992. *Empowering Young Black Males.* Ann Arbor, MI: ERIC Counseling and Personnel Services Clearinghouse.

Madhubuti, H. R. 1990. *Black Men: Obsolete, Single, Dangerous?* Chicago: Third World Press.

Majors, R. 1986. "Cool Pose: The Proud Signature of Black Survival." In M. S. Kimmel and M. A. Messner (eds.), *Men's Lives.* New York: Macmillan.

Majors, R., and J. Billson. 1992. *Cool Pose: The Dilemmas of Black Manhood in America.* New York: Lexington.

Mancini, J. K. 1981. *Strategic Styles: Coping in the Inner City.* Hanover, MA: University Press of New England.

Mauer, M. 1990. *Young Black Men and the Criminal Justice System.* Washington, DC: The Sentencing Project.

McCord, C., and H. Freeman. 1990. "Excessive Mortality in Harlem." *New England Journal of Medicine* 322: 173–77.

Mincy, R., and S. Wiener. 1990. *A Mentor, Peer Group, Incentive Model for Helping Underclass Youth.* Washington, DC: Urban Institute.

Newport, J. P., Jr. 1991. "Steps to Help the Urban Black Man." In J. A. Krombowski (ed.), *Race and Ethnic Relations 91/92.* Guilford, CT: Duskin.

Poda, P. A. 1992. "Most MPS Suspensions Involve Conduct in Class." *Milwaukee Sentinel,* May 16.

Thomas, K. L. 1991. "Raising Black Boys in America." *Atlanta Journal/Atlanta Constitution,* Oct. 2.

Trotter, A. 1991. "Rites of Passage: In an Urban School, Students Build on Their Roots." *Executive Educator,* Sept., pp. 48–49.

Union Institute. 1990a. *A Structural Impediment to Success: A Look at Disadvantaged Young Men in Urban Areas.* Washington, DC: Union Institute.

———. 1990b. *Long-Term Investments in Youth: The Need for Comprehensive Programs for Disadvantaged Young Men in Urban Areas.* Washington, DC: Union Institute.

United Way of America. 1990. *A Youth Mentoring Program Directory.* Alexandria, VA: UWA.

Wilkins, R. 1991. "The Underside of Black Progress." In John Kromkowski (ed.), *Annual Editions: Race and Ethnic Relations 91/92.* Guilford, CT: Dushkin.

Wilkinson, D., and R. Taylor. 1977. *The Black Male in America.* Chicago: Nelson-Hall.

CONTRIBUTORS

William L. Andrews, Ph.D., is Joyce and Elizabeth Hall Distinguished Professor of American Literature at the University of Kansas. He received his doctorate in 1973 from the University of North Carolina at Chapel Hill and has taught at Texas Tech University and the University of Wisconsin–Madison. He is the author of *The Literary Career of Charles W. Chesnutt* and *To Tell a Free Story; The First Century of Afro-American Autobiography, 1760–1865*. He has edited a number of books on African-American literature and culture, including *Critical Essays on W. E. B. DuBois, Sisters of the Spirit: Three Black Women's Autobiographies of the Nineteenth Century, Six Women's Slave Narratives, Three Classic African-American Novels* and *Critical Essays on Frederick Douglass*. He was awarded the Norman Foerster prize from *American Literature* and the William Riley Parker prize from *Publications of the Modern Language Association*.

Fabricio E. Balcazar, Ph.D., is a senior research specialist at the University Affiliated Program in Developmental Disabilities at the University of Illinois in Chicago. He earned his doctorate in developmental and child psychology in 1987 at the University of Kansas and was a research associate at the Research and Training Center on Independent Living there for four years. Dr. Balcazar has focused his research efforts in the areas of empowerment of consumer advocacy organizations and mentoring as a mechanism to attain personal goals.

Benjamin Bowser, Ph.D., is associate professor of sociology and social services at the California State University at Hayward. He earned his doctorate at Cornell University in 1976 and has specialized in race relations and community studies. His recent work has focused on community based AIDS prevention. He is co-editor of *Impacts of Racism on White Americans* and editor of *Black Male Adolescents*. He is also associate editor of *Sage Race Relations Abstracts* (London).

William C. Brooks, M.B.A., is group director of personnel for General Motors Corporation's Truck and Bus Group. He is responsible for personnel activities, including labor relations, salaries personnel administration, medical activities, organizational development and training, and administrative services. In July 1989, Brooks was appointed assistant secretary of labor for the Employment

Standards Administration, the largest agency in the Department of Labor. He was responsible for laws and regulations setting employment standards for most U.S. workers. He resigned in November 1990 to return to General Motors. Prior to joining General Motors in 1973, Brooks held positions in the Office of Management and Budget in the executive office of the President, Department of Defense, Department of Labor, and the Department of the Air Force. Brooks earned an M.B.A. from the University of Oklahoma in 1966. In 1985, he completed the Harvard Business School's Advanced Management Program and in 1987, he was awarded an honorary Doctor of Humane Letters degree from Florida A&M University. Brooks is the recipient of numerous awards and honors including the National Black MBA Association's "Outstanding MBA of the Year" in 1980, and in 1988 he was presented the Detroit City Council's "Recognition Award," as well as the "Spirit of Detroit" award.

Vincent P. Christmas was appointed director of the Residential Development Unit of the New York City Department of Mental Health, Mental Retardation and Alcoholism Services in the Spring of 1987. Prior to this, Christmas served for two years as senior consultant in the department's Bureau of Rehabilitation/Special Services. He has also served as program planning analyst in the department's Office of Planning and Project Management. Before joining the department in 1983, Christmas worked for the New York State Office of Mental Health as a certification specialist/site development specialist. He was instrumental in the development and certification of the first certified community residences for the chronically mentally ill in New York City. Christmas is a graduate of Earlham College, Richmond, Indiana.

Stephen B. Fawcett, Ph.D., is professor of Human Development and Family Life and director of the Work Group on Health Promotion and Community Development of the Schiefelbusch Institute for Life Span Studies at the University of Kansas. Fawcett has been honored as a Fellow in both Division 27 (Community Psychology) and Division 25 (Experimental Analysis of Behavior) of the American Psychological Association. He is co-author of over 80 articles and book chapters in the areas of community development, empowerment, competence building, social policy, health promotion, independent living, and self help. Fawcett has served on the board of editors or as a consulting editor for various journals including the *American Journal of Community Psychology*, the *Journal of Applied Behavior Analysis*, the *Journal of Community Psychology*, *Prevention in Human Services*, the *Journal of Primary Prevention*, *Behavioral Assessment*, *Behavior Therapy*, *ETC (Education and Training of Children)*, and the *American Psychologist*. He is co-author of *Learning Counseling and Problem-solving Skills*, *Matching Clients and Services*, and *Evaluating and Optimizing Public Policy*.

Clyde W. Franklin, II, Ph.D., is professor of sociology at the Ohio State University, Columbus. He has been teaching for twenty-three years, including courses in social psychology, race relations, sex roles, and men's studies. Franklin has written numerous articles on topics in social psychology, male sexuality, Black female–Black male relationships, Black male studies, male socialization, and male friendships. He is the author of *Minority Group Relation* (with James G. Martin), *Theoretical Perspectives in Social Psychology*, *The Changing Definition of Masculinity*, and *Men and Society*. Currently, he is conducting research in the area of Black men's lives.

Edith M. Freeman, Ph.D., ACSW, is a professor in the School of Social Welfare at the University of Kansas. She is chair of the clinical concentration in the school. Freeman received her doctorate in Human Development and Family Life in 1982 from the University of Kansas. She has conducted research in the areas of substance abuse, multicultural communities, and teenage parenthood. Her books and articles in professional journals have focused on those areas of research along with other issues related to children, youth, and families such as identity development and culturally relevant family treatment.

Jewelle Taylor Gibbs, Ph.D., received her undergraduate degree (*cum laude*) at Radcliffe College and three graduate degrees from the University of California at Berkeley: M.S.W. in social welfare (1970), M.A. (1976), and Ph.D. in clinical psychology (1980). Gibbs joined the faculty of the University of California at Berkeley in 1979 and is professor in the School of Social Welfare. She is also a licensed clinical psychologist. Her areas of research include adolescent psychosocial adjustment, minority mental health, and brief treatment methods. She has authored a number of articles and book chapters and is a frequent lecturer and consultant on these topics. She is editor of *Young, Black and Male in America: An Endangered Species* and co-author of *Children of Color: Psychological Interventions with Minority Youth*. Gibbs was a Fellow at the Mary I. Bunting Institute, Radcliffe College, in 1985. She has received numerous awards for her research and advocacy on behalf of Black youth, including citations from the Michigan state legislature, the City of Detroit, the National Association for Equal Opportunity in Higher Education, and the National Black Child Development Institute.

Jacob U. Gordon (Jake), Ph.D., is a professor of African and African American Studies, Research Fellow in the Institute for Life Span Studies and Executive Director of the Institute for Black Leadership Development and Research at the University of Kansas. He received his doctorate in history at Michigan State University. Gordon came to the University of Kansas in 1970 and served as assistant to the dean of the College of Liberal Arts and Sciences. That year, he founded the Department of African and African-American Studies and chaired the department until 1980. The Black History Collection at the Spencer Research Library was established under his direction in 1984, and he founded the Black Leadership Research Center in 1986, which is now known as The Institute of Black Leadership Development and Research. He currently serves as the president and chief executive officer of the National Council of African American Men (NCAAM), a national organization he co-founded in 1990, and he is deputy editor of the *Journal of African American Male Studies*, an NCAAM publication. Among his scholarly publications are three books, numerous monographs, research reports, and more than 100 articles in professional journals. Serving on several state and national boards, including the Kansas Citizens Advising board on Alcohol and other Drug Abuse, Gordon is a member of the Executive Committee of the Kansas Coalition on Alcohol and other Drug Programs and Services and is consultant to the State Alcohol and other Drug Services and Disability Services within the Kansas Department of Social and Rehabilitation Services.

Ronald E. Hall, Ph.D., is assistant professor of social work at the University of Wisconsin–Eau Claire. He received his doctorate in social work from Atlanta University, Atlanta, Georgia. Hall's work on the implications of cutaneo-chroma (skin color) has generated national attention. He testified as an expert witness in the landmark skin color case, *Morrow vs. IRS*, for the United States Federal Court in Atlanta. Hall's most recent research has appeared in the *Journal of Multicultural Social Work* and *Research in Social Work Practice*.

Billy E. Jones, M.D., M.S., is the commissioner of New York City's Department of Mental Health, Mental Retardation and Alcoholism Services. He has served as medical director of Lincoln Medical and Mental Health Center in the Bronx and was senior associate dean of New York Medical College, where he was a tenured professor of Psychiatry. Jones received his medical degree from Meharry Medical College and his M.S. as a Kellogg Fellow in Health Care Policy at New York University's Robert Wagner School of Public Service. Jones is the author of numerous articles on African Americans in urban centers. He is a member of the New York State Alcohol, Drug Abuse and Mental Health Block Grant Advisory Council, serves on the Department of Mental Health's Community Services Board, is a fellow of the American Psychiatric Association, the American College of Psychiatrists, and is a founder and former director of the Minority Task Force on AIDS. A former president of the Black Psychiatrists of America, Jones maintains a private practice and teaches at the Sophie Davis School of Bio-Medical Education of the City University of New York.

Merlin R. Langley, Ph.D., is an assistant professor of Counseling and Psychology at the Lesley College Graduate School in Cambridge, Massachusetts, and a Clinical Fellow in psychology (psychiatry) at the Trauma Clinic affiliated with Massachusetts General Hospital, Department of Psychiatry, Harvard Medical School. His areas of research include cultural determinants of personality, issues in minority mental health, men's issues, treatment of psychological trauma, and psychotherapy process and outcome research. Langley earned a master's degree in counseling and guidance from Boston University, a master's degree in clinical psychology from the Florida State University, a Certificate of Advanced Graduate Study (C.A.G.S.) in counseling psychology and family systems therapy from Northeastern University, and a doctorate in clinical psychology from the Florida State University in Tallahassee.

Ken Lawrence is director of the Anti-Repression Resource Team in Jackson, Mississippi. He has been an activist in the civil rights movement for more than thirty years and is a writer, researcher, organizer, and lecturer on politics, history, and culture. His scholarly works include five volumes on slavery in Mississippi, several chapters in *Dirty Work: The CIA in Africa*, and a number of books and pamphlets on political repression. Since 1978, he has specialized in investigating the Ku Klux Klan and neo-Nazi resurgence in the United States and Europe. He served as an investigator for and consultant to the American Friends Service Committee concerning the Ku Klux Klan murders in Greensboro, North Carolina, in 1979. His pamphlets "Fighting the Klan" and "The Ku Klux Klan and Fascism" have been widely distributed by the anti-Klan movement.

Richard Majors, Ph.D., is assistant professor in the Department of Psychology, University of Wisconsin–Eau Claire, and co-author of *Cool Pose: The Dilemmas of Black Manhood in America*. An American Psychological Association Predoctoral Minority Award recipient in research, Majors received a doctorate in counseling psychology from the University of Illinois, Urbana-Champaign. After postdoctoral work at the University of Kansas, Majors was a Clinical Fellow in psychiatry at Harvard Medical School. Majors is co-founder of the National Council of African American Men (NCAAM), co-founder and deputy editor of the *Journal of African American Males Studies (JAAMS)*, and founder of the *Annual State of Black Male America*. Recently, he was appointed by Rep. Major Owens (NY) to the Executive Committee of the National Citizen's Commission on African-American Education.

Manning Marable, Ph.D., is professor of political science, history, and sociology and is affiliated with the Center for Studies of Ethnicity and Race in America at the University of Colorado, Boulder. He received his doctorate in 1976 from the University of Maryland, College Park, in the field of American history. He has served as professor of sociology and director of the Africana and Hispanic Studies Program, Colgate University (1983–1986); professor of political science and sociology, Purdue University (1986–1987); and professor of history and political science, and chairperson of the Department of Black Studies, Ohio State University (1987–1989). Marable is the author of eight books, including *The Crisis of Color and Democracy* (1991); *Race, Reform and Rebellion: The Second Reconstruction in Black America, 1945–1990* (Revised Edition, 1991); *W. E. B. DuBois: Black Radical Democrat* (1986); *Black American Politics* (1985); and *How Capitalism Underdeveloped Black America* (1983). He advises members of the Congressional Black Caucus and other political organizations. His newspaper column on public policy, *Along the Color Line*, appears in over two hundred newspapers in the United States, the United Kingdom, Canada, the Caribbean, Europe, and India. A radio version of *Along the Color Line* is also distributed to stations across the United States.

Marc Mauer, M.S.W., has directed programs on criminal justice reform for over fifteen years and has served as assistant director of the Sentencing Project since 1987. Prior to that, he directed state and nationwide efforts in criminal justice for the American Friends Service Committee from 1975–1986 and served as that organization's National Justice Communications Coordinator. Mauer is the author of numerous publications on criminal justice issues, including *Black Men and the Crimi-*

nal Justice System and *Americans Behind Bars: A Comparison of International Rates of Incarceration.* Mauer received his M.S.W. from the University of Michigan.

John Lewis McAdoo, Ph.D., is associate professor of social work and community planning at the University of Maryland. Previously, he was a visiting associate professor at Howard University and is now serving on the Nominating Committee for the National Conference on Marriage and the Family, and is chair of the Review Panel of the Society for Research in Child Development. McAdoo received his doctorate in 1970 from the University of Michigan. He has supervised first and second year graduate students in field work at the University of Maryland's School of Social Work and has published numerous books and professional articles on Black males and families. Currently, he is part of the Publications Committee for the American Psychological Association.

Julia B. McAdoo is a Ph.D. Candidate in the Department of Psychology, University of Michigan, Ann Arbor.

Vera S. Paster, Ph.D., is a clinical psychologist. She has served as director of the mental health agency that served the New York City school system, the Bureau of Child Guidance. She developed and served as executive director of the Washington Heights—West Harlem Community Mental Health Center and was the associate commissioner responsible for child and adolescent services at the Department of Mental Health of the Commonwealth Psychology Program of the City University of New York at the City College. A past president of the American Orthophychiatric Association, she has focused on primary prevention and was a member of the Task Panel on Primary Prevention of President Carter's Commission on Mental Health. Her work has emphasized the psycho-social issues concerning Black Males.

Blaine F. Peden completed his undergraduate training at California State University–Fresno and graduate education at Indiana University. His research interests include animal learning and behavior, applying psychology to teaching, and the application of quantitative methods in social psychology.

Chester M. Pierce, M.D., is professor of education and psychiatry at Harvard University and psychiatrist at Massachusetts General Hospital and Massachusetts Institute of Technology. A member of the Institute of Medicine, National Academy of Sciences, he has lectured and consulted on all seven of the earth's continents, including over one hundred colleges and universities in the United States. Among the national offices he has held are president of the American Board of Psychiatry and Neurology, president of the American Orthopsychiatric Association, and founding president of the Black Psychiatrists of America. Pierce Peak in Antarctica honors biomedical research performed by Pierce at the geographical South Pole.

Wesley E. Profit, Ph.D., is a licensed clinical psychologist. He received his doctorate in clinical psychology and public practice from Harvard University in 1977. Profit has worked at the Institute for Law and Psychiatry at McLean Hospital, a Harvard teaching facility, and became one of the first psychologists in Massachusetts authorized to do forensic examinations. He helped develop clinical services at Bridgewater State Hospital, a maximum security forensic facility, and throughout the correctional system. He established and directed the first comprehensive emergency mental health service in the state's prison system. As the forensic director at Bridgewater State Hospital, Profit has overseen the development of a highly rated forensic program. His research interests include behavior in extreme stressful environments, interpersonal violence reduction, and murder.

Gary A. Sailes, Ph.D., is assistant professor of sport sociology at Indiana University. He is founder and director of the Indiana Sport and Education Foundation. Considered an authority on the Black athlete in American sport, he has lectured both nationally and internationally, written several articles, books, and status reports on the Black athlete, appeared on national and international radio and television talk shows, served as moderator for a congressional panel examining the status of the Black athlete in intercollegiate sport, and served as consultant to the NBC special "The Black Athlete: Fact or Fiction."

James B. Stewart, Ph.D., is vice provost and professor of labor studies and industrial relations at Penn State University. Previously, he was director of the Black Studies Program and served two terms of office as vice chair of the National Council for Black Studies. Dr. Stewart received his doctorate in economics (1976) from the University of Notre Dame. He is co-editor of *Black Families: Interdisciplinary Perspectives* and has published extensively in economics and Black Studies journals. He is currently the editor of the *Review of Black Political Economy*.

Yolanda Suarez-Balcazar, Ph.D., is assistant professor in the Department of Psychology at Loyola University, Chicago. Previously, she was a research associate at the University of Kansas where she received her doctorate in 1987. She has conducted several research projects in the areas of community needs assessment, self-help, and empowerment in collaboration with minority groups such as people with disabilities and Hispanic families.

Ronald L. Taylor, Ph.D., is professor and former chair in the Department of Sociology at the University of Connecticut–Storrs. He received his doctorate in 1973 from Boston University. He is the co-author and editor (with Doris Y. Wilkinson) of *Black Male in America* and has published in such journals as the *American Journal of Sociology, American Journal of Orthopsychiatry, Social Science Quarterly, Journal of Adolescent Research,* and *Youth and Society.* He has served on the editorial board of the *American Journal of Orthopsychiatry, Contemporary Sociology,* University Presses of New England, and as guest editor for special issues of *Youth and Society* and the *Journal of Adolescent Research.*

Richard B. Tyler, Ph.D., is an assistant professor of Psychology at the University of Wisconsin–Milwaukee. He received his doctorate from Princeton University in 1986. He has taught in the Afro-American Studies and Psychology Departments at Colgate University and Carleton College, where he also served as director of Multicultural Affairs. As a social psychologist, Tyler's research has primarily focused on attribution, stereotyping, and discrimination. He has also conducted numerous workshops and seminars on racism and cultural diversity in the workplace and on the college campus.

NAME INDEX

SUBJECT INDEX